be returned on

Modern Architecture
and Design

Modern Architecture and Design

An alternative history

Bill Risebero

The Herbert Press

Contents

List of illustrations 6

Acknowledgements 9

1 The modern Prometheus 11
The industrial revolution

2 Contrasts 19
Britain and America in the early 19th century

3 The philosophy of right 50
Continental Europe in the early 19th century

4 How we live and how we might live 78
Europe in the mid 19th century

5 The will to power 106
Europe and America in the late 19th century

6 The light that failed 119
The turn of the century

7 The state and revolution 162
The First World War and after

8 Brave new world 213
The Second World War and after

Select bibliography 246

Index 248

List of illustrations

The 18th century cultural revolution	12
The Industrial Revolution	17
Early 19th century British society	20
Robert Owen and the factory children	22
The contractual system	24
Nash's London	26
The classical revival	27
Luxury and comfort	28
Pugin and Scott	30
The Houses of Parliament	31
The bourgeois country house	33
Coal and iron	35
The engineers · 1	37
The engineers · 2	39
Republican values	42
The move westwards	44
Southern Democracy	46
Shaker and Windsor furniture	47
The American engineer	48
Royal Bavaria · 1	51
Royal Bavaria · 2	52
Imperial Prussia · 1	54
Imperial Prussia · 2	55
The July Monarchy	57
The architect-engineer	59
Viollet-le-Duc	60
The Italian states	62
Biedermeier and Thonet	64
Neo-Classicism in Scandinavia	66
The timber tradition	68
The rural poor	70
Industrial Manchester	71
The Crystal Palace	74
The Great Exhibition	75
Haussmann's Paris	80
The Second Empire	81
The Paris Opéra	83
The French engineers	85
The Risorgimento	87
The Galleria	88
The Battle of Styles	90
Railway travel	92
London stations	93
Ruskin	95
Victorian High Gothic	96
Social pretension in architecture	98
Philip Webb	100
Shaw and Nesfield	101
William Morris	103
Vienna and Berlin	107
Wagner's Bavaria	109
Neo-Gothic in America	112
The art of iron construction	113
American Renaissance	115
John Roebling	116
The late Victorian great house	120
Arts and Crafts	122
The American bourgeoisie · 1	124
The American bourgeoisie · 2	125
Fin-de-siècle grandeur	127
Masterpieces of iron and steel construction	129
The Chicago School	131
Adler and Sullivan	132
Sullivan	133
The concentric city and Ciudad Lineal	135
Philanthropy and paternalism	137
Voysey and Lutyens	139
Early Wright	141
Art Nouveau in Belgium and France	144
Art Nouveau in central Europe	145
The Catalan Renaixença	147
Mackintosh and the Sezession	149
The use of concrete	151
Berg and the Werkbund	153
The value of tradition	156
Urban theory and practice	159
The Werkbund Exhibition 1914	163
The October Revolution	165

VKHUTEMAS	168	Aalto and Finnish design	204
Expessionism	170	New Deal USA	206
L'Esprit Nouveau	173	Nazi Germany	209
The use of historicism	175	The Second World War	210
Suburbia and Radburn	177	Rebuilding the city	212
Constructivism	179	Houses in the USA · 1	216
The Paris Exposition 1925	181	Houses in the USA · 2	217
Le Corbusier's maisons blanches	182	The property boom · 1	219
De Stijl	183	The property boom · 2	220
Fascism in Italy	185	Neo-Liberty	222
Die Neue Sachlichkeit	188	Public buildings · 1	225
VKHUTEMAS and the Bauhaus	189	Public buildings · 2	227
The end of Constructivism	191	Industrial architecture	229
Soviet town planning principles	192	Housing design · 1	232
The modern movement in Britain	196	Housing design · 2	233
London Transport	197	Problems of housing design	236
Public housing	198	The squatter settlement	238
International modern in the thirties	200	The architecture of ecology	241
Scandinavia in the thirties	203	The new historicism	243

Acknowledgements

Many friends and colleagues have helped me to form the
ideas and attitudes in this book, among them Graham
Dowell, Luis Fernández-Galiano, Dougie Gordon and
David Pike. The text itself has been much improved by
the criticism of Tim Sturgis in London and of Roger
Conover and his colleagues at MIT Press. David and
Brenda Herbert have again been both patient and encouraging, Jasmine Atterbury has compiled the index
with her usual skill, Ayeshah Abdel-Haleem has typed
and re-typed the less tractable parts of the manuscript,
and Erica Hunningher has been a very sympathetic
editor. I am grateful to everybody involved but once
again, and most of all, to my wife Christine for making it
all possible, in so many ways.

To
Sophie
James
Peter
Joanna
and
John
whose future
it is

The modern Prometheus
The industrial revolution

The first premise of human history is, of course, the existence of living human individuals. Thus, the first fact to be established is the physical organisation of these individuals and their consequent relation to the rest of nature. . . . The writing of history must always set out from these natural bases and their modification in the course of history through the action of men. . . . By producing their means of subsistence men are indirectly producing their actual material life. (Marx and Engels, *The German Ideology*, part 1, 1846)

Material conditions – that is, social systems, political institutions and culture in general, including art and architecture – are dependent ultimately on the way a society earns its living. Modern architecture and design must thus be seen in the context of, and defined by, the modern economic system, a system which began in effect when the great revolutions of the 18th and 19th centuries brought the bourgeoisie to power, creating a new world society based on industrial production.

In the mid-18th century very little of this change had yet taken place; the predominantly agrarian economics of Europe and colonial America were dominated by the traditional land-owning classes, and their politics by the kings and aristocracies of the old regime. Most typical was France, superficially powerful, with a vast population and an enormous army, rigidly controlled by the seemingly enduring power of the Bourbon court. Yet France's semi-feudal social structure, its static and inefficient peasant economy and its poorly-developed internal trade remained great barriers to the industrialisation on which economic progress ultimately depended. The same was true in greater or lesser degree throughout the western world, from the antiquated and divided German states, in which Hohenzollern Brandenburg alone was beginning to emerge from feudalism, to Austria-Hungary where the elitism and inertia of the Habsburg court sapped the vitality of all the empire's institutions, to the aspiring colonial states of America, still in economic subjection to the ruling class of Britain.

The attitudes and ideas of the aristocracy dominated not only the economics and politics of the West, but also its culture. A long, unbroken intellectual tradition, which looked back for its origins and inspiration to ancient and Renaissance Rome, had created a kind of hieratic language, which united the ruling classes of all countries and set them apart from their own working classes. Writers, musicians and artists were required to collaborate, to assist in the creation of the arcane vocabulary used by the wealthy to communicate with each other. Among them was the gentleman architect, educated, cultured, enjoying a high social status and willingly assisting in this process of class expression by designing palaces, great houses and public buildings. Both he and his art were essentially products of the Renaissance, when it had first become possible – and also desirable for the social standing it brought – to design buildings without also being a craftsman on the site. His education was theoretical and antiquarian rather than practical, and what he gained in intellectualism he lost in alienation from the building process itself and from its roots in common society.

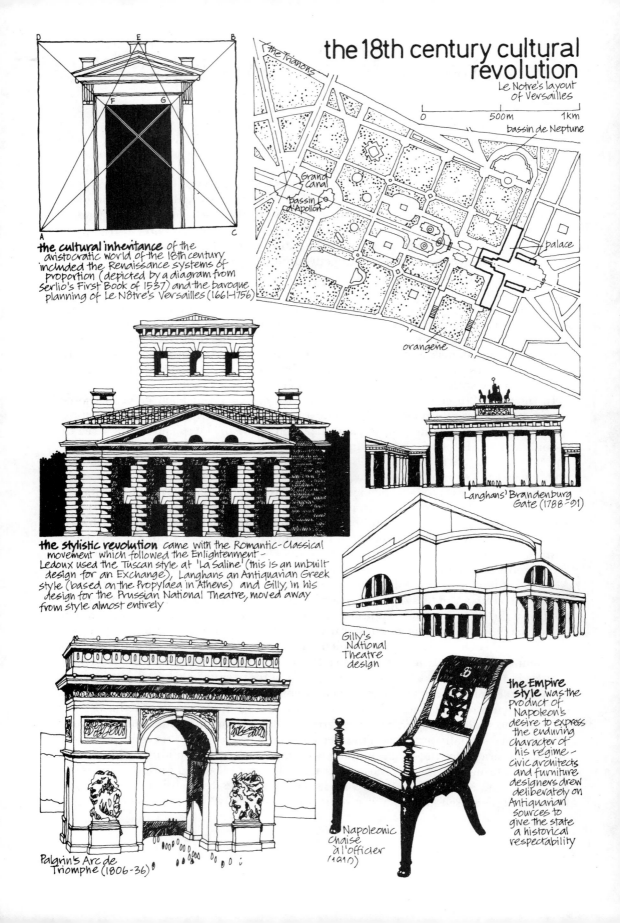

the 18th century cultural revolution

Le Notre's layout of Versailles

the Trianons

Grand Canal

bassin d'Apollon

bassin de Neptune

palace

orangerie

0   500m   1km

the cultural inheritance of the aristocratic world of the 18th century included the Renaissance systems of proportion (depicted by a diagram from Serlio's First Book of 1537) and the baroque planning of Le Nôtre's Versailles (1661-1756)

the stylistic revolution came with the Romantic-Classical movement which followed the Enlightenment – Ledoux used the Tuscan style at 'La Saline' (this is an unbuilt design for an Exchange), Langhans an Antiquarian Greek style (based on the Propylaea in Athens) and Gilly, in his design for the Prussian National Theatre, moved away from style almost entirely

Langhans' Brandenburg Gate (1788-91)

Gilly's National Theatre design

Palgrin's Arc de Triomphe (1806-36)

Napoleonic chaise à l'officier (1810)

the Empire style was the product of Napoleon's desire to express the enduring character of his regime – civic architects and furniture designers drew deliberately on Antiquarian sources to give the state a historical respectability

At the lower end of the social scale was the craftsman architect, who produced the humbler houses and cottages which form the bulk of any country's building activity. Though now no more than a shadow of his forerunners, the medieval master-mason and carpenter, he had nevertheless inherited skills from the middle ages, passed down by oral tradition and developed through practical example. It was a tradition with obvious limits, lacking intellectual stimulus and outside ideas, but it also had its strengths. In particular, it allowed architectural design to grow naturally and appropriately out of the practicalities of building construction. Unlike the intellectual tradition, it was also a genuine folk art, belonging to the ordinary people. Amid the increasing class polarity of the 18th and 19th centuries and the intensification of industrialism, the craftsman architect and his building methods would come increasingly under threat. In Britain, the unity and militancy of the building trade unions, as they fought back against the destruction of their traditions and livelihoods, were foundations on which the early labour movement was to be built.

The intellectual tradition too, if not exactly threatened, was about to see great changes; as the bourgeoisie gained in economic power, the cultured architect, belonging by definition to the aristocratic world, was faced with problems of identification which demanded major adjustments. In the 17th and 18th centuries, the cultural tradition seemed stable enough; Louis XIV's Versailles was the symbol of the age, a vast baroque composition in which a great palace was surrounded by miles of formal garden whose radiating avenues symbolically extended the king's domain to every horizon. It was a concept of a grandeur which in previous centuries had been offered only to God – the world's greatest memorial to absolute kingship and symbolic of the permanence of royal power. But the grandeur and power were based on insecure foundations; conspicuous consumption of this kind could not be maintained indefinitely merely on the extorted taxes of an inefficient agrarian economy. The courts of Europe and their powerful, corrupt bureaucracies were aware of the need to modernise, even if the task itself was beyond them: under Peter the Great and Catherine the Great, Russia took tentative steps towards industrialisation; in the emerging state of Prussia, Frederick the Great significantly improved agriculture, trade and industry; even Bourbon France, under Louis XV and Louis XVI, developed a network of major roads, enlarged the textile and metallurgical industries, imported coal for fuel and introduced the steam engine from Britain. But there was no disguising the fact that the very institutions of the old regime stood in the way of economic development. These were increasingly challenged during the 18th century by a new bourgeois spirit of inquiry, criticism and change, the intellectual stimulus for which came from the 'enlightenment' of Voltaire and Rousseau, of Hume, Locke and Bentham, of Jefferson and Paine. The idea of revolution gained a universal currency. The ideology spoke of 'freedom', 'equality', 'brotherhood', concepts of the widest possible appeal, but underneath lay the ambitions of the bourgeoisie to remove from their path anything which barred the way to political and economic power.

In common with the other arts, architecture began to reflect the new humanistic spirit. Ideas were developed which by referring back to a pre-Roman past expressed the primitive dignity of a world uncorrupted by the Renaissance sophistication of the current regime. The development of archaeology, from Winckelmann onwards, and the dramatic architectural designs of Giovanni Battista Piranesi (1720–78), assisted in the rediscovery of primitive architectural forms. In France, Etienne Louis Boullée (1728–99) and Claude Nicolas Ledoux (1736–1806) developed a simple cosmic geometry for their numerous unbuilt designs. Ledoux, in his two main built works, the state chemical works of 'La Saline' near Besançon (1775–9) and the toll-gates around Paris (1785–9), made good use of the Tuscan style for its primitive, un-Roman associations. In Berlin, Carl Gotthard Langhans (1732–1808) designed the neo-Greek Brandenburg Gate (1788–91), the first of the many ceremonial archways to be built all over Europe in the 19th century. Here too, Friedrich Gilly (1772–1800) designed a monumental memorial to Frederick the Great and a Prussian National theatre, neither of which was built but both of which expressed the essential sublimity for which all such 'revolutionary' architects were searching. In England, this search was pursued by the architect John Soane (1753–1837), who had known Piranesi in Italy and had later come under the influence of Ledoux. Soane's early affection for the neo-Greek style, during the 1780s, developed in later years into a quest for an architecture of pure geometric forms, from which all but the merest hint of classical ornament was removed. Among the representative work of this later period were his extensions to Wren's Chelsea Hospital (1809–17), the Dulwich Picture Gallery in South London (1811–14), St John's Church, Bethnal Green (1825–8), and his masterpiece, The Bank of England in the City of London (1791–1833). The English architect-engineer Benjamin Latrobe (1764–1820) imported Soane's ideas into America. Following an early association with President Jefferson, himself a talented designer in the Italian style, Latrobe introduced the neo-Greek style into the country, designing public buildings in Philadelphia (1798–1800) and in the new federal capital of Washington. He moved towards Soane's later severe style in his own masterpiece, Baltimore Cathedral (1804–18).

This architectural pilgrimage from the Italianate to the Greek and Tuscan, this continual search for greater primitivism and sublime simplicity, was part of what we know now as the Romantic movement, then gaining ground all over Europe. Its beginnings can be seen in the poetry of early 18th-century England, but it came to a climax in the late 18th and early 19th centuries in the work of poets such as Wordsworth, Byron and Keats, of dramatists like Goethe, Schiller and Lessing, and of novelists as various as Scott, Manzoni, Dumas, Georges Sand, the Brontës and Poe. As the movement grew, it attracted contributions from artists and musicians: the wildness and exoticism of Delacroix; Constable's passion for Nature and Turner's for both Nature and Antiquity; Schubert's view of life as an epic pilgrimage; Beethoven's joyful vision of human freedom. Romanticism made a major intellectual break away from aristocratic, courtly modes of expression towards those representing bourgeois values; uppermost was the concept of man as a free individual, rather than a creature of State or church. Individualism was inherent in every major Romantic theme: man's return to the simplicity of Nature or Antiquity, from which the false values of civilisation had estranged him; his rediscovery of those literary classics – Dante, Shakespeare, Cervantes – in which human rather than abstract values could clearly be seen; the desire to supplant the intellectual elitism of the court circle with the universality of new 'schools of thought'; and a new liberty of expression which allowed him to ask questions about human life, destiny, the past, the world itself, and many other things previously beyond question or above criticism. The Romantics were concerned essentially with *ideas*, above all the liberal ideas of liberty, equality and brotherhood which both stimulated and in turn took their stimulus from a series of political revolutions on both sides of the Atlantic.

In the period of reconstruction which followed the American Revolution of 1776, architects had a major part to play in expressing a spirit of resurgence. The establishment of the city of Washington on the banks of the Potomac, a location specially chosen symbolically to unite the agrarian south with the newly industrialising north and the cultured eastern states with the barbarous west, virtually demanded the use of the neo-Greek style to avoid any associations with the aristocratic British past. Latrobe worked on the reconstruction of the Italian-style White House into a Greek Ionic mansion (1807) and in 1815 began an extensive rebuilding of the United States Capitol, completed in 1829 by his prolific associate Charles Bulfinch (1763–1844). Inherent in the architectural message was a parallel between the new state apparatus and Athenian democracy of the 5th century BC. Paradoxically though, the new city plan into which these new symbols were fitted, designed by the French engineer Pierre Charles L'Enfant (1754–1825), was inspired by nothing more democratic than Louis XIV's Versailles; its wide, baroque vistas, though beautiful, remained both functionally inappropriate for a living city and symbolically wrong for a new democratic order. But then, the bourgeois freedom itself was illusory; despite the revolution, the tensions between the interests of the north and south remained a hindrance to the free expansion of the northern industrial system. It would not be till their resolution in the Civil War of 1861 that true economic freedom would be obtained.

The same was true of France where, though the Revolution of 1798 became a universal Romantic symbol of liberty, the events of the post-Revolution years proved otherwise. After a series of wild political changes, Napoleon stabilised the constitution and the law, but at the expense of popular democracy. Academically Roman-style public buildings, such as Vignon's church of the Madeleine (1806–43) and Palgrin's Arc de Triomphe at the Etoile (1806–36) began to emphasise Napoleon's imperial pretensions abroad and despotism at home. The new 'Empire' style of design created for the Napoleonic court by the architects Percier and Fontaine, drew heavily on Roman, Greek and Egyptian sources for its inspiration , in a conscious attempt to reject the modes, however splendid, of Bourbon France. But though the style itself spoke of progressivism and modernity, it continued to be an expression of the power of the state over the people, and the denial of any kind of freedom, bourgeois or otherwise.

At the end of the 18th century there was only one country in the world where bourgeois freedom existed. During the 17th century the Revolution in England had permanently ended the absolute power of the royal court, making it possible for the bourgeoisie to grow in political power; then during the 18th century there had developed all the essential pre-conditions for the industrialisation on which the basic economic power of the bourgeoisie ultimately depended: a rural population from which peasant tenure had almost disappeared and which was therefore capable of moving into new work; agricultural reforms which increased food production and with it the working population; a highly developed market economy across the whole country based on agriculture, urban commerce and rural manufacturing; the existence of a developing overseas trade network into which the market could expand; and above all the opportunity and willingness of the newly emancipated middle class – in distinct contrast to the spendthrift aristocracy – to amass capital for investment in new industries. The French Revolution might be the symbol of the new age, but the industrial revolution was the reality.

Since 1688 Parliament at Westminster had been the supreme decision-making body, a political arena in which the struggle for power between the declining aristocracy and the emerging middle class had become formalised into a contest between the land-owning Tory party, monarchist, anti-republican and reactionary, and the Whigs, progressive, constitutional monarchists who demanded supremacy of Parliament over the king and supported the urban bourgeoisie. As bourgeois power grew, so did the fortunes of the Whigs; one feature of the shift of economic power was the formation during the 17th century of the Bank of England by a powerful group of Whig financiers willing to underwrite the considerable debts of the government in return for the exclusive right to print banknotes. Each successive war or crisis increased the National Debt, as the loan became known, increasing the strength of the Bank and the power of the Whigs. Soane's building for the Bank of England, alone among the works of the 'revolutionary' architects, was indicative of a genuine revolution in progress.

New industries were beginning to grow, creating what was to become an unending demand for human labour-power. The coal and iron industries in Britain had led separate existences for centuries. Both were located in rural areas, the coal-mines wherever a seam came conveniently to the surface to be worked by hand by a small team of men, the furnaces in steep, wooded valleys which provided the charcoal for smelting and the fast-flowing water for rudimentary power. In the 18th century both processes were picturesque, fit subjects for Romantic landscape painters such as Paul Sandby or Joseph Wright. Then, towards the end of the century, experiments in coke-fired smelting by the Darby family, the ironmasters of Shropshire, made iron production more efficient and ensured that in future the coal and iron industries would go hand in hand. Iron production moved quickly away from Shropshire to the larger coalfields of South Wales, Clydeside and Tyneside, but it left one major monument: the Iron Bridge, built by Abraham Darby III at Coalbrookdale in 1779. This cluster of arched iron trusses carrying a narrow roadway over the river Severn was technologically primitive but an unusual achievement for its time. As architecture it was a dramatic and Romantic intrusion into the 18th-century landscape; as a structure it was unsophisticated but direct; historically it was the first major example in the world of the structural use of cast iron.

Although coal and iron were to dominate the second phase of the industrial revolution, it was through the cotton industry that the changes seriously began, and that both the advantages and disadvantages of the capitalist system became apparent. The technology of cotton has two main elements: the spinning of the yarn and the weaving of the cloth. In the traditional cottage industry of the early 18th century a simple partnership existed between the women and child spinners and the male craftsmen-weavers. Various improvements were made to the cottage process, for example the flying shuttle (1730) and the spinning Jenny (1760), but the main change came when the water-frame in 1768 and the Mule in 1780 brought spinning into the factory, vastly increasing the output of yarn and creating an insatiable demand for women and children to serve the machines. There was also now a demand for the mechanisation of weaving, to keep pace; when the power loom, invented in 1780, was widely applied after the turn of the century, it created widespread unemployment among the craftsmen-weavers. The logic of over-production also demanded the rapid creation of markets both at home and overseas to justify the capital invested and the increased output. As the development of transport and technology began to emancipate industry from its rural location, the advantages of concentration became apparent, and towns entered their period of most dramatic growth. After the Napoleonic wars, Lancashire, centre of the cotton industry in Britain and stronghold of the Whig bourgeoisie, became for a time the economic focus of the world.

Great Britain's industry in 1760-1830

0   100km

Clydeside **ships**

Tyneside **coal**

Leeds and Sheffield **cloth, coal, steel**

Manchester **cotton**

Liverpool **port**

Hull **port**

Stoke **pottery**

Ironbridge **iron**

Birmingham **metalwork**

South Wales **iron**

Bristol **port**

London **port**

James Watt (1736–1819) originator of the steam engine

Darby's **Iron Bridge** (1779) and Jedediah Strutt's **Milford** cotton mill in Derbyshire (1780)

1750   1800   1850

300

200

100

a
b
c

Consumption of raw cotton in
a Britain
b France and
c Germany
in thousands of tonnes

consol offices

Threadneedle Street

court

stock room (rotunda)

great hall

court

transfer office

Lothbury

Soane's great monument to Whig power, the **Bank of England** in London (1791–1833)

consol office

On the one hand, as Marx and Engels said, industrial capitalism brought undoubted benefits to some:

> The bourgeoisie, during its rule of scarce one hundred years, has created more massive and more colossal productive forces than have all preceding generations together. Subjection of Nature's forces to man, machinery, application of chemistry to industry and agriculture, steam-navigation, railways, electric telegraphs, clearing of whole continents for cultivation, canalisation of rivers, whole populations conjured out of the ground – what earlier century had even a presentiment that such productive forces slumbered in the lap of social labour? (The 'Communist Manifesto', 1848)

On the other hand, industrialisation, the factory system, rapid urbanisation, the destruction of local economies and with them local crafts and cultures, brought great misery to many more. With the creation of the industrial city came both over-work and chronic unemployment, squalid living conditions, poverty, ignorance and disease. This contrast between affluence for some and misery for others has remained the fundamental contradiction of the modern world, and an all-pervading feature of its 200-year history.

Contrasts

Britain and America in the early 19th century

In 1815, the Treaty of Amiens brought the Napoleonic Wars to an end. In England, many great public events were commissioned to celebrate the peace. The Prince Regent marked the occasion in his own way by asking his recently-appointed architect John Nash (1752–1835) to build a long-awaited new palace, in the fashionable 'oriental' style, at his favourite seaside resort of Brighton. This was the celebrated Royal Pavilion (1815–21), a confused, extravagant, tasteless and completely charming re-interpretation of Indian and Chinese architectural ideas as they were understood at the time. In a country suffering from the effects of the war it was a flamboyant gesture, worthy of any European prince seeking to recapture the glamour of pre-war days. But it belied the fact that Britain was not, and never could be again, a monarchic state of the old style, of the kind which still existed all over Europe. It was the middle-class capitalist who kept the English king on the throne, who paid for the war he had just won and for the palace his son was building. And it was the middle class which was about to make his country into the most powerful the world had yet seen.

The years 1815 to 1840 saw the spread of factory production throughout British industry, and brought the cotton towns of Lancashire to the economic forefront of the world. The population of Manchester and Salford, about 40,000 in 1750, was over 100,000 at the beginning of the 19th century and still growing rapidly. Though by now the second largest city in England, Manchester still bore traces of the medieval market town it so recently was, with an old centre, containing the spacious 18th-century houses of the rich manufacturers, separated from the outlying areas by a ring of toll-gates. But by now the drastic changes were apparent: the fifty or sixty new mills on the banks of the river discharged their effluent straight into the water, and the damp, verminous cottages and hovels of the workers were already clustering in large numbers in the districts of New Cross and Newtown. In 1822 a splendid town hall was built in the city centre. Designed in the Greek-revival style by Francis Goodwin, it was a slightly belated recognition of the civic status which the cotton industry had thrust upon the town.

Life in Manchester had little dignity. Urban society was becoming stratified into two opposed groups: the employers who, in effect, owned everything, and the labourers who owned nothing but their own labour-power to sell for wages, and who worked not at the self-regulated pace of the 18th century but in a totally new situation in which human activity was dictated by the requirements of the machine. The layout of towns was determined by the most efficient and economic location for the factories; developments in building technology, in particular the use of iron and glass, were for the improvement of commercial and industrial buildings rather than houses; and the application of scientific discovery to technology, such as the introduction of gas-lighting to lengthen the working day, had a commercial basis. Even education was denied to most of the population. The mindlessness of factory toil did not require an educated workforce, and England remained without an elementary school system for most of the 19th century. The economic and social life of the workers flooding into the

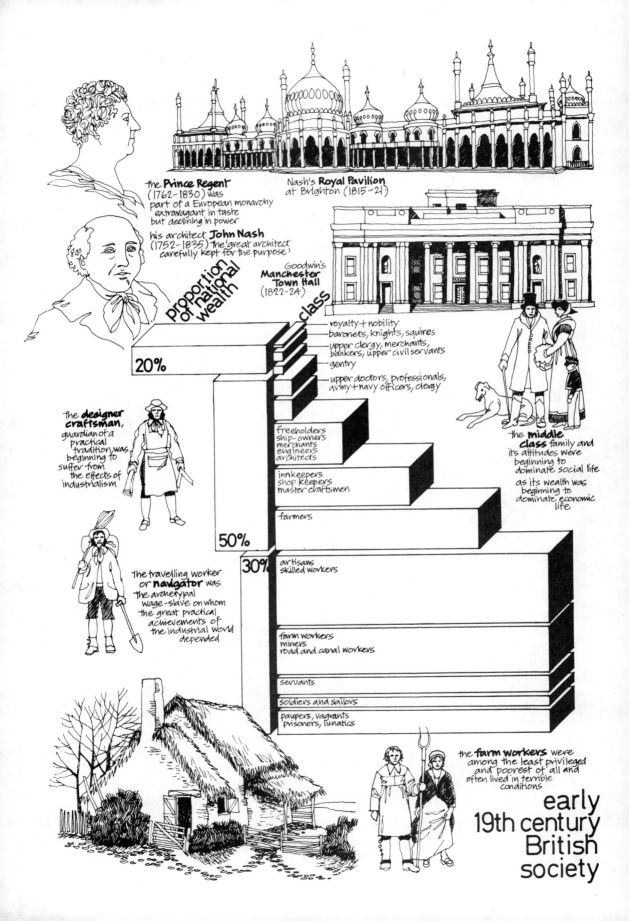

the **Prince Regent** (1762-1830) was part of a European monarchy extravagant in taste but declining in power

Nash's **Royal Pavilion** at Brighton (1815-24)

his architect **John Nash** (1752-1835) the 'great architect carefully kept for the purpose'

Goodwin's **Manchester Town Hall** (1822-24)

proportion of national wealth

class

20%

— royalty + nobility
— baronets, knights, squires
— upper clergy, merchants, bankers, upper civil servants
— gentry
— upper doctors, professionals, army + navy officers, clergy

the **designer craftsman**, guardian of a practical tradition, was beginning to suffer from the effects of industrialism

freeholders
ship-owners
merchants
engineers
architects

innkeepers
shop keepers
master craftsmen

farmers

50%

the **middle class** family and its attitudes were beginning to dominate social life

as its wealth was beginning to dominate economic life

the travelling worker or **navigator** was the archetypal wage-slave on whom the great practical achievements of the industrial world depended

30%

artisans
skilled workers

farm workers
miners
road and canal workers

servants

soldiers and sailors

paupers, vagrants
prisoners, lunatics

the **farm workers** were among the least privileged and poorest of all and often lived in terrible conditions

early 19th century British society

towns was determined by the manufacturers' profit-motive. Workers were not yet thought of as consumers who could contribute to an expanding market by buying its goods, still less as people with human rights, and there was little thought that they should live at anything other than subsistence level.

The reactions of the Romantic artists to all this exploitation and ugliness exemplified the contradictions of capitalism. They celebrated the opportunity offered by the bourgeois world for the growth of individualism, yet they hated the results of capitalism and the way, in practice, the individual spirit was crushed by it. A movement which had begun by celebrating the virtues of the modern world ended by rejecting them in favour of the past or of more primitive societies. The Romantic poets, such as Wordsworth, sought to discover

> In nature and the language of the sense
> The anchor of my purest thoughts, the nurse
> The guide, the guardian of my heart, and soul
> Of all my moral being.

With some notable exceptions, such as Shelley, their political perception was not developed enough for them to realise that the fault lay not with 'the present' but with the system that had created it, the antithesis of which was not Nature or the past but the strength of the emergent working class.

Individual reformers tried to obtain better conditions for the working class, among them Shaftesbury, seeking to curb the worst excesses of the factory system for women and children, and Cobden and Bright, working for the repeal of the Corn Laws. The greatest visionary was Robert Owen (1771–1858), a Welsh industrialist who benefited at an early age from the gigantic profits to be made from cotton. Through marriage with the owner's daughter, he became manager in 1800 of a large mill at New Lanark near Glasgow, where he began to put into practice the utopian theories, later expressed in *A New View of Society* (1813), which were to bring him world renown. His idea that 'man's character is made for him, not by him' was a new concept in the early 19th century, when it was believed that the poor merited poverty through being idle and vicious. Owen's firm view was that if the poor were inadequate it was only *because* they were poor, and he attempted to amend this at New Lanark by improving both living and working conditions and by attending to his workers' spiritual needs, especially through education.

At the centre of the little town, which at its height housed 2,500 people, was the mill, dominating its surroundings. From the profits, Owen was able to provide a cooperative food-store and market, a bakery, an abattoir and a laundry. At an Institute for the Formation of Character the workers were offered daily callisthenics, and at the schoolhouse children aged between five and ten were educated full-time – an unheard-of practice. At the edge of the town were the houses, which like all the other buildings were built dully but well in the gritty local stone. Attracted by tales of its commercial success and social innovation, as many as 15,000 admiring visitors came to New Lanark each year.

The factory children were Owen's first concern, and he expanded his work at New Lanark into a national campaign for a law to improve their working conditions and shorten their hours. He never lost faith in his cause, nor, despite much opposition, did he lose his belief in the essential humanity of the ruling classes. He was sure – against all the evidence – that if he could only get his message across, the capitalist system

Robert Owen
and the factory children

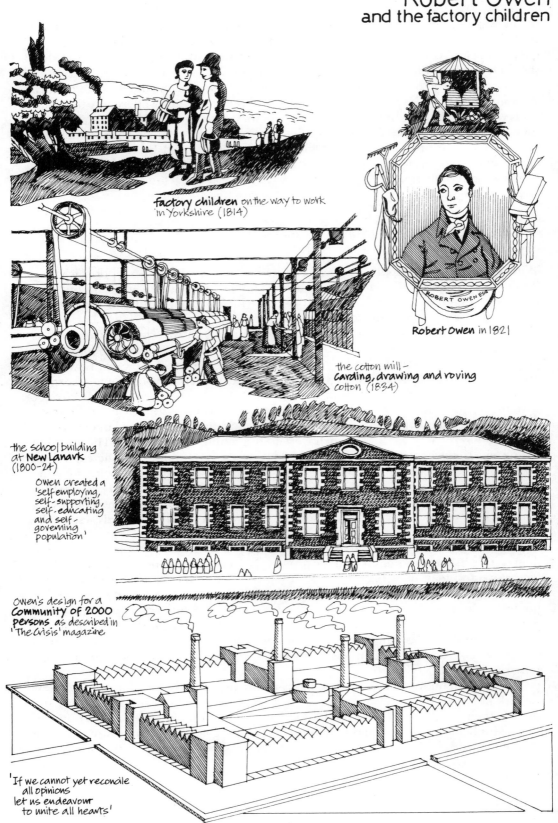

factory children on the way to work in Yorkshire (1814)

Robert Owen in 1821

the cotton mill—
Carding, drawing and roving
cotton (1834)

the school building
at **New Lanark**
(1800-24)

Owen created a
'self-employing,
self-supporting,
self-educating
and self-
governing
population'

Owen's design for a
**Community of 2000
persons** as described in
'The Crisis' magazine

'If we cannot yet reconcile
all opinions
let us endeavour
to unite all hearts'

would begin to reform itself. In 1824 he left Lanark for Indiana, USA, where he founded New Harmony, 40,000 acres of land which he hoped to turn into a model agricultural community; but by 1827 the venture had failed. Back in Britain, he devoted the rest of his life to expanding the cooperative and trade union movement, which had at last been made legal in 1824. Owen's lifetime achievements, great as they were, fell far short of his ambition, but he left behind a legacy of ideas which others were able to expand: that a change in the social order was necessary; that it was possible to use industry for the benefit of the workers as well as for their exploitation; that dignified labour could be a source of human happiness; that it was necessary for the workers to be more conscious of themselves as a class.

Capitalism, meanwhile, continued to accelerate. Cheap labour, especially that of women and children, allowed rapid capital accumulation within the cotton industry, which in turn stimulated investment in the associated chemical, metallurgical and engineering industries, and property speculation and building.

As building activity grew more intense, existing methods of architectural design were stretched to the utmost. An enormous volume of new building was required and much of it was unprecedented in form and technique. Factories, mills and warehouses, bridges and aqueducts, coal-mines, iron-foundries and gas-works required structures of unusual size, height, strength and complexity. As buildings of pure function and utility, they were generally outside the scope of the academically-trained gentleman architect who, even if he had the interest, had little of the practical skill required. At the same time they were too sophisticated and new to be dealt with wholly within the 18th-century craft tradition. New skills and methods of organisation were needed.

The first to emerge were those of the engineer, a new profession established during the late 18th century. Up to that time, large-scale engineering and surveying tasks had been mainly military, and extensive experience had been gained in the construction of bridges and earthworks, and used to great advantage by the canal engineers between 1760 and 1800. Now the technologist of the industrial revolution took the name 'civil engineer' to emphasise his civilian role. His task required a practical mind, an education and, above all, the numeracy necessary to apply the developing science of structural mechanics to practical problems.

Structural accuracy also allowed costs to be more accurately calculated, in the interests of economical design. The emergence of the quantity-surveyor to carry out this specific task was a direct response to the increased competitiveness of building. So too was the growth of the system of competitive tendering, in which rival teams of builders bid against each other to obtain a contract. Increased cost-consciousness also made it important for builders to manage themselves efficiently, and the early 19th century saw the emergence of the general contractor to fill this administrative and co-ordinating role. The contractor's claim to become leader of the building team was at first strongly resisted by the craftsmen, who saw him as an unnecessary interloper in the straightforward relationship between themselves and their client. The growing strength of the building unions was tested on this very issue. The early 19th century saw many strikes and even riots in favour of the old methods – but competitive tendering was demanded by the capitalist system and the craftsman architect's days were almost over.

Functional design was all very well for factories and warehouses, seen by their owners in purely economic terms, as having little social significance: the niceties of architectural design were not to be wasted on a workforce which was not worthy of

the Contractual system

the 18th and 19th century **architect** — often a craftsman himself — had a close contact with the labourers and craftsmen on the site who were employed directly by him but fixed their own rates

this was the system of Soane and Nash the system which made the townscape of the 18th and early 19th centuries like Langham Place (1813-25)

the great achievements of the road and canal **engineer** like Telford's Menai bridge (1819) and his Pont Cysy lltau aqueduct (1805)

were the result of an equally close relationship between the engineer and the navigators on the site

but with the growth of capitalism and the introduction in the early 19th century of the contract system

the architect or engineer began to share responsibility with the **quantity surveyor** — in charge of the costing of the project

and with the **contractor** — who directly employed and controlled the workers

in the case of a building contract the labourers and craftsmen had all now become wage labourers

and in the case of an engineering work — this is Church Tunnel on the London to Birmingham railway — the gangers and navvies contracted to do a 'piece' of the work

consideration. Architectural design, in the academic sense, was therefore confined mostly to buildings regarded as socially important and as indicators, erroneous or not, of the status and significance of the owners and institutions they represented. The gentleman architect's cultured skills were therefore still much in demand. He was able increasingly to concern himself with architectural imagery and to leave the practicalities of structure, of costing and of the building process to the engineer, the quantity surveyor and the contractor. In 1834 the Institute of British Architects, later the Royal Institute, was founded. This significant step towards professionalism was a rejection of the informal architectural methods of the 18th century and a logical means of protecting the architect's status from challenge by the other new building professions.

The meaning and significance of different architectural styles became the architect's chief preoccupation. Scholarly debates ensued on the style most suitable for a church, a town hall, or a bank. The aim was to give dignity to the present by reference to a splendid past, so the styles advocated were those of past ages, chosen for their political and social connotations. During the early part of the century, the styles of ancient Greece and Rome remained dominant.

The most spectacular example of their use was in the extensive reconstruction of central London begun in 1818. The developer was the Prince Regent, wishing to realise the assets of the Crown's large holdings of land and to share, in a dignified way, in the current scramble of speculation. From the royal palace of Carlton House broad processional avenues, lined with elegant neo-classical buildings, were cut through the city to its northern edge where a large area of agricultural land was laid out as a park: it was recognised that an open landscape would enhance the value of the stately terraced houses and detached villas built around its edge. A summer palace, to be located in the park, was never built, but the rest of the grand design was and remains an imaginative sequence of routes and spaces, one of the finest achievements of English town planning. The designer, following his success with the Brighton Pavilion, was John Nash; energetic and cynical, he could produce any architectural style to order. Here he responded with buildings of a conservative dignity: Regent Street, Portland Place, Park Crescent and the terraces of Regents Park itself, including the magnificent Cumberland Terrace (1829). To the north the elegant villas of Park Village, the first recognisable examples of suburban housing, added a light-hearted touch.

As the Bank of England grew in importance, Charles Cockerell (1788–1863), its official architect, designed its branch offices in Plymouth (1835), Bristol (1844), Liverpool (1845) and Manchester (1845). An admirer of both Greek architecture and of Wren, Cockerell developed a style that brought rich baroque touches to sober neo-classical designs. The more conventional side of neo-classicism was seen in the monumental London buildings of William Wilkins (1778–1839) – University College (1827) and the National Gallery (1834), and Robert Smirke (1781–1867) – the British Museum (1823). The finest neo-classical public building of the time was St George's Hall in Liverpool, begun in 1840 by the young architect Harvey Lonsdale Elmes (1813–47) and completed by Cockerell after Elmes' early death. Elmes obtained the commission after winning two separate design competitions, for a concert hall and a law-court. These two functions were then brilliantly combined in a single monumental building on a prominent island site. Its success as a design comes from its simple, logical form, the severity of its classical symmetry and the restrained gravity of its Corinthian-style details.

A feature of 19th-century commercial life was the growth of the gentleman's club as

Nash's London

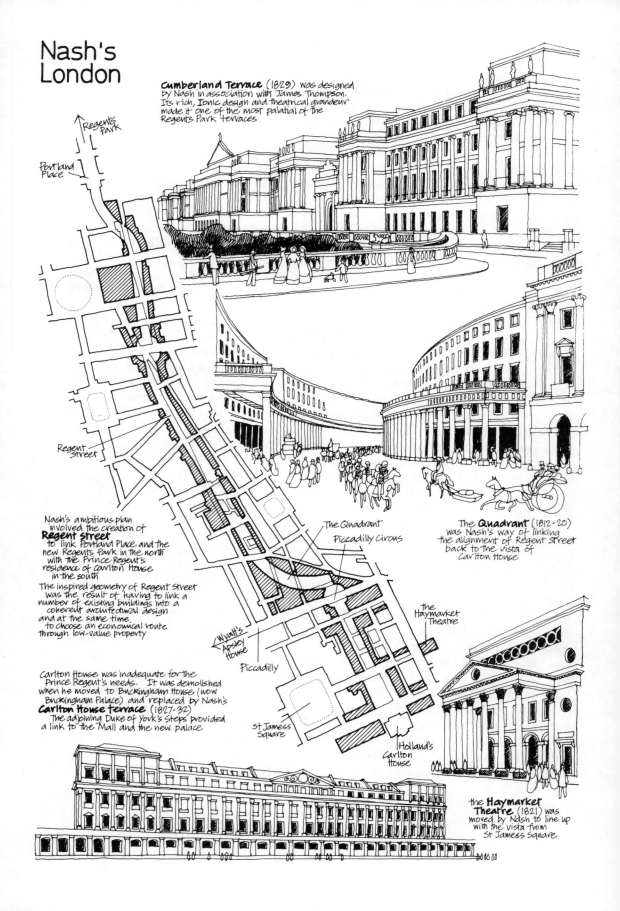

Cumberland Terrace (1829) was designed by Nash in association with James Thompson. Its rich, Ionic design and theatrical grandeur made it one of the most palatial of the Regents Park terraces

Regents Park

Portland Place

Regent Street

Nash's ambitious plan involved the creation of **Regent Street** to link Portland Place and the new Regents Park in the north with the Prince Regent's residence of Carlton House in the south

The inspired geometry of Regent Street was the result of having to link a number of existing buildings into a coherent architectural design and at the same time. to choose an economical route through low-value property

Carlton House was inadequate for the Prince Regent's needs. It was demolished when he moved to Buckingham House (now Buckingham Palace) and replaced by Nash's **Carlton House terrace** (1827-32) The adjoining Duke of York's Steps provided a link to the Mall and the new palace

The Quadrant

Piccadilly Circus

The **Quadrant** (1812-20) was Nash's way of linking the alignment of Regent Street back to the vista of Carlton House

Wyatt's Apsley House

Piccadilly

the Haymarket Theatre

St Jamess Square

Holland's Carlton House

the **Haymarket Theatre** (1821) was moved by Nash to line up with the vista from St Jamess Square

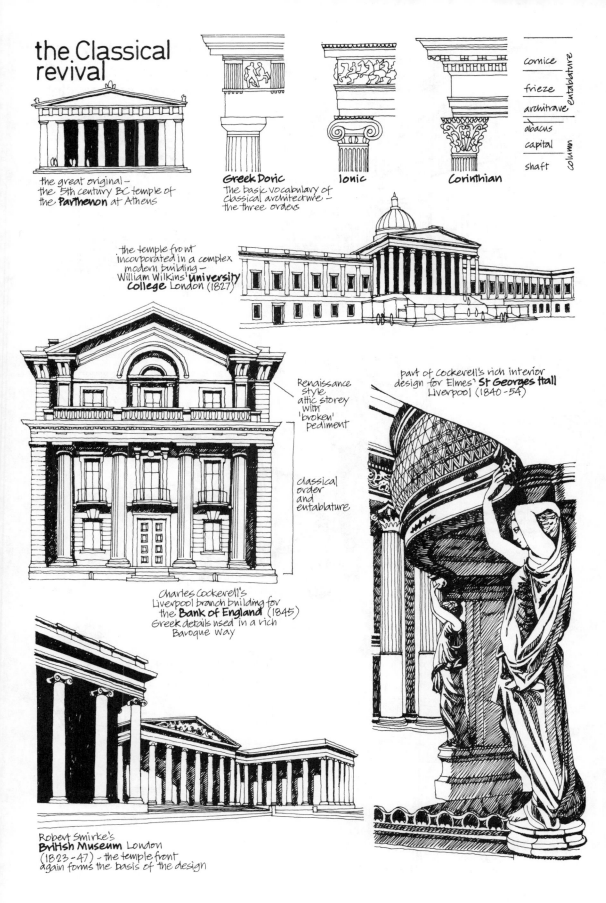

the Classical revival

cornice
frieze
architrave } entablature
abacus
capital } column
shaft

the great original –
the 5th century BC temple of
the **Parthenon** at Athens

Greek Doric   **Ionic**   **Corinthian**

The basic vocabulary of
classical architecture –
the three orders

the temple front
incorporated in a complex
modern building –
William Wilkins' **University
College** London (1827)

Renaissance
style,
attic storey
with
'broken'
pediment

classical
order
and
entablature

Charles Cockerell's
Liverpool branch building for
the **Bank of England** (1845)
Greek details used in a rich
Baroque way

part of Cockerell's rich interior
design for Elmes' **St Georges Hall**
Liverpool (1840-54)

Robert Smirke's
British Museum London
(1823-47) – the temple front
again forms the basis of the design

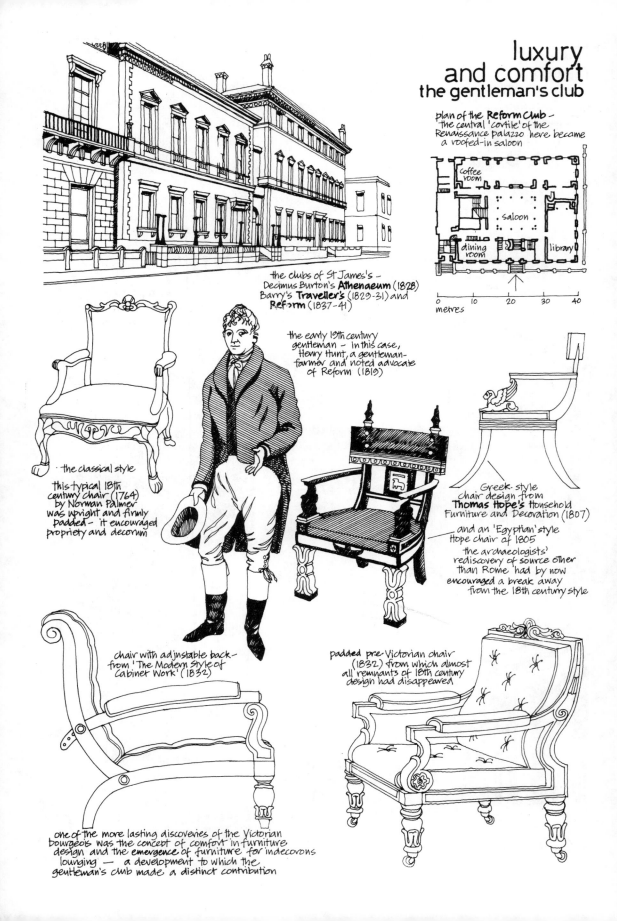

plan of the **Reform Club** — the central 'cortile' of the Renaissance palazzo here became a roofed-in saloon

coffee room

saloon

dining room

library

0 10 20 30 40
metres

the clubs of St James's — Decimus Burton's **Athenaeum** (1828) Barry's **Traveller's** (1829-31) and **Reform** (1837-41)

the early 19th century gentleman — in this case, Henry Hunt, a gentleman-farmer and noted advocate of Reform (1819)

· the classical style

this typical 18th century chair (1764) by Norman Palmer was upright and firmly padded — it encouraged propriety and decorum

Greek-style chair design from **Thomas Hope's** Household Furniture and Decoration (1807)

_ and an 'Egyptian' style Hope chair of 1805 the archaeologists' rediscovery of source other than Rome had by now encouraged a break away from the 18th century style

chair with adjustable back — from 'The Modern Style of Cabinet Work' (1832)

padded pre-Victorian chair (1832) from which almost all remnants of 18th century design had disappeared

one of the more lasting discoveries of the Victorian bourgeois was the concept of comfort in furniture design and the **emergence** of furniture for indecorous lounging — a development to which the gentleman's club made a distinct contribution a place for personal contacts to be made and business deals concluded in an atmosphere of privileged seclusion. The early 18th-century coffee-house, often a converted private house, had fulfilled much the same function, so when purpose-built clubs such as Robert Adam's Royal Society of Arts (1772) or John Crunden's Boodle's Club (1775) first appeared, the architectural style was similarly restrained and domestic. But the merchants of the 19th century had grander ideas. During the 18th century, clubs had become increasingly specialised and sectarian. By the 19th century it had become a matter of pride to any one group that its club was better-appointed and more imposing than any other. In London, several major clubs were founded between 1813 and 1834: the Guards', the United Services, the Athenaeum, the Travellers', the Carlton – for the Tory party, and the Reform – for Whigs and Radicals. The buildings which housed them were massive and splendid, located in the affluent St James's district where they vied with each other in magnificence. Most notable architecturally were the Travellers' (1829) and the Reform (1837), both designed by Charles Barry (1795–1860). By using as his model the *palazzo* of 16th-century Florence, Barry incidentally brought a revival of the Italian renaissance style to Britain. More immediately, he was able to create yet another association of ideas, establishing a flattering link between his clients and the Renaissance merchant-princes.

During the early 19th century, the pre-eminence of the neo-classical style was challenged by the phenomenon of the Gothic revival. The gothic style of the high middle ages was an integral part of European culture and had persisted as a living tradition in parts of Europe until the 17th century. Thereafter it was used only in a spirit of conscious imitation and, generally speaking, in a superficial and misunderstanding way. The growing interest in medievalism marked the start of an attempt by European artists and musicians to revive folk art and to rediscover 'the people', an idealised concept which offered, as an alternative to industrialism, a world of clear, if feudal, social relationships and a more homogeneous society. This interest was stimulated by the growth of archaeological research, the rapidly expanding Romantic movement and, in the 1830s, by the development within the English church of the Catholic 'Tractarian' Movement, with its emphasis on spirituality, the sacraments and the traditional ritual of pre-Reformation Christianity.

Protestant churches of the 18th century had been designed for a post-Lutheran form of worship in which ritual played little part. The Tractarians or ecclesiologists required a new form of building, with a prominent choir and chancel and a ceremonial high altar. They sought to raise church design to an exact science and to invest it with the greatest moral purpose. Gothic churches were built whose designers had made genuine attempts to understand the form and function of medieval building: in Manchester, St Wilfred, Hulme (1839); in Staffordshire, St Giles, Cheadle (1841); and in London, St Giles, Camberwell (1842). The designers of these buildings, Augustus Welby Pugin (1812–52) and George Gilbert Scott (1811–78), were to make a major contribution to the Gothic revival. Pugin was manic, volatile and passionate, a fervent convert to Catholicism; Scott was worthy, competent and evangelical; in their different ways they promoted gothic architecture as a matter of religious principle, through their enthusiastic and scholarly writings and through the convincing quality of their buildings.

Pugin's most seminal contribution to the debate on Gothic was his recognition of its essential 'truth'. In *The True Principles of Pointed, or Christian Architecture* (1841) he wrote, 'The two great rules for design are these. First, that there should be no features about a building which are not necessary for convenience, construction or propriety; second,

Pugin and Scott

Salisbury Cathedral (1220-65) the archetype of 13th century English gothic which Pugin knew well from his early days

Augustus Pugin (1812-52)

Pugin's church of **St Wilfred Hulme** (1839-42)

plan of St Wilfred's
vestry
high altar
chapel
font
tower

Gilbert Scott (1811-78)

Pugin's **St Giles Cheadle** (1841-6)

main porch of St Giles Cheadle

Missal designed in velvet and brass by Pugin for St Giles Cheadle

Scott's church of **St Giles Camberwell** (1842-4)

Pugin's silver **chalice** (1849) for the church of St Marie Hadfield

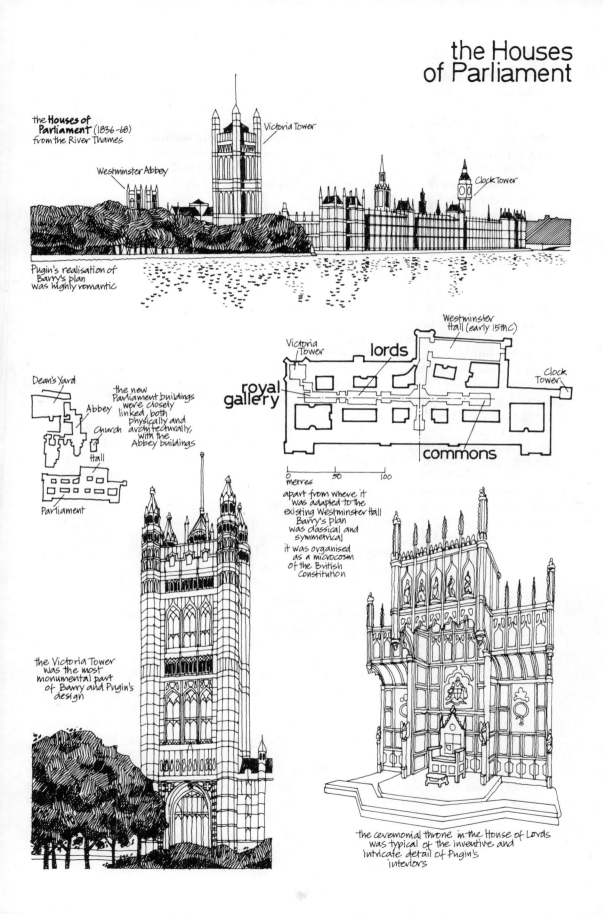

the Houses of Parliament

the **Houses of Parliament** (1836-68) from the River Thames

Westminster Abbey

Victoria Tower

Clock Tower

Pugin's realisation of Barry's plan was highly romantic

Dean's Yard

Abbey

Church

Hall

Parliament

the new Parliament buildings were closely linked, both physically and architecturally, with the Abbey buildings

Westminster Hall (early 15th C)

Victoria Tower

lords

royal gallery

commons

Clock Tower

0 50 100 metres

apart from where it was adapted to the existing Westminster Hall Barry's plan was classical and symmetrical

it was organised as a microcosm of the British Constitution

the Victoria Tower was the most monumental part of Barry and Pugin's design

the ceremonial throne in the House of Lords was typical of the inventive and intricate detail of Pugin's interiors

that all ornament should consist of enrichment of the essential construction of the building.' For him, the forms of gothic architecture derived not out of any external notion of surface symmetry but out of the functional needs of structure, materials and honest craftsmanship. This truthfulness made Gothic so superior a style as to be suitable, Pugin said, for all types of building, both sacred and secular. As the revivalist movement expanded, the style was to become accepted for the new town halls and law-courts in the fast-growing cities, the university colleges and private schools, the libraries and museums endowed by rich manufacturers for the benefit of their sons. It became embedded in middle-class culture in the way that the Palladian style had been intrinsic to the life of the 18th-century aristocracy. It is particularly ironic that a movement born in a spirit of conscious rejection of the mundane – by the Anglo-Catholics searching for greater spiritual truth and the Romantics reliving a past full of human dignity – should so quickly have been turned into a commodity by the material forces from which it represented an escape.

The earliest and most significant example was the result of a fire in 1834 which destroyed the medieval Palace of Westminster, the centre of parliamentary government. The architect appointed for the rebuilding was Charles Barry, the confirmed classicist. However, in remembrance of the original building and as a response to the genuine Gothic of the nearby Westminster Hall and Westminster Abbey, a medieval design seemed appropriate. There was also an unscholarly view that Gothic, unlike neo-Classical, had originated in England and thus had the authority of a national style. Barry provided the basic plan, a symmetrical, classical composition, and Pugin, with great zeal, gave this the appearance of a 15th-century gothic building. The result was a splendid failure: one of the most poetic and picturesque buildings of the 19th century, yet lacking the internal structural dynamism and the grotesque animation of detail of a genuine gothic building. As a design, it looked back to the 18th century rather than towards the realisation of Pugin's theories. Nevertheless, it created an important precedent for designing secular buildings in the gothic style.

In the elections of 1830 the Whigs regained power; but any hopes that a Whig government within a newly reformed parliament would bring further social justice were dispelled by the Corporations Act of 1835, which increased bourgeois power in the cities, and by the notorious Poor Law Amendment Act of 1834. This rationalised all the existing local laws into a monstrously unfair new system which sought to make poverty as unattractive as possible, by keeping relief well below the level of the lowest wage and by confining the poor to workhouses in which families were split up to prevent the birth of more children. The poorest grew poorer, the agricultural labourers suffering the most of all – especially the Irish, of whom a million starved to death in the famine of 1846.

In the early 1840s, the poor at their poorest contrasted poignantly with the rich at their richest. The process of industrialisation was diverting capital from consumption into investment. Both relatively and absolutely there had never been so much capital available, and not all of it was re-invested in industry. Much of it went into speculation and into the construction of the built environment within which the entrepreneur operated: not only the commercial and civic buildings of the city centres but also lavish country houses.

For the successful manufacturer seeking status and power, ownership of a large country estate was essential. The great country house became an extension of his commercial and political life – not merely somewhere to live, nor merely for display,

the bourgeois country house

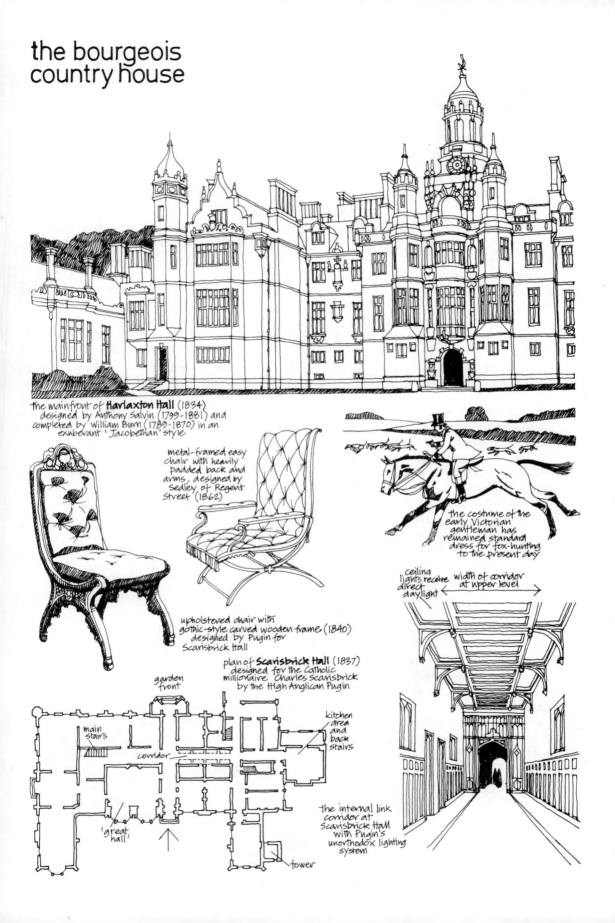

the main front of **Harlaxton Hall** (1834)
designed by Anthony Salvin (1799-1881) and
completed by William Burn (1789-1870) in an
exuberant 'Jacobethan' style

metal-framed easy
chair with heavily
padded back and
arms, designed by
Sedley of Regent
Street (1862)

the costume of the
early Victorian
gentleman has
remained standard
dress for fox-hunting
to the present day

upholstered chair with
gothic-style carved wooden frame (1840)
designed by Pugin for
Scarisbrick Hall

plan of **Scarisbrick Hall** (1837)
designed for the Catholic
millionaire Charles Scarisbrick
by the High Anglican Pugin

garden
front

main
stairs

corridor

kitchen
area
and
back
stairs

'great
hall'

tower

ceiling
lights receive
direct
daylight

width of corridor
at upper level

the internal link
corridor at
Scarisbrick Hall
with Pugin's
unorthodox lighting
system

but to provide an environment for social gatherings at which contacts could be made and business done. It was therefore designed to meet the needs not only of the family and its household staff but also of numerous guests and their servants. The planning was often highly complex, with separate corridors and stairways for masters and servants and for men and women. Gas-lighting, central heating and hot water added to the comfort, and games, blood-sports and all the adopted *machismo* of the aristocratic way of life provided the entertainment.

Several architects specialised in the design of country houses, among them Barry, whose Trentham Hall in Staffordshire (1834) was characteristically in the classical style. Generally, though, a more 'English' style was preferred: Gothic, Elizabethan or Jacobean. Harlaxton Hall in Lincolnshire (1834) by Anthony Salvin (1799–1881) was designed in a mixture of styles which became known as 'Jacobethan' and which Barry later used in the design of Highclere in Hampshire (1842). Pugin not surprisingly used the gothic style in Scarisbrick Hall, Lancashire (1837), which he designed to look like a medieval manor. The form of a medieval castle provided an even more romantic effect, as at Peckforton Castle, Cheshire (1844), by Salvin, and at Dunrobin Castle, Sutherland (1844), by Barry and Leslie.

House interiors were equally varied in style. During the first half of the 19th century interior design began to reflect the increased stylistic freedom in architecture generally. At the same time, the architect's strong influence on furniture design was diminishing, now that workshop production was growing. The increasing scale of production and the ever-growing middle-class market stimulated the production of cheap as well as expensive furniture in a wider variety of types and styles: gothic, Elizabethan, French baroque and rococo. Trade and travel brought back ever more exotic materials and ideas: papier-mâché, painted simulated lacquer, synthetic mother-of-pearl, encrustation with sea-shells. Important technical innovations included the invention of sprung upholstery, which encouraged the design of soft, fat chairs and sofas, and the increasing use of iron instead of wood for framing, especially in bedsteads. The general trend was towards extravagance and variety, intended like the rest of the house to provide for the owner's comfort and to emphasise his wealth.

Coal was now greatly in demand as a fuel for industry, in both engines and iron-furnaces, as a source of coal-gas, and for thousands of domestic fireplaces. Annual production increased from 11 million tonnes in 1800 to 50 million by mid-century. Coal mines began to scar the landscape; the mining process was becoming too large in scale to remain,compatible with any romantic view of nature. The typical mine of the early 19th century was an alien feature in the countryside, with its large, free-standing beam engine for turning the wheels of the pit-head gear, run from the steam of a 'beehive' boiler, its tall brick chimney pouring smoke. Spoil-heaps of shale began to spread over the hillsides. Yet the visual squalor of the mines, and the working and living conditions of the miners and their families, were totally outside the experience of those who benefited most from what coal had to offer. As coal production grew, the demand for iron also increased – for factory machinery, railway engines, ships, industrial buildings and structures. From about 250,000 tonnes in 1800, annual production grew to over 2 million tonnes by 1850. The increased use of machinery encouraged the development of both the metallurgical industry, by demanding ever more specialised metals and alloys, and of the machine-tool industry, by requiring ever greater precision.

As a result, the industrial centre of gravity shifted slightly from the cotton towns

coal and iron

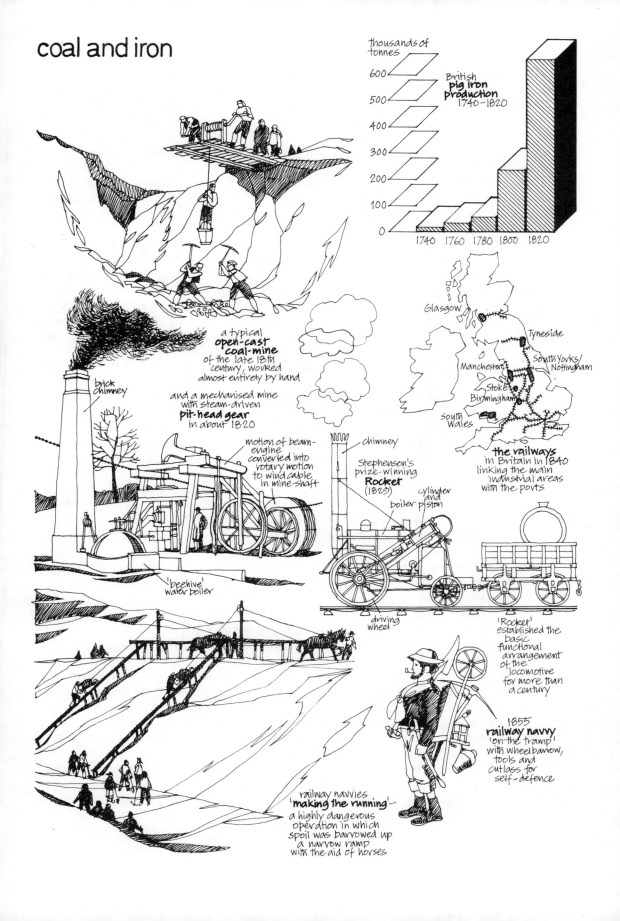

thousands of tonnes

British **pig iron production** 1740–1820

600
500
400
300
200
100

1740 1760 1780 1800 1820

a typical **open-cast coal-mine** of the late 18th century, worked almost entirely by hand

and a mechanised mine with steam-driven **pit-head gear** in about 1820

brick chimney

motion of beam-engine converted into rotary motion to wind cable in mine-shaft

'beehive' water boiler

chimney

Stephenson's prize-winning **Rocket** (1829)

cylinder and boiler piston

driving wheel

Glasgow

Tyneside

Manchester

South Yorks/ Nottingham

Stoke

Birmingham

South Wales

the railways in Britain in 1840 linking the main industrial areas with the ports

'Rocket' established the basic functional arrangement of the locomotive for more than a century

1855 **railway navvy** 'on the tramp' with wheelbarrow, tools and cutlass for self-defence

railway navvies **'making the running'** a highly dangerous operation in which spoil was barrowed up a narrow ramp with the aid of horses towards the mining areas, iron towns and ship-building towns of South Wales, Tyneside and Clydeside. In a frantic upsurge of speculation, the railways developed from a local form of transport serving the mining areas into a national passenger and goods network. The pattern of industry had begun to make cities heavily interdependent and good communications became vital to economic expansion. As trains could carry passengers faster than the fastest stagecoach and goods in greater bulk than the largest barge, investment which might have gone into roads or canals was switched quickly to railways. With the dramatic 'railway mania' of the 1840s, an unseemly speculative scramble took place, and new lines were opened on almost any route for which willing investors could be found. Traffic did not always materialise to justify investment and the failure rate was high.

A newly-formed railway company appointed an engineer to design and supervise the work, who in turn selected the contractor. The scale of the work was gigantic and the best contractors, such as Thomas Brassey or Samuel Peto, were capable of prodigious feats of management. The contractor appointed an agent for each section of the line who in turn appointed sub-contractors to carry out each element of the work: a bridge, a cutting, an embankment, a tunnel. The work was done by teams of men, usually as 'piece-work' – an agreed amount of work for an agreed sum, both shared evenly among them.

The railway mania made great demands on the manual workers. The urgency of competition, the simple technology of the time and the great size of the constructional task required a large force of labourers, working at great speed with the simplest of tools: picks, shovels and wheelbarrows. Canal workers had been known as 'navigators', and 'navvies' became the name applied to all constructional labourers; many were Irish, attempting to escape poverty, unemployment and hunger at home. The railway gangs lived a life of privation and danger; to the employers, profit was more important than industrial safety. Every possible corner was cut in the interests of economy and haste, and accidents were frequent. The navvies' appetite for work, drink and fighting became legendary. With their families in tow, they moved across the country like a marauding army, bringing a taste of the violence and alienation of industrial capitalism, as well as a demonstration of its achievements, to every village through which they passed.

The engineers too were placed under great pressure; the demand for speed often prevented designers from giving sufficient thought to technical problems, and too much knowledge came through the bitter experience of collapse and disaster. The more able engineers did what they could to calculate their designs, or test them in mock-up beforehand, pooling their knowledge with fellow-engineers with whom they were supposedly in competition. The science of statics thus developed simultaneously with the experience on site and a formidable body of theory allied with practice was gradually built up, resulting in a startling succession of engineering achievements.

The use of iron in heavy industrial technology had spread to include more conventional structures, especially those like factories and warehouses in which resistance to fire was important. Benyon and Marshall's flax mill in Shrewsbury (1796), constructed with iron columns and beams for this very reason, is the earliest surviving example. Iron was used in more pretentious architecture also, from the early 19th century: by Thomas Hopper in 1811 for his gothic-style fan-vaulted roof to the conservatory at Carlton House in London, and for the gothic-style roof of the church of St George, Everton, in Liverpool (1812) by Rickman and Cragg. The conservatory at Chatsworth

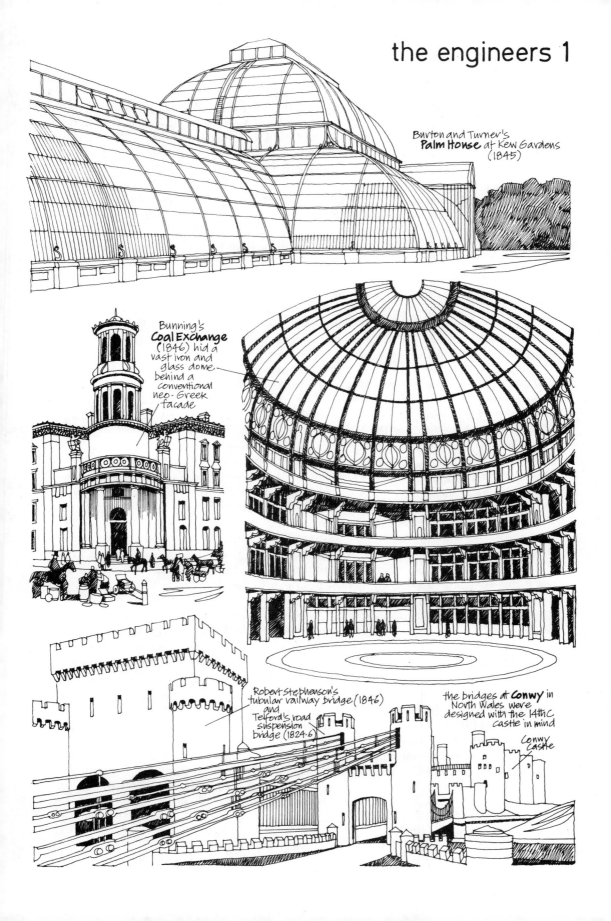

Burton and Turner's
Palm House at Kew Gardens
(1845)

Bunning's
Coal Exchange
(1846) hid a
vast iron and
glass dome,
behind a
conventional
neo-Greek
facade

Robert Stephenson's
tubular railway bridge (1846)
and
Telford's road
suspension
bridge (1824·6)

the bridges at **Conwy** in
North Wales were
designed with the 14thc
castle in mind

Conwy
Castle

House, Derbyshire (1836), was an early and spectacular example of glass building, distinguished by its great size – 84 metres long – and its imaginative double-vaulted shape. Designed by Joseph Paxton and Decimus Burton, it was the precursor of several large-span glass roofs, including those of the Palm House at Kew Gardens near London (1845) by Burton and Richard Turner, the Coal Exchange in London (1846) by James Bunning, and Sidney Smirke's Reading Room at the British Museum (1852).

The most imaginative use of iron, however, was seen in the work of the great road and railway engineers. Between 1819 and 1829 Telford extended the Holyhead road over the Menai straits on the first great suspension bridge of the modern world, a span of 140 metres in which, in addition to cast iron, he used wrought-iron chains for their higher tensile strength. At the same time he was building the Conwy suspension bridge (1824–6) to a similar design. Telford's career was almost at an end and these were his two last great works, but he shared his experience on them with the young Isambard Brunel (1806–59) who was designing a road bridge over the 80-metre-deep gorge of the river Avon at Clifton near Bristol. Strong gales had nearly destroyed the Menai bridge and Telford's advice was against risking another suspension bridge in an exposed location; but Brunel went ahead, achieving a daringly successful design in which masonry piers, built for greater grandeur like the pylons of an Egyptian temple, carried a deck slung on iron chains across a span of over 200 metres.

Telford, the 18th-century canal and road builder, belonged to an earlier age. Brunel epitomised the confidence and ability of a new generation, who would be given great opportunities by the rapid industrialisation and whose achievements in railway and steamship construction would be major contributions in themselves to capitalist expansion. Railway design in the 1830s and 1840s was dominated by a small group of engineers: Brunel, George Stephenson and his son Robert, Charles Vignoles, Joseph Locke and William Cubitt. Their widely varying talents and personalities were reflected in their designs. Brunel, for example, was the most brilliant technician, whose regard for cost-control was secondary to his desire to find the best technical answers. His choice of a 7-foot gauge (2.13 metres) for the Great Western Railway, though safer and more comfortable than the more usual gauge of 4 feet 8½ inches (1.43 metres), posed problems which Brunel met head-on: tunnels, embankments and cuttings needed extra width, and the great tunnel at Box, near Bath, was an epic achievement. Locke was the most efficient administrator and most capable of predicting cost and working to a budget. Applying what would now be known as cost-benefit techniques, he chose a short, steep route over the mountainous Shap Fell, arguing that the extra cost of developing and running a more powerful locomotive would be less than that of building a level but more circuitous route. George Stephenson's main attribute was his unassailable conviction of his own abilities, which inspired confidence in others. During the construction of the Liverpool and Manchester line on which his famous locomotive 'Rocket' made its first appearance in 1829, the peat bog of Chat Moss presented a seemingly impossible barrier which only he was capable of crossing; his long, low embankment built on a carpet of wattle hurdles was inspired in its simplicity.

Robert Stephenson (1803–59) was in some ways the most accomplished civil engineer of all; educated, cultured and charming, he combined at his best the talents of Brunel with greater economic realism. He designed many locomotives, built several railways including the important London and Birmingham line, and constructed a number of magnificent bridges, including the High Level at Newcastle (1846), the last great cast-iron bridge, in which the bow-and-string principle of the main girders was

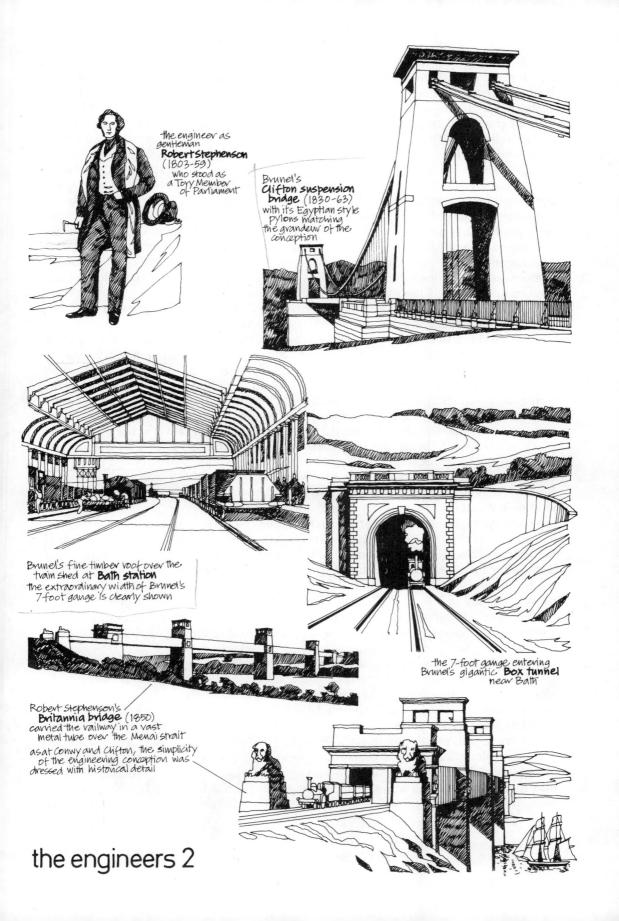

the engineer as gentleman **Robert Stephenson** (1803-59) who stood as a Tory Member of Parliament

Brunel's **Clifton suspension bridge** (1830-63) with its Egyptian style pylons matching the grandeur of the conception

Brunel's fine timber roof over the train shed at **Bath station** the extraordinary width of Brunel's 7-foot gauge is clearly shown

the 7-foot gauge entering Brunel's gigantic **Box tunnel** near Bath

Robert Stephenson's **Britannia bridge** (1850) carried the railway in a vast metal tube over the Menai strait

as at Conwy and Clifton, the simplicity of the engineering conception was dressed with historical detail

the engineers 2

developed to reduce the tensile forces in the cast-iron members. The Britannia railway bridge over the Menai Straits (1850) was his greatest achievement, consisting of two spans of box-girder construction, large square tubes of wrought iron through which the railway track ran, supported on tall masonry piers. This unprecedented design, based on both theoretical calculation and practical tests, was an important contribution to structural knowledge.

In 1850, with the population of Britain around 20 million, the middle class numbered no more than 1.5 million, yet this tiny group, whose final emergence was the most significant social feature of the 19th century, was beginning to achieve economic domination of the world. It was this increase in middle-class power which made the railways both possible and necessary; the railway revolution thus epitomised the greater social revolution then taking place. The resistance of aristocratic landowners to the railways crossing their estates was one aspect of the losing battle they were now fighting on all fronts against middle-class incursion. The grim living and working conditions of the navvies and their families were one particularly graphic example of what was happening to the working class everywhere. And the frequently-expressed feelings of pride in the engineering marvels of the age were those of a middle class discovering its identity.

In one respect, middle class identity was hard to attain: as Marx wrote, 'the separate individuals form a class in so far as they have to carry on a common battle against another class; otherwise they are on hostile terms with each other, as competitors.' The work of sympathetic writers, artists, architects and engineers was important in countering this fragmentation. Through them could be formulated the main tenets of bourgeois philosophy: the organisation of society to obtain the greatest social efficiency; the importance of the 'useful arts'; and the elevation of the idea of work to a high moral plane. Also through them came the main propaganda message of liberalism: that what was right for the middle class was right for society as a whole. Early in the century, the workers who had helped the Whigs to power had been ready to believe this, but the Reform Act and its consequences had broken the illusion. If they were to achieve any kind of freedom it must be through their own efforts.

One way lay through the organisation of labour. The urban proletariat was growing at a faster rate than the middle class and though it comprised only a small proportion of the total workforce – perhaps one in ten – it had the bargaining power which came from being at the centre of economic life, and its concentration in small local areas made union a practical possibility. The union of Carpenters and Bricklayers was formed in 1827, followed in 1829 by Manchester Unity, a national society of bricklayers, and in 1832 by the Operative Builders' Union, a multi-craft organisation which tried to circumvent the exploitation of the contractual system by establishing the co-operative as a means of building.

It is significant that these early steps towards union were taken by the building trades and by the other traditional craft industries – saddlers, shoemakers, weavers. It was they rather than the workers in the new heavy industries whose experience of organisation was longest and whose jobs were most vulnerable to the effects of industrialisation. Apart from farm-labourers, the building workers formed the largest workforce in the country, some 400,000 in the 1830s. Their main source of discontent was the exploitation the new economic system had brought. The intervention of the contractor had reduced the valued autonomy of individual craftsmen and turned them into wage-slaves. It had also divorced the design process from the building process, with unfortunate effects on both the practicality of architectural designs and the creative potentialities of craftsmen who were no longer involved in design decisions. Having finally reduced buildings to the status of commodities, the system hit particularly hard at the poorer sections of society. The increasing urgency of the profit-motive, together with high building costs caused by inflation and taxes on materials, placed even the shoddiest buildings at a premium, and priced the poorer families out of the housing market. Building workers, among whom traditionally there was a hierarchy of elitism – the 'society' craftsmen, the 'cheap' craftsmen, the apprentices, the labourers – sank many of their differences during the 1820s and 1830s in a concerted attack on the system. Along with the other craft workers, among whom many conspiracies to rebellion were conceived, they became radical and militant unionists, not only on their own behalf but in the class-struggle in general. The main focus of radical politics was the Chartist movement, which was developed in the early 1830s by Owen and others, dissatisfied with the slow pace of reform, and which became the world's first national working-class movement seriously to challenge the underlying attitudes of the capitalist world.

Many American industrialists professed horror at the appalling conditions in English cities. Exploitation, it was said, was not only contrary to republican ideals, but also likely to bring discontent and revolution. It became a matter of pride to the American industrialist that by as much as the English city failed to create good working and living conditions, by so much should his succeed. The archetype was the cotton town of Lowell, MA, begun between 1810 and 1820 by Francis Cabot Lowell, Nathan Appleton and Patrick Jackson. It is likely that New Lanark was a model, but the town of Lowell was taken further, both in the efficiency of its production and in the paternalism of its owners. The mill was laid out in a logical production sequence: cotton was carded on one floor, spun on the next and woven on the next two, with the machinery housed in the basement. Over the next few years, mill-towns and factories grew up on every riverside: Waltham and Chicopee in Massachusetts, Nashua in New Hampshire. Bay State Mills at Lawrence, MA (1845), was one of the best examples of a purpose-designed complex of mills, administrative offices, housing, dormitories and local stores. Rapid improvements in machine design began to put New England's productive efficiency on a level with Lancashire's.

Unlike New Lanark, Lowell and many of its successors were not family towns. Although some steam-power was available, most early factories were rural rather than urban phenomena, sited by rivers in remote valleys. Having no urban workforce, the industrialist had to create his own, capable of co-existing wih the local rural system which was still the backbone of the economy and which still had a lot of political support. Yankee farm-girls were persuaded to leave their brothers and fathers on the land and work in an industrial community for a fixed term, perhaps five years, a period short enough to discourage the formation of unions. In hostel dormitories supervised by matrons *in loco parentis*, the girls led lives of strict discipline, with a strong religious bias designed to overcome the misgivings of their parents. The aggressively Christian ethic of Lowell contrasted strongly with Owen's enlightened humanism, and did not conceal the fact that, like urban workers in Manchester, the girls were exploited by low wages, long hours and empty lives.

American industrialism received additional stimulus when an incursion of new settlers escaping the European depression of the 1820s and 1830s rapidly increased the population and created an instant demand for goods and services. Many immigrants got no further than the eastern states, where they formed a pool of cheap labour. Those

Republican values

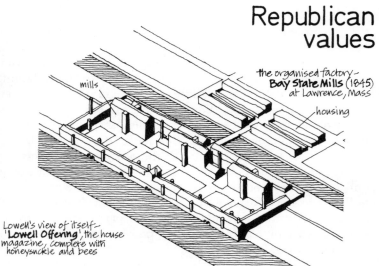

the organised factory—
Bay State Mills (1845)
at Lawrence, Mass

mills

housing

Lowell's view of itself—
'**Lowell Offering**', the house
magazine, complete with
honeysuckle and bees

Quincy Market (1825)
at Boston, Mass
by Alexander Parris

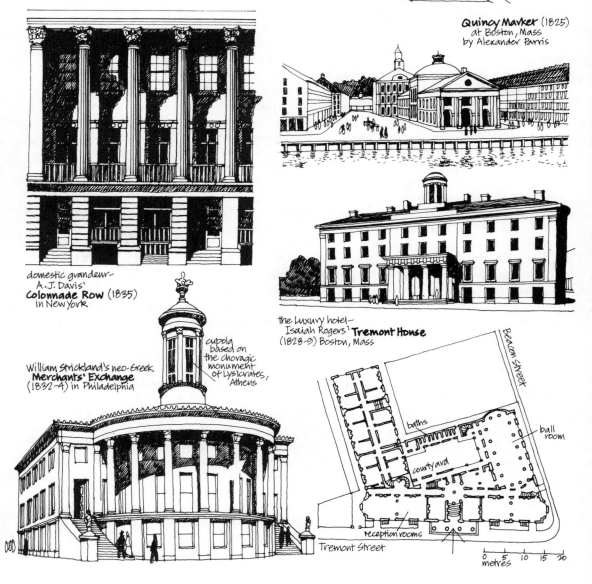

domestic grandeur—
A.J. Davis'
Colonnade Row (1835)
in New York

the luxury hotel—
Isaiah Rogers' **Tremont House**
(1828-9) Boston, Mass

William Strickland's neo-Greek
Merchants' Exchange
(1832-4) in Philadelphia

cupola
based on
the choragic
monument
of Lysicrates,
Athens

Beacon Street

baths

ball
room

courtyard

reception rooms

Tremont Street

0 5 10 15 20
metres

who moved west to settle as farmers became part of the process of opening up a vast agricultural hinterland which in time was to supplant the farmlands of the east, creating even more spare labour for the eastern cities. As factory production increased, domestic prices fell, making it less economic to import British goods. The mechanisation of factories increased; the textile industry expanded tenfold and the coal and iron industries of New Jersey and Pennsylvania began to grow. As in England, investment was poured into new railways; in 1830, the Baltimore and Ohio, the Mohawk and Hudson and the Charleston and Hamburg were opened; by 1850 the eastern seaboard was well served and lines stretched as far west as the Mississippi and as far south as Tennessee.

Republican power in the federal government helped industrial growth; during the 1820s and 1830s the eastern cities began a new phase of civic improvement, reconstructing their town centres to celebrate their new wealth and political power. Republican idealism demanded the Greek-revival style. Bourgeois housing of the period is typified by Colonnade Row in New York (1835) designed by A. J. Davis as a terrace of fine brownstone houses with double-height Corinthian columns. City halls, museums, art galleries, concert rooms and all the panoply of the cultured city appeared at this time. Among these was Quincy Market in Boston (1825), an elaborate stone building designed by Alexander Parris to combine shops with exhibition halls and reception rooms, as if to emphasise the link between bourgeois affluence and bourgeois culture. The grand hotel, as a building type, appeared abruptly in the late 1820s to cater for the large number of wealthy entrepreneurs travelling through the eastern sea-ports. Isaiah Rogers, the Boston architect, earned himself an international reputation by the magnificence of his Tremont House hotel in Boston (1828) and his Astor House in New York (1832).

Northern capitalists were also making money from the development of the west. Here railways were the key to economic expansion. Already they had taken urban culture across the Appalachians and, in a single generation, towns which at the beginning of the century had been timber-built frontier posts had acquired Greek-revival city halls built in stone. The architects Town and Davis designed the new State Capitol in Indianapolis (1831) as a peripteral Greek temple surmounted incongruously by a Roman dome. Neo-classical buildings appeared in every large town – the cathedral in St Louis, MO, the Capitol in Columbus, OH, the court-house in Cleveland, another of Rogers' luxury hotels in Cincinnati – and the style spread west to Illinois and crept south to Kentucky and Tennessee.

Frontier society was at first mobile, impersonal and self-contained, having few links with the east and certainly not enriching it with raw materials or produce. But as the railways came they brought banks, factories, stores and all the trappings of middle-class capitalism to service the local areas and, in return, to extract a profit from them. Those who benefited most were the financiers of the east and of Britain whose capital underwrote the land acquisition and the development of the railway lines; those who lost most were the Indians. By the mid-19th century the tribes east of the Mississippi and on the western seaboard had been 'pacified'; only in the plains were the Indians still relatively free, and even here they were now under pressure from colonisation. The Sioux leader Crazy Horse said, 'a man does not sell the land on which the people walk', but in 1834 the founding of the Bureau of Indian Affairs was a major step towards the total control of their land.

The growing prosperity of the north also affected the cotton-growing south, which

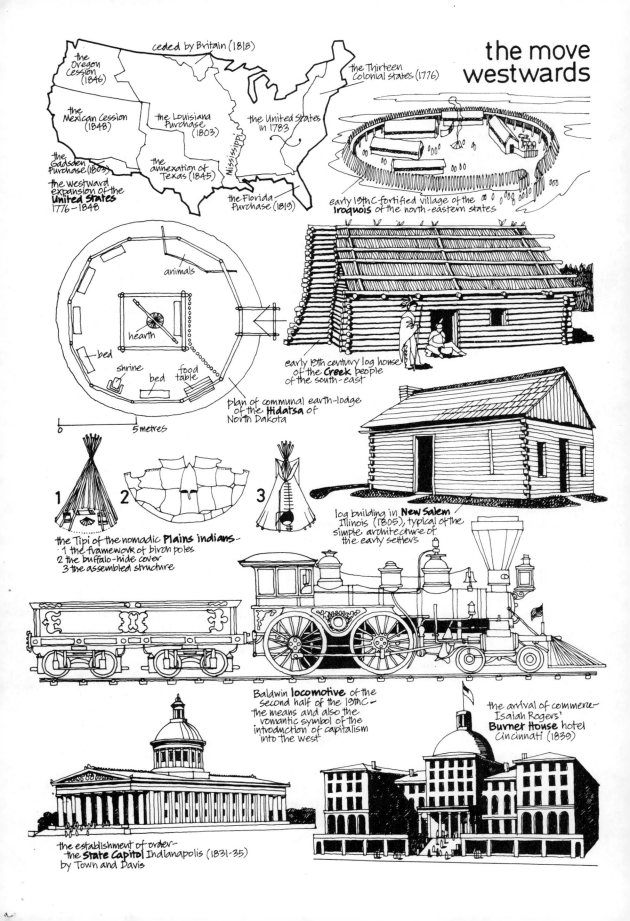

the move westwards

ceded by Britain (1818)

the Oregon Cession (1846)

the Mexican Cession (1848)

the Louisiana Purchase (1803)

the United States in 1783

the Thirteen Colonial states (1776)

the Gadsden Purchase (1853)

the annexation of Texas (1845)

Mississippi

the westward expansion of the **United States** 1776-1848

the Florida Purchase (1819)

early 19thC fortified village of the **Iroquois** of the north-eastern states

animals

hearth

bed

shrine

bed

food table

0   5 metres

plan of communal earth-lodge of the **Hidatsa** of North Dakota

early 19th century log house of the **Creek** people of the south-east

the Tipi of the nomadic **Plains indians**
1 the framework of birch poles
2 the buffalo-hide cover
3 the assembled structure

log building in **New Salem** Illinois (1805), typical of the simple architecture of the early settlers

Baldwin **locomotive** of the second half of the 19thC - the means and also the romantic symbol of the introduction of capitalism into the west

the arrival of commerce - Isaiah Rogers' **Burnet House** hotel Cincinnati (1830)

the establishment of order - the **State Capitol** Indianapolis (1831-35) by Town and Davis

during the 18th century had dominated economic life but was now falling behind. It relied on the north not only as an outlet for its exports but also for imports of food and consumer goods, all of which were nearly doubled in price by shipping duties and taxes. Among the southern whites a mood of resentment began to grow, leading them ever more strongly to defend their culture and institutions and aggressively to expand them where necessary.

In an attempt to create confidence in the southern system, both among themselves and others, the rich plantation-owners adopted a life-style of cultured gentility and chivalry. Neo-classical architecture, which in the north represented federalism, republicanism and freedom, took on a new meaning in the south. The apologists noted that Plato's Athens had been dependent on slavery: the use of the Greek architectural style was therefore one way of linking the present with an admired past, and of implying that slavery was an essential part of any great democracy. Robert E. Lee's own house at Arlington, VA (1802–26), was in the Greek revival style, but there were few others till the 1830s. Then came several major examples, with their characteristic giant porticos in Doric or Corinthian style: the Hermitage, Nashville (1835), the Ralph Small house, Macon, GA (1835), Gaineswood, Demopolis, AL (1842), and the Polk mansion, Rattle and Snap, in Tennessee (1845).

The workers of the industrial north, though technically free, were as enslaved to the system as the cotton pickers. Even within the Lowell system, life was hard; outside it, working conditions were bad and housing in very short supply. The labour movement first grew up among the male workers in the heavy industries of New Jersey and Pennsylvania and, as in England, among the workers in the declining craft industries. The social changes taking place in America were mirrored by the furniture industry. At the beginning of the century a strong craft base persisted, and was responsible for such classic products as the 'Windsor' fan-back farmhouse chair, which together with the contemporary ladder-back associated with the Shaker religious communities, a design of comparable simplicity and purity, contrasted strongly with the flamboyance of the revivalist styles then current in wealthy homes both in America and Europe. However, as factory production began to affect the industry, technical innovations – such as the laminating, steam-bending and machine carving carried out by the manufacturer John Henry Belter – resulted in designs of technical excellence but little originality: ornate rococo-revival styles adapted for machine production.

In 1837 came depression, part of the characteristic sequence of booms and slumps by which industrial capitalism developed. The cyclical pattern was typical. Continued expansion, and reinvestment in the hope of further profits, resulted in a shortage of both capital and labour, causing costs and lending-rates to rise and profits to fall. Lower profits caused investors to withdraw from the capital goods industries, creating a downward spiral of lower production, increased unemployment and panic. The new class of wage-labourers was helpless; totally dependent on outside sources for both housing and food, with no welfare system to protect them, they relapsed into a vicious circle of poverty, starvation and disease. For the first time, the problem of insanitary, overcrowded inner areas, worsened by the ever-present danger of fire among the wooden shacks, was brought home to city authorities.

The depression was part of a world-wide economic crisis which lasted until 1841, bringing bankruptcy to many financiers and unemployment and hunger to workers and their families. In America, the immediate effect was the withdrawal of European finance from the industries and railways; it was now necessary to create new industrial

the city

plan of **Savannah**, Georgia, in 1856 – laid out with the order and regularity of an ancient Greek colonial town

city hall

waterfront

market

church

park

1km

500m

0

typical Savannah house of 1819

Savannah house of 1840 – a wide variety of treatment was possible within the strict dimensional framework and the limits of the classical style

typical neighbourhood unit of 44 building lots with central open space

typical town house with iron balconies (1837) **New Orleans**

the plantation

plantation house **Chalmette**, Louisiana (1820)

basic form of the Louisiana **plantation house** 19th century

wide eaves

'parasol' roof sheds rain and shades house from sun

balconies encourage air-flow

full-height windows increase ventilation and 'jalousies' give both air and privacy

the George Polk mansion 'Rattle and Snap' (1845) at **Columbia**, Tennessee

Shaker and Windsor furniture

Shaker Barn (1823)
Hancock, Mass

early British Chippendale
comb-back Windsor
(1800)

'cabriole' legs

'splat' bow back

'ladder' back

mid 19th century
Shaker side-chair
in maplewood

comb

American
**fan-back
Windsor**
arm-chair
(1800)

'H' shaped stretcher

turned legs

English **bow-back Windsor** (early 19th century) with wheel-shaped 'splat'

'saddle' seat

scroll

American
Belter side-chair
in laminated
rosewood (1850)

English
mid 19th century
**Scroll-back
Windsor**
side-chair
from the High
Wycombe
furniture factories

American
**bow-back
Windsor settee**
(1800)

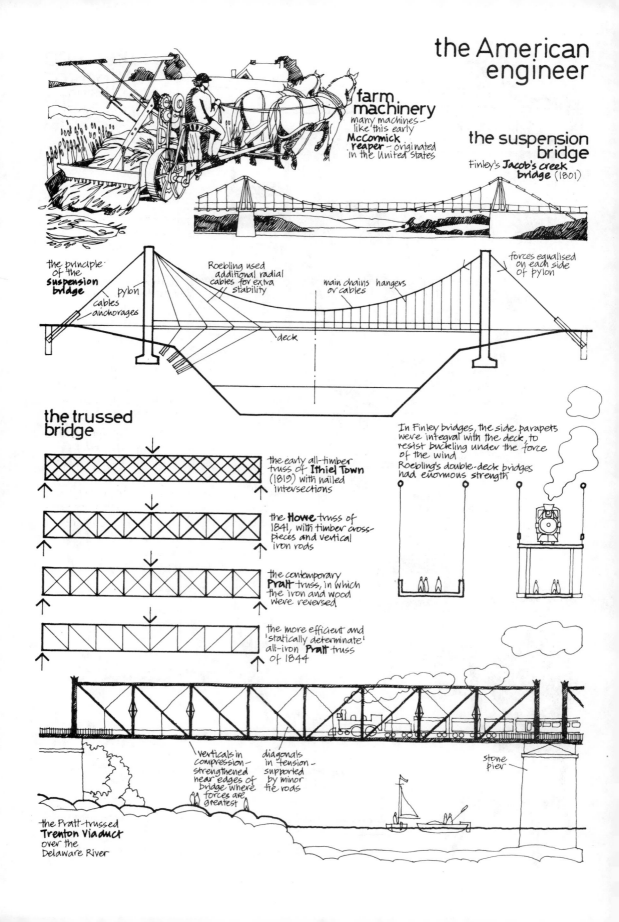

the American engineer

farm machinery

many machines – like this early **McCormick reaper** – originated in the United States

the suspension bridge

Finley's **Jacob's creek bridge** (1801)

the principle of the suspension bridge

pylon
cables
anchorages

Roebling used additional radial cables for extra stability

deck

main chains or cables   hangers

forces equalised on each side of pylon

the trussed bridge

the early all-timber truss of **Ithiel Town** (1819) with nailed intersections

the **Howe** truss of 1841, with timber cross-pieces and vertical iron rods

the contemporary **Pratt** truss, in which the iron and wood were reversed

the more efficient and 'statically determinate' all-iron **Pratt** truss of 1844

In Finley bridges, the side parapets were integral with the deck, to resist buckling under the force of the wind
Roebling's double-deck bridges had enormous strength

verticals in compression – strengthened near edges of bridge where forces are greatest

diagonals in tension – supported by minor tie rods

stone pier

the Pratt-trussed **Trenton Viaduct** over the Delaware River

and financial institutions, less dependent on outside aid and more capable of with-standing economic crisis. As the railways had opened up the continent for mining, farming and lumber, other mechanical inventions had followed: pumps, drills and winding-engines, harvesters, threshers and mechanical saws. Machines were expensive to buy and it was necessary to make them earn their cost-price by keeping them productive through both good times and bad. It became usual for competing manufac-turers to join together in mergers and cartels in order to adjust the market and keep production flowing smoothly. The introduction of monopoly in place of competition was thus the first major adjustment in the capitalist system.

The second was the development of the corporation, also introduced during the 1840s and 1850s. No single American financier had sufficient capital to build a rail-way, but a corporation, by selling shares to investors, large and small, could create the capital out of other people's money. As in England, there was over-investment in railways and many schemes failed. The investors had illusory rights and the real profits were made by a very few. Also as in England, the railways stimulated the development of structural engineering. Before Telford's Menai bridge was begun, the American engineer James Finley had constructed eight suspension bridges, incorporating extra stiffening to counteract the oscillation caused by the wind. In 1844, the introduction of high-tensile steel cables by the engineer John Roebling established the suspension bridge as a common form, though its inherent flexibility of construction made it more appropriate for roads than railways. An alternative was the trussed bridge, a simple lattice of straight members of regular length. Iron was in short supply at first, and the earliest versions were in wood, simply nailed at the junctions and capable of being put together quickly and cheaply in remote sites. Later versions used timber for the com-pression members with iron tie-rods. In 1844, Thomas Pratt patented an all-iron ver-sion which became the standard design for medium-span railway bridges for the next hundred years.

America was developing a cultural identity separate from that of Europe, which allowed its technology to develop in different directions where necessary. At the same time, the continuing economic link stimulated the interchange of ideas, to the benefit of capitalism on both sides of the Atlantic.

The philosophy of right
Continental Europe in the early 19th century

In 1825 Ludwig I (1786–1868) came to the Bavarian throne and resolved to make his remote, economically backward state one of the cultural centres of Europe. Within twenty years, influenced by the neo-classical ideas of Napoleonic France, and stimulated perhaps by the recent completion (1824) of the elegant Marktplatz in Karlsruhe by Freidrich Weinbrenner, his architects had transformed the old city centre of Munich with formal squares and routes, churches, palaces and above all the galleries and museums deemed essential to a cultured regime. Principal among them was Leo von Klenze (1784–1864) who had studied in Paris and had already distinguished himself as a neo-Classicist with the Glyptothek sculpture hall (1816–30) and, more daringly, as a neo-renaissance designer with the Alte Pinakothek art gallery (1826–33). For Ludwig he laid out the Königsplatz, a formal square in which a ceremonial Greek propylaeon (1846–63) formed the central feature. He developed his neo-renaissance ideas in the Königsbau at the Royal Palace (1826) where, like Barry in England, he took the Florentine palazzo as his model. He even ventured, at the King's insistence, into a neo-Byzantine style for the Allerheiligen royal church (1827). His finest work, however, was probably his memorial temple for national heroes, built at Regensburg in the Bavarian Forest and known portentously as Walhalla: a peripteral Greek temple stood on a hill-side artificially enlarged with ceremonial ramps, stairs and walls in a composition which looked back not only to Gilly's monument to Frederick the Great but also to Jefferson's hilltop Capitol at Richmond, VA.

Klenze's main rival for Ludwig's attention was Freidrich von Gärtner (1792–1847) who had also studied in Paris. Gärtner's speciality was not French neo-classical but the *Rundbogenstil*, a style incorporating Romanesque round-headed arches, which he used, again at Ludwig's behest. The development of the processional Ludwigsstrasse, with its Ludwigskirche (1829–40), its state library (1831–40) and its university (1835–40), was his chief work. The opportunity for another major work came in 1829, at the end of the Greek struggle for independence from Turkey, when the north-European powers placed a puppet king on the Greek throne. There was some difficulty in finding a candidate, but Ludwig's temerity in taking on the job on behalf of his son, who became Otto I of Greece, was matched by Gärtner's in the building of the Royal Palace in Athens (1837–41) in which he exported the classical style back to its place of origin.

Ludwig's interests were not confined to buildings. In 1835 he built the first railway line in Germany. He was motivated more by interest and enthusiasm than by any sense of the railway's economic significance, but others could see that railway development was crucial to solving the problem of Germany's desperate political and economic disunity. The industrialist Friedrich Liszt wrote, 'I could not see the astonishing effects of the railways in England and North America without wishing that my German fatherland would partake of the same benefits.' By 1860, 5,500 kilometres of track had been laid, cutting across state boundaries and linking the inaccessible Danube-orientated south with the canal system and Baltic ports of the lowland north; Germany was well on the way to being the greatest industrial nation of continental Europe and

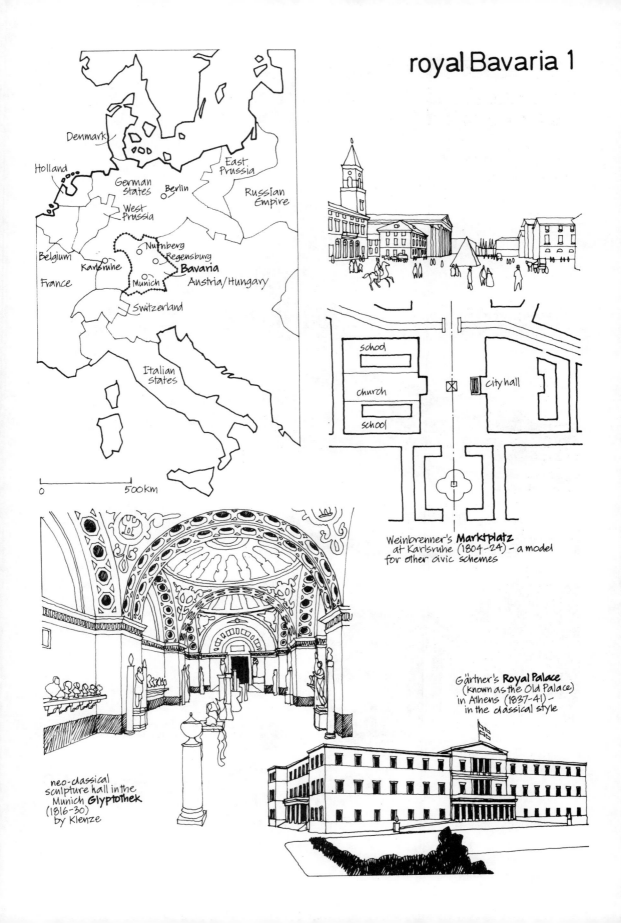

Denmark

Holland

East Prussia

German States   Berlin

Russian Empire

West Prussia

Belgium   Karlsruhe

Nurnberg   Regensburg

France   Munich   **Bavaria**

Austria/Hungary

Switzerland

Italian states

0   500km

school

church

school

city hall

Weinbrenner's **Marktplatz** at Karlsruhe (1804-24) - a model for other civic schemes

Gärtner's **Royal Palace** (known as the Old Palace) in Athens (1837-41) - in the classical style

neo-classical sculpture hall in the Munich **Glyptothek** (1816-30) by Klenze

Klenze's Romanesque-influenced
building for the **War Office**
(1824-26) on the
Munich Ludwigsstrasse.

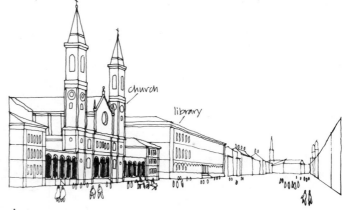

church

library

the **Ludwigsstrasse** in Munich with
Gärtner's Ludwigskirche (1829-40) and
Staatsbibliothek (1831-40)

the hill-top temple -
Klenze's **Walhalla** near
Regensburg (1831-42)
and two of its precursors -

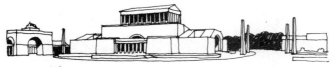

Gilly's project for a monument to
Frederick the Great (1797) and

the **Capitol** at Richmond, Virginia
(1789) by Jefferson and Latrobe

royal Bavaria 2

the world's only serious rival to Great Britain and the USA. Two further developments made this possible: the establishment in 1834 of the *Zollverien*, or customs union, which removed internal trade barriers, protected local industry and encouraged the transference into Germany of enterprises from outside; and the growing political strength of Prussia which, with its greater potential for economic development, was finally to crush Austria in the war of 1866.

These dramatic developments brought economic growth but, by comparison with Britain, no great changes in the social structure of Germany; the old political elite remained firmly in control. Reforms were introduced, including peasant emancipation and certain commercial freedoms – not in the libertarian way of Britain or France, but through the equal application of state laws to all citizens, a process in which the middle class need play no revolutionary part. The fundamental basis for the economic growth was a demographic one: a massive rise in population from 25 to 35 million between 1815 and 1850, concentrated mainly in Saxony and Prussia, which increased demand, stimulated production and supplied new labour. Here especially, technical schools were set up to supply industry with qualified personnel, loans and subsidies were offered to assist in the importation of machinery, state industries were begun, and railway-building, heavily underwritten by state money, was pushed ahead. The work of one architect in particular coincides with this expansive period in the development of state economic power.

Karl Friedrich Schinkel (1781–1841) was a native Prussian, most of whose work was carried out in and around Berlin. Educated in Italy and Paris, he was brought up within the neo-classical architectural tradition, though his initial approach to architecture was an oblique one, through painting and stage design, media which gave full rein to his feeling for dramatic, romantic-classical effects. He came to the notice of Humboldt, the chief minister, through an unsolicited design for a mausoleum for the Queen Louise, and in 1810 was appointed to the new Department of Public Works. By 1830, he had produced his main works: the Neue Wache guard house on the Unter den Linden (1816); the Schauspielhaus (1812–21); Tegel, Humboldt's country house (1822–4); and the Altes Museum (1823–30). His means of expression was severe and neo-classical though the effects he obtained in his interiors, with dramatic lighting, changes of level and spatial fluidity, show an original mind at work. The Altes Museum demonstrates this well. Its exterior is restrained and academic neo-Classicism; internally it is a *tour de force* of spatial effects: a two-story entrance space within the portico, incorporating a fine double staircase; a splendid domed sculpture hall; the ingeniously arranged picture galleries with hanging-screens at right angles to the windows for the best lighting effect.

Schinkel travelled widely, to France, Italy and England, researching into architectural design and also into industrial production, which was one of his responsibilities. In 1830 he became director of the department and about this time his architectural style became freer and increasingly romantic. The Charlottenhof Palace, built for the Crown Prince at Potsdam (1826), the court gardener's house (1829) and the tea-house and Roman bath on the same estate, are picturesque and irregular, intimately related to the naturalistic landscaping of P. J. Lenné.

Schinkel's pupils and successors tended to follow the informality of his later work rather than the rigidity of the neo-classical style. The Friedenskirche in Potsdam (1845–8) by Ludwig Persius (1803–45) is a romantic evocation of an early Christian basilican church, subtle and refined in detail. The 1840s saw an increasingly eclectic

imperial Prussia 1

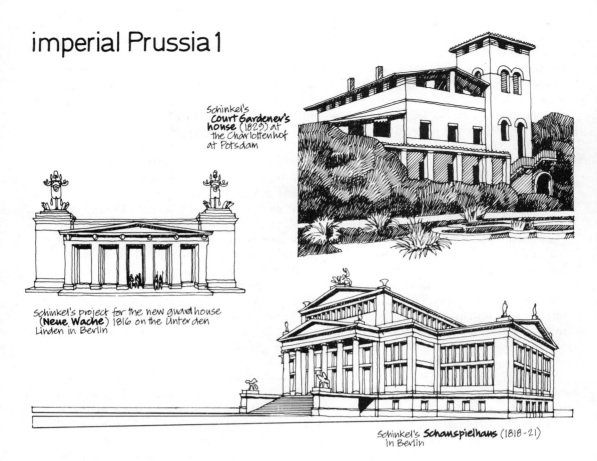

Schinkel's **Court Gardener's house** (1829) at the Charlottenhof at Potsdam

Schinkel's project for the new guard house (**Neue Wache**) 1816 on the Unter den Linden in Berlin

Schinkel's **Schauspielhaus** (1818-21) in Berlin

Schinkel's **Altes Museum** (1823-30) in Berlin

entrance facade

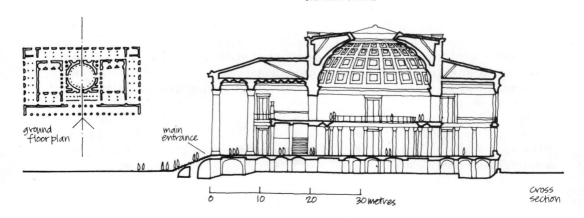

ground floor plan

main entrance

cross section

0   10   20   30 metres

Persius'
Friedenskirche
(1845-48) at Potsdam
followed the court
gardener's house in
evoking the spirit
of early Christian
architecture

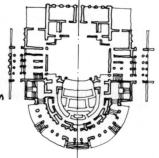

plan of
Semper's building for
the **Dresden opera**
(1838-41) where
The Flying Dutchman
and **Tannhäuser**
were first performed

Gilbert Scott
assimilated the
style of the German
High middle ages
for the Hamburg
Nikolai kirche
(1845-63)

compare with the
cathedrals of Ulm
and Cologne

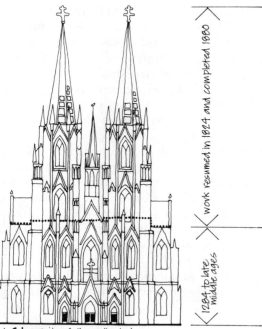

work resumed in 1824 and completed 1880

1284 to late
middle ages

at **Cologne** itself the cathedral
was completed to the original design
after an effective delay of 400 years

approach to design: *Rundbogenstil* and early Christian designs proliferated, to be followed by medieval and even Islamic ones. This is seen particularly in the work of Gottfried Semper (1803–79) who used Italian renaissance, Byzantine, Islamic and romanesque ideas in a succession of buildings in Dresden: the opera house (1838–41), the synagogue (1839–40), the Villa Rose (1839), the Oppenheim Palace (1845), the art gallery (1847–54) and the Albrechtsburg villa (1850–5). Neo-Gothic already enjoyed an interested academic following, including that of Schinkel who had tried it out in two of his buildings. It was given added impetus in 1825 with the resumption of work on the unfinished 13th-century cathedral of Cologne and by the construction in Hamburg of the Nikolaikirche (1845–63) to the winning competition design of Gilbert Scott. It was to Germany's advantage that the industrial revolution, rather like Scott's neo-Gothic, could be imported from Britain wholesale. Although industrialisation could not be through the textile industry, now that Britain dominated the world market, Germany could take advantage of the technology available from Britain; in addition, Germany could go straight into the second, heavy-industrial and chemical phase of development, without being impeded by those now-outmoded early capital investments which in Britain's case would eventually become a barrier to progress.

In France, the pattern was different: the chronic lack of coal and iron-ore for heavy industry made it necessary to compete with Britain in textile production – with some success. The invention of the Jacquard loom allowed weavers to produce intricate designs and to concentrate on the sophisticated European market instead of the colonial one dominated by Britain. For the same reason, big advances were made in bleaching, dyeing and printing; indeed the application of France's developed chemical knowledge to industry brought progress in several fields: the manufacture of wood-pulp for paper-making, and of coal-gas for lighting and the mechanical processing of beet-sugar. The shortage of coal for metallurgy produced some original ideas: the large-scale use of wood-burning furnaces; the recovery of hot gases for recycling; the development of turbine-assisted machinery. The first railway, the St Etienne–Loire opened in 1827, helped to unite the coal-regions with the canal-system and with Paris; and the first passenger line, Paris–St Germain, opened in 1837.

Yet despite this activity, economic progress was slow, affected above all by the dispersed, piecemeal character of French industrial life, which allowed no great concentrations of industry such as Pittsburgh, Clydeside or the Ruhr valley. Capital was scarce in the aftermath of the Napoleonic period, and investors were interested more in the safety of land and property than in industrial speculation. The mainly rural form of life persisted: industries were mostly family affairs, restricted in size and incapable of attracting large-scale investment.

In common with much of Europe, French politics had moved to the right in the years following Waterloo. Charles X, who came to the throne in 1824, attempted to restore many of the features of the pre-revolutionary regime – church and aristocratic privilege, heavy taxes and censorship. Stretched to breaking-point by the world economic recession of 1829, the patience of the liberals and the endurance of the workers finally snapped in July 1830, and France was once more in a state of revolution. Charles fled; the ministers Talleyrand and Lafayette succeeded in preventing civil war by placing Louis Philippe on the throne, a professed liberal proud to be called 'bourgeois'. His 'July Monarchy' carried out a number of reforms to satisfy bourgeois opinion, and though none of these helped the plight of the urban proletariat, sporadic outbreaks of violence from the workers could now be savagely suppressed, this time

the July Monarchy

Percier and Fontaine's shops and apartments in the **Rue de Rivoli** (1811-35) in Paris

St Germain • Paris

Loire coalfields

St Etienne • Lyon

France

Manchester

Great Britain

London

Holland

Belgium

German states

Berlin

Switzerland

Austria

Italian states

Spain

French railways in 1846

0   500 km

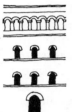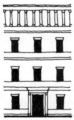

Designs from Durand's **Précis et leçons d'architecture** (1802)

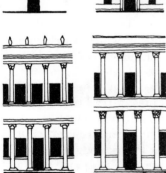

the 'vertical combinations' provided a wide variety of repetitive treatments for elevations

Berlioz whose **Symphonie Funèbre** celebrated the inauguration of the July Column in the Bastille, and the dead of the 1830 Revolution

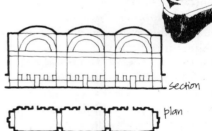

section

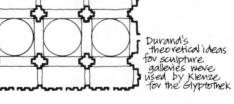

plan

Durand's theoretical ideas for sculpture galleries were used by Klenze for the Glyptothek

Labrouste's **Bibliothèque Ste Geneviève** (1843-50) with its repetitive Durand-like elevation

with bourgeois support. France entered two decades of relative harmony during which it was possible for the middle class to expand in a burst of economic activity.

Most of this was centred on Paris, which dominated its country's commercial life more completely than any other capital city. A concentration of middle-class investment in buildings and services began to convert it into a bureaucratic and commercial stronghold, with its public buildings, railway stations, shopping streets and bourgeois housing. Typical of the period were a number of commercial developments: streets lined with regular terraces consisting of shops on the ground floor and apartments above. The topmost storey was generally treated as a mansard roof with dormers and the ground storey as an elegant arcade. Percier and Fontaine's Rue de Rivoli (1811–35) is the best-known example, but there were several others, including Pellechet's Place de la Bourse (1834). The Galérie d'Orléans (1829–31) by Fontaine was an early example of a glass-roofed shopping arcade, which influenced similar schemes elsewhere in Europe.

The look of the new buildings in Paris was determined largely by the work of J.-N.-L. Durand (1760–1834), a theoretician who was professor of architecture at the new Ecole Centrale des Travaux Publiques from 1795 to 1830. He built very little, but his two books, *Receuil et parallele des édifices en tout genre* (1800) and *Précis et leçons d'architecture* (1802), influenced a whole generation of architects trained at the Ecole, but also had an effect on the work of Schinkel, Gärtner, Klenze, Persius and Semper. Durand's theories were perfectly in tune with the time: his ideas that buildings could be planned in repetitive 'modular' units, that their basic framework could be clad in different styles of architecture according to function or taste, and that rich decoration was not essential to architectural effect, were a perfect formula for building a large number of urban developments quickly, effectively and cheaply. At worst, the formula ensured an acceptable, if anonymous, standard; at best, in the hands of Schinkel, it achieved architectural dignity.

One of the best post-Durand buildings in Paris is the Ste Geneviève library (1843–50) by Henri Labrouste (1801–75), a long, rectilinear building in which an elegant neo-renaissance façade in two tiers conceals an interior that is a fine early example of iron engineering: a double row of semicircular iron vaults carried on iron columns. French architects were more than ready to adopt the use of cast iron. The technical tradition fostered by the Ecole Centrale des Travaux Publiques, a tradition which stretched back through the 18th century, gave them a familiarity with engineering techniques denied their colleagues in Britain where the rift between architect and engineer was almost complete. In major French buildings of the period, style and structure were often highly integrated in a way rare in England. This is particularly true of the Ste Geneviève library, and also of the Gare de l'Est (1847–52) by F.-A. Duquesney (1800–49) and the Gare du Nord (1862–3) by Jakob Ignaz Hittorf (1792–1867), in both of which the curving iron roof of the train shed finds visible expression on the entrance façade by means of a soaring stone archway. It is also true of Labrouste's other main work, the Bibliothèque Nationale in Paris (1862–8). The roof of the main reading room is a cluster of nine domes faced with ceramic panels, with circular openings for lighting the interior. The elegance of the cast-iron roof structure contrasts with the masonry walls round the perimeter.

Durand's catholic attitude to architectural style reflected – and no doubt helped to promote – a growing eclecticism among architects and their clients, who sought inspiration ever more widely, both geographically and historically, for architectural effects.

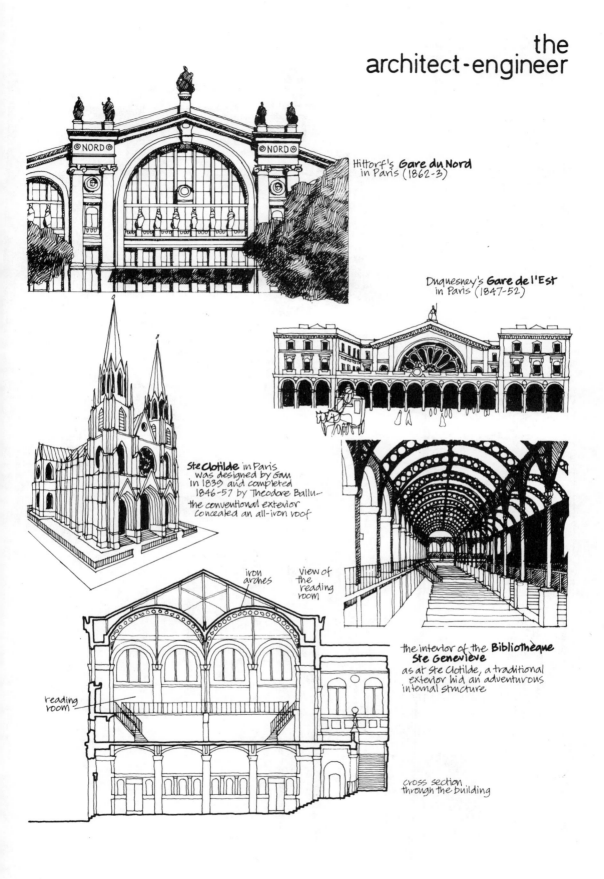

the architect-engineer

Hittorf's **Gare du Nord** in Paris (1862-3)

Duquesney's **Gare de l'Est** in Paris (1847-52)

Ste Clotilde in Paris was designed by Gau in 1839 and completed 1846-57 by Theodore Ballu — the conventional exterior concealed an all-iron roof

iron arches

View of the reading room

the interior of the **Bibliothèque Ste Geneviève** as at Ste Clotilde, a traditional exterior hid an adventurous internal structure

reading room

cross section through the building

Viollet-le-Duc

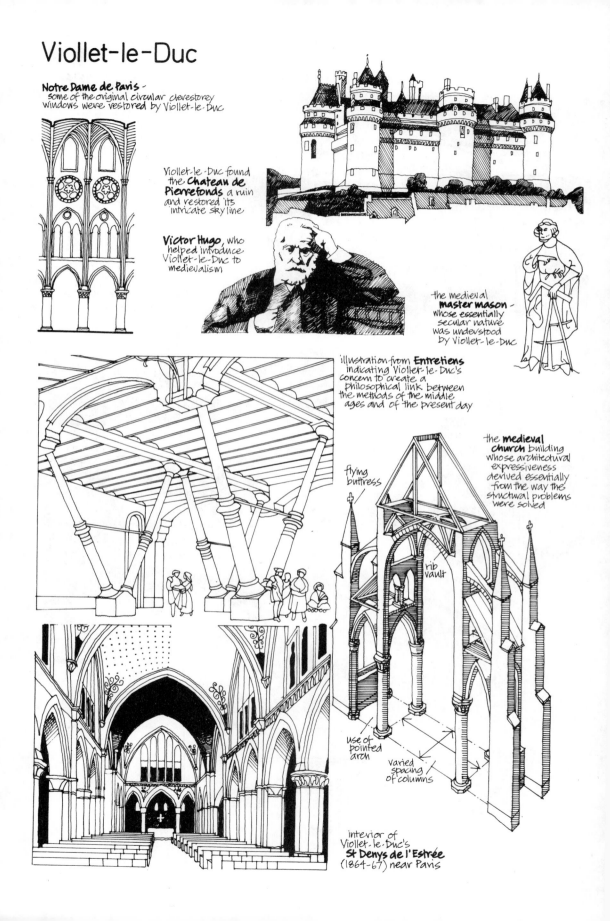

Notre Dame de Paris - some of the original circular clerestorey windows were restored by Viollet-le-Duc

Viollet-le-Duc found the **Chateau de Pierrefonds** a ruin and restored its intricate skyline

Victor Hugo, who helped introduce Viollet-le-Duc to medievalism

the medieval **master mason** - whose essentially secular nature was understood by Viollet-le-Duc

illustration from **Entretiens** indicating Viollet-le-Duc's concern to create a philosophical link between the methods of the middle ages and of the present day

the **medieval church** building whose architectural expressiveness derived essentially from the way the structural problems were solved

flying buttress

rib vault

use of pointed arch

varied spacing of columns

interior of Viollet-le-Duc's **St Denys de l'Estrée** (1864-67) near Paris

As with Pugin and Scott in England, there was a growing interest in the gothic style which in France also was considered suitable for churches. The appointment of the writer Prosper Mérimée, an enthusiastic medievalist, as Inspector of National Monuments in 1834 began a period of restoration of France's incomparable legacy of cathedrals and castles which had stylistic effects on the design of new buildings. Typically, the French neo-gothic church of the period made use of cast iron for columns or vaulting or both. Among many such examples the best are probably Ste Clotilde, Paris (1846–57), by Franz Christian Gau (1790–1854) and Ste Eugène, Paris (1854–5), by Louis Auguste Boileau (1812–96).

The most important figure in the French neo-gothic movement was Eugène-Emanuel Viollet-le-Duc (1814–79) who, like Pugin, did much to awaken an appreciation of medieval architecture. Born into a wealthy family, he was introduced to the study of the middle ages by Mérimée and Victor Hugo and from about 1840 became a scholar and restorer of cathedrals and châteaux, beginning with Ste Madeleine at Vézelay and including, among scores of restorations, Laon, the Sainte Chapelle and Notre Dame de Paris. He developed a number of perceptive theories about the gothic style which he set down in two influential books, *Dictionnaire raisonné de l'architecture française* (1854–68) and *Entretiens* (1863–72).

As a liberal and an active revolutionary who had fought at the barricades in 1830, he saw Gothic first of all in its social context, as the style of a growingly secular world trying to throw off the church domination of the early middle ages. Secondly, he appreciated its structural integrity: the way the ribs of a vault concentrated the stresses on piers and buttresses and allowed the spaces between to be filled with lightweight, non-loadbearing panels of stone or glass – all clearly visible to the onlooker. He appreciated, in other words, that architectural expression emerged directly from the way structural problems were solved. Thirdly, he drew a parallel between the structural truth of gothic buildings and the iron and glass architecture of his own day, of which he was a firm advocate. At a time when historical buildings were studied to provide styles for architects to copy, Viollet was attempting to study the past for its own sake, for a keener appreciation of the social factors which had given the buildings birth. At the same time, by linking the past and the present, he used historical study in a dynamic way, as a springboard to the future. Apart from his restorations, some of which were imaginative and spectacular, going at times beyond mere scholarship, he built a small number of new buildings, somewhat unworthy of his theories, of which St Denys-de-l'Estrée near Paris (1864–7) is the best-known.

Germany and France were thus beginning to make economic progress through industrialisation, leaving behind those parts of Europe slowest to emerge from their peasant economies – Scandinavia, eastern Europe, the Balkans and the Mediterranean countries. In Italy, for example, industrialisation was almost impossible. During the Napoleonic occupation the Italians had experienced temporary unity but, after the Congress of Vienna, the country had been divided into eight small despotic states, some controlled by Austria, others by the Vatican. Between them, Metternich and the Pope barred all progress to bourgeois freedom. Italy's main product was raw or spun silk of high quality, produced in Piedmont and Lombardy and exported to northern Europe for weaving. Italy did not develop a weaving industry of its own nor, at this stage, any alternative industries other than cotton-weaving. Railways, too, were late to develop; a few lines were built in the 1830s in Lombardy, Piedmont and Veneto, linking with France and Switzerland, but the south remained cut off.

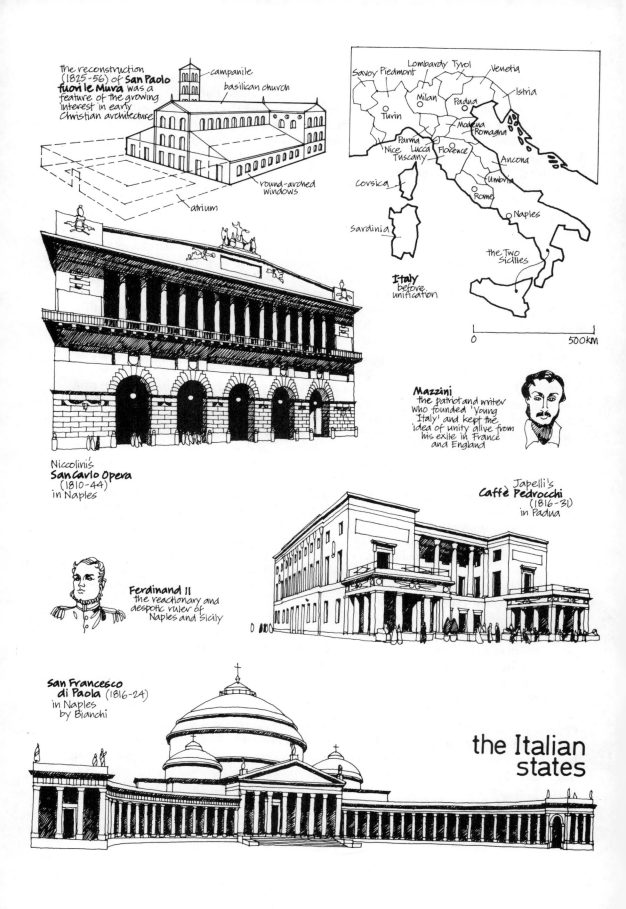

the reconstruction (1825-56) of **San Paolo fuori le Mura** was a feature of the growing interest in early Christian architecture

campanile

basilican church

round-arched windows

atrium

Savoy   Piedmont   Lombardy   Tyrol   Venetia

Turin   Milan   Padua   Istria

Modena
Romagna

Parma
Nice   Lucca   Florence   Ancona
Tuscany

Corsica   Umbria

Rome

Sardinia   Naples

the Two Sicilies

Italy before unification

0   500km

Niccolini's
San Carlo Opera
(1810-44)
in Naples

Mazzini
the patriot and writer who founded 'Young Italy' and kept the idea of unity alive from his exile in France and England

Japelli's
Caffè Pedrocchi
(1816-31)
in Padua

Ferdinand II
the reactionary and despotic ruler of Naples and Sicily

San Francesco di Paola (1816-24)
in Naples
by Bianchi

the Italian states

Architecturally it was a productive period, with each tiny state continuing, for the sake of prestige, the traditions of Italian civic architecture whose reputation was still high despite the fact that the great days were now past and the cultural centre of gravity had moved to Paris and Berlin. In Rome itself, the Pope initiated the building of a new sculpture hall at the Vatican Museum (1817–22) by Raffaelle Stern (1774–1820) and the reconstruction by a number of architects of the early Christian church of San Paolo fuori le Mura (1825–56). The independent kingdom of the Two Sicilies, backward, feudal and corrupt, produced two minor architectural masterpieces, both in Naples: the San Carlo Opera House (1810–44) by Antonio Niccolini (1772–1850) and the church of San Francesco di Paola (1816–24) by Pietro Bianchi (1787–1849). Both were grandoise conceptions, the former a monumental building with a colonnaded façade rising on a high rusticated base, the latter a Pantheon-like building with a great shallow dome and a pedimented portico, flanked by colonnades linking it to the public piazza in front.

In the Piedmontese city of Turin the Piazza Vittorio Veneto (1818–30) and the Piazza Carlo Felice (1823 and later) were laid out by Giuseppe Frizzi (1797–1831) as part of a gigantic scheme of civic improvement. They were lined with repetitive, arcaded, Parisian-style buildings by Frizzi and by Carlo Promis (1808–73) but the general conception, involving a variety of spatial effects, was within the Italian tradition of civic design. Equally Italian in its originality and charm was the Caffè Pedrocchi in Padua (1816–31) designed by Giuseppe Japelli (1783–1852), a purpose-built restaurant on a prominent street-corner, in the neo-classical style. It has none of the solemn grandeur of Schinkel's buildings; with its broken forms, varied planes and discreet decoration it was one of the most light-hearted neo-classical buildings in existence.

The Austrian Empire, whose politics completely dominated those of Italy at this time, was hardly more advanced industrially. The period from 1815 to 1848 was dominated by Metternich, whose repressive policies included the deliberate de-industrialisation of Vienna to avoid creating a dangerous proletariat, and the refusal to allow railways to be built up to the northern frontiers. A desultory proposal for Austria to join the *Zollverein* was strenuously opposed until worsening relations between Austria and Prussia made such a union impossible anyway. Some industrialisation did take place: wool and cotton manufacturing in Brno and Liberec; coal-mining in Bohemia, Moravia and Silesia. In these declining years of Habsburg power, Vienna remained a wealthy, cultured, imperial capital, continually being improved. Josef Kornhäusel's Schottenhof (1826–32) was typical of the development of Vienna: a large complex of five-storey apartment blocks built above shops and around a series of square court-yards. One can imagine it fitted out with the simple, monumental Biedermeier furniture of the 1820s or possibly the bent-wood furniture which Michael Thonet had begun to develop in the 1830s. Thonet's 'Viennese chair', constructed from dowels of beechwood steamed into shape in factory presses, was one of the main Austrian contributions to 19th-century design. Beautifully conceived within the limitations of the material, quick and cheap to produce, it found its way into bourgeois and well-to-do working-class homes all over Europe and earned a popularity which remains today.

In northern Europe, another great empire was in decline. Denmark, which from the middle ages had attempted to dominate the whole of the Scandinavian area, finally lost Norway to Sweden. At the same time, Finland's close links with Sweden ended when it was incorporated as a Grand Duchy into the Russian empire. This new ar-rangement, which lasted throughout the 19th century, brought important economic

Biedermeier and Thonet

Austria Hungary before 1848

0   500 km

early **Biedermeier** chair from the Rhineland (1820) showing the influence of English Regency and French neo-Classicism

later **Biedermeier** chair of about 1835 manufactured in Prague

early **Thonet** chair showing Biedermeier influence – made in Thonet's home town of Boppard-am-Rhein (1836) – a complex design, not suited to mass-production, but already demonstrating the Thonet bent-wood technique

later chair in developed **Thonet** style – this is the 'Viennese chair' of 1859, designed simply, for large-scale production – to date over 50 million have been sold

the classic **Thonet** rocking chair of 1850 – like the Viennese chair it was made in turned and bent wood, with cane seat, and was suitable for large-scale production

readjustments. Today, all the Nordic countries are highly industrialised; at the beginning of the 19th century they were all predominantly agricultural and – apart from Denmark – among the poorest countries of Europe. Norway and Finland produced timber in large quantities but little else. Sweden had a small iron and steel industry, based on its rich deposits of iron ore; during the 18th century it had, like Russia, been a major producer but had now been displaced in the European market by Britain. Denmark had few raw materials and little industry, but for centuries had contested with Sweden the economic and political leadership of the area.

The social structure of the Nordic countries was typical of all societies of the old regime: a local peasant economy, dominated by a feudal aristocracy, with a growing bourgeoisie on which economic growth largely depended but which had not yet attained any great degree of power. Copenhagen and Stockholm were the two major cities, though Gothenburg, Oslo and Turku (Åbo) also had economic and social importance. Scandinavia had one of the world's richest and most sophisticated traditions of timber construction, within which all rural buildings and most of those in the towns were built, but this was overshadowed by the international, classical culture of the aristocracy and upper middle class, and the main cities and their outskirts were rich with royal palaces, châteaux and public buildings in stone.

In 1814 came the political break-up. Among the direct effects on architecture and planning was a new life for Oslo, long dominated by Copenhagen. A number of public buildings by the architect Christian Heinrich Grosch demonstrated the city's new economic independence: the neo-classical Exchange building (1826), designed in collaboration with Schinkel, the University (1840) and the more eclectic and romantic Market Hall (1840). Another major effect was the foundation of a new Finnish capital at Helsinki (Helsingfors), for which an ambitious rebuilding plan was drawn up by Albert Ehrenström, a friend of King Gustav. In the ancient capital of Turku, Carlo Bassi, in succession to Gjörwell, built the 'New' Academy (1823), but in 1827 the city was devastated by the worst fire in Scandinavian history, with the loss of 2,500 timber buildings. Turku's functions were transferred direct to Helsinki, where a minor architectural renaissance took place under the direction of Bassi's successor, the architect Carl Ludwig Engel (1778–1840).

Born in Germany, Engel was influenced both by Schinkel and by his early training in St Petersburg. In his work in Helsinki, from 1815 onwards, these two strands of architectural thought were interwoven; his style, at first rich and decorative in the imperial tradition, moved towards greater restraint and severity. In collaboration with Ehrenström he designed the monumental Senate Square and the public buildings which surrounded it, including the Senate (1818), the University building (1828), the University library (1836), and most spectacular of all, the cathedral (1830) with its high dome and gigantic flight of steps. Engel's informal style was seen in his country houses and churches. The former included the early timber-built Ala-Urpala in Karelia (1815) and the somewhat grander stone-built mansions of Vuojoki (1836) and Viurila (1840), both near Turku. The latter included the medieval church at Hollola, near Helsinki, where a dome of Engel's design was added after his death, and the attractive 'Old' Church in Helsinki (1826) which had a centralised plan, in the long-standing Nordic tradition.

Medieval church-building in Scandinavia had been subject to many influences. The thousands of parish churches, especially in outlying areas, displayed a wide variety of plan forms, including not only the basilica of western Christianity but also the central-

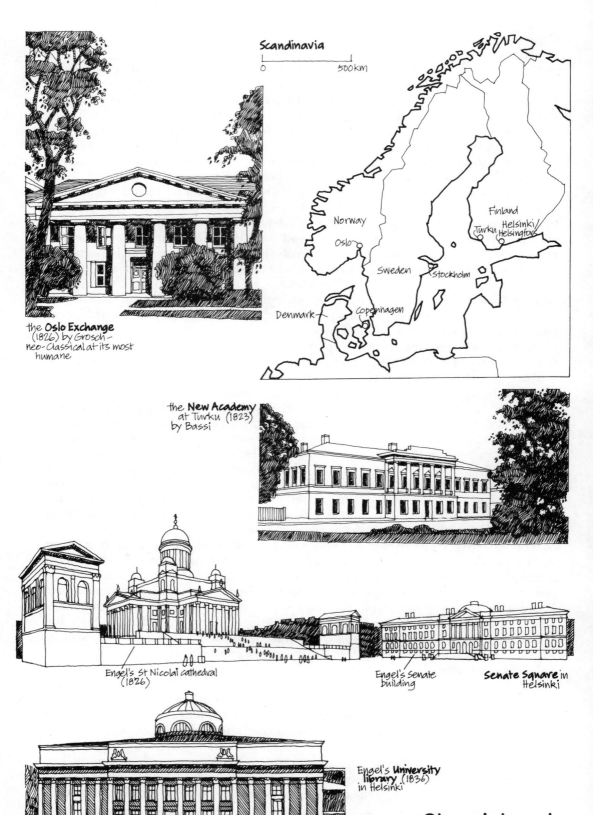

Scandinavia

0   500km

the **Oslo Exchange**
(1826) by Grosch—
neo-Classical at its most
humane

Norway

Oslo

Sweden

Denmark

Copenhagen

Stockholm

Finland

Turku

Helsinki/
Helsingfors

the **New Academy**
at Turku (1823)
by Bassi

Engel's St Nicolai cathedral
(1826)

Engel's Senate
building

Senate Square in
Helsinki

Engel's **University
library** (1836)
in Helsinki

neo-Classicism in
Scandinavia

ised Greek-cross of the Byzantine church. Foremost among the latter were the wooden 'stave' churches of Norway, which reached their greatest spatial and decorative richness in the Sogne area, near Bergen, during the 12th century. This vernacular timber tradition persisted in the rural areas for many generations, and families of carpenter–designers continued building parish churches all over Scandinavia well into the 19th century. Examples could be seen at Keuruu (18th century) by the master-builder Antti Hakola, in the late-18th- and early-19th-century work in Ostrobothnia of Matti Honka and Jacob Rijf, and above all in the twenty-sided 'double cruciform' churches of early-19th-century Karelia developed by the builders of the Salonen family and typified by Kivennapa (1804) and Kirvu (1815–16).

The character of Scandinavian society was determined by its peasant economy, which emphatically distinguished it from contemporary Britain and the USA. The social system had developed very slowly over ten centuries, with only small differences in the life-style of the early middle ages and the 19th century. Even by the mid-19th century, urbanisation was minimal: less than 20% in Denmark, the most industrialised country, and 5% in Finland, the least. National income was similarly low, but the Nordic countries were in some respects far from backward, suffering from few of the intense contradictions which capitalism had created in highly industrialised countries.

The robust tradition of timber building created by this slowly developing rural way of life was most remarkable in Norway, where medieval society was feudal, with a mass of peasant farmers both protected and exploited by a predominantly Danish church and aristocracy. During the high middle ages a succession of plagues devastated social life, destroying the source of income of the overlords and permitting adjustments in the feudal relationships. Organising for protection into the *grannelag* farming communities, the peasants created economic and cultural siege conditions for themselves, which few outside influences were able to penetrate. Overall ownership remained with the church and aristocracy until the 17th and 18th centuries, when large debts incurred during the Danish wars with Sweden forced the widespread sale of land and began to create not only a class of land-owning farmers, but also the landless labouring class necessary to the process of industrialisation. Between 1810 and 1825 a sudden growth in population coincided with increased agricultural output, which stimulated demand and increased economic growth. Norway, like the rest of Scandinavia, entered the industrial revolution in a relatively humane and gradual way; public health standards were high and the level of education remarkably advanced, all four countries having introduced compulsory schooling in the late 18th century, some 100 years before Britain.

The rural timber building known as the *laftehus* was Norway's particular contribution to the local vernacular tradition. Unlike the stave church, which was of framed construction with lightweight infill panels, the *laftehus* was of load-bearing log construction, with the familiar notched joints at the corners. This type of joint could form only a right-angle junction, and the need to use timber of uniform thickness resulted in sides of roughly equal length, so that the plan-form was almost always square. A farm group would consist of a number of nearly identical buildings – house, granary, byre, storeroom – arranged around a central courtyard and fenced or walled for security. Carved decoration, though often very ornate, was limited to features of particular significance, such as the door-frame of the main house.

Over the centuries, the original single-cell, single-storey plan-form gradually changed, with the addition of side extensions and upper floors. In the 18th century, a symmetrical plan-form, obviously derived from that of the Georgian town house, made

67

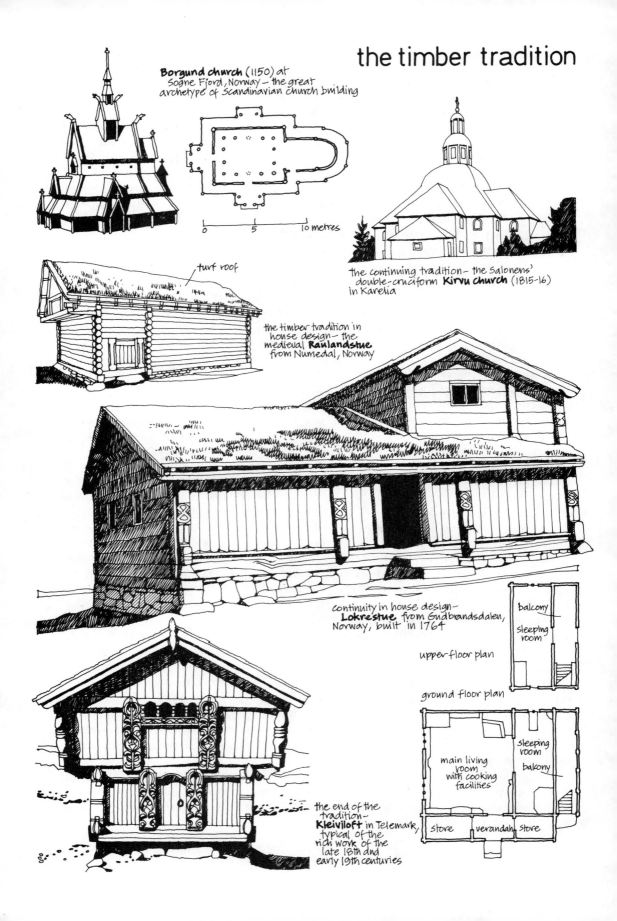

the timber tradition

Borgund church (1150) at Sogne Fjord, Norway – the great archetype of Scandinavian church building

0   5   10 metres

the continuing tradition – the Salonens' double-cruciform **Kirvu church** (1815-16) in Karelia

turf roof

the timber tradition in house design – the medieval **Raulandstue** from Numedal, Norway

continuity in house design – **Lokrestue** from Gudbrandsdalen, Norway, built in 1764

balcony

sleeping room

upper-floor plan

ground floor plan

sleeping room

main living room with cooking facilities

balcony

store   verandah   store

the end of the tradition – **Kleiviloft** in Telemark, typical of the rich work of the late 18th and early 19th centuries

a brief appearance. During the 18th and early 19th centuries, land reforms, improved agricultural methods, the foundation of agricultural and veterinary colleges, all had their effect on the *laftehus* building tradition. New methods demanded new buildings and an increased variety and sophistication of construction which the rural craftsman was not able to provide. *Laftehus* construction soon came to an end in favour of more complex buildings by specialist designers. The local tradition of building of which the *laftehus* was part existed all over the western world, from the stone-built farmhouses of the western Mediterranean with shuttered windows and shallow pan-tiled roofs, to the English 'black and white' buildings with exposed oak box-frames and the American balloon-framed houses protected by clapboard sheathing. All these local building forms were profoundly affected by industrialisation: some were adapted to new techniques, others persisted only in the remoter geographical fringes or died out completely. The collective loss of the rural skills which had produced them was one of the many social disasters caused by industrialisation. Nevertheless, it is unjustifiable to imagine a pre-industrial world of unqualified self-fulfilment and simple architectural excellence. These buildings by no means represent the bottom of the social scale. The general agricultural reforms of the 18th and 19th centuries had widened the gaps between the social classes of the countryside, creating on the one hand farm-owners and relatively wealthy tenants, and on the other a dispossessed labouring class owning little or nothing, a prey to homelessness and unemployment. Most country people lived in buildings so plain and conditions so poor that any talk of architectural simplicity and honesty is a mockery. Farmers might live in the well-built houses of the rural tradition, tenants in cottages designed in the picturesque style of the moment, but the landless often lived in hovels of birch-poles and brushwood, hastily thrown up at night by the road-side to take advantage of the laws on squatting.

For the thirty years following the Treaty of Vienna Europe had been held in a political vice by rulers fearful of a repetition of 1789. Both conservatives and liberals recognised that revolution was increasingly likely: sixty years of industrialisation had created not only a dispossessed rural population but also an urban working class whose misery might easily turn them towards revolution. Cities all over Europe had districts of dreary factories and squalid slum housing. Manchester, the notorious archetype of human dereliction, was now just one among the many towns which had expanded beyond all recognition through industrialisation. By mid-century it bore very little resemblance to a Georgian market town.

Judging by Engels' vivid description in *The Condition of the Working Class in England* (1844), Manchester had clearly become a modern city, displaying all the essential architectural and spatial features we now associate with big cities and introducing all those persistent social problems which industrialisation, even today, has remained unable to solve. The old Georgian centre was replaced by a new commercial centre, a square kilometre in extent, and consisting almost entirely of offices and warehouses: 'Nearly the whole district is abandoned by dwellers, and is lonely and deserted at night; only watchmen and policemen traverse its narrow lanes with their dark-lanterns. This district is cut through by certain main thoroughfares upon which the vast traffic concentrates, and in which the ground level is lined with brilliant shops.' Around the centre lay the economic generators of the city: the factories, mills, gasworks and railway yards; between them huddled the houses and shacks of the workers. The middle classes now lived further out to the west, mainly on the heights of Cheetham Hill, Broughton and Pendleton, away from the stink of the city. The main radial roads linking these

the rural poor

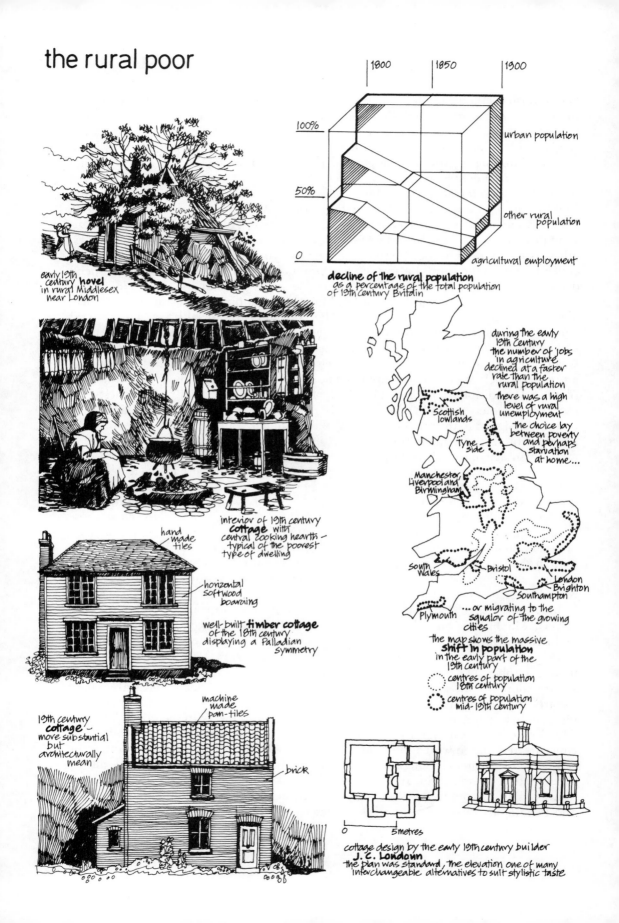

early 19th century **hovel** in rural Middlesex near London

decline of the rural population as a percentage of the total population of 19th century Britain

1800 1850 1900

100%

50%

0

urban population

other rural population

agricultural employment

interior of 19th century **cottage** with central cooking hearth – typical of the poorest type of dwelling

hand made tiles

horizontal softwood boarding

well-built **timber cottage** of the 18th century displaying a Palladian symmetry

19th century **cottage** – more substantial but architecturally mean

machine made pan-tiles

brick

during the early 19th century the number of jobs in agriculture declined at a faster rate than the rural population

there was a high level of rural unemployment

the choice lay between poverty and perhaps starvation at home…

Scottish lowlands

Tyne side

Manchester, Liverpool and Birmingham

South Wales

Bristol

London Brighton

Southampton

Plymouth

…or migrating to the squalor of the growing cities

the map shows the massive **shift in population** in the early part of the 19th century

⚬⚬⚬ centres of population 18th century

●●● centres of population mid-19th century

0   5 metres

cottage design by the early 19th century builder **J. C. Loudon** the plan was standard, the elevation one of many interchangeable alternatives to suit stylistic taste

industrial Manchester

Engels – author of 'The Condition of the Working Class in England' (1844)

Engels' Manchester – the archetype of the modern industrial city

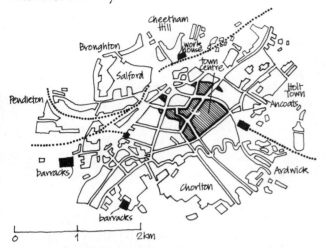

Cheetham Hill
Broughton
Salford
workhouse
town centre
Pendleton
Holt Town
Ancoats
barracks
Ardwick
Chorlton
barracks

0   1   2km

Todd Street
Long Millgate
Fennel Street

housing in Manchester in 1844 – the twisted streets and courtyards of the old town, and the regimentation of the new

this **working class housing** in mid-19th century London was typical of most big industrial cities

LODGINGS FOR TRAVELERS
LODGINGS
A SINGLE BED

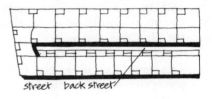

street   back street

model houses designed 1848 for the Society for Improving the Condition of the Working Classes

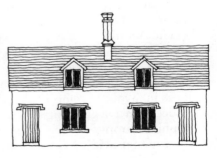

Edwin Chadwick repressive Poor Law administrator and effective campaigner for sanitary reform

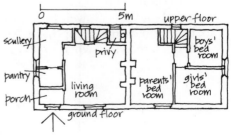

0   5m   upper floor
scullery
privy
boys' bed room
pantry
parents' bed room
girls' bed room
porch
living room
ground floor

suburbs to the centre were lined with shops whose neat frontages hid the squalor of working-class housing in the areas behind them. Lack of direct contact enabled the middle classes to ignore the appalling reality, though socially-conscious authors like Elizabeth Gaskell in her early novel *Mary Barton* (1848) tried to bring them the truth at second hand.

> It was very dark inside. The window panes were many of them broken and stuffed with rags, which was reason enough for the dusky light that pervaded the place even at mid-day . . . they began to penetrate the thick darkness . . . and to see three or four little children rolling on the damp, nay wet, brick floor, through which the stagnant, filthy moisture of the street oozed up; the fireplace was empty and black; the wife sat on her husband's chair, and cried in the dank loneliness.

Engels' survey of working-class housing in Manchester identified a number of distinct types of building. In the Old Town, just north of the centre, remained two or three hundred houses from the city's mercantile past, now overcrowded with poor families living six, eight or ten to a room. The maze of yards and courts was crowded with shacks and lean-to extensions. There was nowhere for refuse but the alleys themselves, through which pigs foraged, 'whence the swine grow fat and the atmosphere, confined on all four sides, is utterly corrupted by putrefaction'. The nearby New Town was purpose-built by speculative builders to take the rapid influx of population. Here Engels found a more regular layout, but living conditions just as poor. Groups of houses were built around small, square courtyards on which the windows opened and into which all the refuse had to be thrown. Others were built in long, straight rows, back to back and side to side, making through-ventilation impossible. Some had brickwork walls only 10cm thick through which the rain penetrated, and many were built with habitable basements into which seeped the liquid refuse of the streets.

In mid-19th century Britain, despite the ruthless efficiency of the industrial sector and the vast profits it was making, the tenuous urban life it had propagated seemed on the point of collapse. If working-class housing was bad, so too were the overcrowded workhouses, orphanages and insane asylums, the inadequate and primitive hospitals and public wash-houses provided through the parish rates and by sporadic charity. The level of public health was appallingly low, with inadequate sewerage and polluted water supplies, but widespread cholera epidemics in 1832 and 1848 encouraged earlier progress in public health than in working-class housing. In 1848 a major Public Health Act made provision for main drainage and the protection of water supplies from pollution in all cities and towns.

The Act did not have the unanimous approval of the upper ranks of society; many questioned not only the cost to the tax payer but also the very principle. All over Europe, reforms in general were looked on with great suspicion by the conservatives, who feared that any increase in the power of the workers might overturn society. Even those in favour of reform felt that concessions should be made less for reasons of social justice than as a guard against possible revolution. Whether from motives of conciliation or philanthropy is not clear, but certainly in England numerous charities grew up with the aim of providing better housing for the workers. In 1848 the society for Improving the Condition of the Labouring Classes, with Prince Albert as its president, published model plans for neat, well-built dwellings which would house, for example, a family of six in 45 square metres of space. Modest as they were, very few were built.

In the same year, when the economic crisis pervading Europe was at its height, the

'Communist Manifesto' appeared. As if it were a signal, a revolt began in France and Louis Philippe lost the throne; the Austrians were driven out of northern Italy and several Italian states achieved constitutional liberty; in Austria itself Metternich was deposed and a Hungarian uprising won independence; Poland rose against Prussia and Bohemia against Austria; the king temporarily lost control of Prussia and the Austrian emperor fled the country. By the end of the year only Frederick William had made it back to the throne, and everywhere the bourgeoisie had taken a step nearer to total economic control. Everywhere too, as Marx had suspected, the workers and their leaders had been firmly checked before they could get used to the idea of freedom: in France, the government workshops set up by Le Blanc for the unemployed were discontinued almost before they had begun. With Louis Napoleon Bonaparte as its president, a Second Republic was established to preserve bourgeois freedom and socialist leaders joined the deposed kings in exile.

Ironically, the English working class, though large, articulate and the best organised of all, failed fully to capture the revolutionary spirit. A Chartist uprising at Newport in Wales in 1839 was crushed by the army and stimulated no further revolutionary violence. The celebrated demonstration in London in 1848 at which 200,000 Chartists presented their 'monster petition' for constitutional reform was fervent but peaceful. Britain had weathered its own economic storm in 1842, and it is significant that when the European crisis of 1848 brought revolution to the continent, Britain was already experiencing an economic revival which stimulated the railway boom and provided employment. Marx and Engels had expected England, where the problems of capitalism were most acute, to be in the forefront of the revolution, but realised in retrospect that the marginal benefits of industrialisation were reaching at least some of the workers, giving them less to fight for and more to lose. A century of exploitation had encouraged an autonomous, self-reliant attitude of mutual help and education which had created a class in some respects more cultured than the bourgeois merchants for whom it worked; Shelley and Byron, Proudhon and Diderot, Bentham and Godwin were better known in working-class than middle-class homes. Apart from the one example of Chartism, when as Engels said, 'the English workman marched at the head of the European working class', there was a strong tendency towards exercising class strength through union alone, rather than through political action. The British worker's main weapon was the strike rather than revolt; his main enemy the employer rather than the state.

After 1848, British industry was able to capitalise on the country's relative social harmony. In the next twenty-five years, steady economic expansion and changes in the pattern of labour relations put the bourgeoisie in an ever stronger position. The symbolic beginning of this period was the Great Exhibition of 1851, brainchild of the energetic Prince Albert, who saw as well as any ruler that the crown would benefit from giving support to industrialism. It was to be an international exposition of 'Machinery, Science and Taste', the first of its kind in the world, a demonstration not only of Britain's superior manufacturing skill but also its peace and prosperity in a troubled world.

The building to house the exhibits had to be enormous and only London's Hyde Park could hold it. The competition therefore stipulated a building capable of being taken down afterwards. Of the hundreds of entries, many were highly imaginative, including several designed in iron and glass; but the distinguished committee of architects and engineers, which included Barry and Brunel, rejected them all and designed their own in an impractical mixture of brick, stone and cast iron which would have cost

the Crystal Palace

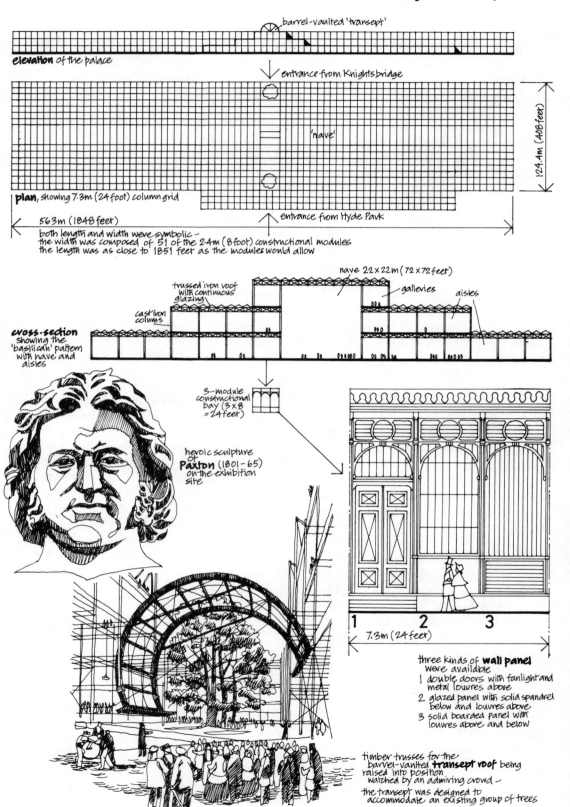

barrel-vaulted 'transept'

elevation of the palace

entrance from Knightsbridge

'nave'

124.4m (408 feet)

plan, showing 7.3m (24 foot) column grid

563m (1848 feet)

entrance from Hyde Park

both length and width were symbolic –
the width was composed of 51 of the 2.4m (8 foot) constructional modules
the length was as close to 1851 feet as the modules would allow

nave 22 × 22m (72 × 72 feet)

trussed iron roof with continuous glazing

galleries

aisles

cast iron columns

cross-section showing the 'basilican' pattern with nave and aisles

3-module constructional bay (3 × 8 = 24 feet)

heroic sculpture of **Paxton** (1801–65) on the exhibition site

1 2 3

7.3m (24 feet)

three kinds of **wall panel** were available
1 double doors with fanlight and metal louvres above
2 glazed panel with solid spandrel below and louvres above
3 solid boarded panel with louvres above and below

timber trusses for the barrel-vaulted **transept roof** being raised into position watched by an admiring crowd –

the transept was designed to accommodate an existing group of trees

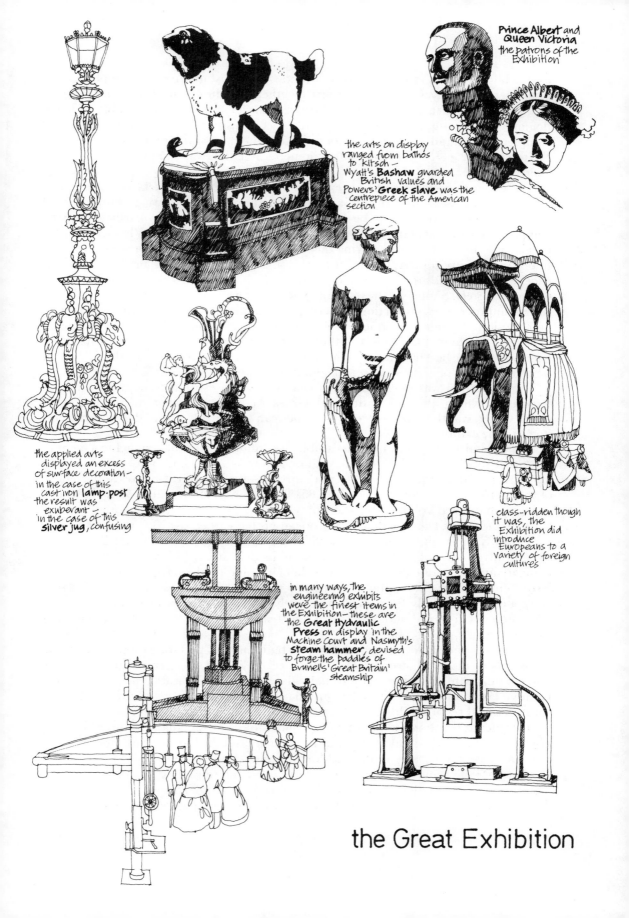

Prince Albert and **Queen Victoria** the patrons of the Exhibition

the arts on display ranged from bathos to 'kitsch' — Wyatt's **Bashaw** guarded British values and Powers' **Greek slave** was the centrepiece of the American section

the applied arts displayed an excess of surface decoration — in the case of this cast iron **lamp-post** the result was exuberant — in the case of this **silver jug**, confusing

class-ridden though it was, the Exhibition did introduce Europeans to a variety of foreign cultures

in many ways, the engineering exhibits were the finest items in the Exhibition — these are the **Great Hydraulic Press** on display in the Machine Court and Nasmyth's **steam hammer**, devised to forge the paddles of Brunel's 'Great Britain' steamship

the Great Exhibition

as much to demolish as to build. It was almost at the last minute that Joseph Paxton, designer of the Chatsworth conservatory, together with the engineers Fox and Henderson, offered an idea for a building cheaper, quicker to erect and capable of being demounted as easily as it was put up. At Albert's insistence Paxton was appointed; complete working-drawings were done within nine days and within eight months of Paxton's first sketch a building half a kilometre in length was completed and handed over.

The exhibition consisted of an extraordinary collection of artefacts, from heavy industrial machinery to furniture and domestic appliances, painting, sculpture and other works of art. It is easy to be dismissive about the general lack of artistic taste, by comparison with that of the unreproachable 18th century. But to the Victorian middle class, taste – in the sense of observing theoretical rules of design for their own sake – was not of prime importance. The technological exhibits were chosen for their technical excellence, from the great lathes and presses to the bizarre pen-knife with 1,851 blades of Sheffield steel. Similarly, the main purpose of a work of art was extra-artistic: didacticism, improvement, correction, the creation of a middle-class ethos through parable and allusion. Wyatt's grotesque marble sculpture of a Newfoundland dog standing on a snake – 'Bashaw, man's most faithful friend, crushes underfoot his most insidious enemy' – might be taken as a warning allegory of any of the fears of the Victorian bourgeoisie: sin, poverty, disease, social unrest, the working class.

The exhibition was international in character, with exhibits from as far afield as Russia and China. Powers' sentimental 'Greek slave', standing against a background of red velvet, was the centrepiece of the American section and one of the most popular items in the exhibition.

The Crystal Palace, and not the exhibits it contained, was the real achievement of the Great Exhibition and the demonstration *par excellence* of what industrialism was all about. It was an enormous building, with an over-all width of 125 metres and a length of 563 metres, as close to the symbolic 1,851 feet as the 8-foot module would allow. For a single, undivided volume, this was unprecedented: over twice as long and twice as wide as the longest and widest of European gothic cathedrals. But unlike a gothic cathedral, with its dramatic, self-assertive structural system, the Crystal Palace was structurally anonymous, the only function of its delicate, repetitive grid of ironwork being to support an outer membrane which, being nine-tenths glass, was itself light and insubstantial. There was a practical reason for using so much glass: a building so large could not be artificially lit; the exhibition relied on daylight and was closed at dusk. The internal effect, it is said, was one of the greatest lightness and of almost unending spaciousness.

The key to the rapid construction of the building was prefabrication: each of the thousands of identical structural elements was delivered pre-formed to the site for immediate assembly. This extraordinary departure from traditional practice gave Paxton, Fox and Henderson a revolutionary role in the history of design. It took constructional responsibility away from the craftsman on the site and gave it firstly to the designer at the drawing-board and secondly to the off-site manufacturer. The site assembly of the ready-made parts thus became an unskilled job, at one more remove from the age-old creativity of the building process.

After the exhibition, the building was dismantled and re-erected in an adapted form in south London, remaining till its destruction by fire in 1936. Historically, it represents the culmination of cast-iron building technology: from the mid-century onwards, cast iron, with its brittle cell-structure, was increasingly replaced by the higher tensile strength of wrought iron. It was the precursor of a large number of wide-span iron buildings, including the great railway stations of the 1850s and 1860s. And the exhibition itself was first in a long line of international expositions, from Paris to Philadelphia, for the stimulation of trade and economic growth. Over the years, these spectacular shows would involve ever greater expenditure of money and expertise, and require the creation of ever greater structural masterpieces. The growth of capitalism demanded the allegiance of the most able technical minds of the age, then as now.

How we live and how we might live
Europe in the mid 19th century

Tolstoy's description in *The Cossacks* of a Caucasian village in the 1850s gives a picture of a feudal life unknown in western Europe since the early middle ages: 'The village is encircled by ramparts of earth and thorn hedges, and is entered at each end through high gates . . . the dwellings are all raised off the ground on posts. They have decorated gables and are carefully thatched with reeds.' Tolstoy goes on to describe how the villagers spend their days outside the compound, farming, fishing, hunting and raiding: at night they crowd back down the mud streets with their animals, light the fires and close the gates against marauders and wild beasts. This way of life formed the basis of Russia's multi-racial medieval economy which Tsar Nicholas I attempted to mobilise in a military assault on industrial Europe. Russia's defeat in the Crimean War of 1854–6 by inferior French and English forces prompted the new Tsar Alexander II to re-examine his country's backward institutions and, in the face of opposition from Boyars and bureaucrats, to embark on a vast programme of reform. Economically, the main problem of the feudal system was its stagnation, though progressive social critics like Herzen and Bakunin – often necessarily in exile – also attacked its social injustice. For tens of millions of peasants the combination of local exploitation and insensitive central bureaucracy was a heavy weight to bear.

A package of reforms, aimed at solving the economic problems and incidentally at alleviating the social ones, was put into effect in 1861. The feudal system was abolished, a new taxation and banking system set up, greater freedom given to educational establishments, and district councils, known as zemstvos, were set up to meet local needs. Although this formed the basis of a modern industrial economy, in practical terms the hoped-for social reforms were long in coming. The emancipation of 23 million serfs was to create two classes of peasant: the wealthy kulaks, able to amass vast areas of land, and a dispossessed labouring class owing allegiance to the village collective, or *mir*, unable to increase productivity or improve the conditions of life and prey to continued discontent.

Intellectually it was a time of introspection, with the great novelists like Gogol, Turgenev, Tolstoy and Dostoievsky searching deeply into human psychology. At the same time an increasing national self-consciousness encouraged the discovery of an essentially Russian idiom, in literature, in the music of Glinka and Tchaikovsky, and in civic architecture. The Cathedral of the Redeemer in Moscow (1839–83) by Konstantin Thon was the first important example of a neo-Byzantine approach to architecture, rejecting classicism and returning to local tradition.

All industrial countries were attempting colonial expansion. The politician Joseph Chamberlain, speaking with the authentic voice of the Victorian industrialist, said, 'The day of small nations has long passed away. The day of Empires has come.' By the middle of the 19th century European industrial countries could no longer supply all their own needs; these included not only staple foods, such as corn and meat from Australia, Argentina, India, Canada and America, but also a wide range of new and exotic foodstuffs to satisfy an increasing expectation of good living. Industry needed imported raw materials: cotton from America, India and Egypt; silk from the Far East; wool from Australia and South America; timber and iron ore from northern Europe. In return, the finished products were exported ever more widely, to satisfy the urge for economic growth. Newly-industrialised countries were the first targets, and British iron and steel went to build machinery and railways all over the western world. Then came the export of textiles to underdeveloped countries, which were drawn into the nexus through the familiar colonial process of military conquest and social and economic demolition and reconstruction. The imperial world became dominated by a few major powers, vying with each other for supremacy, seeking to capture markets, establish trade routes and build navies to defend them.

In the 1850s and 1860s, British capitalists anxiously watched the emergence of bourgeois France, which seemed their most likely competitor. In 1852, the new president Bonaparte attempted to recapture France's imperial grandeur by abandoning the constitution and declaring himself Emperor Napoleon III, but neither he nor the bourgeoisie were blind to the fact that it was on them rather than him that imperial power would rest. He was shrewd enough to offer concessions to all the main power groups – military glory to the officer class, higher salaries to the bureaucracy, and to the bourgeoisie the law and order necessary for economic growth. With minority groups, the universities and the press he was repressive and unjust, but for ten years his military successes against Russia and Austria, colonial expansion in Senegal and a programme of development at home increased his popularity with the establishment. He encouraged the building of railways and telegraphs, the development of banks, credit facilities, industry and agriculture, and the negotiation of helpful trade treaties.

The new emperor needed an imperial capital, and through the energy of his Prefect Baron Eugène Georges Haussmann (1809–91) and the wealth of his new industrial state he created a city more splendid than that of Napoleon I. Between 1853 and 1868 the centre of Paris was ruthlessly reshaped into a grand design of new routes and spaces. The baroque planning of Versailles and Washington was again put to use, not only for its associations of grandeur but also for the more practical purpose of controlling working-class unrest. From a *rond-point* at the centre of a web of radial avenues a small detachment of artillery could control an entire district; troops and police could move swiftly about the city on the ring of *boulevards extérieurs*; the new ceremonial spaces which provided dignified settings for public buildings could also protect them from surprise attack. The Paris of today, in which every celebrated vista bears the mark of Haussmann's influence, makes it difficult to imagine the medieval city in which the 1848 revolution took place, with its rookeries of working-class housing where rebellions could be hatched and fugitives sheltered. The new boulevards not only destroyed areas of potential trouble but also separated those that remained.

The reconstruction of the city was part of a much bigger programme of civic improvement in which Haussmann overhauled the local government system, provided a new water supply and drainage, laid out parks – including the Bois de Boulogne and the Bois de Vincennes – and constructed new bridges, fountains and public buildings. One of these was the Ecole des Beaux-Arts (1860–2) by J.-F. Duban, its large windows expressive of the studios and galleries inside, its exterior detail restrained and elegant like that of the Bibliothèque Ste Geneviève. The new regime also introduced a new mode of architectural expression, the style known as *Deuxième Empire*, which originated with the enlargement (1852–7) of the Palais du Louvre by the architects Visconti and Lefuel to provide new government offices. This Nouveau Louvre, taking its inspiration

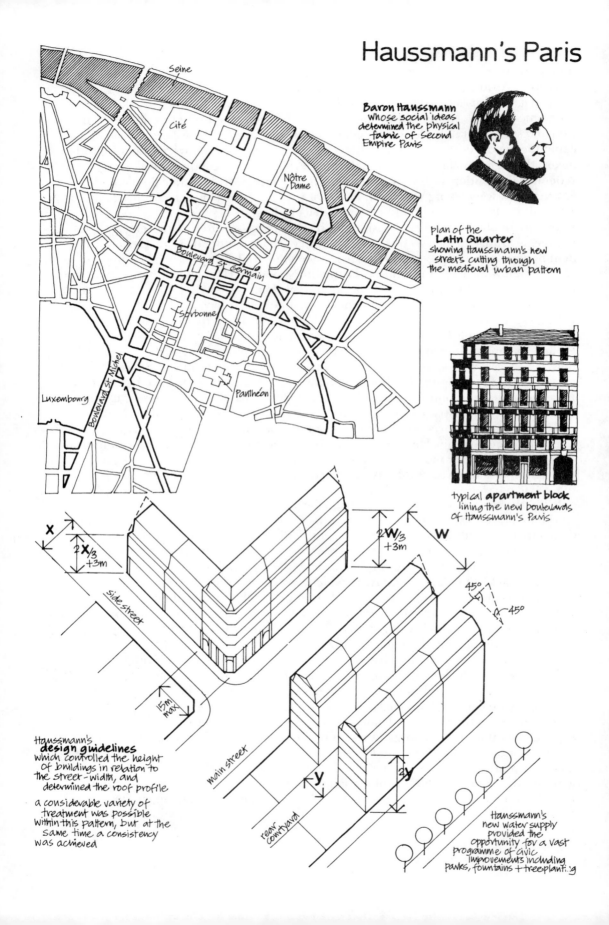

Haussmann's Paris

Baron Haussmann
whose social ideas determined the physical fabric of Second Empire Paris

plan of the
Latin Quarter
showing Haussmann's new streets cutting through the medieval urban pattern

Seine

Cité

Nôtre Dame

Boulevard St Germain

Sorbonne

Boulevard St Michel

Luxembourg

Panthéon

typical **apartment block**
lining the new boulevards of Haussmann's Paris

X

2**X**/3 +3m

side street

15m max

2**W**/3 +3m

W

45°

45°

main street

y

2y

Haussmann's
design guidelines
which controlled the height of buildings in relation to the street-width, and determined the roof profile

a considerable variety of treatment was possible within this pattern, but at the same time a consistency was achieved

rear courtyard

Haussmann's new water supply provided the opportunity for a vast programme of civic improvements including parks, fountains + treeplanting

Pavillon Turgot

rusticated pilasters

heavy baroque style decoration

Pavillon Richelieu

'mansard' roof

Pavillon Colbert

Vieux Louvre

the **Nouveau Louvre** (1852-7) by L.T.J. Visconti and H.M. Lefuel

the 17th century **Pavillon de l'Horloge** by Jacques Lemercier which provided the pattern for the Second Empire additions

the **Palais du Louvre** – showing Visconti and Lefuel's new blocks linking the old Louvre with the Tuileries

Rue de Rivoli

Pavillon Richelieu

Pavillon Colbert

Arc du Carrousel

Pavillon Turgot

Place Louis Napoléon

Vieux Louvre

Pavillon de l'Horloge

former Palace of the Tuileries

Quai du Louvre

River Seine

0   100   200   300
metres

Napoléon III

Second Empire planning –

the 1848 revolution began in the Boulevard des Capucines, so there was a more-than-architectural reason for reconstructing it

Blondel and Fleury's scheme for the **Place de l'Opéra** was built 1858-64

monuments like Rudé's sculpture of **Marshal Ney**, Napoléon I's general, recalled a more glorious past

Rue du 4 Septembre

Avenue de l'Opéra (later)

Rue de la Paix

Boulevard des Capucines

Place de l'Opéra

Rue Halévy

Rue Auber

from the old building and in particular from Lemercier's 17th-century Pavillon de l'Horloge, created a vogue both inside and outside France for baroque-style buildings with rusticated pilasters, heavily-carved ornament and high mansard roofs. Haussmann laid down strict design rules for the buildings lining his streets, determining their height in relation to the street-width, the level of the cornice, the position of balconies and the shape of roofs. But within this over-all pattern, architects were free to experiment with detail, and the result was a street scene regular yet lively. The prevailing architectural treatment was a simplified and domesticated version of that of the new Louvre. The Place de l'Opéra (1858–64) by de Fleury and Blondel, the Boulevard de Sébastopol (1860) and Mortier's Rue de Milan (1860) were typical of the variety that could be obtained within a standard dimensional framework.

But the most spectacular monument to the Second Empire was conceived in 1861, when Charles Garnier won a competition for the building of a new Paris Opéra. Previously intended to entertain 18th-century aristocrats with intimate comedies of manners, opera developed a wider appeal around the beginning of the 19th century, becoming much more associated with the middle class and ideologically with the liberal struggle for freedom. Operas with political themes began with Beethoven's *Fidelio* (1805) and Spontini's *La Vestale* (1807), followed by Auber's *Masaniello* (1828), Rossini's *Guillaume Tell* (1829) and Meyerbeer's *Les Huguenots* (1836). Set in ancient or medieval times to escape the censors, the stories of prison rescues and of oppressed peoples throwing off foreign domination had unmistakable contemporary relevance. At the same time the new and larger audiences demanded grander and more spectacular operas, which needed high fly-towers for numerous changes of scene and stage areas vast enough for triumphal processions, battles and ballet. Garnier (1825–98) responded well to the importance of the commission. The site was a prominent one not far from the Louvre, at the focal point of a network of new streets which met in an enormous civic square. Garnier continued the baroque mood of the new Louvre, even exceeding it in elaboration of decoration. The building itself was gigantic, with a stage and backstage area almost as large as the front-of-house. Internally the most impressive feature was the entrance hall, a conception of appropriately theatrical grandeur comprising an *escalier d'honneur*, statues, ornate lighting and painted ceilings, which created an attractive *mise en scène* for the fashionable clients.

As the wealth and prestige of middle-class culture grew, so did the opposition to it. Out of the Romantic movement emerged the realist school of writers, dedicated to exposing the contradictions of bourgeois life. Balzac's *Comédie Humaine* and the novels of Stendhal, particularly *Lucien Leuwen*, criticised the materialistic values of the July Monarchy, and Flaubert's *Madame Bovary* and the Goncourt novels the opulence of the Second Empire. The Realists described life as it really was, attempting to represent it dialectically and without any bourgeois mystification, though as yet there was little appreciation of underlying economic causes or of political solutions.

The basis for all this opulence was the steady growth of industrialisation. The spread of the railways had enlarged and unified the home market. The textile and metallurgical industries, despite the lack of raw materials, were making big advances through improved techniques and the stimulus of foreign competition. Steel production expanded after 1855 with the adoption of the Bessemer process. State investment in industry, begun before the revolution, continued under Napoleon III and industries began to concentrate together into groups – collieries, blast furnaces, factories – forming consortia like that of the Compagnie des Forges de Franche-Comté. This enabled

the Paris Opéra

Théâtre de l'Opéra (1861-74) by Charles Garnier

1

2

only the Italian baroque style was sufficiently grand and opulent for Garnier – the double columns, and the contrast between large orders and small, had their precedent in Perrault's Louvre (1) and Michelangelo's Campidoglio (2)

Rossini

heroic scene from **Guillaume Tell** first performed in Paris (1829)

the **escalier d'honneur** was the centre-piece of the composition

fly tower

backstage, with ceremonial salon

dome with borrowed light to auditorium

stage

auditorium

escalier d'honneur

foyer

entrance

long section through the building

considerable diversification within the same group: smelting, steel-plate, girders, rails, rolling-stock, engines and machinery.

One result was the rapid expansion of the use of iron and steel in building. The long French tradition of excellence in technical education continued throughout the 19th century through the Ecole Centrale des Travaux Publiques, producing a number of distinguished architect-engineers. Victor Baltard (1805–74) was commissioned by Haussmann to design a new wholesale food market in Paris, on its traditional site near St Eustache. Baltard's first effort was a solid stone building – soon pulled down as being unsuitable – which he then replaced between 1854 and 1866 with ten interconnected pavilions of iron and glass. Provided with vast cellars and internal streets, Les Halles covered an area of 50,000 square metres, and remained in use as *le ventre de Paris* till its demolition in 1971. Outside Paris, at Noisiel, Seine-et-Marne, the architect Jules Saulnier designed a turbine building (1871–2) for the Menier chocolate company. Perched on heavy stone piers above the river, it was the first French example of a masonry building completely framed by an iron skeleton. This feature, combined with its ornate, polychromatic appearance, earned the approval of Viollet-le-Duc, coinciding as it did with his rationalist views on structure and decoration.

After 1860, the Napoleonic regime went into decline. Greater press freedom and more liberal labour laws (including in 1864 the right to strike), a series of costly military exploits in Morocco, Syria and Mexico and a massive programme of spending on the Suez Canal all combined to loosen the emperor's autocratic grip at home and reduce his standing abroad. His dethronement came in 1870 during the short, brutal Franco-Prussian war which ended with the siege and capitulation of Paris. For the people, this military débâcle was less traumatic than its immediate aftermath, when they expelled the defeated bourgeois government and for a few heroic months during 1871 ran Paris as a Commune. For the first time, the proletariat and its socialist leaders had moved against their new class enemy. For their temerity, they were put down by government troops in a brutal action which left a perpetual legacy of hatred. The bourgeoisie could accept defeat more readily from the Germans than from their own working class. In fact, they and their system survived both the war and the Commune unscathed and even strengthened. During the 1870s, French industry was transformed, achieving those levels of financial concentration, of integrated production and of industrial employment which brought it into the modern age.

The work of two great engineers exemplifies this economic expansion. The first was Ferdinand de Lesseps (1805–94), the French consul whose negotiations with the Viceroy of Egypt allowed the building of the Suez Canal – a project anticipated for centuries but which only the 19th century could realise. The English stood to gain most – their Indian empire would be 8,000 km nearer – but their capitalists were uninterested, and it was mainly with Egyptian and French money that the Suez Canal Company was formed in 1858. The Khédive provided forced labour for the project, which de Lesseps supplemented with heavy modern machinery. De Lesseps' well-chosen route involved joining up a number of existing lakes and valleys and was so level that it required no locks. In ten years the canal was built.

If de Lesseps represents the entrepreneurial skill of the 19th-century engineer, no one typifies his technical ability better than Gustave Eiffel (1832–1923). His early work included the railway viaducts at Busseau (1864) and Douro (1876) and the structural design of the iron and glass Bon Marché department store in Paris (1876) whose architect was Boileau, designer of Ste Eugène. The *chef d'oeuvre* of his early career

the French engineers

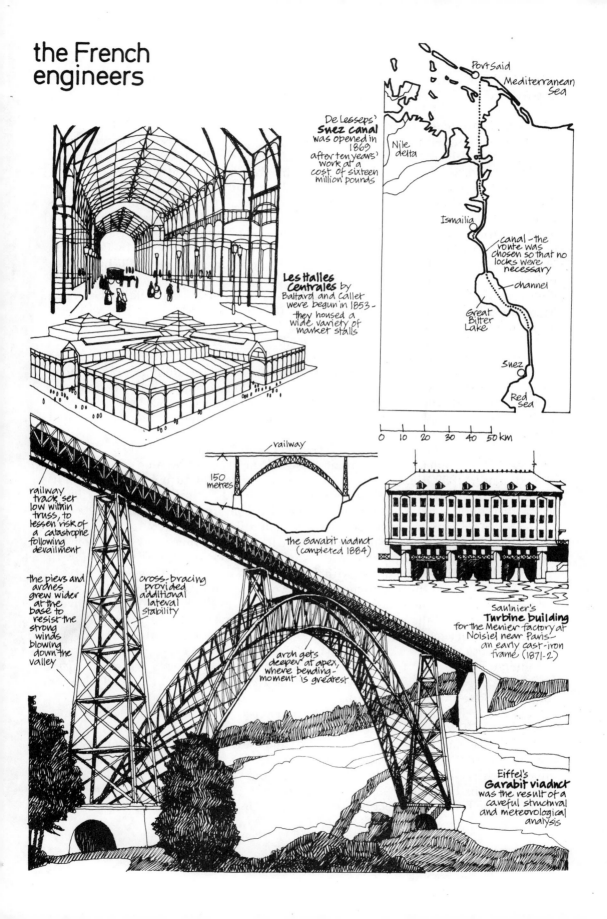

De Lesseps' **Suez Canal** was opened in 1869 after ten years' work at a cost of sixteen million pounds

Port Said
Mediterranean Sea
Nile delta
Ismailia
canal – the route was chosen so that no locks were necessary
channel
Great Bitter Lake
Suez
Red Sea

0 10 20 30 40 50 km

Les Halles Centrales by Baltard and Callet were begun in 1853 – they housed a wide variety of market stalls

railway
150 metres
the Garabit viaduct (completed 1884)

railway track set low within truss, to lessen risk of a catastrophe following derailment

the piers and arches grew wider at the base to resist the strong winds blowing down the valley

cross-bracing provided additional lateral stability

arch gets deeper at apex, where bending-moment is greatest

Saulnier's **Turbine building** for the Menier factory at Noisiel near Paris – an early cast-iron frame (1871-2)

Eiffel's **Garabit viaduct** was the result of a careful structural and meteorological analysis

was the Garabit railway viaduct (1880) in which he supported the flat deck of lattice construction on a gigantic latticed arch. Eiffel was continually pushing forward the technology of bridge design, moving from wrought iron into steel, perfecting design, off-site fabrication and erection techniques, and gaining the experience which was to give him the confidence, later, to build the engineering masterpiece of the century.

As in Britain, the commercial community also soon saw the possibilities of iron, and began to use it in warehouses, shops and shopfronts. Small, glass-roofed shopping arcades has been common in France in the 18th century; now the increasingly ambitious use of iron allowed larger arcades and department stores to be built. Fontaine's Galérie d'Orléans (1829) in Paris had been an early example, followed by the Bazaar de l'Industrie (1830) by Lelong, the Galéries du Commerce et de l'Industrie (1838) by Grisart and Froelicher, and by the Passage Pomeraye in Nantes (1843) by Buron and Durand-Gasselin. A French-style arcade, the Galleria de Cristoforis built by Andrea Pizzala in the Lombardic capital of Milan in 1831, was a smaller local forerunner of the finest of all 19th-century arcades, the Galleria Vittorio Emanuele by Giuseppe Mengoni (1829–77), built between 1865 and 1877 with English money by an English firm but magnificently Italian in design. Cruciform on plan, it consisted of two intersecting iron vaults with a domed crossing, lined with stone façades four storeys in height in a rich neo-Renaissance style. It linked the Piazza del Duomo and its great medieval cathedral with a number of other urban spaces including the Piazza della Scala, in which the 18th-century opera house stood. The decorative scheme was one of elegant richness, from the ornate ironwork of the roof to the entrance façade designed as a Roman triumphal arch. The whole was a convincing demonstration of municipal dignity, culture and wealth.

Between the building of the Galleria de Cristoforis and the Galleria Vittorio Emanuele, Italy underwent a dramatic change. When Cavour became prime minister of Piedmont in 1852 he saw Italy's lack of economic development as a function of its disunity, a condition fostered by its foreign overlords and by the Pope and perpetuated by the ineptitude of its own rulers. He turned Piedmont into a liberal state, promoted bourgeois interests, negotiated trade treaties, built railways and encouraged links with France. For international prestige he allied Piedmont with France and England in the Crimean War and subsequently, with Napoleon's backing, provoked a war with Austria which resulted in union with Lombardy. This liberal *Risorgimento* rapidly expanded when the Central Provinces also revolted against Austria and voted to join the new union, and when Garibaldi's 'Thousand' occupied Sicily and Naples, giving Piedmontese troops the opportunity of seizing part of the Papal States. In 1861 Vittorio Emanuele of Piedmont was able to declare himself king of the new Italy, lay down a constitution and set up a capital in Florence. The composer Verdi demonstrated the intense aspirations of the period in his 'revolutionary' operas *I Vespri Siciliani, Simone Boccanegra, Un Ballo in Maschera* and *La Forza del Destino*, composed between 1855 and 1862, which all express the current bourgeois idealism.

The civic architecture of the *Risorgimento* period was primarily that of Piedmont and Lombardy: of Turin and Milan. In Turin the architect Alessandro Antonelli (1798–1888) built the tall Mole Antonelliana (1863) and the domed spire of the church of San Gaudenzio (1875). The city centre was enlarged and reshaped with new roads and squares such as Giuseppe Bollati's Piazza del Statuto (1864). New railway stations, the Porta Nuova in Turin (1866–8) by Mazzuchetti and Ceppi and the Centrale in Milan (1857) by the French architect Bouchot among them, typified northern Italy's efforts

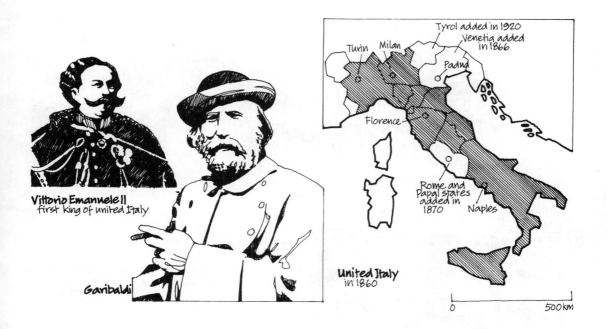

Vittorio Emanuele II
first king of united Italy

Garibaldi

United Italy
in 1860

Tyrol added in 1920
Venetia added in 1866
Turin
Milan
Padua
Florence
Rome and Papal states added in 1870
Naples

0   500km

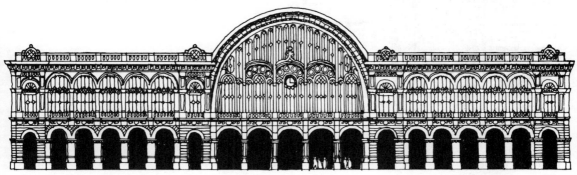

Ceppi and Mazzuchetti's
Porta Nuova station
(1866-68)
in Turin

Manzoni
and **Verdi**

VIVA VERDI!

Verdi's name, used as a
political slogan, contained
a hidden message –
Vittorio Emanuele, Rè d'Italia

Manzoni, author of the great modern
novel **I Promessi Sposi**, symbolised
the potential achievements of
bourgeois Italy

Gaetano Koch's **Esedra** (1880)
in Rome was one of many
architectural celebrations of its
becoming the capital of a
united Italy

the Risorgimento

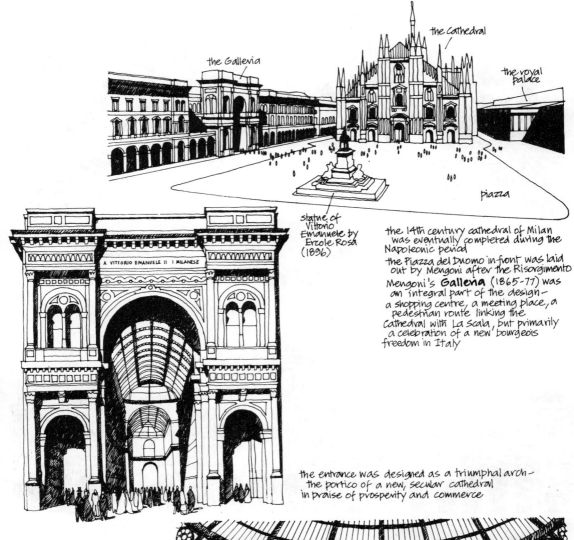

the Galleria

the Cathedral

the royal palace

piazza

statue of Vittorio Emanuele by Ercole Rosa (1896)

A VITTORIO EMANUELE II I MILANESE

the 14th century cathedral of Milan was eventually completed during the Napoleonic period

the Piazza del Duomo in front was laid out by Mengoni after the Risorgimento

Mengoni's **Galleria** (1865-77) was an integral part of the design – a shopping centre, a meeting place, a pedestrian route linking the Cathedral with La Scala, but primarily a celebration of a new bourgeois freedom in Italy

the entrance was designed as a triumphal arch – the portico of a new, secular cathedral in praise of prosperity and commerce

the interior was an extraordinary unity between architecture and engineering – the cruciform plan and the domed crossing emphasised the religious imagery

the Galleria

to link itself with the rest of industrial Europe. Expansion continued; when in 1866 Prussia crushed Austria, Italy was able to seize Venice. Similarly, when in 1870 Napoleon III was defeated by the Prussians and could no longer protect the Pope, Italy was able to incorporate the Papal States, ending their centuries-old political power and making Rome the capital of a united nation.

During the few years in which Florence had been capital the northern part of its city centre had been rebuilt with formal avenues and squares to a design by Giuseppe Poggi (1811–1901). During the 1870s and early 1880s an even larger rebuilding took place in Rome to celebrate its new capital status. The ideological significance of an ancient city aspiring once again to its great destiny was not forgotten, and the new additions were monumental in scale and traditional in style: the Via Venti Settembre and the Via Nazionale (both began in 1871), the Palazzo delle Belle Arti (1878–82) by Pio Piacentini (1846–1928), and the Esedra (1880), the Palazzo Boncampagni (1886–90) and the Banca d'Italia (1889–92) by Gaetano Koch (1849–1910). As an expression of economic and political strength all this architectural activity had a certain air of bravado: both politically and financially the country was still at a low ebb, even though unification had at last opened the door to economic progress. In 1870, Italy's gross domestic product was less than 1% of that of Britain, which during the 1850s and 1860s underwent its 'golden age' of capitalist expansion.

Britain was still the world leader in cotton, and output continued to grow, though at a lesser rate than in the early years. The British share of the world market was declining, however, and the industry was losing its pre-eminent place to steel, engineering and shipbuilding, which were not only growing faster but also beginning to dominate the export market. The enhancement of Victorian Manchester with a series of splendid civic buildings – Edward Walters' palazzo-style Free Trade Hall (1853–4), the neo-gothic Assize Courts (1859–64) and new Town Hall (1868–77), both by Alfred Waterhouse (1830–1905) – thus came slightly too late to celebrate the city's one-time industrial supremacy, now shared with Birmingham, Glasgow, Sheffield, Leeds and a number of other northern and midland cities which exerted an influence on British political life during the 1850s and 1860s through a long succession of Liberal governments. Cuthbert Brodrick's neo-classical Town Hall in Leeds (1853–9) and Alexander 'Greek' Thomson's Caledonia Road Free Church in Glasgow (1856–7) were among the finest public buildings of this affluent period. In one respect, the cotton industry was a victim of its own success. Competition and rapid expansion required frequent improvements in technology, and British capital assets, both buildings and machinery, were soon to become out-dated; a reluctance to rebuild and re-tool assisted the industry's long-term decline. This was less true of the railways, whose technology lasted over a century without any fundamental changes, attracting continuous and massive investment. Unlike Germany and the USA, Britain did not open up uncharted areas by building railways: the country was small and already well covered by canals and roads. Railway-building was therefore less a functional need than a convenient channel for speculative investment. Too many lines were built, and much capital was sunk without trace; the average return on investment, per mile of track, was only one-fifth of that in the USA.

To succeed, the railways had to attract travellers. Speed and cheapness were selling-points, but the public's suspicion of the discomfort, danger and sheer novelty of railway travel had to be overcome. The development of Samuel Morse's electric telegraph improved signalling and safety, and better rolling-stock was quickly developed to

the Battle of Styles

Scott's **Albert Memorial** (1863-72) in London— neo-Gothic was used for a quasi-religious effect

Brodrick's **Leeds Town Hall** (1853-59) was one of the finest English buildings of the period— the severity of its neo-Classical style was enriched by Second Empire decoration

Waterhouse's **New Town Hall** in Manchester (1868-77) was among the best of a growing number of neo-Gothic town halls

In Glasgow, Greek Thomson's **Caledonia Road Free church** (1856-7) was academic yet original, in keeping with Scottish scholarship at the time

committee rooms

main hall

tower

dining room reception room committee room council chamber

0 10 20 30 40 50 metres

protect passengers from the weather and fumes. In addition, a reassuring image was provided by the station buildings, in which the Victorian passion for allusion and representation was put to good use. The finest early example was Philip Hardwick's Euston station in London where the entrance screen (1835–7) and the Great Hall (1846–9) invited the traveller to experience the excitement of some Homeric journey and appeased the faint-hearted or the critical by alluding to a familiar cultural tradition. At King's Cross station (1850–2), designed by the engineer Lewis Cubitt, the main train shed consisted of two 30-metre-wide cast-iron barrel vaults, with the principal arches in laminated timber, and the entrance façade of a massive brick screen in which two gigantic arched recesses matched the vaults behind. Cubitt also designed the adjoining Great Northern hotel in a simplified Italian style. The Great Western hotel at Paddington (1852–4), designed by M. D. Wyatt, formed a dignified front to the train shed, which was one of Brunel's finest works: three parallel iron vaults intersected at right-angles by subsidiary cross-vaults lent an almost cathedral-like aspect to the design.

Iron buildings became quite common between 1850 and 1880, as the industry expanded. Among the most notable were the Jamaica Street warehouse in Glasgow (1855–6) by John Baird, the naval boat-store at Sheerness (1858–60) by G. T. Greene, and Peter Ellis's Oriel Chambers in Liverpool (1864–5). For these fairly modest structures cast iron was appropriate, but the collapse of Stephenson's Dee Bridge in 1847 had underlined the deficiencies of cast iron in highly-stressed structures. Stephenson's own Britannia bridge and Brunel's great Royal Albert bridge over the Tamar at Saltash (completed 1859), which relied on vast, hollow tubes of wrought iron, created a considerable corpus of advanced structural knowledge. In Paddington, in John Dobson's great curved roof at Newcastle Central (1850) and in the superb roof designed by W. H. Barlow for London's St Pancras station (1863–7), wrought iron was used for its greater tensile strength.

Barlow's roof was a structural *tour de force*, a gigantic parabolic vault 30 metres high with a span of 75 metres, at that time the largest in the world. Yet George Gilbert Scott, architect of the Midland hotel (1865–71) which formed its façade, looked on it with disdain. Between 1860 and 1875 Scott was building the Foreign Office in London, designed much against his will in the renaissance style; he would have preferred the design which he later used in the Midland hotel, an ornate concoction of English, Italian and Flemish Gothic, with a large central tower. He clearly felt it was too good for a railway station and that Barlow's great building was a poor neighbour for his own. Yet unrelated as the two parts are, and indicative of the gap between the philosophies of the engineer and the architect, the building as a whole remains an extraordinary masterpiece whose vastness of scale, romantic appearance, structural dynamism and sheer brilliance of planning typifies everything that was best in Victorian design.

Gilbert Scott, whose practice was the largest and most active of the day, covered Britain with neo-gothic buildings; it is said that on one occasion, seeing a church under construction, he asked the name of the architect and was told 'George Gilbert Scott'. More than any other designer, he represents the commercial turn taken by Pugin's holy crusade; prolific and able, he was the archetype of the successful modern architect, to whom professionalism consisted of responding readily to any commission, sacred or secular, commercial or ideological. In his London memorial to Prince Albert (1863–72), for a quasi-religious effect he placed a statue of the prince within an outsize ciborium of granite, marble, mosaic and bronze; groups of symbolic figures around the

during the 1860s developments like the **block system** in which signals and points were interlinked, and **first class** coaches with heavily padded seats, brought increased safety and luxury to railway travel

the Great Hall at Hardwick's **Euston station,** London (1846-49) turned a railway journey into a ceremonial experience

the train sheds too, like Dobson's at **Newcastle Central** (1850), with its great curving roof, and...

... Brunel's at London's **Paddington** (1852-54), with its elegantly designed structure, synthesised architecture and engineering in a way worthy of Viollet-le-Duc

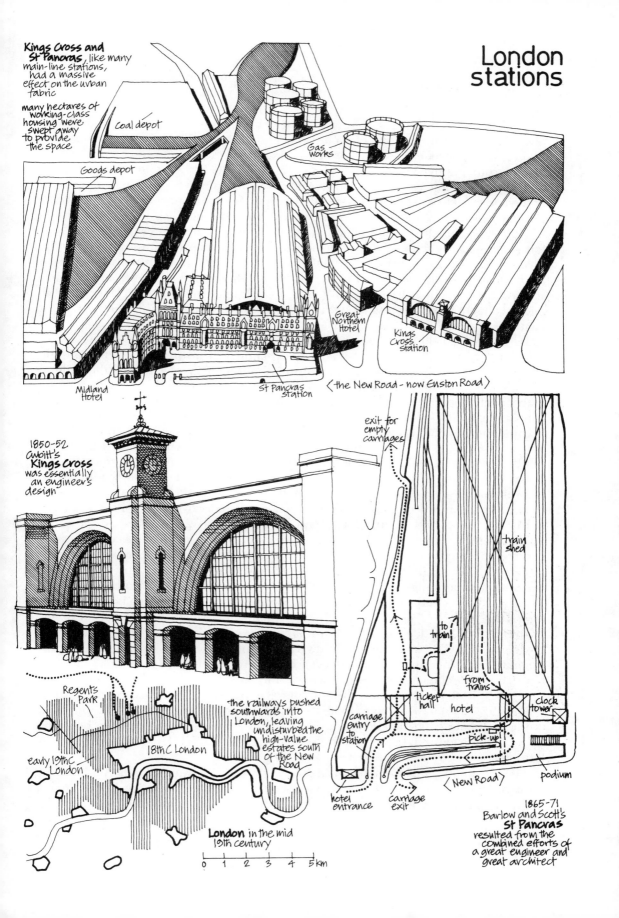

London stations

Kings Cross and St Pancras, like many main-line stations, had a massive effect on the urban fabric

many hectares of working-class housing were swept away to provide the space

Coal depot

Gas Works

Goods depot

Great Northern Hotel

Kings Cross station

Midland Hotel

St Pancras station

⟨ the New Road - now Euston Road ⟩

1850-52 Cubitt's **Kings Cross** was essentially an engineer's design

exit for empty carriages

train shed

to train

from trains

ticket hall

clock tower

hotel

Regents Park

the railways pushed southwards into London, leaving undisturbed the high-value estates south of the New Road

carriage entry to station

pick-up

early 19thC London

18thC London

hotel entrance

carriage exit

⟨ New Road ⟩

podium

London in the mid 19th century

0 1 2 3 4 5km

1865-71 Barlow and Scott's **St Pancras** resulted from the combined efforts of a great engineer and great architect

base represented the continents over which British dominion extended, and a frieze of notables, from Socrates to Mendelssohn, placed the monarchy at the head of a 2000-year cultural tradition.

The later stages of the gothic revival were dominated by the art critic John Ruskin (1819–1900). At an early age, like many other young romantics, he came to appreciate nature, to despise the false and pretentious and to embark on a lifelong search for artistic truth. His five-volume book *Modern Painters* (1836–53) was famous for its defence of Turner, in whose work Ruskin discovered a 'truth to nature' which gave reality to his own ideas. These he developed in 1849 with his book *The Seven Lamps of Architecture*, putting forward seven basic precepts for the designer: the 'sacrifice' involved in striving for excellence; the 'truth' in the honest use of materials; the 'power' of simple, grand forms; the 'beauty' imparted by the use of nature as a source of inspiration; the 'life' given by hand-craftsmanship; the 'memory' offered to future generations by a work of art built for posterity; and the 'obedience' of disciplining oneself to use only the finest styles of the past – which, in Ruskin's view, were Italian Romanesque, Italian Gothic and – as Pugin and Scott also thought – English Gothic of the late 13th and early 14th century.

In *The Stones of Venice* (1851–3) he examined Venetian Gothic in more detail and also developed his ideas on craftsmanship, explaining the artistic achievements of the middle ages in terms of the medieval craftsman's intimate involvement in the building process and conversely the ugliness of the modern world in terms of the modern crafts-man's denied opportunity for self-creation through fulfilling work. He developed this concept in the 1850s during his association with the Pre-Raphaelite painters, and it became the basis of his own favourite work, *Unto this Last* (1862), which cut sharply across the established ethic of the capitalist world. To him, riches were less important than privilege and to demand uncreative work from one's fellows was immoral.

In his own time, as today, Ruskin was recognised as an eminent figure, a fine writer of profound insight. He had an immediate though superficial influence on many contemporary architects and builders, to whom his rediscovery of Venice and Lombardy was novel and exciting. The post-Ruskin period was marked by the use of Italian details – particularly the plate-tracery of the Doge's Palace, of decorative carving in natural vegetable forms, and by the mixing of materials to achieve polychromatic effects. In Oxford, where he lived and taught, his ideas affected a whole generation of buildings as diverse as the University museum (1855–9) by Deane and Woodward, the church of St Philip and St James (1860–2) by George Edmund Street and Keble College chapel (1867–83) by William Butterfield. Street (1824–81) and Butterfield (1814–1900), together with Samuel Sanders Teulon (1812–73) and John Pearson (1817–97), took the gothic revival in a new direction, less academic, more original, concerned with dramatic, even brutal architectural effects. Street designed numerous churches but is best-known for the Royal Courts of Justice in London (1871–82). Butterfield designed the fine church of All Saints, Margaret Street, London (1849–59), and new buildings (1858–84) for Dr Arnold's Rugby School, cornerstone of the bourgeois educational system. Teulon and Pearson are each known best for a single London church, the former for St Stephen's on Rosslyn Hill (1869–76) and the latter for St Augustine's in Kilburn (1870–80).

Though many of his architectural followers tended towards High Anglicanism, Ruskin's own view of Gothic was essentially anti-Catholic; he developed Pugin's relatively narrow, religious view of architectural truth into a more expansive secular

Ruskin

Ruskin (1819-1900)

from a drawing by Ruskin

Ruskin's
Seven Lamps of Architecture and **Stones of Venice** celebrated Italian Romanesque and Gothic craftsmanship

the 12thC church of San Michele at Lucca (1) and the 14thC gothic Doge's Palace in Venice (2) displayed the use of multi-coloured masonry, the use of simple geometric tracery and the use of natural forms for decoration

Deane and Woodward's
Oxford Museum (1855-59) on which Ruskin collaborated for a time

Street (1824-81)

church of
SS Philip and James in Oxford (1860-62) by Street was rich in Ruskinian polychrome masonry

typical
north Oxford villa of the late 19thC displaying Ruskin's influence

Victorian High Gothic

Teulon's **St Stephen's**, Rosslyn Hill, London
(1869-76)

Pearson's **St Augustine's**, Kilburn,
London (1870-80)

Butterfield's **All Saints**, Margaret Street, London
(1849-59) and
Keble College chapel, Oxford
(1867-83)

Butterfield
(1814-1900)

ideology which in the long term had a considerable influence on designers and theorists. The concepts of truth and power expressed in *The Seven Lamps of Architecture* became a fundamental part of the development of modern architectural theory. And many of his broader social concepts, especially his insights into alienation, have even more relevance today, though he himself never took this particular idea to its logical conclusion. He criticised capitalism as vehemently, more penetratingly and less negatively than his contemporary, Carlyle, but like Carlyle he was ultimately unable to step outside his bourgeois role and offer a genuine alternative to the capitalist world.

Neo-Gothic, in all its forms, remained the architecture of the middle class, an outward and visible sign that the industrial revolution had now become institutional and permanent. The work of Carlyle and Macaulay, amid an increasing national consciousness of history, helped the middle class to see itself not as a temporary phenomenon but as an integral part of human development and the very core of the 19th-century class structure. Culturally and spiritually, even the monarchy had become bourgeois. For the working class, living conditions remained appalling and wages did not generally improve. Nevertheless, through a number of reforms which limited hours of work, introduced incentive bonuses and developed the factory inspectorate, working conditions slowly improved. As the engineering and shipbuilding industries grew, the highly skilled workers who manned them began to form an aristocracy of labour, better paid and better housed than the working class as a whole. In the early days there had been the sustaining hope that industrial capitalism might prove short-lived; now, by contrast, at least part of the working class had an interest in the continuation of the system, and there was an over-all lessening of class tension. The unions concentrated on the development of self-help, of cooperatives and friendly societies; Chartists and revolutionaries appeared to have gone underground or died out.

The development of the joint-stock company and of limited liability allowed a more adventurous use of money: an over-zealous investor stood to lose no more than his investment, and not his entire fortune as hitherto. Banks and stock exchanges allowed an easy flow of capital anywhere in the world. They also made it possible to invest for a living, rather than to work, thus creating a new class of *rentiers* existing on the surplus profits of the railway age. The stuccoed terraces of Leamington and Cheltenham, vast hotels like the Grand at Scarborough, the Metropole at Brighton and the Cecil in London, and Thomas Cook's tours to Italy, Egypt and the Alps represent the prosperous and slightly ostentatious life-style of this leisured group. On the more attractive edges of every large town suburbs grew, as the speculators built for middle-class customers of varying levels of affluence. Some demanded the new gothic style; the more traditional clung during the 1860s and into the 1870s to that of the Italian Renaissance. Contemporary with the gothicised houses built for progressive Oxford dons on the Woodstock and Banbury Roads, deriving at second or third hand from the ideas of Ruskin, were the large stuccoed villas of Belsize Park in London, or the tightly-packed terraces of North Kensington, tricked out with vestigial Italianate details to awaken faint echoes of the Grand Tour for stock-jobbers and bank clerks. Railway transport brought materials from various parts of Britain, and even Europe, to displace the local brick and timber. In place of the local stocks and hand-made tiles of the south of England came glazed red bricks, yellow-green bricks, glazed green tiles and the ubiquitous Welsh roofing slate, while local brick fields and quarries closed down.

It is symptomatic of the speculative process that many of the newly-built areas were

social pretension
in architecture

the **Hotel Cecil** (1890)
in London, one of
many luxury hotels
designed in a
monumental second-
Empire style

mid-19th century house in
Cheltenham, in a gracious
Italianate style, commensurate with
the town's image as a fashionable spa

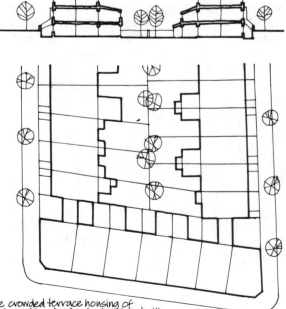

the crowded terrace housing of
North Kensington in London, built
speculatively in the 1860s and intended
for lower-middle-class owners

0   10 metres

like Cheltenham and
North Kensington and
many other places, the
terraces of **Kentish
Town** in London were
also in an Italian style

never settled by the middle-class clients they were intended for, and became from the start 'twilight' areas of workers' rooming-houses. The Marx family, living in a house in Grafton Terrace in the new London suburb of Kentish Town, among streets as yet un-paved and un-lit, paid an annual rent of £70, but were still unable to live a lower-middle-class life without pawning most of the furniture. The average worker could not aspire even so high; a London building craftsman in 1861 earned 32 shillings a week, and was unable to pay as much as £10 a year in rent. For him, the choice could lie only between a room in a multi-occupied house, a Model Dwelling run by a charity, costing 3 shillings a week, or his own hovel on a scrap of wayside land.

In 1859, the year in which Marx, living in poverty, finished writing the *Grundrisse*, a large, comfortable middle-class house was built at Bexleyheath outside London. The designer used neither the rhetoric of the Italian style not the superficial gothic dec-oration of Ruskin's imitators, but attempted instead to rediscover the forms of the age-old craft traditions which industrialisation had all but destroyed. It was a building almost without style, in the academic sense. Faintly medieval in appearance, its forms were derived directly from the character of the materials used and were designed carefully and artfully to resemble the work of skilled but simple craftsmen; its plain brick walls and steeply-pitched clay-tile roofs gave it the name 'Red House'. The architect, Philip Webb (1831–1915), had worked in Street's office in Oxford where he had come to understand Ruskin's theories – their essence, not the superficialities which surrounded them – and to wish to take them further. Webb was an uncompromising, even brutal, designer, devoid of academicism and prepared to use any styles or mixture of styles without too much regard for their orginal context but merely for the functional appropriateness of the motifs they contained. Confining himself almost entirely to the design of houses, in town and country, he produced 1 Palace Green and 19 Lincoln's Inn Fields in London (both 1868), Joldwyns, Surrey (1873), Clouds, Wiltshire (1876), Smeaton, Yorkshire (1878), and Conyhurst in Surrey (1885).

Webb's successor as Street's chief draughtsman was Richard Norman Shaw (1831–1912). He developed a similar interest in craftsmanship and the honest use of traditional materials, but in the context of a style more obviously charming and attrac-tive, which brought him wider success and a bigger, more varied output. Much of his work was carried out in collaboration with his partner Eden Nesfield (1835–88) and included country houses such as Leys Wood and Glen Andred in Sussex (both 1868) and Cragside in Northumberland (1870), and London houses such as Lowther Lodge, Kensington (1873), his own house in Ellerdale Road, Hampstead (1875), and the Swan House in Chelsea (1876). He also designed commercial buildings in London, among them New Zealand Chambers (1872) and New Scotland Yard (1886) and the development during the 1870s of the world's first garden suburb, Bedford Park in west London.

From mid-century, for sixty years and more, progressive architects, first in Britain then in Europe and America, were discovering the virtues of informal, organic design and the imaginative re-use of forms of the pre-industrial tradition. The Red House was a landmark in the development of this movement, though not for its architectural distinction alone. Architecturally it was not wholly without precedent: Pugin's own house at Ramsgate (1841–3) for example, and Butterfield's vicarage at Coalpitheath (1844–5) had been early attempts to invoke the spirit of honest craftsmanship. More important, and more influential, was the philosophical background from which it emerged, whose creation and development was essentially the work of one man, owner

Philip Webb

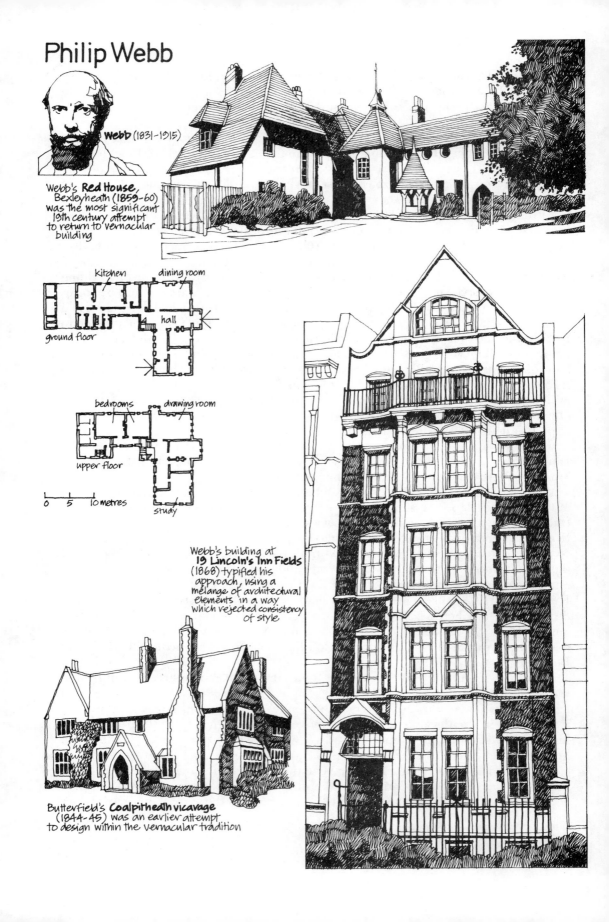

Webb (1831–1915)

Webb's **Red House**, Bexleyheath (1859–60) was the most significant 19th century attempt to return to vernacular building

kitchen

dining room

ground floor

hall

bedrooms

drawing room

upper floor

0 5 10 metres

study

Webb's building at **19 Lincoln's Inn Fields** (1868) typified his approach, using a mélange of architectural elements in a way which rejected consistency of style

Butterfield's **Coalpithealth vicavage** (1844–45) was an earlier attempt to design within the vernacular tradition

Shaw and Nesfield

Shaw (1831-1912)

Shaw's **Cragside** (1870), designed for a Northumberland factory-owner in an 'Olde English' style

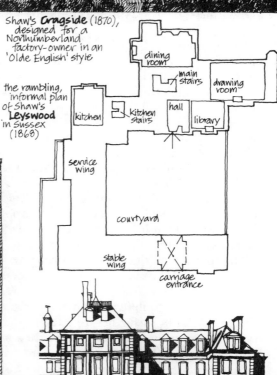

the rambling, informal plan of Shaw's **Leyswood** in Sussex (1868)

dining room

main stairs

drawing room

kitchen

kitchen stairs

hall

library

service wing

courtyard

stable wing

carriage entrance

Nesfield's **Kinmel Park** in North Wales (1868) and his tiny lodge building at **Kew** near London (1867), whose high-pitched roofs, tall chimneys and dormers were reminiscent of the age of Wren, and helped establish the so-called 'Queen Anne' style

Shaw's elegant **Swan House** in Chelsea (1875) was his personal version of the Queen Anne style

of the Red House, friend of Webb, working colleague of Shaw and numerous other architects, and the most significant theoretician of art and architecture of the 19th century.

William Morris (1834–96) came from a comfortable middle-class family and was educated at the new Marlborough public school – where he learned little more than love for the countryside and old churches – and at Oxford – where he discovered Ruskin and Carlyle and established a friendship with the painter Burne-Jones, who shared his revulsion for the ethical values of the 1850s. For Burne-Jones, for the Pre-Raphaelite Brotherhood of painters which he helped to found, and indeed for the young Morris, this revolt took the form of a fascination with the middle ages, but Morris soon saw the hollowness and inadequacy of fake medievalism. What for Pugin, the neo-gothic architects and the Pre-Raphaelites remained an end, for Morris was merely a beginning: for them the enemy was 19th-century industrialism, its squalor and ugliness; for him, through the exploitation and alienation it brought, the enemy was capitalism itself.

The Red House, built for his marriage in 1859 to Jane Burden, was designed according to his principles. Having built the house, he needed furniture and decorations neither pretentious nor shoddy – which was all that capitalism could provide – and in 1861 he founded 'the Firm' to produce honest workmanlike furniture, wallpaper and fabrics for himself and others. Later he expanded into stained-glass, books, tapestries and carpets, making characteristic use of stylised, two-dimensional designs which emphasised the character of the materials he was working with, in contrast to the exaggerated chiaroscuro of the contemporary machine-produced design typified by the Great Exhibition. As a designer he achieved international fame, which was further enlarged by his poetry, mostly – like *The Earthly Paradise* (1868) – with epic, historicist themes, and by his foundation in 1877 of the Society for the Protection of Ancient Buildings. Yet each success left him unsatisfied, and he particularly resented that capitalism had made hand-production so inherently costly that it turned the Firm into a purveyor of attractive goods for the rich.

This particular question has been the subject of much misconception and misrepresentation. There is a persistent view of Morris as a hater of the modern age, impossibly concerned with the creation of some medieval utopia, whose aim of bringing art to a wider public was somehow frustrated by his hatred of machine production. This could hardly be further from the truth: he hated not the age itself but the exploitation of its powers by a privileged class; he was concerned less with the past than with the future, and used the middle ages as some vast allegory of what the common man had once been capable of before capitalism crushed him, and could be once again; and far from hating the machine he was almost unique among the great social critics in recognising the potential of technology in relieving man of drudgery and creating a better world. As he said, 'our epoch has invented machines which would have appeared wild dreams to the men of past ages, and of those machines we have as yet *made no use*'. To him 'use' meant social use, for the benefit of many, not mis-use, for the benefit of a few.

The idea that art can be brought to the people only by machine production is one that only a capitalist could conceive. To Morris art was not an elitist pursuit, nor a commodity to be peddled by entrepreneurs, but an integral part of every man and woman's self-development. Only in a society in which decisions were taken to benefit the community as a whole could ordinary people find the opportunity to develop their own skills to their full potential; clearly capitalism was unable to create this kind of

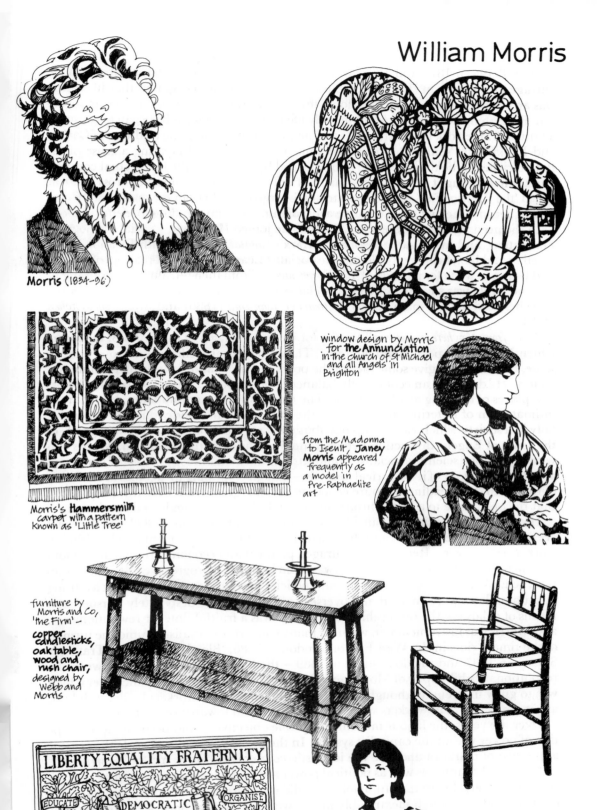

William Morris

Morris (1834-96)

window design by Morris for **the Annunciation** in the church of St Michael and all Angels in Brighton

Morris's **Hammersmith** carpet with a pattern known as 'Little Tree'

from the Madonna to Iseult, **Janey Morris** appeared frequently as a model in Pre-Raphaelite art

furniture by Morris and Co, 'the Firm' –

copper candlesticks, oak table, wood and rush chair, designed by Webb and Morris

LIBERTY EQUALITY FRATERNITY

EDUCATE

ORGANISE

DEMOCRATIC FEDERATION

AGITATE

Morris's design for a membership card for the Democratic Federation; and **Eleanor Marx**, one of the co-founders

The will to power
Europe and America in the late 19th century

In 1858 the emperor Franz Josef, taking his cue from Napoleon III, began to reconstruct the centre of Vienna. The medieval city walls were replaced by the Ringstrasse, forming round the city centre a wide horse-shoe of protective avenues, its open end enclosed by the Danube canal. In 1848 the city had been a perpetual invitation to insurrection, with working-class housing existing alongside highly accessible public buildings and palaces, including the Hofburg itself. Now the Ringstrasse was lined with open spaces and public buildings – parliament, university, city hall, stock-exchange, opera house – and created a line of demarcation between the ceremonial city centre and the new residential suburbs, middle-class in the immediate vicinity and working-class, cut off by another ring-road, further out.

Franz Josef's efforts to keep peace in the city were part of his strenuous attempts at over-all political reconstruction. In the interests of holding together his disintegrating empire he offered increased autonomy to the rebellious Hungarians and renamed the empire Austria-Hungary. Outwardly he still commanded immense power and resources but his country, bound by the ideas and attitudes of the old regime, contrasted with Prussia's single-minded industrialisation, on which military power really depended. Unlike the hedonistic Viennese upper classes, building luxury apartments such as von Hansen's Heinrichshof (1861–3), the Prussians were investing heavily in railways, steel and armaments. In 1866, after a surprisingly short war, the Prussians defeated the Austrians decisively at Sadowa and became undisputed leaders of the new Germany.

The personification of Germany's military strength was Otto von Bismarck (1815–98) who became chancellor in 1862. The strength itself rested on Germany's economic base; the *Zollverein*, currency reform, the railways and the military adventure all contributed to the economic unity which was Bismarck's prime concern. Scientific researches and their technological application allowed the industrial system to expand and diversify: Friedrich Bayer's development of new dyeing techniques (1860), as well as his contribution to the manufacture of medicines, photographic materials and plastics; Werner von Siemens' invention of the dynamo (1866), used to generate electricity for street-lighting, factories and tramways; the application of the Gilchrist-Thomas process (1878) which compensated for Germany's lack of non-phosphoric ore; and the introduction (1883) of Gottlieb Daimler's automobile. The end-product of these links between research, design, technology and industrial production was the growth of the giant combines: in Berlin, Egell's iron and engineering works and Borsig's locomotive works; Klett's locomotive works in Nuremberg and the iron and steelworks of Krupp in Essen. Rapidly they all expanded and diversified from metallurgy and railways into structural steelwork, steam boats or armaments. With investment and intellectual effort concentrated in more functional directions, it is not surprising that architectural styles tended towards the pedestrian and derivative, ranging from that of the Parisian Second Empire typified by Heise's military hospital in Dresden (1869) and Cologne Opera House (1870–2) designed by Julius Raschdorf, to the Schinkel-like neo-

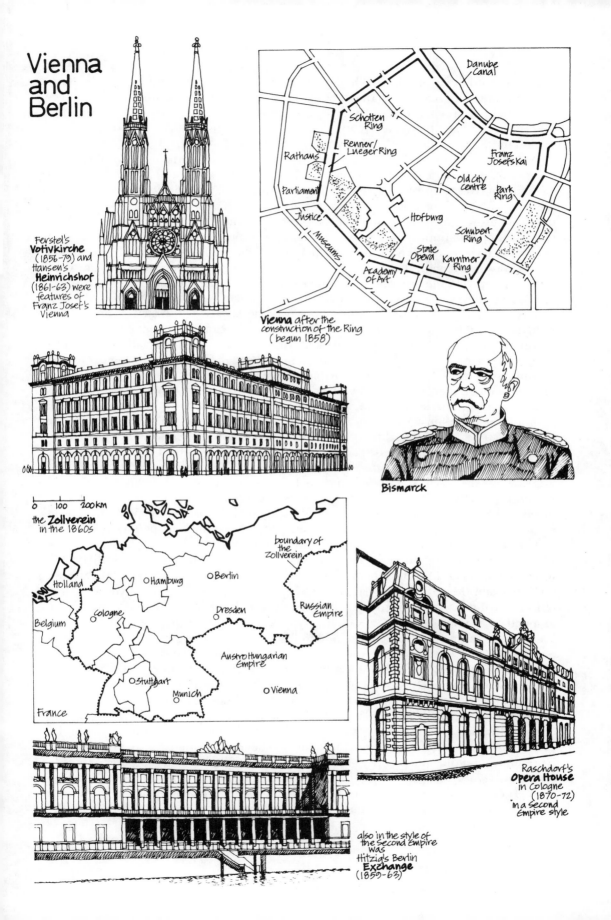

Vienna and Berlin

Ferstel's **Votivkirche** (1856-79) and Hansen's **Heinrichshof** (1861-63) were features of Franz Josef's Vienna

Vienna after the construction of the Ring (begun 1858)

Danube Canal

Schotten Ring

Renner/ Lueger Ring

Rathaus

Parliament

Justice

Museums

Academy of Art

State Opera

Hofburg

Old City centre

Franz Josefs Kai

Park Ring

Schubert Ring

Karntner Ring

Bismarck

0 100 200km
the **Zollverein** in the 1860s

Holland

Belgium

France

Cologne

Hamburg

Berlin

Dresden

Stuttgart

Munich

boundary of the Zollverein

Russian Empire

Austro Hungarian Empire

Vienna

Raschdorf's **Opera House** in Cologne (1870-72) in a Second Empire style

also in the style of the Second Empire was Hitzig's Berlin **Exchange** (1859-63)

Classicism of Hitzig's Berlin Exchange (1859–63). More significant than style, however, were the industrial techniques finding their way into traditional-looking buildings in the form of iron or steel frames, heating systems and passenger lifts. The most successful marriage between old style and new technique was the Anhalter railway station in Berlin (1872–80) by Franz Schwechten (1841–1924).

At Gotha in 1875 the Social Democratic Party (SPD) was formed. From the first it was dominated by the moderate policies of Lassalle's followers rather than the marxist Liebknecht. Marx himself expressed disappointment that the new party was seeking alliance with traditional landed interests rather than challenging them. As in Britain, the rapid growth of cities brought poor housing and disease; the system itself brought bad working conditions, long hours and child labour. Though in their fight against exploitation the marxists gained strength and in 1890 challenged for the leadership of the socialist movement, the eventual improvement of food, clothing and working conditions dampened the fires of revolution among the workers themselves.

Concessions to the workers by Bismarck's government were part of its over-all drive towards industrial transformation: it reformed the laws which restricted growth; it nationalised industries of doubtful profitability; it developed the banking system to encourage long-term loans; it promoted education at all levels, especially in technical subjects; it made Germany self-sufficient in food through agricultural protection; and it stimulated the 'cartel' system which deliberately reduced wasteful competition, creating monopoly capitalism at home and more efficient exporting abroad. All this was in marked contrast to Britain, where reluctance to apply new techniques, together with a preference for competiton and a resistance to state intervention, allowed the industrial base to decline during the Great Depression, never to recover its early strength. The most curious social feature of Germany's industrial revolution was its strongly aristocratic aspect. After 1848, in both Austria and Germany, the bourgeoisie was slow to take political initiative and the land-owning class regained much of its old power, especially in Prussia. The middle classes could create an industrial state only through the authority of the land-owners who, by their control of the peasants – from whose ranks the industrial workforce was drawn – determined the pattern of labour.

The architecture of the period is rich with the houses and palaces of powerful aristocrats and princelings, whose Ruritanian way of life persisted anachronistically in the world of Krupp and Daimler-Benz. The most spectacular examples were not Prussian but Bavarian, the result of the partnership between the architect Georg von Dollman (1830–95) and his eccentric royal employer Ludwig II (1845–86). The king was ready to spend enormous sums of money on his vivid ideas, in whose realisation Dollman was little more than an agent. Schloss Linderof near Oberammergau (1870–86) was an essay in the rich Bavarian baroque of Neumann and Fischer, and Ludwig's spiritual identification with Louis XIV was the inspiration for Herrenchiemsee (1878 and later) in the style of Versailles. Most fantastic of all was Neuschwanstein (1869–81), a flamboyant medieval-style castle on a mountain-side, Ludwig's romantic response to Wagner's opera, *Der Ring des Nibelungen*. Infatuated with the music, Ludwig had become Wagner's patron in 1864, one of his aims being to stage the great music-dramas in the way the composer intended. The Festspielhaus at Bayreuth, near Nuremburg, unique among opera houses in being designed by the composer expressly for his own work, was opened in 1876 with the first complete performance of the *Ring* cycle. It embodied Wagner's rigorous and revolutionary philosophy of art, and was as sober as the Paris Opéra was magnificent. Attention was focused entirely on the

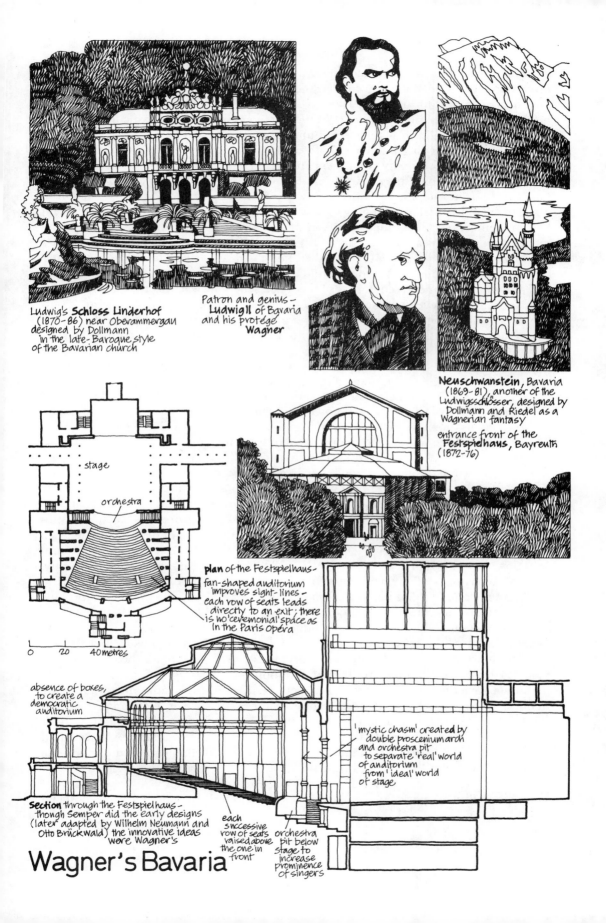

Ludwig's **Schloss Linderhof** (1870–86) near Oberammergau designed by Dollmann in the late-Baroque style of the Bavarian church

Patron and genius – **Ludwig II** of Bavaria and his protégé **Wagner**

Neuschwanstein, Bavaria (1869–81), another of the Ludwigsschlösser, designed by Dollmann and Riedel as a Wagnerian fantasy

entrance front of the **Festspielhaus**, Bayreuth (1872–76)

stage

orchestra

plan of the Festspielhaus – fan-shaped auditorium improves sight-lines – each row of seats leads directly to an exit; there is no 'ceremonial' space as in the Paris Opera

0   20   40 metres

absence of boxes, to create a democratic auditorium

'mystic chasm' created by double proscenium arch and orchestra pit to separate 'real' world of auditorium from 'ideal' world of stage

Section through the Festspielhaus – though Semper did the early designs (later adapted by Wilhelm Neumann and Otto Brückwald) the innovative ideas were Wagner's

each successive row of seats raised above the one in front

orchestra pit below stage to increase prominence of singers

Wagner's Bavaria

drama. The interior was plain and undecorated; boxes were abolished, and all the seats faced the stage; latecoming and conversation were discouraged and for the first time in any theatre the auditorium was darkened during performances; even the orchestra was hidden from view behind Wagner's *Schalldeckel*, a curved wooden baffle to diffuse the orchestral sound and throw the stage into prominence.

Wagner's far-reaching influence, both on the development of theatrical procedure and stagecraft and on many composers and writers, pervaded the work of Nietzsche, who played a dominant part in western philosophy. Nietzsche's concept of creating a new society by developing the individual was directly opposed to Marx, who sought to liberate the individual by changing society. Nietzsche was totally opposed to socialism; to him, democracy meant mediocrity, and his main preoccupation was the enhancement of mankind as a species. He saw history as a sorry tale of the jealous masses repeatedly destroying the great men in their midst who alone were capable of extending human development – an obvious parallel with Wagner's heroic innocent, Siegfried, killed by the envy and greed of lesser men. Nietzsche's answer was the concept of the *Ubermensch* – the development both genetically and intellectually of an élite group capable of exercising its 'will to power' and of leading society forward. His deliberate separation of ethics from the restraining morality of religion encouraged the determination of a personal code of values by the *Ubermensch*. These ideas continued to influence western thought well into the 20th century. Open to misconstruction by the ambitious and unprincipled, they strengthened the intellectual respectability of élitism and autocracy, becoming the implicit justification of a succession of European dictators.

To those of Christian principle, however, such self-justification was more difficult. Western civilisation was founded on a religion according to which the earth belonged to the poor and meek, yet its economic system was one which favoured only the rich and powerful. One way round this was adherence to Christian values in theory but not in practice: the honouring of personal freedom in an exploitative system; the veneration given to simple, thrifty living in a society of conspicuous consumption; and the ideal of self-development within a monopolistic economy whose effect was to crush the individual. The writings of Herbert Spencer and Charles Darwin provided further justification. Where Nietzsche tried to show that the strongest were destroyed by the weak and placed his hopes in a new race yet to be developed, Darwin's principles of natural selection, as outlined in *The Origin of Species* (1859), showed that the strongest were the natural inheritors of the earth. Turned from a biological into a moral argument to justify the economic domination of one group by another, this appeared to make capitalism part of some natural order of creation.

In architecture, the effect of such philosophical arguments was to reinforce the general trend of the profession towards social and intellectual élitism, and to help perpetuate what Morris called 'the great architect, carefully kept for the purpose, and guarded from the common troubles of common men'. The growing complexity of planning, structural design, mechanical services and contract administration made building an ever more specialised task, outside the experience of the layman. Capitalism had created this situation, making demands for larger or higher buildings, built more quickly or more cheaply than those of a competitor. It had also brought rapid change; growth required continual reinvestment and so technologies quickly became obsolete. The useful life of buildings tended to become shorter, and towns to change shape with ever greater speed. The successful architect or engineer drew assurance from his ability to perform well under such high-pressure conditions, and social confidence from being an integral part of an economic system which itself was gaining strength. Technology was the outward and visible sign of the success of capitalism, seducing the technologist himself by allowing him to realise his grandiose dreams and the layman by showing him, in the words of Marx and Engels, 'wonders far surpassing Egyptian pyramids, Roman aqueducts, and Gothic cathedrals'.

In America, structural ideas were becoming more adventurous and even in the most traditional-looking buildings use was made of new materials and techniques, to an extent still rare in Britain. Thomas Walter's great neo-classical dome added to the Capitol in Washington between 1855 and 1865 could only have been built in cast iron. The philosophical gap between architecture and engineering was less pronounced in America than in Britain; the three most significant American architects of the time were able to turn their hands with equal facility to engineering projects. William Strickland (1788–1854), designer of the Philadelphia Exchange (1834) and the United States Mint in Washington (1829–33), was also an engineer of canals, railways and the Delaware breakwater. Robert Mills (1781–1855), like Strickland an engineer and former pupil of Latrobe, designed the United States Treasury (1836–9), the Patent Office (1836–40) and the Post Office (1839), all dignified additions to Washington's collection of neo-classical buildings. He was also the designer of the Washington monument (1836–84), a spectacular 170 metre obelisk in white granite, for some years the tallest structure in the world. James Renwick (1818–95), the son of an engineer, designed the Smithsonian Institution in Washington (1846), St Patrick's cathedral in New York (1853–87) and Vassar College (1865). The romantic Romanesque of the Smithsonian inspired W. C. Cumberland's University College of Toronto (1856–8); the most splendid Canadian building of the period, however, was the Ottawa parliament building (1861–7) by Thomas Fuller (1822–98), an ebullient exercise in High Victorian neo-Gothic on a fine riverside site. Increasingly the neo-classical style was supplemented by other imported styles from Europe. The National Academy of Design in New York (1862–5) by P. B. Wight was Venetian Gothic and Trinity Church, Boston (1872–7), by Henry Hobson Richardson (1838–86) in his own distinctive version of Romanesque. John McArthur's City Hall in Philadelphia (1874–1901) was in the style of the French Second Empire, and McKim, Mead and White's Boston Public Library (1887–93) in that of the Italian renaissance, in the manner of Labrouste's Bibliothèque Ste Geneviève. The Pennsylvania Academy of Fine Arts in Philadelphia (1871–6) by Frank Furness was in no particular style at all, but in a liberal mixture, from a variety of sources.

In America more than anywhere, with its irresistible economic pressures for innovation, industrialists were eager to write off and replace capital works of all kinds. From the mid-century onwards, cast iron was one of the most favoured materials for new commercial buildings. John Haviland (1792–1852) made his name as a designer of prisons, such as the Eastern State Penitentiary in Philadelphia (1821–9) and the Tombs in New York (1836–8), but for the Farmers' and Mechanics' Bank at Pottsville, PA (1830), he designed the first major example of an all-iron façade, some twenty-five years before the British equivalent. The commercial buildings of James Bogardus (1800–74) made extensive use of iron and included the Laing Stores (1849), the Harper Brothers' printing works (1854), both in New York, and his unbuilt competition entry for the Crystal Palace exhibition building, also in New York: a vast tent of sheet-iron, suspended from a 90-metre-high prefabricated tower, that would have surpassed the Great Exhibition building. A less imaginative – and less costly – design

111

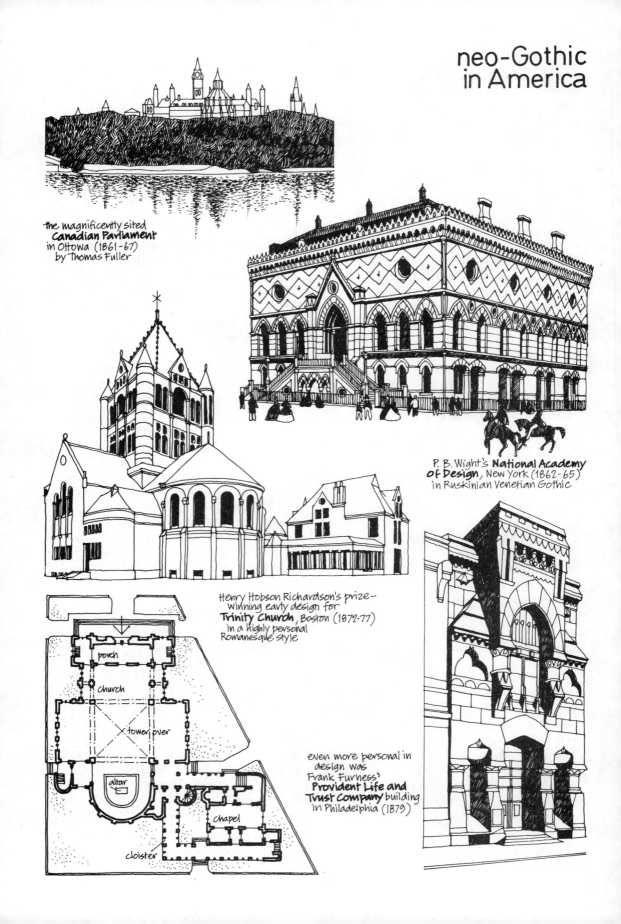

the magnificently sited
Canadian Parliament
in Ottawa (1861-67)
by Thomas Fuller

P. B. Wight's **National Academy
of Design**, New York (1862-65)
in Ruskinian Venetian Gothic

Henry Hobson Richardson's prize-
winning early design for
Trinity Church, Boston (1872-77)
in a highly personal
Romanesque style

porch

church

tower over

altar

chapel

cloister

even more personal in
design was
Frank Furness'
**Provident Life and
Trust Company** building
in Philadelphia (1879)

the art of iron construction

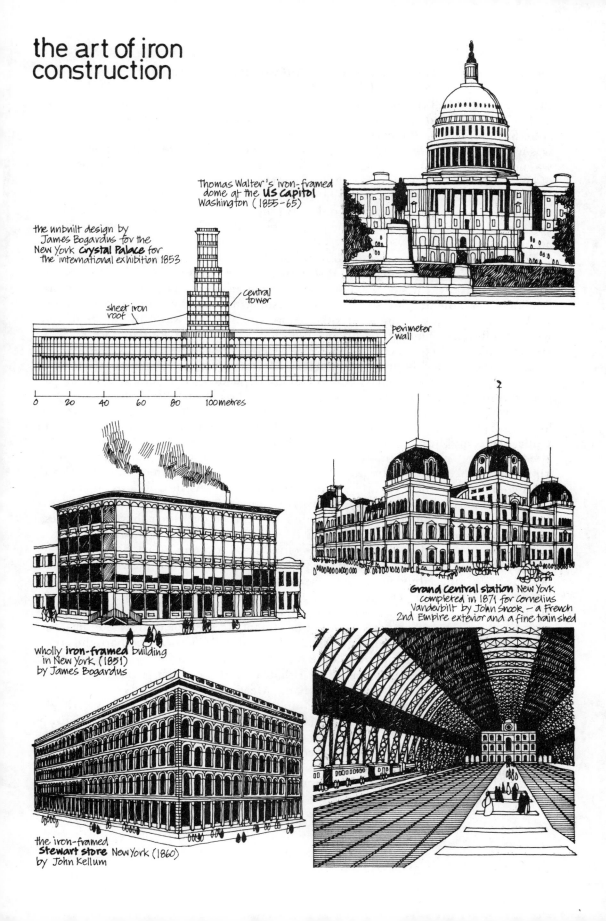

the unbuilt design by James Bogardus for the New York **Crystal Palace** for the international exhibition 1853

sheet iron roof

central tower

perimeter wall

0   20   40   60   80   100 metres

Thomas Walter's iron-framed dome at the **US Capitol** Washington (1855-65)

wholly **iron-framed** building in New York (1851) by James Bogardus

Grand Central station New York completed in 1871 for Cornelius Vanderbilt by John Snook — a French 2nd Empire exterior and a fine train shed

the iron-framed **Stewart store** New York (1860) by John Kellum

by Carstenson and Gildermeister, based firmly on Paxton's original, was built for the exhibition in 1853, and burned down in 1858. Among many other fine iron buildings of the period were the Penn Mutual Life Insurance Building in Philadelphia (1850–1) by G. P. Cummings and the A. T. Stewart Store (Wanamaker's) in New York (1860) by John Kellum. During this early phase in the history of iron construction, the material was used in a relatively primitive way. Though cheaper and lighter than masonry, it was nevertheless brittle, suitable only for buildings of limited height and in conditions of low tensile force; it was used mainly as a direct substitute for masonry, in external load-bearing walls where the stresses were simple. It was not till the widespread use of the Siemens-Martin open hearth and, later in the century, the Gilchrist-Thomas process that structural steelwork became practicable and heights and spans became more adventurous.

Following the financial panic of 1857, technological development received dramatic impetus from another, unexpected direction with the outbreak in 1860 of the Civil War. Ideologically, the lines of battle were drawn around the issue of slavery; more fundamentally, the struggle was for economic supremacy, and with its superior industrial base the North was almost predestined to win. The war was ruthless, the first in which a full range of modern weaponry was used; casualties on both sides were heavy and the cities and countryside of the South were devastated. It also brought great profits to the railroad builders, armaments manufacturers and above all to the telegraph companies on whom communications depended. The long-term effect of northern supremacy was considerably to advance the industrial revolution; once the Union was re-established the South too was able to benefit from the agricultural reforms and protective tariffs offered by the Federal government by way of reparation. Under the Republicans whose politics, both as the party of industrialism and as the saviours of the Union, dominated the post-war period, the country entered a phase of rapid and – unconstrained by the shortage of raw materials common in many European countries – of careless and exploitative expansion. As in Germany, monopoly capitalism was developed: competition was minimised and monopolies created by the formation of trusts, whereby groups of companies turned over their shares to trustees, who obtained control of the market and rewarded the shareholders with dividends. Corruption, too, became a major feature of industrial expansion, particularly in the railway industry. Between 1867 and 1873 some 30,000 miles of track were built, and it became important to buy out landowners, secure water rights and win mail contracts. From 1875 to 1885 the Central Pacific Railroad spent $500,000 a year on bribes. The archetypal figures of the time were men such as Jay Gould and Jim Fisk, the first great speculators on the growing stock market, not manufacturers or railway builders but gamblers with other people's money. The archetypal buildings were perhaps the great houses of the new rich, such as the Vanderbilt Mansion (1879–81) designed by Richard Hunt in the style of a French renaissance château and the Villard houses (1883–5), brownstone Italian-style *palazzi* by McKim, Mead and White, in New York; the luxury hotels of J. A. Wood such as the Grand Union at Saratoga Springs, NY (1872), which catered for a wealthy clientele made mobile by the railways; and the railway stations themselves, of which the finest was John Snook's Grand Central in New York (1871) with its great arched roof of latticed beams.

Perhaps the greatest technological achievements of the time, however, were the late works of John Roebling, who had continued his work on high-tensile steel cables and produced between 1851 and his death a number of splendid suspension bridges, in-

114

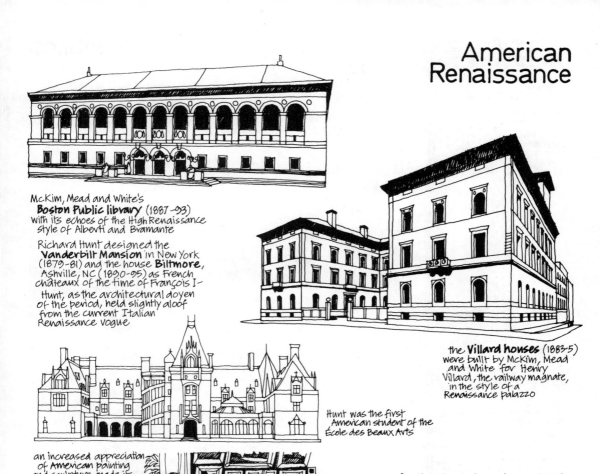

McKim, Mead and White's
Boston Public library (1887-93)
with its echoes of the High Renaissance
style of Alberti and Bramante

Richard Hunt designed the
Vanderbilt Mansion in New York
(1879-81) and the house **Biltmore**,
Ashville, NC (1890-95) as French
châteaux of the time of François I -
Hunt, as the architectural doyen
of the period, held slightly aloof
from the current Italian
Renaissance vogue

the **Villard houses** (1883-5)
were built by McKim, Mead
and White for Henry
Villard, the railway magnate,
in the style of a
Renaissance palazzo

Hunt was the first
American student of the
École des Beaux Arts

an increased appreciation
of American painting
and sculpture made it
seem that a general
artistic Renaissance
had arrived -

the Art Gallery of the
Vanderbilt houses in
Fifth Avenue opened
its doors to the public
in 1884

the **Vanderbilt houses**
(1879-84) by Charles Atwood
and John Snook

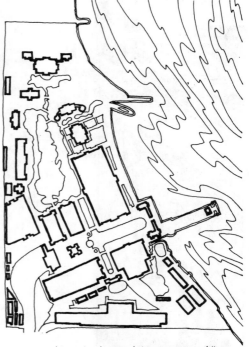

Atwood, with Daniel Burnham and the
landscape architect Frederick Olmstead,
was involved in the design of the **Chicago
World's Fair** ground (1893) - Renaissance
buildings in a Beaux Arts layout

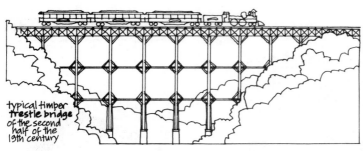

John Roebling

typical timber **trestle bridge** of the second half of the 19th century

double deck forming box section for additional stability

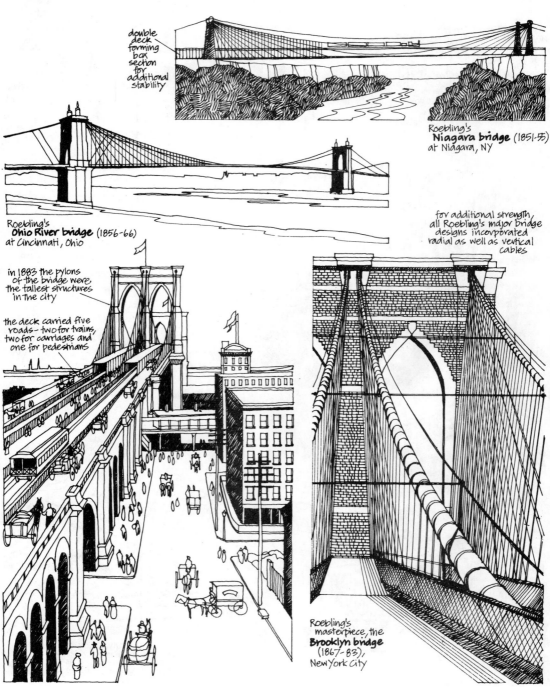

Roebling's **Niagara bridge** (1851-55) at Niagara, NY

Roebling's **Ohio River bridge** (1856-66) at Cincinnati, Ohio

for additional strength, all Roebling's major bridge designs incorporated radial as well as vertical cables

in 1883 the pylons of the bridge were the tallest structures in the city

the deck carried five roads – two for trains, two for carriages and one for pedestrians

Roebling's masterpiece, the **Brooklyn bridge** (1867-83), New York City

cluding the Niagara railway bridge (1851–5), the Ohio River bridge at Cincinnati (1856–66) and, finest of all, the Brooklyn bridge in New York. This massive project cost Roebling his life in 1867, with construction scarcely begun. Nevertheless, his mastery of large-scale design, his intricate attention to crucial details such as the weaving of the cables, and the devotion of his son who succeeded him brought the work to a spectacular conclusion in 1883. These great bridges were only part of the massive engineering problem of providing a vast sub-continent with roads and railways; the sheer volume of engineering work, much of it in remote, badly-supplied sites, demanded simple, standard solutions for standard problems. The trestle bridge, familiar from western movies, belongs to this period; originally built as a lattice of timber-work, it was replaced where possible in steel to guard against fire.

The political unity of the country and the growth of its economic system depended on good communications, in themselves often profitable contributions to economic expansion. As well as basic physical communications – roads, railways, canals, riverways – there were many other developments: the commercial use of Morse's telegraph and of Bell's telephone; Henry Ford's automobile and Goodyear's rubber tyre; the rotary press in newspaper printing; the typewriter, the dictaphone, the press agency, the advertising profession, the mail-order house. In every commercial field, inventions and improvements were accelerating production and affecting people's lives: the Otis elevator, the Singer sewing machine, Woolworth's retail stores, meat processing, fruit canning, the ring-spinning of textiles, the automatic loom, the use of standard sizes in clothing and footwear. More significantly, the industrial process itself was undergoing a radical change. The production-line system was first introduced in the Chicago meat-packing industry and at once its efficiency and susceptibility to control appealed to industrialists as preferable to the politically more dangerous craft system. Mass-production became common in most industries, especially the newer ones: in the automobile factories, in Whitney's armaments works, at Rockefeller's Standard Oil, in the railway works of Cornelius Vanderbilt and throughout the Pennsylvanian iron and steel empire of Andrew Carnegie. Typical of the factory buildings of the period was Carnegie's Lucy Furnace at Pittsburgh (1872), a gigantic assemblage of sheds, furnaces, cooling towers, railway yards and belching chimneys, offering a vision of the kind of industrial future which prompted the novelist Richard Bellamy to depict in *Looking Backward* (1888) a utopian future based on state control.

To the worker, the loss was enormous: a dramatic strengthening of the alienating effects of industrialism. He now worked in a large corporation or factory with no view of his employer, at a desk or on an assembly line which even denied him an understanding of what he was producing. He was also exploited by the system as a whole: bad working conditions, low pay, grim housing in crowded urban tenement blocks. Immigrant families were treated worst, deliberately chosen for the most menial jobs because they were less likely to organise for higher wages. Each successive wave of immigrants entered at the bottom of the social scale, cut off by custom and language from the support of their slightly wealthier fellow-workers.

Throughout the 1850s and 1860s the labour unions remained relatively small and poorly organised; activity was stronger in the dying craft industries – printers, building workers, hatters and cobblers – than among the workers in large-scale industries. However, in 1877, after the first effects of the Great Depression, the railway barons reduced their workers' wages. The result was a series of violent revolutionary strikes, supported by all unions, throughout the main cities of both coasts, which reminded fearful bourgeois opinion of the Paris Commune six years earlier. The rising was re-pressed by state and Federal troops, but it strengthened working-class unity and resulted in the formation in 1878 of the socialist-led Knights of Labor, like Owen's Grand National an attempt to draw workers of all industries into a single, great move-ment. In the long-term, the depression also assisted the development of monopoly capitalism, as smaller companies went bankrupt and were swallowed by the trusts and giant corporations. John D. Rockefeller, the greatest monopolist of the time, defended the trend towards consolidation as a matter of principle: 'The time was ripe for it. It had to come, though all we saw at the moment was the need to save ourselves from wasteful conditions. . . The day of combination is here to stay. Individualism has gone, never to return.'

The individualism in question was, of course, that of the competitive individual capitalist of the early industrial revolution, an ideology which persisted in Britain but was recognised as out-dated in both Germany and America. It is perhaps understand-able that the increasingly monolithic nature of capitalism should engender a com-parable view of socialism; in place of the revolutionary views of Marx, Engels and Morris came a doctrine in which the enemy was not capitalism but merely the outworn dogma of *laissez-faire*, and in which capitalism need not be overthrown but merely controlled and directed into proper channels by a benevolent state. The reformism of the SPD in Germany or of the Fabians in Britain created another scenario of the future to set beside that of the revolutionaries: one of state-controlled social democracy. Morris's *News from Nowhere*, contrasted with Bellamy's *Looking Backward*, expresses this dichotomy: on the one hand, a truly free society in which the state has been phased out of existence, and on the other, state-control as a utopian ideal. It was not only capital-ism which threatened the individual.

The light that failed
The turn of the century

The growth of competitive capitalism in 19th-century Britain was reflected in the development of the building industry. The contractual system institutionalised competition and created numerous small firms competing with one another to win one contract in every six or eight for which they tendered. Unlike the manufacturing sector, the building industry was not capital-intensive; it was unnecessary and even disadvantageous to invest in capital goods and plant beyond the relatively simple, basic equipment required. Building technology did not in itself create chronic unemployment to the extent that this occurred in manufacturing industry, where labour-saving technology released skilled and unskilled manpower into industries in which there was little mechanisation. Building, together with mining, docking, brick-making, railway building and the gas industry, was thus able to draw on an enormous pool of under-employed labour. These industries could afford to be profligate with manpower, to avoid mechanisation and to keep wages down. Another reason for the lack of mechanisation was the peripheral place of the industry in the national economy. Buildings were a convenient outlet for surplus capital, the very commodity which dries up in times of recession. Totally at the mercy of the market, building firms could slip easily into bankruptcy; recognising this, governments tended to use the fluidity of the industry as an economic regulator, as the simplest way to adjust levels of investment and employment in the economy as a whole. In times of unemployment, the building industry is one of the worst affected.

These problems, imposed on the industry by the capitalist system itself, have always been a major burden, tending to create uncertainty, inefficiency and under-employment as a matter of course. The bourgeois view, however, has generally been that the main barrier to efficiency is the workforce – the reluctance of apprentices to come forward for training as craftsmen, for example, or the problem of trade 'demarcation' within the building process, created by the multiplicity of craft unions. The long hours, poor working conditions, low pay and above all the uncertainty of the work, explains the question of 'reluctance', and the 'division of labour' within the industry is not confined to the workers.

During the late 19th century, as middle-class institutions grew in power and prestige, new professions began to multiply within the industry. In Britain, the civil engineers, contractors and architects were joined by professional surveyors (1868), municipal engineers (1873), heating and ventilating engineers (1897) and structural engineers (1908). In 1865 a contractors' federation, the General Builders' Association, was founded, becoming in 1878 the National Federation of Building Trades Employers. Like most professional organisations it claimed that its objectives were in the best interests of society at large: 'to uphold the best traditions of the building industry in its service to the community; to participate in the government of the relations between the various sections of the industry along well-ordered and jointly-agreed lines; and to afford protection to its members . . . should their common interests be assailed or interfered with by the action of others.'

Shaw's **Wispers** at Midhurst in Sussex (1875) was rambling and informal in design, with something of the late-medieval character of houses like Compton Wynyates

170 Queen's Gate (1888), one of Shaw's London houses, had a more formal, classical flavour akin to the original 'Queen Anne' style of the 17thC

by the time Shaw designed **Bryanston** in Dorset (1890) the prevailing style had become more consciously classical, grandiose and formal

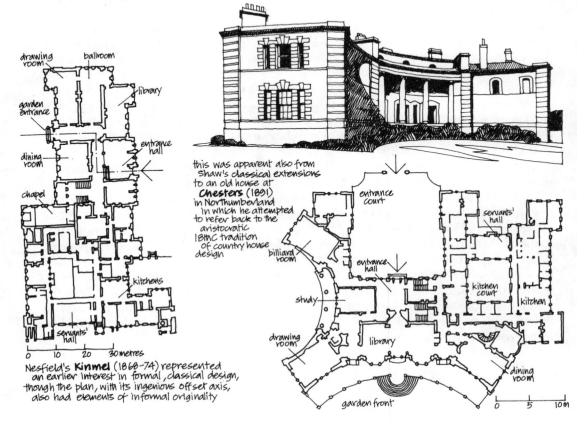

this was apparent also from Shaw's classical extensions to an old house at **Chesters** (1891) in Northumberland in which he attempted to refer back to the aristocratic 18thC tradition of country house design

drawing room · ballroom · library · garden entrance · entrance hall · dining room · chapel · servants' hall · kitchens

0 10 20 30 metres

Nesfield's **Kinmel** (1868-74) represented an earlier interest in formal, classical design, though the plan, with its ingenious offset axis, also had elements of informal originality

entrance court · servants' hall · billiard room · entrance hall · kitchen court · kitchen · study · drawing room · library · dining room

garden front

0 5 10M

It is significant, of course, that while the employers' federations were free to develop, the growth of the manual workers' trade unions was discouraged during most of the century. For much the same reason, the economic system began to make financial provision for middle-class housing much earlier than it came to terms with the problem of housing the working class. The institution known as the building society was first formed in England in 1775: individual members subscribed regularly to a fund which, when big enough, would finance a house for one of them. The process continued until all the members were housed, upon which the society was terminated. By 1825 there were 250 such societies, and between 1836 and 1856 a further 4,000 were set up. As well as 'terminating' societies, 'permanent' ones were established, with a continuing life for the purpose of investment and loan. The Building Societies Act (1874) set the basic rules of finance and organisation which are essentially still in use, and by 1900 there were 1,400 terminating and 850 permanent societies, the latter growing in importance and beginning to monopolise the field. Over the years, building societies became the biggest single factor encouraging the growth of home ownership among the lower middle class and those aspiring to it.

The upper middle classes required no such assistance; self-made fortunes were numerous in both Europe and America as the industrial corporation expanded, and great houses like Nesfield's Kinmel Park in Denbighshire (1868–74), Shaw's Lowther Lodge, Kensington (1873–4), and Hunt's Biltmore, Ashville, NC (1890–5), demonstrated the heights of splendour attainable. Architects permitted themselves great freedom: Biltmore was designed as a 16th-century French château, Kinmel and Lowther Lodge in the mixture of renaissance detail and informal gothic planning which became known inappropriately as 'Queen Anne'. Shaw's other important London house of the period, 170 Queen's Gate (1888), was nearer in approach, with its 'Wrenaissance' detail and symmetrical, classical plan form, to the original Queen Anne style of the 17th century. In his later country houses such as Bryanston in Dorset (1890) and Chesters in Northumberland (1891) he used a grandiose, classical style in buildings as far removed as they could be, both socially and architecturally, from the ideas of Morris.

Architecturally, if not politically, the banner of Morris was taken up by the Arts and Crafts movement, whose formal beginning was the formation in 1884 of the Art Workers' Guild. Central to the movement were the brilliant teacher and theorist William Lethaby (1857–1931) and the architect E. S. Prior (1852–1932) whose most representative work was a house called The Barn at Exmouth, Devon (1895–6). The movement developed a distinctive approach to design deriving from that of the uncompromising Webb: building layouts determined by function rather than by theoretical ideas of symmetry; the honest use of local materials and methods to relate building to landscape; the sparing use of ornament, except in features of particular importance; the use of elements of historical style for their functional appropriateness, if any, rather than for their associations. These ideas affected a whole generation of architects, among them E. W. Godwin (1833–86), designer of the White House in Chelsea (1878–9) for James McNeill Whistler, Arthur Mackmurdo (1851–1942), best-known for his furniture designs, and Charles F. Annesley Voysey (1857–1941) whose early house, The Cottage at Bishop's Itchington in Warwickshire (1888–9), used traditional materials and forms in an original way.

The architects of the Arts and Crafts movement and their clients, though unashamedly bourgeois, nevertheless stood apart from the ostentatious world of the successful industrialist and his commercially-minded architect. Comfortable, even wealthy,

121

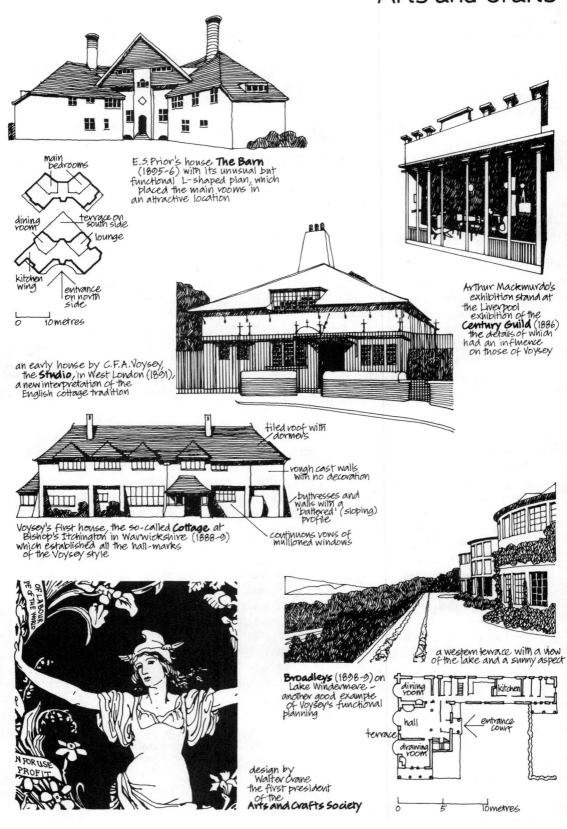

E.S. Prior's house **The Barn** (1895-6) with its unusual but functional L-shaped plan, which placed the main rooms in an attractive location

main bedrooms

dining room

terrace on south side

lounge

kitchen wing

entrance on north side

0   10 metres

an early house by C.F.A. Voysey, the **Studio**, in West London (1891), a new interpretation of the English cottage tradition

Arthur Mackmurdo's exhibition stand at the Liverpool exhibition of the **Century Guild** (1886) the details of which had an influence on those of Voysey

tiled roof with dormers

rough cast walls with no decoration

buttresses and walls with a 'battered' (sloping) profile

continuous rows of mullioned windows

Voysey's first house, the so-called **Cottage** at Bishop's Itchington in Warwickshire (1888-9) which established all the hall-marks of the Voysey style

a western terrace with a view of the lake and a sunny aspect

Broadleys (1898-9) on Lake Windermere – another good example of Voysey's functional planning

dining room

kitchen

hall

entrance court

terrace

drawing room

0   5   10 metres

OF LABOUR
PE OF THE WORLD

N FOR USE
PROFIT

design by Walter Crane the first president of the **Arts and Crafts Society**

yet politically liberal and culturally progressive, they formed a clique within the middle class, economically and socially belonging yet intellectually aloof. They had their counterparts in the suburbs of New England – where, in the late 19th century, the long tradition of domestic timber building culminated in the construction of a number of fine houses, including most notably the H. F. Stoughton house at Cambridge, MA (1882–3), and the W. G. Low house at Bristol, RI (1887). Built in traditional east-coast materials – timber framing clad with shingles – yet without any self-conscious historical associations, these houses represent a new departure in American design comparable with the Arts and Crafts movement. The prime mover was the architect Henry Hobson Richardson (1838–86), who trained in Paris in the Beaux Arts system, worked with Labrouste and Hittorf, and first became known as a designer of public buildings in a massive, romanesque style. He was attracted by the idea of functional design, as the Stoughton house demonstrates, with its free-form planning and simplicity of detail. In his Glessner house in Chicago (1886) he used stone in place of timber, but achieved a similar freedom of form. His ideas had a considerable influence on American architects, especially the young Frank Lloyd Wright (1869–1950), whose early Winslow house at River Forest, IL (1893), was a formal, symmetrical building, but who increasingly turned towards free-form planning in his later bourgeois houses. Richardson's ideas also influenced his pupils Charles McKim and Stanford White, whose Low house (1887), designed in collaboration with W. R. Mead, represents a short, informal phase in their professional career, before they became successful enough to specialise in civic architecture of great pomposity.

'It is the customary fate of new truths', said Thomas Huxley, 'to begin as heresies and end as superstitions.' As the foremost disciple of Darwin, Huxley was well-placed to observe how *The Origin of Species*, at first an outrageous challenge to Victorian morality, gradually became assimilated into the conventional wisdom of the time. To the complacent middle class of the late 19th century, Darwinism was a justification of bourgeois ideology: as in evolution, struggles for supremacy between nations or commercial enterprises were inevitable and natural; class-struggle, on the other hand, was not, and efforts to redress the balance between the weak and the strong could never succeed; state welfare was an interference in man's natural liberty to fend for himself. Nevertheless the state did intervene where it saw fit, recognising that welfare was as much an instrument of state control as any judicial system. It is significant that the first steps towards a welfare state were taken not by a liberal regime but in Germany by Bismarck, who abhorred socialism but insisted equally strongly on the logic of social engineering. Germany's programme of staggered income-tax and of state accident, old-age and health insurance was introduced by 1889 and was imitated by France and Russia during the 1890s. Britain and America were slower to respond: the former had enacted some social legislation by 1911, but the latter made no moves till the 1930s.

The growth of the state apparatus was reflected, despite the economic depression of the 1870s and 1880s, in the continued public building programmes of the period. Public control in the guise of civic or national pride required the reconstruction of city centres on the pattern of Paris or Vienna. New formal avenues, punctuated with parliament buildings, city halls, museums, churches and court-houses and lined with repetitive blocks of apartments and shops, created a new urban image, with great variety of style and presentation ranging from the monumental to the informal.

The formal Second Empire style, though it no longer had any political meaning in its country of origin, persisted elsewhere in Europe well into the 1870s and 1880s. In

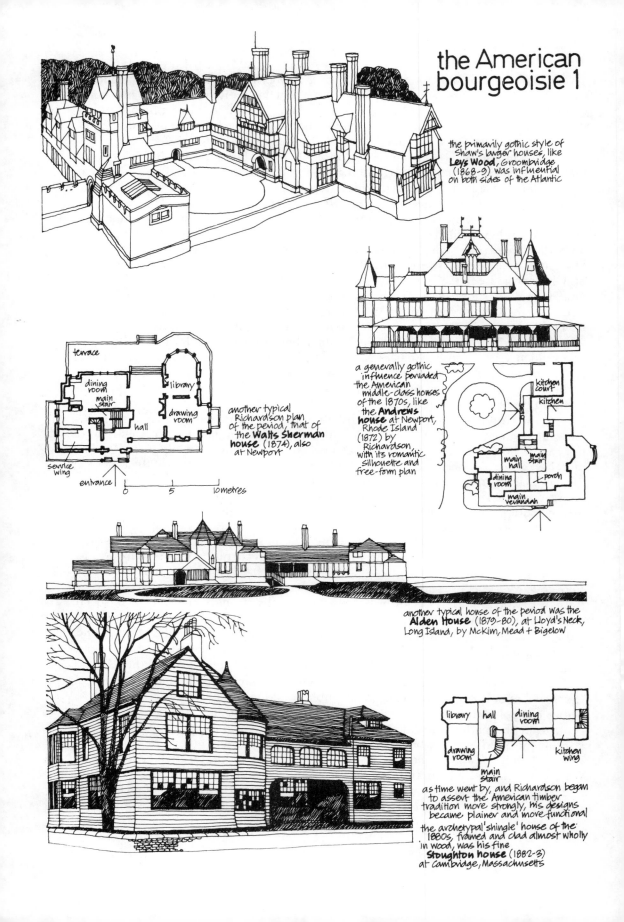

the primarily gothic style of Shaw's larger houses, like **Leys Wood**, Groombridge (1868-9) was influential on both sides of the Atlantic

another typical Richardson plan of the period, that of the **Watts Sherman house** (1874), also at Newport

terrace

dining room

library

main stair

drawing room

hall

service wing

entrance

0 5 10 metres

a generally gothic influence pervaded the American middle-class houses of the 1870s, like the **Andrews house** at Newport, Rhode Island (1872) by Richardson, with its romantic silhouette and free-form plan

kitchen court

kitchen

main hall

main stair

dining room

porch

main verandah

another typical house of the period was the **Alden House** (1879-80), at Lloyd's Neck, Long Island, by McKim, Mead + Bigelow

library

hall

dining room

drawing room

main stair

kitchen wing

as time went by, and Richardson began to assert the American timber tradition more strongly, his designs became plainer and more functional

the archetypal 'shingle' house of the 1880s, framed and clad almost wholly in wood, was his fine **Stoughton house** (1882-3) at Cambridge, Massachusetts

the American bourgeoisie 2

Richardson's inventive planning could also be seen in masonry-built houses, like the **Glessner house** (1886), on its small urban site in Chicago

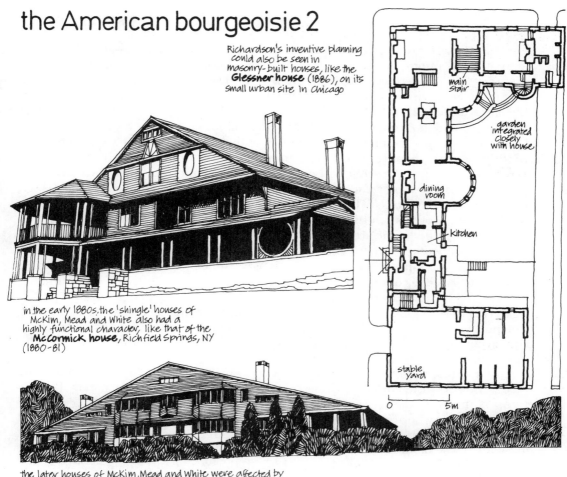

main stair

garden integrated closely with house

dining room

kitchen

stable yard

0   5m

in the early 1880s, the 'shingle' houses of McKim, Mead and White also had a highly functional character, like that of the **McCormick house**, Richfield Springs, NY (1880-81)

the later houses of McKim, Mead and White were affected by their involvement in the 'American Renaissance' movement, like the symmetrically designed **Low house** (1887) at Bristol, Rhode Island...

... and the axially planned **Taylor house** (1885-6) at Newport, in which they reverted to an almost literal reproduction of the style of colonial New England

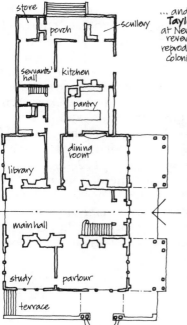

store

porch   scullery

servants' hall   kitchen

pantry

dining room

library

main hall

study   parlour

terrace

this classical influence affected the early houses of Wright, as in his axially planned **Charnley house** in Chicago (1891) and...

... in his consciously simple and refined **Winslow house** (1893) at River Forest, Illinois, a house in the spirit of a classical temple

Holland, Cornelis Outshoorn (1810–75), designer of an iron-and-glass Palais vor Volksvlijt in Amsterdam (1856), used the Second Empire style in his numerous hotels: the Amstel in Amsterdam (1863–7), the Berg-en-Dal in Nijmegen (1867–9) and the Orange in Scheveningen (1872–3). In Brussels, whose reconstruction began to earn it the name 'little Paris', L.-P. Suys (1823–87) used the style for the Exchange building (1868–73), and in Zurich, Theodore Geiger (1832–82) used it for his Rütschi-Bleuler house (1869–70). Parisian influences spread to the geographical fringes of Europe: to Madrid, and the Spanish National Library and Museum (1866–96) by Francisco Jareño y Alarcón (1818–92); to London, and the terrace at 1–5 Grosvenor Place (1867) by the Grosvenor Estate Office; to Copenhagen, where Petersen and Jensen built Søtorvet, four blocks of bourgeois apartments (1873–6); and to Stockholm, where the Kumlien brothers built the Jenkontovets building (1873–5). Amid this conventional and repetitive civic architecture, a few designers were noticeable for their boldness. The competition-winning entry for the Berlin Reichstag (1884–92) by Paul Wallot (1841–1912) was a ponderous, undistinguished baroque, but Poelaert's vast Palais de Justice in Brussels, completed in 1883, was a different vein of baroque, dramatic, massive and highly personal. Similar in spirit to these weighty designs was the archetypal Italian public building of the time, the gigantic monument in Rome to Vittorio Emanuele II (begun 1885). The designer, Giuseppe Sacconi (1854–1905), set an equestrian statue of the king on a high plinth backed by a giant Corinthian colonnade, in a composition of imperial Roman pretentions.

The informal approach was followed by Norman Shaw in New Scotland Yard (1887–8), a Scottish-baronial-style headquarters for the London police, and by P. J. H. Cuijpers in Amsterdam. Cuijpers (1827–1921), a religious and scholarly restorer of gothic churches who also designed new ones such as the Maria Magdalenakerk (1887), built the two most significant public buildings in 19th-century Amsterdam, the Rijksmuseum (1877–85) and the Central Station (1881–9), both in an eclectic late-gothic style. The Town Hall in Copenhagen (1892–1902), gothic in general character but simpler in detail, represented a move by the architect Martin Nyrop (1849–93) away from revivalist forms and the discovery of a more direct and robust style, parallel with that of Richardson and unusual in monumental civic buildings of the time. One of the most extraordinary of these was the Sacré-Coeur in Paris (1874–1919), designed by the architect Paul Abadie in the style of the 12th-century Byzantine pilgrimage church of St Front at Périgueux. Known also as the church of the National Vow, it demonstrates the continuing close link between Church and state; it was built with government support through the subscriptions of the Catholic faithful, in symbolic expiation of the horrors of 1870–1, and cost 40 million francs, a considerable sum for an act of contrition.

In 1876 an international exposition was held in Philadelphia, birthplace of American independence, to celebrate a century of progress. A vast iron-and-glass exhibition hall was built to resemble the Crystal Palace, though by comparison the design was pedestrian and crude; as yet the structural advances of Roebling had not been taken up by architects. This changed in 1883 when William Le Baron Jenney (1832–1907) built the Home Insurance Company office in Chicago. The first of Chicago's famous 'skyscrapers' had been the Montauk building, by Burnham and Root, two years earlier, but Jenney's was the first ten-storey tower to use a structural wrought-iron frame. Jenney readily confronted the theoretical problems and practical possibilities of this new material, versatile because it could be used equally well in tension as in compression and quick to erect because it could be riveted.

fin-de-siècle grandeur

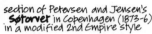

section of Petersen and Jensen's **Søtorvet** in Copenhagen (1873-6) in a modified 2nd Empire style

Joseph Poelaert's extraordinary **Palais de Justice**, Brussels, (1866-83), a Piranesian conception of great vitality

Martin Nyrop's elegant, gothic-style **Town Hall** in Copenhagen (1892-1902)

Count Giuseppe Sacconi's vast Roman **Monument to Vittorio Emanuele II** begun 1885 and completed by other designers in 1922

St Front, Périgueux (1120)

the prominent **church of the Sacré Coeur**, Paris, begun by Paul Abadie in 1874 and completed eventually in 1919

It was Gustave Eiffel who took wrought-iron design to its functional limits. Following the success of his brilliant design for the Garabit viaduct, he was appointed engineer to the Paris exposition of 1889 –to celebrate this time the centennial of the French revolution – for which he proposed a 300-metre iron tower. He had to face not only the practical problems of building the tallest structure in the world but also the concerted opposition of politicians, rival engineers and architects, and numbers of Parisian intellectuals from Maupassant to Verlaine. His persistence – and money – overcame the political problems and his ingenuity and experience the structural ones; the design of the four spread feet on their reinforced stone pads owed much to lessons learned at Garabit. The organisation of the contructional process itself was exemplary in its thoroughness: Eiffel provided shop-drawings for the fabrication as well as assembly-drawings for the site; he designed and detailed the temporary scaffolding; he carefully recorded each stage of the tower's growth in photographs. The tower is the only remaining feature of the 1889 exposition, but a magnificent contrast to it was provided by the Galérie des Machines, built by the engineer Victor Contamin (1843–93) and demolished in 1910. Half as long again as the tower was high, its width of 114 metres and height of 45 metres were spanned by a series of vast steel principal arches, hinged at the base and apex and braced for longitudinal rigidity with steel ribs. Comparable in volume with the Crystal Palace, the Galérie was structurally much more dynamic and the first major example of the advantages of steel over iron. The earliest important steel construction still in existence today was the Firth of Forth bridge in Scotland, begun in 1883 and opened in 1890. A suspension bridge had been proposed, but after the collapse in 1879 of Thomas Bouch's similar bridge over the Firth of Tay, a revised design was prepared by Benjamin Baker and John Fowler, consisting of three 100-metre latticed steel towers, on either side of which rigidly cantilevered platforms joined together to form the base for the railway track. The towers, made of a network of hollow steel tubes, were supported on vast concrete piles constructed below the water-line inside steel caissons.

The use of steel in important engineering works extended the designer's understanding of the material and made its everyday use a practical possibility. This was seen nowhere better than in Chicago, where in 1871 fire had destroyed almost the whole of the wood-built city and provided both the need and the opportunity for a new start. Chicago's importance in railway construction, in iron and steel making, in meat-processing and as a gateway between the eastern cities and the plains of the mid-west had made it very prosperous – the city of Pullman, the railway king and of Armour, the meat-packing millionaire. It was rapidly re-built, with considerable ingenuity and style; in the Loop area, the downtown business district, the use of steel-frame construction, together with the new Otis elevator, allowed the development of commercial buildings of unprecedented height, which were also of great architectural quality. They were not the only high buildings of the area – they shared the skyline with the grain elevators of the agricultural mid-west – but it was the first time repetitive floors of commercial accommodation had been piled on one another to a height of ten storeys and more. Richardson's seven-storey Marshall Field warehouse (1885–7), though influential in its powerful external treatment, with romanesque arches and heavily rusticated walls, broke no new structural ground, being built in solid, load-bearing masonry. The same was true of Burnham and Root's sixteen-storey Monadnock building (1889–91); but the freedom of planning and elevational treatment offered by a metal frame, to say nothing of the saving in constructional time, were too valuable to

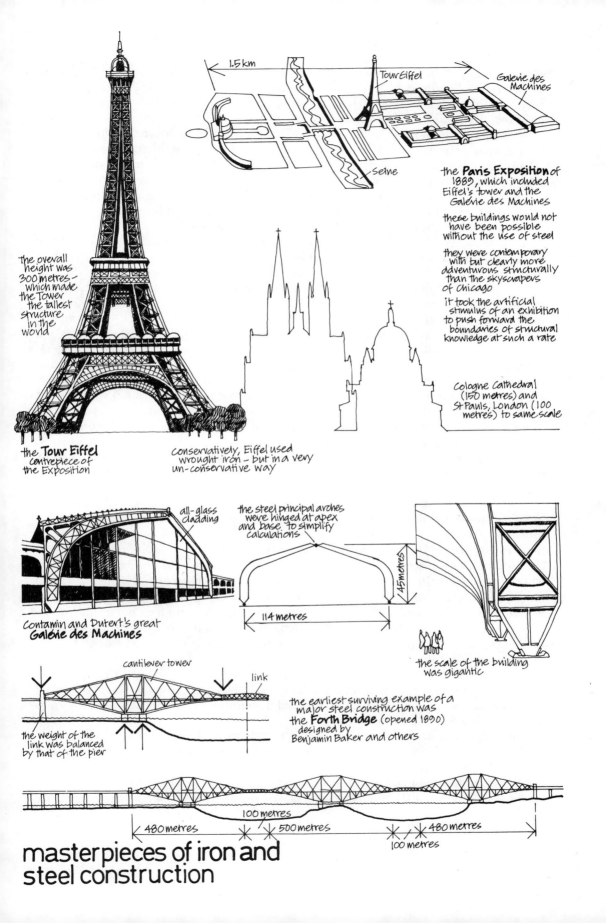

1.5 km

Tour Eiffel

Galerie des Machines

Seine

the **Paris Exposition** of 1889, which included Eiffel's tower and the Galerie des Machines

these buildings would not have been possible without the use of steel

they were contemporary with but clearly more adventurous structurally than the skyscrapers of Chicago

it took the artificial stimulus of an exhibition to push forward the boundaries of structural knowledge at such a rate

the overall height was 300 metres - which made the Tower the tallest structure in the world

Cologne Cathedral (150 metres) and St Pauls, London (100 metres) to same scale

the **Tour Eiffel** centrepiece of the Exposition

conservatively, Eiffel used wrought iron - but in a very un-conservative way

all-glass cladding

the steel principal arches were hinged at apex and base, to simplify calculations

45 metres

114 metres

Contamin and Dutert's great **Galerie des Machines**

the scale of the building was gigantic

cantilever tower

link

the earliest surviving example of a major steel construction was the **Forth Bridge** (opened 1890) designed by Benjamin Baker and others

the weight of the link was balanced by that of the pier

480 metres

100 metres

500 metres

480 metres

100 metres

masterpieces of iron and steel construction

stay unexploited for long. Holabird and Roche's Tacoma building (1887–8), like the earlier Home Insurance building, had a metal skeleton, as did the eight-storey Second Leiter building (1889–91) by Jenney and Mundie and the sixteen-storey Reliance building (1890–5) by Burnham and Company.

Architecturally, however, the biggest advances from 1881 onwards came from the Chicago partnership formed between the experienced Danish architect Dankmar Adler (1844–1900) and the brilliant young Louis Sullivan (1856–1924), to whom the newness and lack of architectural tradition of their adopted city were an invitation to unorthodox forms of architectural expression. At first, Richardson influenced their work; the best-known early example was the Auditorium building (1886–9), a ten-storey tower combining the unlikely functions of office block and opera house, whose solid, load-bearing construction bore a distinct resemblance to the Marshall Field warehouse. But as steel-frame construction became more common, Sullivan began to develop the ideas inherent in his famous aphorism, 'form follows function', by which he intended that an honest expression of use and structure was an essential precondition for the design of a beautiful building. These ideas began with the Wainwright building in St Louis (1890–1) and the Guaranty building in Buffalo, NY (1894–5), reaching Chicago with the Gage building (1898–9) in which Sullivan collaborated with Holabird and Roche, and with Sullivan's finest work, the Schlesinger-Mayer store (1899–1904) known later as Carson, Pirie, Scott and Company. The façades became plainer and simpler, that of the Schlesinger-Mayer store consisting of no more than strips of faience-work covering the repetitive grid of columns and floor-slabs punctuated with rows of identical windows of a size made possible only by the use of a steel frame. This building also illustrated Sullivan's particular hallmark of over-all simplicity with contrasting areas of decoration to draw attention to the principal architectural features: a heavy, overhanging cornice at roof level (now removed) and ornate metal friezes, designed by colleague George Elmslie, marked the shop's display windows and main entrance.

As in any big city centre, the physical form of downtown Chicago with its new skyscrapers was determined by high land values, themselves a reflection of the natural tendency in any commercial centre towards growth and concentration, and of the shortage of available land. It is significant that Chicago, where the mechanics of the modern city were most apparent, was the source of one of the most influential of 20th-century urban sociological theories. Sociology as a discipline had begun, in effect, with Marx's analysis of the world around him, but with Emile Durkheim (1858–1917) and more particularly with Max Weber (1863–1920) it had moved into a bourgeois phase. Social relationships, and with them the structure of cities, were seen not as part of the ever-changing pattern of history, in the marxist sense, but in terms of a relatively static model, peculiar to its own time and place, consistent with the Nietzschean and Spenglerian view that each age determines its own values and points of reference. The Chicago school of urban sociologists, led by Robert Park, developed the 'zonal' or 'concentric' theory of urban form, describing how social and economic factors changed from one part of a city to another and created definable social zones in concentric rings about the downtown business area.

There was a basic contradiction here: the dynamics of capitalism required a city capable of physical growth, but at the same time bourgeois ideologists needed to believe in a stable, unchanging political and social system, while the forces of law and order needed cities they could control and whose very form expressed the dominance of state power. The concentric theory, like most social theories of the day, supported the stability

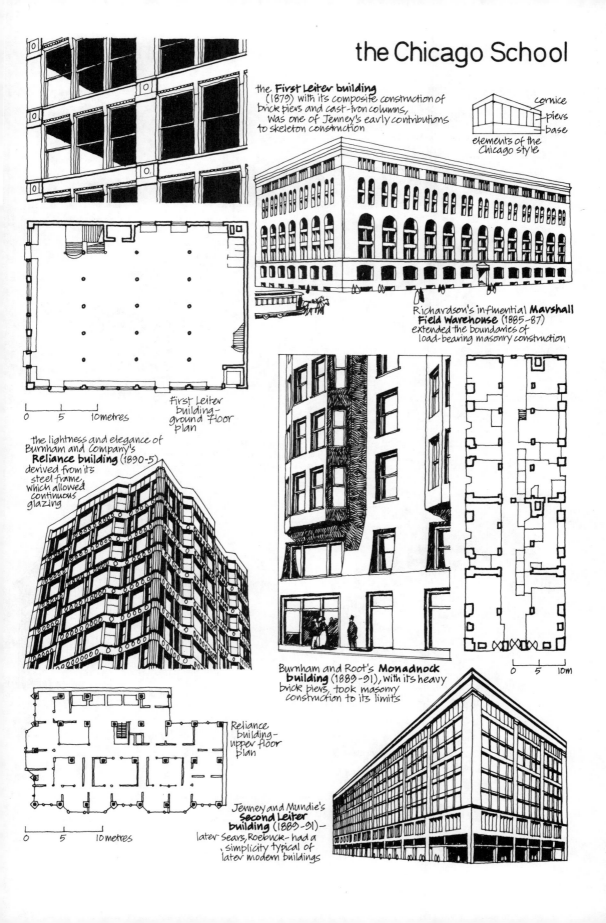

the Chicago School

the **First Leiter building** (1879) with its composite construction of brick piers and cast-iron columns, was one of Jenney's early contributions to skeleton construction

cornice
piers
base

elements of the Chicago style

Richardson's influential **Marshall Field Warehouse** (1885–87) extended the boundaries of load-bearing masonry construction

First Leiter building–ground floor plan

0   5   10 metres

the lightness and elegance of Burnham and Company's **Reliance building** (1890–5) derived from its steel frame, which allowed continuous glazing

Burnham and Root's **Monadnock building** (1889–91), with its heavy brick piers, took masonry construction to its limits

0   5   10m

Reliance building–upper floor plan

0   5   10 metres

Jenney and Mundie's **Second Leiter building** (1889–91) – later Sears, Roebuck – had a simplicity typical of later modern buildings

Adler and Sullivan

the Auditorium building on the Chicago lake shore in 1889

Louis Sullivan
(1856-1924)

entrance to the auditorium

Wright joined the Adler and Sullivan office in 1887 and probably worked on the details of the Auditorium

the Chicago **Auditorium building** (1886-9), in which a concert hall was combined with a hotel and offices - the architects changed their original design for the façade when they saw Richardson's design for Marshall Field

tower

hotel

Lake Shore

auditorium

offices

section through the auditorium building

like Marshall Field, the Auditorium was built in load-bearing masonry; however the **Guaranty building** at Buffalo NY (1894-5) and the...

...**Wainwright building** at St Louis (1890-1) had steel frames with masonry piers externally

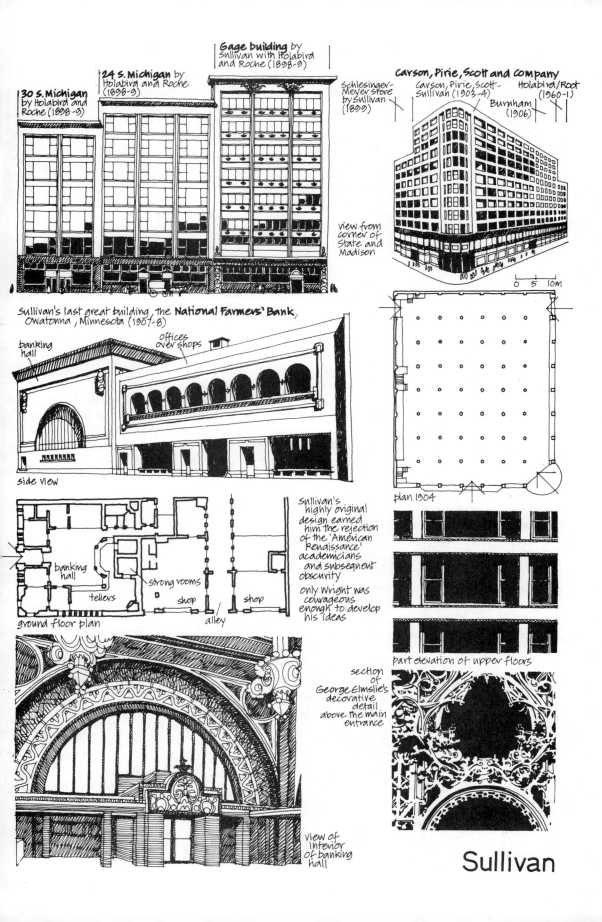

30 S. Michigan by Holabird and Roche (1898-9)

24 S. Michigan by Holabird and Roche (1898-9)

Gage building by Sullivan with Holabird and Roche (1898-9)

Schlesinger-Meyer store by Sullivan (1899) X

Carson, Pirie, Scott and Company

Carson, Pirie, Scott-Sullivan (1903-4)

Burnham (1906) X

Holabird/Root (1960-1) X

view from corner of State and Madison

Sullivan's last great building, the **National Farmers' Bank**, Owatonna, Minnesota (1907-8)

banking hall

offices over shops

side view

plan 1904

ground floor plan

banking hall

tellers

strong rooms

shop

alley

shop

Sullivan's highly original design earned him the rejection of the 'American Renaissance' academicians and subsequent obscurity

only Wright was courageous enough to develop his ideas

part elevation of upper floors

section of George Elmslie's decorative detail above the main entrance

view of interior of banking hall

Sullivan

of the social structure, being essentially static: it described a city at a certain moment in time, largely unconcerned with social change. It also gave pseudo-scientific credibility to the concentric form as a 'natural' one for all cities, thus coinciding with the needs of the state, which had long recognised the political advantages of a centralised city plan.

Yet there is no doubt that the concentric form posed problems of physical growth, especially for the central area which, if wholly encircled by suburbs, could be expanded only through increased densities, building heights and costs, traffic congestion and high land-values. In 1882 the Spanish transport engineer Arturo Soria y Mata had attempted to solve this problem by devising a radically different urban form, a *Ciudad Lineal* or linear city, only 600 metres in width but of indefinite length. Set out on either side of a spinal road and tramway, with no building more than 300 metres from either the road or the open countryside, it was intended to spread across the landscape, joining old and new settlements into a continuous whole. About five kilometres of *Ciudad Lineal* were build outside Madrid (1894–6) but the idea was not developed. The linear form solved the problem of expansion – it could be added to at will; but some critics predicted that the central road, though intended as a main arterial route, would become choked with local traffic, and others anticipated the soullessness and lack of local identity of a city of infinite length. One might add, from the authorities' point of view, the difficulty of keeping such a sprawling monster under political control.

Utopian theories and experiments abounded during the late 19th century as concerned individuals and groups sought to solve urban problems by changing, if not their causes, at least their effects. In America the paternalistic Lowell system was in decline, attracting the scepticism of industrialists and the resentment of workers; but in Britain the tradition of New Lanark was continued by philanthropic, if not entirely disinterested, factory-owners like Titus Salt, whose tied town of Saltaire was begun in 1853 to provide an escape from nearby Bradford. The pleasant rural site chosen by Salt for a new alpaca-weaving mill was remote, like both Lowell and New Lanark, and required the establishment of a captive workforce, so mill and town co-existed from the start. The architects, Lockwood and Mawson, designed 800 little houses in the gothic style, in regular terraces on the hillside. Salt provided almost all his employees' needs, both spiritual and bodily – a church, chapels, almshouses, shops, baths, an Institute, a hospital and a school – though like many industrialists he stopped short of allowing them alcohol. The vast mill dominated the town, a permanent reminder of its *raison d'être*, with 40,000 square metres of floorspace, in bulk as large as St Paul's cathedral, crowned by an 80-metre chimney in the style of an Italian campanile.

In fact Salt represented less the utopian socialism of Owen than the enlightened Toryism of Disraeli, whose social novel *Sybil* had been published a few years earlier. To the British capitalist, a well-run factory and a contented workforce made sound economic sense – and so much the better if economic sense could coincide with Christian duty. In general, it was clear that both the authorities and the private housing market were reluctant to provide good working-class housing, so from the mid-century 'housing associations' began to develop, non-profit-making bodies whose primary aim was the welfare of working-class tenants. They depended entirely on voluntary funds, so had to provide a rate of interest, albeit minimal, to attract bourgeois investors. They therefore had to charge 'reasonable' rents, thereby pricing themselves out of the areas of greatest poverty and need, and also had to apply careful management techniques, exercising strict supervision over their carefully chosen tenants. Association housing was, by definition, for the clean, sober, 'deserving' poor.

the Concentric City and Ciudad Lineal

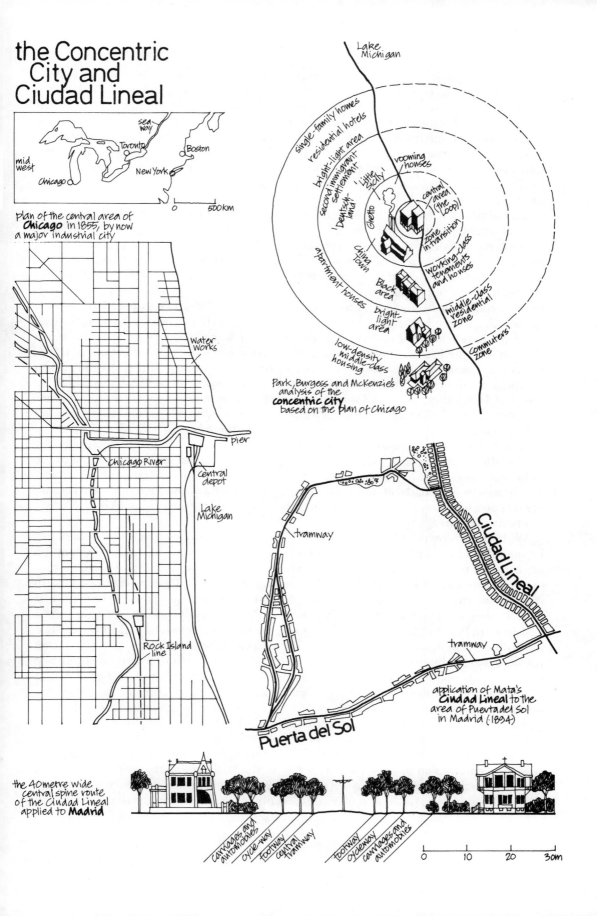

sea way

Toronto

Boston

mid west

Chicago

New York

0   500km

plan of the central area of **Chicago** in 1855, by now a major industrial city

Water Works

pier

Chicago River

central depot

Lake Michigan

Rock Island line

Lake Michigan

single-family homes

residential hotels

bright-light area

second immigrant settlement

'Deutschland!'

'Little Sicily!'

Ghetto

rooming houses

central area (the Loop)

zone in transition

working-class tenements and houses

middle-class residential zone

commuters' zone

china town

Black area

bright-light area

apartment-houses

low-density middle-class housing

Park, Burgess and McKenzie's analysis of the **concentric city** based on the plan of Chicago

tramway

Ciudad Lineal

tramway

application of Mata's **Ciudad Lineal** to the area of Puerta del Sol in Madrid (·1894)

Puerta del Sol

the 40 metre wide central spine route of the Ciudad Lineal applied to **Madrid**

carriages and automobiles

cycle-way

footway

central tramway

footway

cycleway

carriages and automobiles

0   10   20   30m

The earliest public provision for working-class housing came in 1868 with the Artisans' and Labourers' Dwellings Act and in 1875, resulting from the work of the philanthropist Octavia Hill, with the Artisans' and Labourers' Dwellings Improvement Act. Local authorities were charged with the duty of clearing slums and getting new houses built, though from the first housing associations were admitted as equal partners in the process; many of them, set up by rich land-owners and industrialists, were wealthier and more powerful than the authorities themselves. The Guinness Trust, begun in 1889, was soon followed by the Peabody Donation Fund, Sutton Dwellings, the Cadbury family's Bournville Estates and the Rowntree Trust.

The brothers Richard and George Cadbury, cocoa refiners and makers of French-style chocolate confectionery in industrial Birmingham, were prompted in 1878 by professional idealism to move to the country in search of a factory site that would match the vaunted purity of their products. Priority was given to building the factory itself and to working conditions, and at first only a group of semi-detached dwellings was built. As devout Quakers, however, the brothers had a real enthusiasm for bettering the working class in general, and in 1893 George Cadbury began construction of a model village on a 50-hectare site with the aim of 'securing to the workers in factories some of the advantages of outdoor village life'. The river Bourn gave it the name 'Bournville', the French suffix being a gesture to the origins of the confectionery trade. Bournville was never a tied town – it was intended that Cadbury workers would always comprise a minority of its population, and that its benefits should reach as widely as possible. Inevitably, the need for minimal return on investment kept rents too high for the poorest, but for those who could afford it, George Cadbury's rural idealism created a medieval England which had never existed. Two-storey houses with tiled or thatched roofs and decorative barge-boards, with half-timbering and oriel windows applied for Tudor effect, stood in spacious gardens pre-planted with fruit trees. In contrast to the tight terraces of Saltaire, Bournville had all the characteristics of the garden city: low densities, winding roads, an informal building layout and above all a mass of trees and open space which undeniably contributed to the people's health, as well as to their aesthetic pleasure.

W. H. Lever, owner of a soap-works at Warrington near Liverpool, was no idealist; he resembled Ford or Carnegie more nearly than Owen or even Disraeli. The housing he provided was an investment in his own commercial future and was decidedly for his own workers rather than outsiders. It was financed from ploughed-back profits, in recognition that at least some of the surplus-value created by the workers should be used for their own benefit – though not necessarily in a way of their own choosing. The new town of Port Sunlight which he began on the banks of the Mersey in 1888, planned by William Owen, was strongly influenced by Lever's ideas on design, borrowed from the boulevards of Paris and the formal avenues of Versailles. As in Bournville there was plenty of planting, but a wider variety of architectural styles included English Tudor and classical, Flemish domestic and French Empire. Architecturally the town was dominated by a large parish church and by the Lady Lever art gallery whose collection was another outlet for profits and a calculated advertisement for the business. 'The whole village', as one observer remarked, 'is dominated by the spirit of soap.'

These middle-class efforts to gentrify the working class were at least partially successful, accompanied as they were by a rise in the skilled workers' standard of living which formed a protection from the worst effects of the depression. This was generally true of the industrial world as a whole, especially of Germany and the USA; the Russian

philanthropy and paternalism

George Street in Titus Salt's **Saltaire**, centred on Lockwood and Mawson's Congregational church – a perpetual call to sobriety

Benjamin Disraeli (1804–81) Prime Minister of England, social reformer and author of 'Sybil'

well-built Tudor-style houses in Lever's **Port Sunlight**, part of the wide variety of architectural styles available.

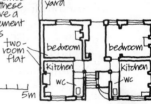

typical association dwellings of the late 19th century – Mermaid Court in south-east London

open staircase

space standards were low and facilities minimal, but these dwellings were a great improvement on the slums

yard

two-room flat

bedroom

bedroom

kitchen

kitchen

wc

wc

0   5m

George Cadbury's original group of cottages (1879) at Cadbury's **Bournville**, located next to the factory building in Bournville Lane

unlike Port Sunlight, Bournville had an unpretentious, informal layout, with a number of humane features which have become axiomatic in modern town planning

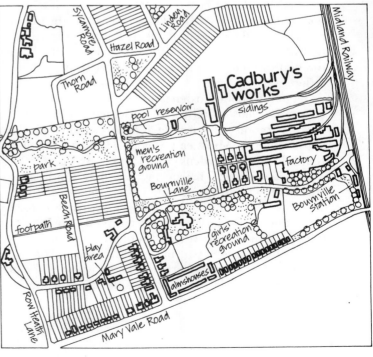

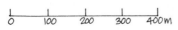

0   100   200   300   400m

regime was almost alone in offering nothing to its urban working class. Nevertheless there remained nearly everywhere a submerged section of the population – in Britain it was about one-third – whose acute poverty was in stark contrast to the growing wealth of the remainder. At the end of the century the gap between the middle and working classes was greater than ever, both economically and culturally. As the depression cleared and the international economy expanded, a spirit of crass scientism flourished, due partly to the increasingly secular philosophy of the post-Nietzschean period – typified by the pragmatism of William James – and partly to deliberate perversion of the undoubtedly real achievements of the scientific community – Planck, Mendel, Pasteur, the Curies, Freud, Adler and many others – which, like Darwinism, were used to give a spurious justification to the philosophy of materialist self-interest. In Germany, the church reacted censoriously by trying to dissociate itself from the state, while the Vatican, though not going quite that far, loudly proclaimed its apartness from political life. In literature, there were rebellions against the corruption of bourgeois morality: powerful and aggressive like that of Ibsen, despairingly pessimistic like Chekhov or Kafka, or satirical like Wilde and Shaw.

In the world of architecture, something of Morris's critical attitude was shown by Charles Ashbee (1863–1942), theorist, reformer, teacher and practical Arts and Crafts designer who in 1888 founded the Guild and School of Handicraft in London's working-class East End. His best buildings were 37 and 38–9 Cheyne Walk (1894 and 1904) in Chelsea, at that time a predominantly working-class suburb gradually becoming fashionable for the middle class. Among architects in general there were few real rebels, especially among those designing elegant houses for the rich. Any echoes of Morris's dissatisfaction with industrial capitalism were generally artistic rather than social, taking the form of a search – like Voysey's, for example – for an architecture of simple informality. Voysey's kind of simplicity was the result of careful contrivance rather than of unsophisticated craftsmanship; he brought a puritanism of a particularly luxurious kind to the lives of his progressive, free-thinking, but wealthy clients – at Merlshanger (1896) and the Pastures (1901). The hallmarks of his influential style typified by the Orchard (1899), were the low, comfortable proportions, the long, horizontal windows divided into casements, the ubiquitous white pebbledash rendering and the slated hipped roof, all of which re-appeared *ad nauseam* in later years in lower-middle-class suburbs. He attended to every detail, including the furniture which, like the houses themselves, was simple yet comfortable and sophisticated without ostentation.

Set in the poetic garden landscapes of Gertrude Jekyll, the opulent country houses of Edwin Lutyens (1869–1944) provided idyllic environments for aristocrats and successful capitalists. Beginning as an Arts and Crafts designer with a number of informal houses such as Munstead Wood (1896), the Orchards and Tigbourne Court (both 1899), Deanery Gardens (1901) and Folly Farm (1905), Lutyens developed a progressive *folie de grandeur* as his success increased. Lindisfarne Castle (1903), Nashdom (1905), Heathcote (1906) and Castle Drogo (begun 1910) were more formal, rhetorical and expensive but less original than his earlier designs. Lutyens was a talented architect who in his early work at least attempted to break away from the long-term historicist trend in 19th-century design – something Shaw, for example, was never able to do – yet socially he remained part of the 19th century. His architecture depended on, and in an oblique way helped to perpetuate, the world of the petty aristocrat and the primitive, self-made industrialist – already anachronistic and soon to be superseded.

Voysey and Lutyens

the gatehouse at Voysey's
Merishanger, Guildford, Surrey
(1896)

elevation of
Voysey's own house,
The Orchard
at Chorley Wood (1899)

view of Voysey's country house
The Pastures, North Luffenham,
Rutland (1901)

Lutyens' house
The Orchards
at Godalming (1899)
was a good
example of the
close integration
of building and
landscape

Lutyens' **Deanery Gardens**,
Sonning (1901), which like The Orchards
owed a debt to Voysey and
the Arts and Crafts movement

In the USA, similar attempts were being made to move the designer of bourgeois houses away from historicism. Sullivan now lived in obscurity but his colleague Elmslie went into partnership in 1909 with William Purcell and carried on the Chicago tradition, mostly in the mid-west and on the west coast. The architects Charles and Henry Greene worked in a similar geographical area, though apparently uninfluenced by the Chicago school. They made much use of traditional Japanese building techniques and the D. B. Gamble house at Pasadena, CA (1909), demonstrated the advantage of light, airy, flexibly planning, with minimum distinction between internal and external spaces. It contrasted with the more staid European approach of the east coast and presaged the suburban Californian house of today.

The most fruitful application of the Chicago tradition was by Frank Lloyd Wright who as a young man worked for Adler and Sullivan, designing private houses while Sullivan concentrated on office blocks. The three-storey Charnley house (1891), simple, symmetrical and solid-looking, was his first work for the firm. But from 1893, in practice on his own in Illinois, he began to develop what he called his 'prairie' houses, whose evolution can be clearly traced between 1893 and 1909. The Winslow house of 1893 had a four-square plan but its elevational treatment was low and horizontal, making the house appear to hug the ground. In the Willitts house (1902) Wright expanded the plan into a cruciform shape extending in all directions into the landscape around. In the Unity Temple and Parish house (1906) he developed, among other things, his ideas on natural lighting, suffusing the interior with the glow of amber glass. The Avery Coonley house (1908) was integrated with external courtyards, a sunken garden and a swimming pool, in a way which blurred all distinction between interior and exterior. In the Robie house (1909) all these elements came together in one fine composition. The narrow suburban lot precluded the expansive plan of the Coonley house but Wright still achieved a sense of close integration with the landscape. The house was three storeys high but low, calm and reposeful in appearance, capped by over-sailing hipped roofs which visually pinned it to the earth. The internal planning was free, with interlocking spaces, enlivened by changes of level, around a solid central core of staircase and fireplaces.

Wright's other major work of the period was the Larkin administrative building (1904–5) in Buffalo, NY. Already, in the hands of the Chicago architects, the form of the office block was becoming almost stereotyped, with repetitive storeys lit be rectangular repetitive windows. Wright re-thought the whole concept, providing offices which looked inwards to a four-storey glass-roofed courtyard, with solid external walls to guard against noise and pollution. It was the first commercial building to be fully air-conditioned, the first to make use of purpose designed steel fittings, and the first in which the staircase 'tower' was an important design feature. The exciting unconventional internal space and the massive, cubist external treatment had a great influence on the European avant-garde.

Purely in design terms, Wright was an innovator of genius who extended architectural thought in many directions: fluid treatment of space; modern use of traditional materials; use of new structural and servicing systems; use of building form to create abstract sculptural effects. In his 'prairie' designs he sought to invent an 'organic' architecture, integrated with the landscape, true to the materials of which it was built, designed to give its inhabitants as close a relationship as possible with the earth and the elements. It is apparent from his writings that this organic architecture was in part an expression of his veneration of the pioneer and of the cult of the frontier, derived from an immigrant

In direct contradiction of the ideas of Morris, Art Nouveau designers promoted art as a commodity; commercialism was fundamental to the movement, and many key designers, such as Tiffany and Lalique, were both artists and shop-keepers selling their own work. The boundaries between the arts were blurred: mixed-media pieces combined the techniques of both artist and craftsman; sculpture and jewellery were applied to consumer goods; even 'pure' art, through the lithography of pictures or the miniaturisation and mass-production of sculpture, was turned into a readily saleable form. The department store played an important part in the process: in Paris, van de Velde's 'L'Art Nouveau' (1883), which gave its name to the movement, and 'Samaritaine' (1904–5); in Brussels Baron Horta's 'L'Innovation' (1901). London's foremost store gave its name in turn to the Art Nouveau movement in Italy: 'Stile Liberty'.

Art Nouveau was a genuinely international movement, the first of the modern age. It belonged to second-generation industrial countries – France, Belgium, Germany and the USA – and to third-generation ones such as Spain, Italy and Hungary, numerous enough by the end of the 19th century to form a significant new international bourgeois community. The movement belonged specifically to urban capitalism; in Spain for example, it flourished in Catalonia, the most advanced industrial area, where it became a focus of nationalist pride against the political dominance of Castile; and in Italy it was the style of Milan, Turin and Udine rather than of the peasant south.

Art Nouveau architecture began in Belgium with Victor Horta (1861–1947) whose Hôtel Tassel in Brussels (1892), with its exotic main staircase in twisting ironwork, was exactly contemporary with van de Velde's early experiments in graphic design. As well as 'L'Innovation', Horta's main works included the Hôtel Solvay (1895–1900) and the Maison du Peuple (1896–9) and helped to establish the classic, flame-like line of Gallic Art Nouveau, achieved by an imaginative and modern use of iron and glass. Henri van de Velde (1863–1957) turned to architecture and interior design at about the same time, beginning in Paris with 'L'Art Nouveau' and then, after an exhibition in Dresden had popularised his work, moving to Germany where he furnished the Folkwang Museum in Hagen (1901) and the Nietzsche Archiv in Dresden (1903), where he also rebuilt the Art School (1904).

In France there were two main centres of Art Nouveau. The forests of Lorraine provided both the timber and the visual inspiration for the furniture of the Nancy workshops of Emile Gallé and his pupils Louis Majorelle and Victor Prouvé. They disregarded the inherent limitations of wood, using it in a highly figurative way, bending it and carving it across the grain into flowing shapes in direct imitation of vegetable and plant forms. Parisian furniture was even lighter and more extravagant. The main practitioners were Eugène Colonna, Eugène Gaillard, Georges de Feure and the architect Hector Guimard (1867–1942) whose Castel Béranger (1894–8), with its intricate ironwork, had established Art Nouveau in France in the same way as Horta had in Belgium. The culmination of French Art Nouveau was the international exhibition of 1900; the event itself – which included the ceremonial opening of the Pont Alexandre III by the Tsar – the exhibition buildings of Charles Girault and the works on display, such as the rich graphic designs of Alphonse Mucha and the beautifully decadent jewellery of René Lalique, seemed to epitomise the extravagant and slightly shocking *fin-de-siècle* bourgeois world of Wilde's *Salomé* and the comedies of Feydeau, of the Théâtre de l'Oeuvre and the Moulin Rouge, of Sarah Bernhardt and Loïe Fuller.

In Germany, the style became popular in the design of manufactured goods, particularly at the Württemburgische Metallwarenfabrik, Daniel Straub's mid-19th cen-

Art Nouveau
in Belgium and France

the main entrance gate at the **Castel Béranger** in Brussels — designed by Guimard in 1896

Baron Horta's **Maison du Peuple** (1896-9) designed for the Brussels branch of the Parti Ouvrier Belge

electric light

METROPOLITAIN

iron and glass sign over one of three standard entrances to the **Paris Métro** by Guimard (1900)

Art Nouveau in furniture — a mahogany dressing table with mirror by Louis Majorelle (1900)

fin-de-siècle Paris at the 1900 Exhibition

Art Nouveau in jewellery — a 1900 bracelet designed for Bernhardt, by Georges Fouquet and Alphonse Mucha, as Cleopatra's asp...

...and a dragon-fly clasp by René Lalique (1898)

Art Nouveau in Munich –
August Endell's
**Elvira photographic
studio** (1897-8)

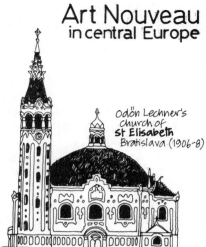

Odön Lechner's
church of
St Elisabeth
Bratislava (1906-8)

Lechner's masterpiece in
decorative brickwork –
the **Post office savings
bank** at Kecskemét
(1899-1902)

the domestic elegance of
the Stile Liberty –
Sommaruga's **Palazzo
Salmoiraghi** in Milan
(1906)

Aladár Árkay's
Calvinist church
in Budapest (1911-13) –
like Lechner, and like
Mackintosh, Árkay drew
on the local folk tradition

Raimondo d'Aronco's
Central pavilion at the
1902 Turin exhibition was
decorative but also
structurally functional

tury foundry, which by the end of the century had grown into a large corporation dominating German production of metalwork and cast-metal sculptures. August Endell (1871–1925) was one of a number of German Art Nouveau architects; his Atelier Elvira, a photographic studio in Munich (1897–8), and his Buntes-theater in Berlin (1901) were notable for their intricate surface decoration. In Budapest, Odön Lechner (1845–1914) and Aladár Arkay (1868–1932) reworked Art Nouveau in terms of the Hungarian folk tradition of which both were part. Lechner began as a neo-gothic architect but his finest work, the Postal Savings Bank in Kecskemét (1899–1902), was pure Art Nouveau of great decorative and spatial variety. Arkay's most significant work was the Calvinist church in Budapest (1911–13), a strong, simple building enlivened by areas of rich decoration. In contemporary Italy, architecture combined the lightness of Art Nouveau, known in Italy as Stile Liberty, with the ponderous baroque of Italian tradition; it was typified by the work of Ernesto Basile (1857–1932), Raimondo d'Aronco (1857–1932) and Giuseppe Sommaruga (1867–1917) whose buildings for the Turin exhibition of decorative arts (1902) established Italian Art Nouveau on the international scene. In America, the ornate decorative metalwork by Elmslie on Sullivan's buildings was certainly a significant influence on the style, but the most important work was undoubtedly the rich and colourful glassware of Louis Comfort Tiffany and his firm, Associated Artists.

The internationalism of Art Nouveau did not prevent it taking on here and there a narrower, more sectarian significance. In Catalonia it was considered a national rather than international style, highly significant to the emergent bourgeoisie of Spain's most industrial region in their fight for cultural identity and political recognition, playing a similar, though more intensely felt, role to that of neo-Gothic in England. It came as part of a bourgeois *Renaixença* in cultural and political life, which also saw the reform of the language, the setting-up of academies and universities and the establishment of a new constitution. In Barcelona, Valencia, Gerona and Mallorca *El Modernisme* drew on a wide variety of local cultural traditions, becoming popular enough to affect all the arts and to result in literally hundreds of new buildings, some of great architectural importance.

The most famous Catalan architect, and one of the most significant figures of the Modernist period, was Antoni Gaudí (1852–1926). He used the experience of decorative metalwork, gained from his craftsman father in his early bourgeois houses, the Casa Vicens in Barcelona (1878–80) and the Capricho at Comillas (1883–5). Sponsored by the successful industrialist Güell, he completed for him the Palacio Güell (1885–9), the chapel of Santa Coloma (1898) and the Parque Güell (1900). Influenced at first by traditional Arabic and gothic architecture, Gaudí quickly developed a personal style. He encased his elemental building forms, like giant concrete crustacea, with a coral of inventive and unconventional decoration of embedded glass and pottery shards and clusters of metal. This was seen at its best in the church of the Holy Family in Barcelona, an existing neo-gothic building which the deeply religious Gaudí had begun to extend in 1884, adding between 1903 and 1926 four extraordinary bottle-shaped transept towers. The same inventiveness was seen in his two other mature buildings, the luxury apartment blocks in Barcelona, Casa Milá and Casa Battló (both started in 1905).

Gaudí's imagination, though boundless in sculptural terms, was not sufficient to encompass the new structural possibilities of the 20th century, and though he was able sometimes to enlarge the scope of traditional means of construction, he could not break away from them. He differed in this respect from his great contemporary Luis Domènech y

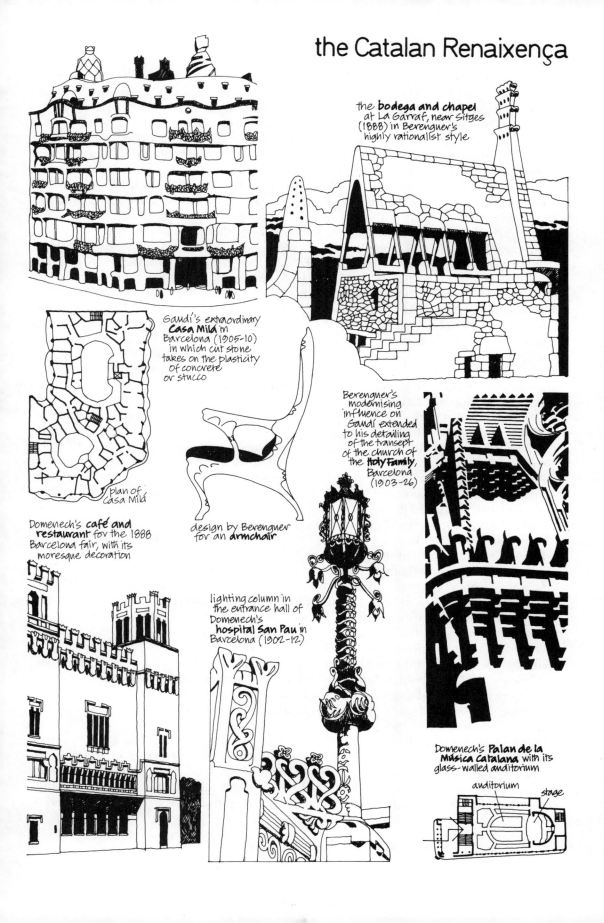

the **bodega and chapel** at La Garraf, near Sitges (1888) in Berenguer's highly rationalist style

Gaudí's extraordinary **Casa Milá** in Barcelona (1905-10) in which cut stone takes on the plasticity of concrete or stucco

plan of Casa Milá

Domenech's **café and restaurant** for the 1888 Barcelona fair, with its moresque decoration

design by Berenguer for an **armchair**

Berenguer's modernising influence on Gaudí extended to his detailing of the transept of the church of the **Holy Family**, Barcelona (1903-26)

lighting column in the entrance hall of Domenech's **hospital San Pau** in Barcelona (1902-12)

Domenech's **Palau de la Música Catalana** with its glass-walled auditorium

auditorium

stage

Montaner (1850–1923) whose use of new materials and techniques represents a more genuinely modernist aspect of Catalan *Modernisme*, in the spirit of Viollet-le-Duc and Morris. Where Gaudí was a holy fool, trying to invoke the spirit of the Catalan people through his own very personal religious expressionism, Domènech was a prominent member of the Cortes, a politician to whom architecture was a means to a better social future. Influenced at least in part by the ideas of Morris, he developed similar theories of structural rationalism and integrity of craftsmanship. His earlier works in Barcelona, such as the Montaner y Simón publishers' office (1881–5) and the café and restaurant building for the 1888 Catalan Fair, paid respects to the Moorish tradition of Spanish architecture, the former with its abstract geometric decoration and the latter with its lacy, crenellated sky-line. His mature works included the Institut Pere Mata (1897–9), the Casa Thomas (1899) and Casa Navás (1901), all at Reus, and three great buildings in Barcelona, the hospital San Pau (1902–12), the Casa Lleó Morera (1905) and the Palau de la Música Catalana (1905–8). These three represented the culmination of his work; the hospital was remarkable for the rationalism of its planning, the Casa Lleó Morera for its severity of architectural treatment, and the Palau de la Música above all for the spatial richness deriving partly from Domènech's imaginative use of steel and glass. Gaudí and Domènech represented two contrasting sides of Catalan *Modernisme*. Together with his pupils, notably Francesc Berenguer (1866–1914), architect of the bodega and chapel at La Garraf (1888), Gaudí was part of a richly sculptural, expressionist strand of architectural development. Both this and Domènech's more severe rationalist approach have continued to influence 20th-century architecture.

The rationalist approach was fundamental to the work of the Scot, Charles Rennie Mackintosh (1868–1928). His greatest and most influential building – the Glasgow School of Art – was also one of his earliest, a commission won in competition in 1897. It contained many light-hearted decorative elements appropriate to his early career as an Art Nouveau graphic artist and furniture designer, but also offered something more fundamental: an uncompromising use of both traditional and new materials, notably stone, wood, metal and glass; a simplicity of surface treatment; and above all a complex and fluid use of space and light, features which became essential to the rational architecture of the 20th century. This spatial awareness set Mackintosh apart from most of his Art Nouveau contemporaries, though it ran consistently through his own work, from his Glasgow tea-rooms in Buchanan Street (1897–8), Argyle Street (1897–1905), Ingram Street (1901–11) and Sauchiehall Street (1904) to his country houses Windy Hill, Kilmalcolm (1899–1901), and Hill House, Helensburgh (1902–3), and to the Glasgow School of Art extension (1907–9). Although at the centre of what became known as the 'Glasgow School' – a small group of Art Nouveau designers which included Margaret and Frances McDonald and Herbert McNair – Mackintosh had little influence in Britain; the Whitechapel Art Gallery (1898–9) and the Horniman Museum (1900–1), both in London, designed by Charles Harrison Townsend (1850–1928), were England's nearest approach to Art Nouveau. It was left to continental Europe to develop Mackintosh's ideas of surface simplicity and spatial richness which pointed towards a rationalist future.

The key figure in introducing Mackintosh's work to Europe was Otto Wagner (1841–1918), a Viennese architect immersed in the bourgeois tradition of Habsburg Austria and eminent enough to be called upon for monumetal civic buildings in the Ringstrasse, yet also liberal enough to believe in the idea of progress and to doubt whether, in architectural terms, the sentimental and derivative styles of imperial

Mackintosh and the Sezession

a new rationalism— the library wing added 1906-7 to Mackintosh's **Glasgow School of Art** (begun 1897)

Mackintosh's Scottish exhibit at the **Vienna Sezession** exhibition (1900) brought a new coolness and restraint to European Art Nouveau

it was echoed in the subsequent attitude of the Sezession designers

with the **Post Office Savings Bank** Vienna (1903-6) Wagner moved away from his earlier classicism towards a steel-and-glass modernity

Olbrich's **Sezession House** in Vienna (1898) was the original statement of the Sezession style

open work dome

'Hoch zeits turm'

Hoffmann's **Palais Stoclet** was a mansion for a Brussels industrialist (1905-11) which brought the Sezession style out of Vienna

hall

dining room

gate

kitchen

the **Kunsterkolonie** Mathildenhöhe Darmstadt (1905-07) by Olbrich and others was the most complete expression of the Sezession philosophy

exhibition buildings

Vienna were adequate for the buildings of the future. He hoped to evolve a style that would pay due respect to Vienna's noble history yet reflect the progressive intellectual stimulus of the city of Schoenberg, Kokoschka and Freud. His statement that 'nothing that is not practical can be beautiful' was a challenge to traditional architectural values; in his stations for the Vienna Stadtbahn (1894–7) he attempted to put this into practice. As professor of architecture at The Academy from 1894, and as a respected employer, he taught and encouraged many younger architects, some of whom went beyond him in their ideas. Two – Josef Maria Olbrich (1867–1908) and Josef Hoffmann (1810–1956) – were members of a breakaway artists' group whose name, the *Sezession*, promised a total rejection of past styles. The group's headquarters in Vienna (1898), designed by Olbrich as a simple cubic building with a light-hearted, openwork dome, led to a commission from the Grand Duke of Hesse in 1899 to design studios, houses and exhibition buildings for the Mathildenhöhe, an artists' colony at Darmstadt near Frankfurt. It was part of the commercial spirit of the *Sezession* that its members made their work the subject of numerous exhibitions; the one in Vienna in 1900 was significant for introducing the work of Mackintosh to Europe.

Hoffmann was particularly receptive to the influence of both Morris and Mackintosh; in 1903 he founded the Wiener Werkstätte in which he tried to bring together the techniques of both architecture and craftsmanship. The same year he built his convalescent home at Purkersdorf, extraordinarily in advance of its time with plain walls, flat roofs and regular, rectangular windows. In 1905 he began his Palais Stoclet in Brussels, a large, comfortable bourgeois house, elegant, richly-designed and full of space and light. Olbrich too was affected; his Hochzeitsturm at Darmstadt (1907) was a tall tower whose clean, smooth lines owed much to Mackintosh. Even Wagner, caught up in the flurry of new ideas from his pupils, built in the Post Office Savings Bank in Vienna (1903–6) a plain, glass-roofed banking hall from which all ideas of historicism had been banished. In Amsterdam, Hendrikus Berlage (1856–1934) was pursuing similar objectives in his designs for the Diamond Workers' Union building (1899–1900) and the Stock Exchange (1897–1903). The simple, monumental treatment of the interiors was reminiscent of Richardson's romanesque, though there was also a distinct affinity in style with Domènech's café and restaurant of 1888. In both buildings Berlage achieved sobriety and dignity by his honest and craftsmanlike use of materials and structure.

The Art Nouveau designer's emphasis on craftsmanship, conceived as a criticism of the industrial world, paradoxically brought him commercial success but achieved nothing in social terms. Somewhere between Morris – who died only in 1896 – and the *Sezession*, the road to socialism had been lost; craftsmanship had become at best an end in itself and at worst a commodity rather than the true reflection of a society which respected and encouraged personal freedom. Morris himself had made clear this difference in emphasis; it was not material standards which mattered but the character and quality of life. In a lecture entitled 'The Society of the Future' (1887), he said: 'Free men, I am sure, must lead simple lives and have simple pleasures: and if we shudder away from that necessity now, it is because we are not free men and have in consequence wrapped up our lives in such a complexity of dependence that we have grown feeble and helpless.' Others recognised the inadequacy of the general Art Nouveau obsession with craftsmanship not because it missed the point of Morris's socialist argument but, on the contrary, because it failed to come to terms sufficiently with the methods of industrial capitalism. The Moravian-born architect Adolf Loos (1870–1933) condemned all hand-craftsmanship and extolled the mechanistic aspects of

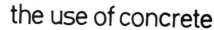

Steinerhaus – view from the garden

street

section through Steinerhaus

garden

entrance

plan of house at piano nobile level

terrace

Adolf Loos's **Steinerhaus** in Vienna (1911) was perhaps the first wholly modern example of reinforced concrete house construction

its cubist appearance, with flat roofs and plain walls, and its freedom of plan-form, were features of the material

Loos

Perret exploited the advantages of reinforced concrete frame construction which allowed greater freedom of plan and of elevational design

Perret

Perret's garage in the **Rue Ponthieu** Paris (1905-6) with its concrete frame and all-glass walls

Perret's flats at **25 bis Rue Franklin** Paris (1902-3) with their free plan-form, wide windows and modest cantilevered beams at the first floor

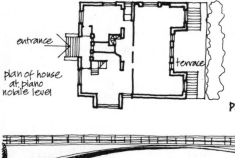

Maillart's early **Zuoz bridge** (1901)

Robert Maillart's contribution was the development of the curved, parabolic slab in bridge design

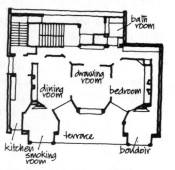

bath room

drawing room

dining room

bedroom

kitchen

smoking room

terrace

boudoir

Maillart's masterpiece – the road bridge over the **Salgina gorge** (1929-30)

modern building. This approach came partly from first-hand study in America of the work of Jenney, Burnham and Root, and Adler and Sullivan, and partly, after his return to Vienna, from exposure to Wagner's theories on honesty. He rejected the ornamental approach of Art Nouveau and with it Olbrich, Hoffmann and the Werkstätte; a series of outspoken books and articles established his name as an evangelist of the practical and utilitarian, a champion of the structural engineer and the plumber. His buildings were correspondingly spartan; the Villa Karma, Montreux (1904), the Steinerhaus (1911) and the Goldman offices (1910), both in Vienna, were essays in straight lines, rectangular shapes and cubic volumes. The Steinerhaus was probably the first private house to be designed in reinforced concrete.

This material, which came to typify more than any other the building methods of the 20th century, had already had a half-century or more of development. It was made practically possible by the discovery of Portland cement in the 1820s and was used in a primitive form in the floor construction of Fairbairn's textile mill in Manchester (1845). In 1861 the French builder François Coignet introduced what is virtually the present-day form: a steel mesh embedded in concrete to obtain two structural virtues in one member – the compressive strength of concrete and the tensile strength of steel. François Hennebique, at the Charles VI mill at Turcoing (1895), translated the principle into a system, using the repetitive grid of columns and beams already common in steel-frame construction. Concrete was a more versatile material, however, capable of assuming any shape according to the form-work in which it was cast. Rectangular, repetitive form-work continued to be used where economy was important, but it was not long before the plasticity of concrete also was explored for architectural effect, as in the church of St Jean-de-Montmartre in Paris (1894–7) by Anatole de Baudot (1834–1915) in association with the engineer Contamin. The most successful marriage between architecture and engineering was made by Auguste Perret (1874–1954) whose buildings were elegant and classical in feeling – and in later years more literally neo-classical – but at the same time were designed to reveal the simple utility of their reinforced concrete skeletons. Early examples in Paris, including a block of flats at 25*bis* Rue Franklin (1902–3), a garage in the Rue Ponthieu (1905–6) and the Théâtre des Champs-Elysées (1911–14), established for years to come the conventional way of using reinforced concrete: a regular grid of columns cast in rectangular form-work, repeated in identical 'lifts' from floor to floor. The Rue Franklin flats introduced modest cantilevers at first-floor level, which also became part of conventional concrete construction. The dramatic and unconventional side was seen in the pure engineering works of the Swiss engineer Robert Maillart (1872–1940). Starting not from the economics of repetitive form-work but from the nature of the calculated forces within the structures themselves, he designed reinforced concrete bridges in dynamic parabolic curves, well-suited to the plasticity of the material. In his early bridges at Zuoz (1901) and Tavenasa (1905) he evolved the technique, seen at its best in his bridge at Salgina Gorge (1929–30), of making the roadway and the arch which supported it integral with one another, so that the road ceased to be so much dead weight and became part of the structural system. His 'mushroom' system (1910) carried this principle into multi-storey buildings; by widening columns at the top he made them an organic part of the floor-slabs they supported.

The most dynamic concrete building of the early 20th century was the Jahrhunderthalle (1911–13) built in Breslau to commemorate the centennial of the rising against Napoleon in 1813. The external appearance was staid and neo-classical but the archi-

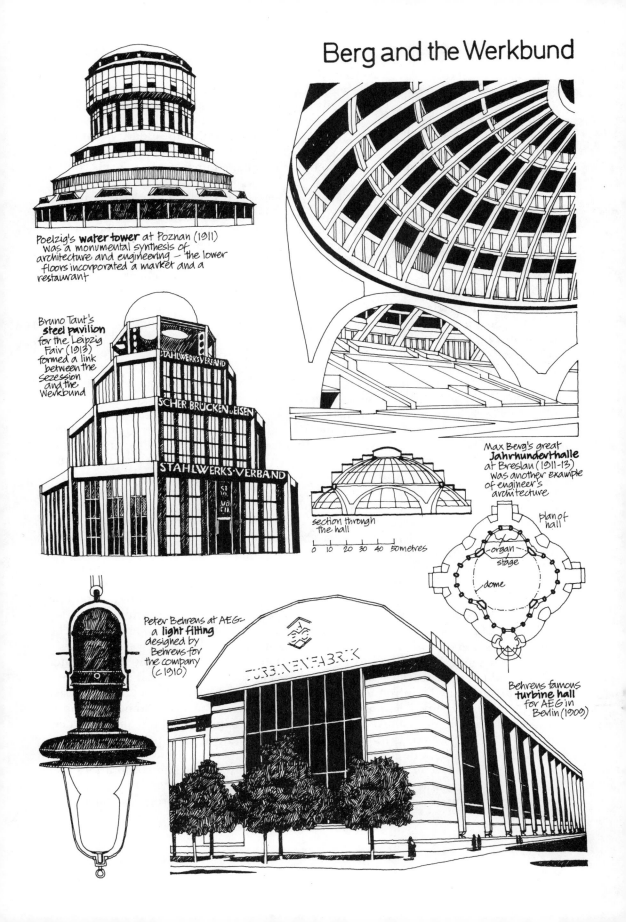

Poelzig's **water tower** at Poznan (1911) was a monumental synthesis of architecture and engineering – the lower floors incorporated a market and a restaurant

Bruno Taut's **steel pavilion** for the Leipzig Fair (1913) formed a link between the Sezession and the Werkbund

STAHLWERKS·VERBAND

...SCHER BRÜCKEN u.EISEN

STAHLWERKS-VERBAND

section through the hall

0 10 20 30 40 50 metres

Max Berg's great **Jahrhunderthalle** at Breslau (1911-13) was another example of engineer's architecture

plan of hall

organ

stage

dome

Peter Behrens at AEG. a **light fitting** designed by Behrens for the company (c 1910)

TURBINENFABRIK

Behrens famous **turbine hall** for AEG in Berlin (1909)

tect, Max Berg (1870–1947), conceived the interior as pure structure, with gigantic arched ribs of reinforced concrete supporting a glass dome over a 65-metre circular auditorium. The new materials brought new methods of construction and with them the learning of new skills such as steel-fixing, welding, riveting and concreting. With the growing complexity of buildings the division of labour within the industry continued to increase, allowing the growth of the production-line principle whereby each worker saw only part of the finished product and often remained unaware of how his contribution fitted into the whole.

Many designers, particularly in Germany where strong links between state and industry made industrialists highly conscious of their national role, were uneasy about this fragmentation. It was considered especially desirable to strengthen the links between the various sides of productive industry: management, design, manufacture and marketing. Much thought was given to creating a unity of effort, notably by Hermann Muthesius (1861–1927) as controller of the Board of Trade for schools of arts and crafts. In 1903 he appointed three avant-garde architects as heads of major art schools: Hans Poelzig in Breslau, Bruno Paul in Berlin and Peter Behrens in Düsseldorf. Poelzig (1869–1936), a brilliant individualist, designed a number of dramatic, highly expressionist buildings including a water tower at Poznan (1911), an office building in Breslau (1911–12), a chemical factory at Luban (1911–12) and a reconstruction for Max Reinhardt of the Grosses Schauspielhaus in Berlin (1918–19). Paul and Behrens were by contrast rationalists; Paul (1874–1954) was best known as a furniture designer and Behrens (1868–1940) for a series of significant buildings which began in 1901 with his own house in the Darmstadt artists' colony, a design of romantic vigour, and continued from 1907 with his appointment as chief designer to the electricity combine AEG Berlin. The same year, Muthesius set up the Deutscher Werkbund, an association of industrialists, designers, architects and craftsmen which aimed to bring industry and design closer together. Paul, Behrens and van de Velde became members, and from then on the ideas of the Werkbund affected their attitudes as designers. Behrens' work for AEG, for example, was to set design standards and give a corporate image to everything from buildings to electrical products and letter-heads. His most memorable work was the turbine hall in Berlin (1909), a severe, powerful design, modern in detail yet neo-classical in mood, unusually serious in intent for an industrial building; but most significant, perhaps, were his relatively anonymous designs for electrical products, which established new industrial norms. Despite resistance from van de Velde, who argued for preserving the designer's individuality, designing for the production line became the basis of the Werkbund philosophy; it was considered important to set standards, obtain adequate levels of peformance and achieve economies of scale. The concept of 'standardisation', applied first to manufacturing industry, was carried over into architecture. The theory of standardisation was that it brought the customer better-quality goods at lower prices; apologists for the Werkbund claimed that it humanised technology by introducing the skilled industrial designer, and democratised good design by bringing beautifully made consumer goods into every home. This must, however, be seen in the context of German monopoly capitalism of the time. The new industrial techniques required increased capital investment and created greater divisions of labour; it became essential to form units of production which were both large and diverse in character, so companies were brought together into corporations and cartels. These were able either to dominate the market by their sheer size or to carve it up between themselves, to manipulate it by inventing special products which they promoted by advertising or salesmanship, or to control it by buying political support. Power became concentrated into the hands of a few monopolists, whose essential aim was to increase profits; in contrast to the competition of earlier days, this was done by restricting rather than increasing output and by keeping prices artificially high. This created a problem of reinvestment, since strict output controls often made it unnecessary to plough capital back; because monopoly capitalism was essentially restrictive, there was no need for development beyond a certain point – and technical progress came in spite of the system rather than because of it. Other fields of investment had to be found: smaller-scale industries, or those of under-developed countries. Monopolism thus exploited not only the worker and the consumer, by artificially maintaining prices, but also the middle classes unable to organise for higher pay, capitalists in other, more vulnerable industries and above all the colonial peoples. As competition within each country decreased it became more acute internationally. One major aspect of this was the arms race in Europe leading up to 1914, in which not only Krupp of Essen but many other corporations were involved, including AEG and its Werkbund designers. Their claims that rational design and standardisation were producing social benefits were perhaps true in a very limited sense, but at the same time gross social iniquities were being perpetrated by the system of which they were willingly a part.

In America, capitalism was making great strides and with it industry and commerce expanded. The first decades of the new century were unremarkable in a formal architectural sense but saw much consolidation of architectural lessons already learnt; the use of steel frames, elevators and air-conditioning spread to every city centre, and skyscrapers grew in height. The Woolworth building in New York (1911–13) by Cass Gilbert (1859–1934), clad in neo-gothic stonework, was architecturally pedestrian but at 240 metres and fifty-two storeys high it was a considerable technical feat. In general, the design of public buildings reflected a revival of interest in the classical style created by the Chicago World's Fair of 1893. In New York the architects Reed and Stem at Grand Central station (1903–13) and McKim, Mead and White at Pennsylvania station (1906–10) were among many contemporaries who looked back to imperial Rome for inspiration. Even Frank Lloyd Wright, in his buildings for the Midway Gardens entertainment centre in Chicago (1913), entered his most eclectic and decorative phase – though his own term 'baroque' represented an attitude rather than a style.

In contemporary Britain the word 'baroque' was taken more literally. Britain's relative decline as a great manufacturing power and the loss of its share in world trade – to which the growing independence of its old empire contributed, with Canada and Australia achieving self-government in 1867 and 1901 respectively – led to a number of ill-considered imperial adventures in search of new markets. This late attempt at colonialism was a succession of military disasters, but was supported at home by the popular myth of an immutable, God-given empire. The work of artists such as Kipling and Elgar, together with the civic architecture of the period, helped to give credence to imperialism and to justify Rorke's Drift, Khartoum and Spion Kop. Colchester Town Hall (1898–1902) by John Belcher was an early example of imperial neo-Baroque applied to a civic building; it was followed by buildings such as Cardiff Civic Centre (1897–1906) and Central Hall, Westminster (1906–12), both by Lanchester and Rickards, and the Law Society in London (1902–4) by Charles Holden. Many accomplished architects adopted the style, including John Burnet, Edwin Cooper, Herbert Baker and Reginald Blomfield; among the most prolific was Aston Webb, designer of

the value of tradition

commercial **academicism** in the United States – McKim, Mead and White's **Pennsylvania railroad station** in New York (1906-10), was an academic essay in classicism, and Napoleon LeBrun's **Metropolitan tower** facing Madison Square (1909) was in the style of an outsize Italian campanile...

...while the **Woolworth building** in New York (1911-13) by Cass Gilbert was elaborated in the style of a 15th C Gothic cathedral

national romanticism in Scandinavia – the **Grundtvig church** in Copenhagen (1913-26) by Jensen Klint, and **Stockholm City Hall** (1911-23) by Ragnar Östberg, both reflected a romantic search for the traditional roots of Scandinavian culture

British **late-imperial baroque** – the last years of the Empire were marked by buildings proclaiming its permanence, like the **Central Hall** in Westminster (1906-12) by Lanchester and Rickards, and like Lutyens' **Viceroy's palace** in New Delhi (1913-30)

the Victoria and Albert Museum in London (1899–1910) and the new east front of Buckingham Palace (1913). The great opulence of the style was also appropriate for commercial buildings such as the Ritz Hotel, London (1905), by Mewès and Davis, and Shaw's nearby Piccadilly Hotel (1905). It reached its ultimate grandeur at New Delhi, the main outpost of British imperialism, where Lutyens and Herbert Baker created a gigantic avenue of civic buildings centred on Lutyens' palace of the Viceroy. Delhi represents more than anywhere the political emptiness of late-imperial architectural gestures; begun in 1913, it took some twenty years to construct, by which time local agitation for constitutional reform had almost completed India's journey to independence.

In Britain, the government was expected to act in an enabling role, and not to interfere too much in the workings of private enterprise. In India, the reverse was true: the Indian Civil Service was a massive centralised bureaucracy, supported by the army and the law. Colonial economics demanded that India act primarily as a producer of raw materials for western factories; great emphasis was placed, for example, on the movement of troops, administrators and raw materials to the ports, but there was little official interest in improving standards of living. Thus the high technology of what was then one of the world's best railway systems existed within a vast, sprawling peasant economy, a prey to over-population, poverty and starvation, which mild agricultural reforms and the famine relief policy of the 1880s eased only partially. As in the early days of the industrial revolution in England, concern for the workers was limited to ensuring a plentiful labour supply and a market for hardware. While conditions in the west slowly improved, the worst exploitation merely shifted across the national boundaries to different groups of workers.

Within the Russian empire a similar kind of colonialism prevailed, with the old regime and the new capitalists jockeying for position and contriving between them to depress the conditions of both the tiny industrial working class and the great multi-racial mass of peasants through low wages and punitive taxation. In 1905 the crude inefficiency and manifest injustice of the system brought about an abortive but prophetic revolution. In one way or another most western countries were also in a state of industrial unrest; depression had been succeeded by expansion, but the workers had no share in it: real wages fell as profits increased and the arms race intensified. The military-industrial machine, amid excesses of middle-class patriotism and increasing opposition from working-class groups, moved towards war. In America William Haywood's 'Wobblies' and in Britain the dock and railway workers, led by men like Ben Tillett and Tom Mann, launched massive strikes which were met by military force.

The revolutionary socialism of the more militant industrial leaders contrasted with the increasingly reformist attitudes of the labour parties and politicians, now dominated by 'revisionists' such as Kautsky in Germany, Jaurès in France and the Webbs in Britain. Their main theoretician was Eduard Bernstein, author of *Suppositions of Socialism* (1899). He 'revised' Marx's scenario of intensifying class-struggle leading to revolution, into a picture of diminishing conflict; capitalists and landlords would gradually see sense, and a conciliatory labour movement would draw society together and create a kind of apolitical socialism. This thinking had many parallels in urban design theory around the turn of the century as architects and planners invented physical forms for the reformist utopia.

Much thought went into housing design. New artisans' dwellings such as the White tenements in Brooklyn, NY, or the Peabody estates in London had only slightly relieved the squalor of city life. The buildings themselves were cheerless barracks, more sanitary but no more hospitable than the slums, and apt to degenerate. It was increasingly clear that private enterprise alone would never be able to deal with the scale of the problem, and in 1890 Britain took a significant step forward with an Act which gave local authorities themselves the responsibility of rebuilding in slum-clearance areas. The new London County Council – many of whose members were reformists, like Sidney Webb – was first in the field and formed a group of young idealistic architects with an enthusiasm for the ideas of Lethaby. In common with all reformist thinkers their attitude was architecturally 'determinist': a better environment would create a better social system. Their innovations, particularly in the Boundary Street estate in Bethnal Green and the Millbank estate in Pimlico, included: the introduction of focal points in their layouts to avoid the featureless repetition of the Peabody and Guinness estates; greater richness of detail, especially the use of the 'Queen Anne' style which, through association with Shaw's bourgeois houses, was intended to upgrade the quality of working-class flats; and a striving for unity of architecture and craftsmanship. This pursuit of unity, already a basic aim of the Arts and Crafts and Art Nouveau designers, seemed to the LCC architects particularly relevant in encouraging building craftsmen to express themselves in buildings intended for their own class.

Like the Peabody estates, the LCC flats were five or six storeys with open, common staircases. Despite the superior layouts, the densities, at 500 or more people per hectare, were still high; and in 1890 *The Builder* magazine commented:

> . . . the crowding of the same number of people in tall blocks of buildings with a certain minimum space between them may be nearly as unhealthy as crowding them in lower houses more closely set. Overcrowding vertically is very little better than overcrowding laterally: it is only another way of arranging the same number of people on an area too small for them.

In 1898 Ebenezer Howard (1850–1928), a clerk in the City of London, offered an answer to this problem in his utopian treatise, *Tomorrow*. Drawing inspiration from Bellamy's *Looking Backward*, he proposed the concept of the garden city, built at a low enough density to obtain for all its inhabitants the space, light and air which the inner city so conspicuously lacked. Unlike the garden suburb, which depended on its parent town, the garden city would be self-contained, both physically and economically; it would also be economically self-sustaining, independent of public ownership, so that the value which in the traditional city accrued to the private landlord came instead to the community. The concept was essentially one of balance: between town and country, obtaining the best attributes of both and the disadvantages of neither; between the constituent land-uses, so that housing, factories and schools were always matched to population; between growth and decline, so that the size of the city was always held around an optimum of 30,000 people; and between the *laissez-faire* freedom of the market and benevolent municipal control. In 1899 The Garden City Association was formed and after the amassing of some capital the first garden city, Letchworth, was begun in 1903 by Barry Parker and Raymond Unwin. Finance – and consequently progress – came only slowly, however. The physical imagery of garden-city planning was realised sooner and with greater effect at Henrietta Barnett's trust-funded Hampstead Garden Suburb near London (1907), with its formal layout by Unwin, its romantic house designs and plentiful vegetation. The original intention was for Hampstead to house a wide social cross-section, but the limitations of private finance ensured that it

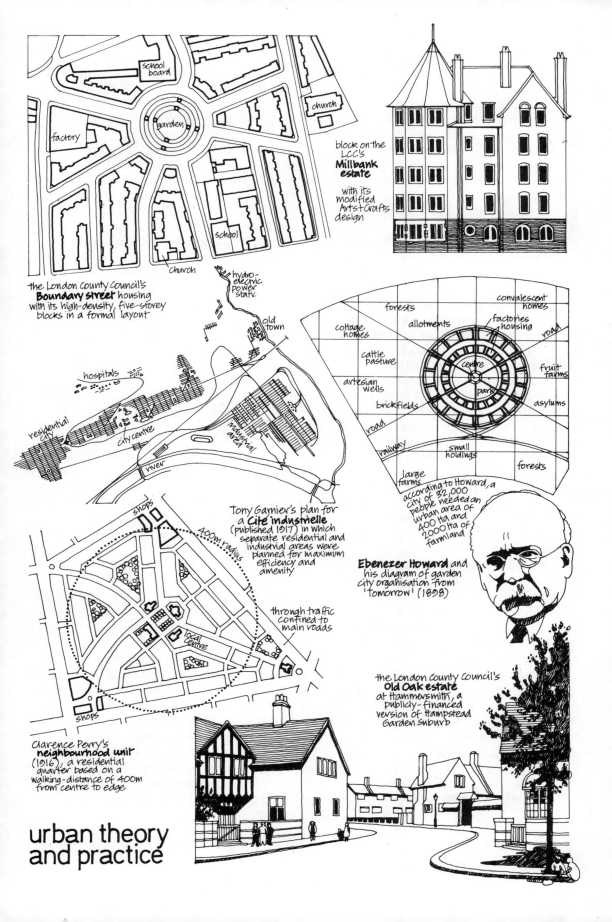

the London County Council's **Boundary street** housing with its high-density, five-storey blocks in a formal layout

school board

garden

factory

church

school

church

block on the LCC's **Millbank estate**

with its modified Arts+Crafts design

hydro-electric power stat.

old town

hospitals

residential city

city centre

industrial area

river

Tony Garnier's plan for a **Cité industrielle** (published 1917) in which separate residential and industrial areas were planned for maximum efficiency and amenity

forests

convalescent homes

cottage homes

allotments

factories housing

road

cattle pasture

centre

fruit farms

artesian wells

park

brickfields

asylums

road

railway

small holdings

forests

large farms

according to Howard, a city of 32,000 people needed an urban area of 400 Ha and 2000 Ha of farmland

Ebenezer Howard and his diagram of garden city organisation from 'tomorrow!' (1898)

shops

400m radius

through traffic confined to main roads

local centre

shops

the London County Council's **Old Oak estate** at Hammersmith, a publicly-financed version of Hampstead Garden Suburb

Clarence Perry's **neighbourhood unit** (1916), a residential quarter based on a walking-distance of 400m from centre to edge

urban theory and practice

began and remained middle-class. However, after 1898 the LCC began to implement another provision of the 1890 Act when, in addition to rebuilding after slum clearance, they also began to acquire empty sites on the cheaper fringes of London for new housing. Taking the opportunity to design to lower densities, they built 'cottage estates' at Tottenham, Kilburn and Wandsworth, the first working-class suburbs and the first to be built with public money. The Old Oak estate at Wormwood Scrubbs was the best, in some ways comparable with Hampstead.

There were further developments in housing design when Clarence Perry and other planners working in Chicago and New York between about 1910 and 1929 advanced the idea of the 'neighbourhood unit'. The question was one of 'identity'. In place of the anonymous grid of streets of the typical American city, with shops, schools and open spaces occurring haphazardly, cities should be planned as a series of district neighbourhoods, each contributing to the whole, but identifiable in itself, with an elementary school, the focus of family and social life, at its centre. Each neighbourhood would contain about 1000 families – the number required to support one school – and its physical extent would be determined by a maximum walking-distance of 400 metres or so from edge to centre. Each area would have local shops, parks and open spaces and, most significantly, a road system designed to exclude dangerous through-traffic.

The most complete urban theory of the period was proposed by the French architect Tony Garnier (1869–1948) between 1901 and 1904 in his model 'Cité Industrielle'. It was designed for a specific site near Lyon, in intricate and workable architectural detail; only the World War prevented its realisation and many of its ideas were later used in Garnier's own buildings. He used the restrained architectural language of Loos, designing predominantly in reinforced concrete and demonstrating its versatility in simple, cubist houses, wide-span industrial buildings, elegant towers and bridges. His architectural vision placed his proposals in a different category from Howard's whose ideas were essentially two-dimensional. Another equally important point of divergence was Garnier's socialism, around which the whole of his urban fabric was constructed. It was the socialism not of Marx but of Proudhon, a philosophy which rejected the idea of class-struggle and sought instead to create utopia through the abolition of private property. Garnier's city therefore had a number of important features: communal ownership of land and buildings, allowing strict control of industry, traffic movement and other intrusions into the domestic environment; an emphasis on communal living, including the provision of flats and an absence of individual gardens in favour of common ones; an emphasis on local centres, sports stadia and other manifestations of the community spirit. The vividness of Garnier's ideas and designs created a persistent imagery for the social architecture of the 20th century and influenced many town planning theorists.

Both Howard and Garnier tried to anticipate and cater for all the essential needs of contemporary life, canalising them into a logical physical form. Howard in particular was sanguine about his theories, fully accepting that they would need adaptation in practice, but perhaps the biggest failure of them both was the most obvious one, inherent in all utopian thinking. The overwhelming lesson of the Victorian city, from Manchester to Chicago, was that though it might aggravate social problems, it was not in itself a cause. Rather was it an effect, itself the product of a society in conflict, competing within itself for land and resources. Capitalism had created a society in which the physical and material were the sole measures of success. It was difficult to conceive of solutions to the problems of society in other than physical terms; capitalism allowed little room for social criticism and none at all for political and economic change. There was pressure to move away from real solutions to the problems of the city towards what in effect, were abstractions.

This tendency towards abstraction could also be seen in contemporary art and architecture. The Impressionists, for example, for all their brilliance and originality, for all that they emancipated art from pretentiousness by their choice of everyday subject-matter, nevertheless increased the objectivity of painting by treating it in terms of colour, light and form rather than for any more human meaning. In architecture too, the growth of the Sullivanian concept of functionalism, though purifying building design of the excessive rhetoric of Beaux Arts classicism and Imperial baroque, had the effect of turning buildings into abstract essays in space and mass, solid and void, light and shadow. With the growing together of architecture and engineering, function and structure were seen as the very essence of architecture. This long-term trend towards abstract formalism was the most retrogressive historical response of the artist to the bourgeois world. It ensured that for all his efforts he would never challenge the system nor begin to resolve any of the conflicts within it; that required more radical measures.

The state and revolution
The First World War and after

The great artistic turmoil at the beginning of the 20th century derived essentially from the gross contradictions of *fin-de-siècle* Europe – stagnant economies which favoured only the rich, old political regimes hanging grimly on to power through their police states, universal industrialism bringing squalor to the cities and poverty to the country-side, destructive and pointless foreign wars – all dressed up in an imperial livery of baroque buildings, resounding poetry and historicist paintings and sculptures. When the 20th-century artists 'declared war' on the art of the past – on romanticism, on neo-Classicism, on the Impressionists or on Art Nouveau – it was undoubtedly a social comment, even if only a few saw it in political terms. In Germany, the Expressionists retreated into highly personal and emotional artistic modes, while in France, the Cubists sought to create a new artistic language by rejecting the bourgeois use of pictorial art for ideological and political purposes and by moving increasingly towards abstraction as a means of purifying the artistic process. Out of the early Cubism of Braque, Picasso and Léger grew a number of distinct movements, as artists developed their ideas: the Purism of Amédée Ozenfant, who took the cubist rules to more severe and rigorous lengths; the work of the Russian Kasimir Malevich whose *Suprematist Manifesto* (1915) was exemplified by the extreme 'supreme' restraint of works such as his *White rectangle on a white ground*; and the neo-Plasticism of Mondriaan and van Doesburg in Holland who created works of pure, rectilinear abstraction. In 1917 Mondriaan and van Doesburg joined De Stijl, an association of designers which produced an influential journal of the same name. Neo-Plasticism, with its straight lines and rectilinear forms, its deliberately limited range of colours and its interlocking, over-lapping planes, was a major influence on early De Stijl, seen in the Red-Blue chair (1917) of Gerrit Rietveld (1888–1964) and the Huis ter Heide at Utrecht (1916) by Rob van t'Hoff.

The Futurists, by contrast, disdained such introspection; the violence of the capitalist world bred counter-violence.

> We must invent and rebuild *ex novo* our modern city as a tumultuous shipyard . . .
> the house of cement, iron and glass . . . rich only in the inherent beauty of its lines
> and modelling, extraordinarily brutish in its mechanical simplicity . . . must rise
> from the brink of a tumultuous abyss . . . the street will . . . plunge storeys deep
> into the earth. . .

These words were part of a *Manifesto dell' Archittetura Futurista* published in Milan in 1914. The Futurist group, led by the artists Marinetti and Boccioni, included the architects Antonio Sant'Elia (1888–1916) and Mario Chiattone (1891–1957). Sant'Elia's life was cut short by the war, and between them they built very little, but their published designs created a vivid and influential picture of the city of the future. Architecturally, they rejected the baroque extravagance of Italian Art Nouveau in favour of the monumental simplicity of the *Sezession*; but their own essential and unique contribution was their fervent sense of the technological dynamism of the modern city,

the Werkbund Exhibition 1914

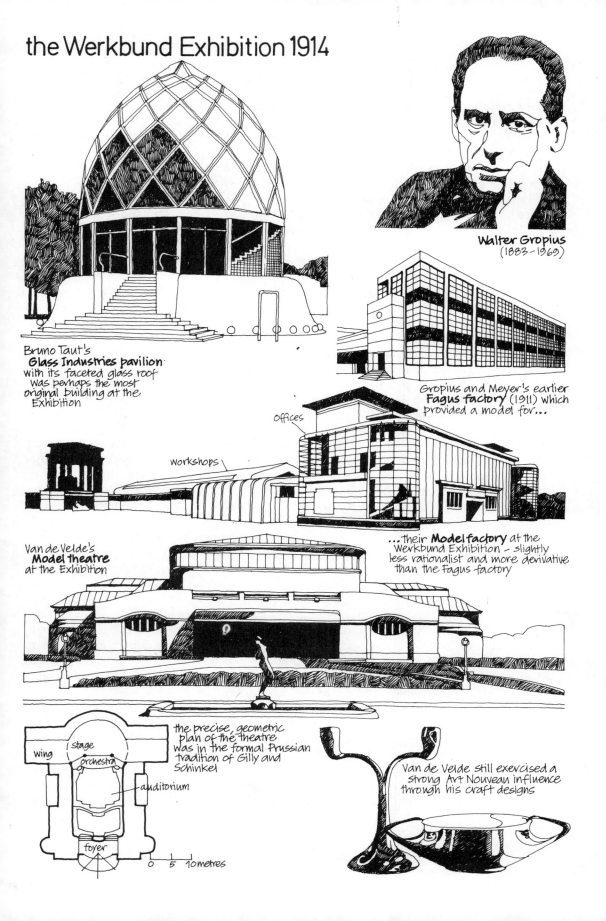

Walter Gropius
(1883–1969)

Bruno Taut's
Glass Industries pavilion
with its faceted glass roof
was perhaps the most
original building at the
Exhibition

Gropius and Meyer's earlier
Fagus factory (1911) which
provided a model for...

Offices

Workshops

...their **Model factory** at the
Werkbund Exhibition – slightly
less rationalist and more derivative
than the Fagus factory

Van de Velde's
Model theatre
at the Exhibition

wing
stage
orchestra
auditorium
foyer

0 5 10 metres

the precise, geometric
plan of the theatre
was in the formal Prussian
tradition of Gilly and
Schinkel

Van de Velde still exercised a
strong Art Nouveau influence
through his craft designs

expressed in projects for office towers, airship-hangars, power stations and transport interchanges consisting of multi-level walkways, roads and railways, which persisted for later generations as powerful, hostile, yet seductive images of utopia.

The Werkbund Exhibition in Cologne (1914) presented another set of images, this time as real buildings. The emphasis was again on technology and the new forms made possible by new materials; Bruno Taut's Glass Industries pavilion with its faceted glass dome, van de Velde's innovatory model theatre building, and the Model factory designed by the young Adolf Meyer (1881–1929) and Walter Gropius (1883–1969). Though eclectic in design, leaning heavily on Wright, the administrative block with its rectilinear outline and large areas of steel-framed glazing had elements of rationalism, as did the same architects' Fagus factory at Alfeld (1911). In both buildings Gropius and Meyer used the distinctive modernist trick of keeping all structural columns away from the corners, as if to emphasise the non-loadbearing function of the external glass walls.

The Werkbund, like so many other European institutions, was overtaken by the other events of 1914 which changed Europe beyond recognition. The final destruction of the old regimes by the First World War altered the political power-base of post-war Europe, just as the loss of a whole generation of young men changed its social structure. Those workers, intellectuals and artists who survived were radically affected by front-line traumas, by feelings of betrayal, resentment and rebellion. Most significant of all were the events of 1917, which saw the creation of the world's first socialist state, an important pointer to the future for those who defined the struggle in terms of class rather than of race or nationality. The Russian revolution of February 1917 deposed the Tsar and established a liberal government, which began to pass laws for social welfare and to promise land to the peasants when the war was over. But the growing strength of the Soviet workers' councils, demanding 'Peace, Land and Bread', brought first the moderate socialist government of Kerensky into power and then, with the uprising of October 1917, the Bolsheviks. Lenin's first act was to secure peace with Germany, his second to meet the need for land and bread by beginning a massive programme of social reconstruction, putting an end to all private property not needed for living in, nationalising the banks and large industries, placing the smaller factories and the farms in the hands of the workers and peasants and forbidding the employment of one person by another. The effects of sudden liberation on an enslaved population were enormous. The task of rebuilding a political and social structure from the bottom upward was approached with trepidation but with great sense of purpose, and intellectuals, artists, poets and architects suddenly found they could make a significant contribution to a major social task. Under Tsarism they had either served the state or lived aimless lives in bohemian café-society; suddenly they had total freedom, and responded by creating the short-lived artistic movement known as Constructivism which, in the words of John Berger, 'for its creativity, confidence, engagement in life and synthesising power, has so far remained unique in the history of modern art'.

The guiding principles of the new revolution were those of Lenin's *The State and Revolution*, written before October 1917 and published the following year. Lenin defined the state as 'a special organisation of force; the organisation of violence for the suppression of some class'. Historically, the state apparatus had been devised by the ruling class specifically for the suppression of the working class; it was therefore impossible for the proletarian revolution merely to take it over – the old machinery must be replaced with new. The more useful functions such as the banks and financial institu-

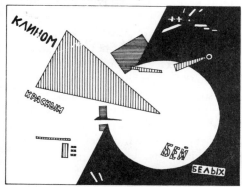

El Lissitzky's Bolshevik
street poster of the
Civil War – **Beat the Whites
with the Red Wedge** (1919)

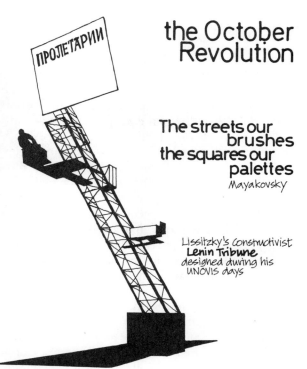

the October Revolution

The streets our
brushes
the squares our
palettes
Mayakovsky

Lissitzky's Constructivist
Lenin Tribune
designed during his
UNOVIS days

Agitprop board at a Vitebsk factory
by UNOVIS (1919)

Malevich   Lissitzky

members of the
UNOVIS group at Vitebsk
in 1919

Tatlin in 1920
when working on the
construction of his
tower

the **Tatlin tower** –
projected
monument to the
Third
International (1920)

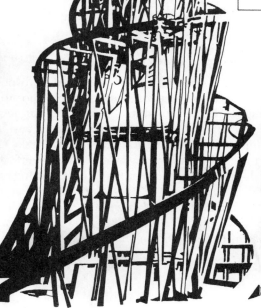

part of Altman's
abstract
decoration
outside the
Winter Palace
during the
symbolic restaging
of the 1917
uprising
in 1918

tions should be transformed and used for the general good; the coercive ones – the police, the standing army and the bureaucracy – must be replaced by the people themselves, exercising their own controls. This could not be accomplished by persuasion; the pressure of established institutions, the ruling-class monopoly of propaganda, the inertia of the people themselves, all negated the idea of democratic change. It could come only through 'the dictatorship of the proletariat', which would deliberately set out to destroy the power of the former oppressors and their allies. The process might take 'a whole historical epoch' but in the end the state would disappear; even democracy, in which the minority bowed to the will of the majority, would eventually be replaced by a society not for the majority but for everyone, in which people would make decisions by rational discussion and consent and would observe elementary rules of behaviour without compulsion.

The Bolshevik party was the key to the creation of this new society, but it could not do it alone. The revolution had to be an international one, supported by the workers of the advanced capitalist countries. Lenin was convinced of the inevitability of socialism but knew it would not be achieved with equal ease everywhere, and even in Russia success still lay far ahead. By 1918 the white counter-revolution, supported by British, French, American and Japanese forces, had cost millions of revolutionaries their lives. The efforts that might have gone into reconstruction had been diverted, and the chance of spreading the revolution to the rest of Europe was receding. Decimated though the party was, it was still essential for it to keep the revolution going and to demonstrate to the people the reality of the new society. Ultimately this could only be done by political and economic means, but in the meantime the artists had a central part to play. Propaganda, communication and education became primary artistic concerns: Meyerhold organised mass festivals and Altman staged a vast re-enactment in Petrograd of the storming of the Winter Palace; Agit-Prop trains and steamers carried the revolutionary message to all parts of the union; Mayakovsky declaimed poetry to open-air audiences:

> Roses and dreams
> debased by poets
> will unfold
> in a new light
> for the delight of our eyes,
> the eyes of big children.
> We will invent new roses,
> roses of capitals with petals of squares.

The colours and techniques of Suprematism adapted readily to posters and broadsheets; the emphasis was on typography, not only for its graphic possibilities but also for its literal message. The cause of the dictatorship of the proletariat never found a better visual expression than in the abstract poster 'Beat the Whites with the Red Wedge' (1919) by the designer, sculptor and architect Eleazar (El) Lissitzky (1890–1941). The international ambitions of the revolution were reflected by the efforts of the artists to promote their work abroad, but the main task remained the raising of consciousness at home and the creation of a utopian vision of the society which revolution had not yet made possible. The most significant work of these early days was the steel tower proposed in 1920 by the sculptor Vladimir Tatlin (1885–1953) to celebrate the communist Third International. It was intended to be half as high again as the Eiffel tower and to contain within its vast spiral framework a conference centre, a radio station and all the paraphernalia of communication. Loudspeakers would address the crowds below, in cloudy weather the slogan of the day would be projected on to the sky, and sections of the vast apparatus would rotate in time with the hours and seasons. The scheme was impossibly heroic, conceived, as Brecht might have said of it, 'with a splendour that only a beggar can imagine'. These were days in which even political posters had to be fixed to walls with wooden pegs because there were no nails, and the flour for the glue was needed for bread. The tower was the conception of a sculptor rather than an engineer; though never built, it remained a powerful symbol of renaissance.

From 1918 to 1921 there was a period of 'war communism'; government was put into the hands of the Soviet central committee and its executive arm the Politburo, supported by the newly-formed Red Army and the Bolshevik-controlled police. Lenin recognised this strong centralisation as a diversion from his original purpose but necessary under the desperate circumstances. At the same time there was no artistic censorship; Lenin was tolerant of what he called 'the chaotic ferment, the feverish search for new solutions and new watchwords' which the circumstances had created. Artists' groups began to spring up to whom the ideology of revolution was central to creative life. In 1919 UNOVIS was founded in Vitebsk by Ermolaeva, with Malevich and Lissitzky. The same year Lissitzky began working on constructions which linked pictorial art with architecture. He called the idea PROUN, an acronym for 'for the new art', and when UNOVIS published its early work in Holland and Germany in 1920 it had a considerable influence on the ideas of De Stijl. As early as 1918 the Free State Art Studios had been founded in Moscow, becoming in 1920 the school for art and technical studies known as VKHUTEMAS; unique for its social commitment, universality and accessibility, it aimed to combine all the plastic arts – architecture, painting, sculpture, graphics and craftwork – in the service of the community and opened its lectures and seminars to anyone who cared to attend. Its members included a number of major architects: Alexander Vesnin, Ilya Golossov, Moisei Ginsburg, Nikolai Ladovsky, Konstantin Melnikov and Vladimir Semenov. The same year INKHUK was founded, an association of artists among whom were Kandinsky and Rodchenko, Varvara Stepanova, Liubov Popova and the theorist Ossip Brik. Between them VKHUTEMAS and INKHUK provided the two main streams of architectural thought of the revolutionary period.

In 1923, Ladovsky and Melnikov founded the Association of New Architects (ASNOVA), dedicated to 'Rationalism' – the use of new materials and techniques, the *rational* expression of structure and the analysis of architectural space. At the same time Vesnin became leader of a large band of 'Constructivists', concerned primarily with purity of expression – by which they meant freedom from representationalism – and with the *heightened* expression of structure, as an end in itself. They included the artists Gabo and Pevsner, as well as Rodchenko, Stepanova and Brik, and a number of VKHUTEMAS students including Mikhail Barsch and Andrei Burov. Mayakovsky and Brik and their newly-found LEF (Leftist Art Front) became associated with the movement, as did Meyerhold and Eisenstein, in whose theatrical productions and films the architecture of Constructivism was first seen. The first major constructivist building design was that of the Palace of the People (1922–3) by Alexander Vesnin and his brother Leonid, a large oval auditorium flanked by a tower, between which were hung radio-masts and aerials, essential features of the architecture of communication.

Europe was never closer to following Russia's revolutionary example than at the end

VKHUTEMAS

Lecturers at VKHUTEMAS

the Constructivist **Alexander Vesnin**

the Rationalist **Nikolai Ladovsky**

the Theorist and Historian **Moisei Ginsburg**

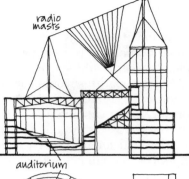

radio masts

auditorium

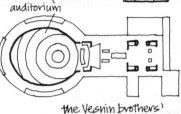

Alexander Rodchenko, head of the Basic Course, dressed in working gear designed by his wife Stepanovna

the Vesnin brothers' **Palace of the people** in Moscow (1922-3)

water tower exercise designed by Lamkov (1921) under the tutorship of Ladovsky

design by Kotchar for **bachelor flats** at VKHUTEMAS

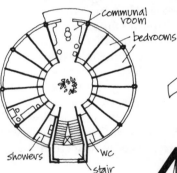

communal room

bedrooms

showers

wc

stair

tower for chemical manufacture (1922) by Gruschenko under the tutorship of Ladovsky

Study for a building for **Izvestia** by Leonidov (1926) under the tutorship of Alexander Vesnin

study for an **art school** (1927) designed by Helfeld under the tutorship of Dokuchaev

the Vesnin brothers' design for the **Pravda building** in Moscow (1923)

of the First World War: in Germany, disaffected soldiers and workers staged a revolution, the Kaiser was deposed and workers' soviets were set up in Berlin and Bavaria; Bela Kun's revolutionaries gained control in Budapest; even in Britain the police and the army were on the verge of strike and mutiny. The civil war in Russia helped to stop the spread of Bolshevism and all over Europe moderate socialists banded together with the right to crush the rebels. In Germany President Ebert's revisionist Weimar Republic (1919) offered moderate reforms and failed, in the event, to appease either the right or the left. The whole of Europe remained politically volatile, reflecting above all its uncertain economic state. A short, post-war burst of economic confidence collapsed in 1922, after which there was an apparent slow recovery – but with the problems of unemployment and depression never far below the surface.

The febrile atmosphere generated great artistic activity. This was further stimulated in March 1921 when the introduction of Lenin's New Economic Policy (NEP) marked the beginning of a short period in which links with the west were actively encouraged. For some time Paris had been the focus of a group of pre-revolution Russian *émigrés* – centred mainly on Diaghilev's ballet and including Stravinsky, Bakst and Soutine – but after 1921 the travels of the new Russian avant-garde made Germany the channel of constructivist ideas into the west. The revolution, though created by the urban workers, had been possible only through the support of the peasants, whose loyalty to the party it was essential to retain. By giving them a bigger stake in their own future Lenin hoped to obtain an immediate increase in food production to raise the country's desperately low standard of living. Trade and some forms of private ownership were restored, some factories de-nationalised and given to co-operatives, and efforts made to create a rapprochement with the west. As the western powers began to lift the economic blockade which had been their answer to the revolution, many Marxists accused Lenin of surrendering to capitalism. However, he was aware of the NEP's limitations and looked on it as a mere expedient, simultaneously making longer-term proposals for increased socialisation, national plans for heavy industry and electric power and for a communal agriculture based on co-operative ownership.

This was the basis on which Kandinsky, Gabo, Pevsner, Chagall, Malevich, Lissitzky and others came to the bourgeois west. The European avant-garde, in the aftermath of war and failed revolution, were enveloped in a neurasthenia of Expressionism which produced the poetry of Becher and Werfel, the plays of Kaiser and Toller and the novels of Kafka, and influenced contemporary architecture. This could be seen in Holland in the rich formalism of the co-operative housing estates built by the architects of the 'Amsterdaamse School', Michel de Klerk (1883–1923) and Piet Kramer (1881–1961), who continued Berlage's expressive brickwork tradition in the Eigenhaard housing at Zaanstraat (1913–21) and in the Henriette Ronnerplein apartments, Amsterdam (1921–22), and the apartments in Amsterdam-Zuid (1918–23), both for the housing association, *de Dageraad*. In Germany it could be seen in the curvilinear Expressionism of Erich Mendelsohn (1887–1953), designer of numerous projects for factories and aircraft hangars and of the symbolic Einsteinturm at Potsdam (1921), and of Ludwig Mies van de Rohe (1886–1969) who produced a number of 'designs for glass skyscrapers' (1919–21). Even Gropius had temporarily abandoned his earlier hesitant steps towards rationalism in favour of the jagged Expressionism of the monument in Weimar to the dead of the March Rising, begun in 1919.

The same year, Gropius had taken over from van de Velde as head of the school of arts and crafts in Weimar. He renamed it the 'Bauhaus', the *Bau* of the title indicating

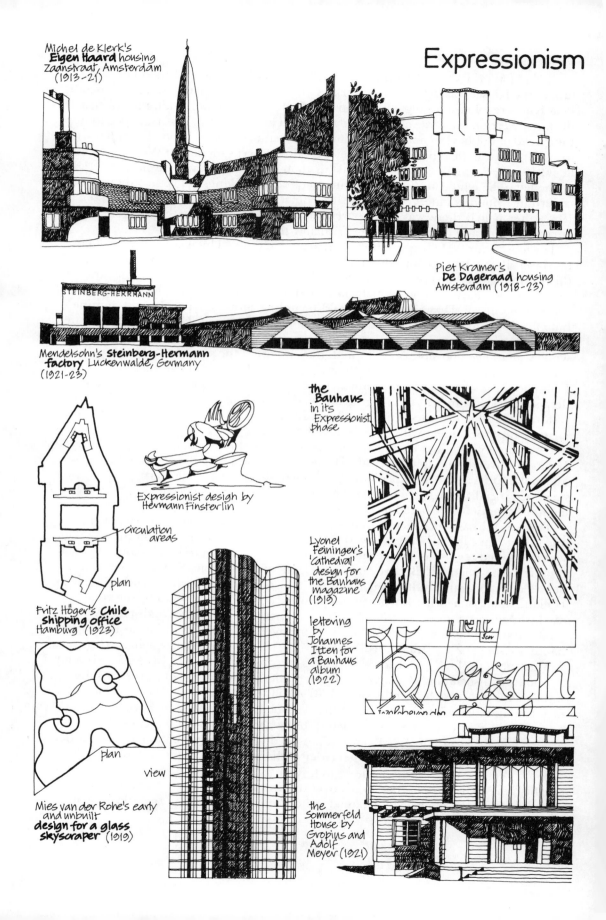

Michel de Klerk's **Eigen Haard** housing Zaanstraat, Amsterdam (1913-21)

Piet Kramer's **De Dageraad** housing Amsterdam (1918-23)

Mendelsohn's **Steinberg-Hermann factory** Luckenwalde, Germany (1921-23)

STEINBERG-HERRMANN

Expressionist design by Hermann Finsterlin

circulation areas

plan

Fritz Höger's **Chile shipping office** Hamburg (1923)

plan

view

Mies van der Rohe's early and unbuilt **design for a glass skyscraper** (1919)

the Bauhaus in its Expressionist phase

Lyonel Feininger's 'Cathedral' design for the Bauhaus magazine (1919)

lettering by Johannes Itten for a Bauhaus album (1922)

the Sommerfeld House by Gropius and Adolf Meyer (1921)

an aim to build not so much buildings as competent designers. From the start the curriculum was biased towards handicraft, in the tradition of Art Nouveau rather than the Werkbund. Largely through the influence of the head of the basic course, the mystically-inclined Johannes Itten, the attitude to design was quasi-religious. In keeping with Gropius' current mood it was also strongly expressionist – too much so for Theo van Doesburg, who was a somewhat critical guest lecturer.

But in 1922 two important artistic events helped to change the Bauhaus. One was an international conference of avant-garde artists held in Düsseldorf, at which van Does-burg and Lissitzky brought together their respective ideas on purity of form and honesty of construction to establish a new 'Constructivist international'. The other was the major exhibition of Soviet design arranged in Berlin by the Russian cultural minister Lunacharsky, which created an immediate general interest not only in Constructivism but also in the social aims which informed it. Gropius was prompted to revise his own views and to overhaul Bauhaus policy, restructuring the course to reject Expressionism and to emphasise rational design, with the slogan 'not cathedrals, but machines for living'. As in Russia, the aim was to form links between all the productive arts, though unlike VKHUTEMAS, the Bauhaus had no architectural course till 1927. Among a number of important appointments to the staff were Kandinsky and the Hungarian engineer László Moholy-Nagy, who replaced Itten. Moholy-Nagy, already an enthusiastic Constructivist, brought a rigorous approach to the basic course comparable with that exercised by Rodchenko at VKHUTEMAS. For the next few years there were close parallels in the development of Russian and German design; as Rodchenko, Stepanova, Tatlin and Popova turned from fine art to the design of furniture, heating equipment and clothing for large-scale production, Moholy-Nagy was laying the foundations at Weimar for a positive co-operation between the Bauhaus designers and German industry.

In a purely artistic sense, Constructivism was innovatory and influential: Eisenstein's montage revolutionised film-making; Meyerhold's theatre had its effects on both Piscator and Brecht; the graphic design of Rodchenko and Lissitzky, especially their use of typography and photography, was developed by a number of European designers, including Moholy-Nagy at the Bauhaus. German architects were jolted from an expressionist into a constructivist mode, notably Gropius and Meyer with their competiton entry for the *Chicago Tribune* office building (1922) and Mies van der Rohe with his 'Project for a reinforced-concrete office block' (1923) and 'Project for a brick country house' (1923).

The unequivocal attention given by the Russian Constructivists to structure as the starting-point for architectural expression became fundamental to the modern movement in architecture. Like the Futurists, the Constructivists celebrated technology, but whereas the former developed their ideas within the context of capitalism, seeking ways to intensify its technological effects, the Constructivists looked for an alternative role for technology, one in which its social value came before its commercial one. Their sense of social commitment contrasted with, say, the Werkbund designers' deliberate retreat from the political consequences of their work, or with the moralising aloofness of 'purifying' movements such as De Stijl. The Russians confronted western designers with the reality of art with a progressive social purpose, though this approach did not necessarily find general support. Van Doesburg for example, to whom the purely visual aspects of Constructivism were of course acceptable, argued against 'committed art' on the basis that art was above questions of class: 'The art we want is neither proletarian nor bourgeois, since the forces developed by it are strong enough to influence the whole of culture and not to be influenced by social conditions.' Moholy-Nagy said much the same thing, claiming for Constructivism itself a commonality which transcended the class struggle: 'Constructivism is neither proletarian nor capitalistic. Constructivism is primeval . . . fundamental, precise and universal.'

In Russia too there was some dissent from the idea of synonymity between modern art and progressive social policy. Some traditionalist designers, such as A. Schussev, tried to adapt to the new ways, but others such as I. Fomin and I. Zholtovsky held fast to neo-Classicism as the source of all that was excellent in architecture. Some dissenting modernists, notably the poet Viktor Shklovsky and the formalist school, attempted like van Doesburg to separate the artistic from the political message, concentrating on the former to the deliberate exclusion of the latter. But to the Bolshevik Constructivists the class-struggle was fundamental to the artistic process though, unlike the Futurists, their attitude was not a violent one. The only real, necessary act of violence was the revolution itself, after which the emphasis was on reconstruction and the creation of a dialogue with the working class. The extent to which the educated, generally middle-class intelligentsia of the constructivist movement identified with the workers and peasants and tried to share their lives was itself unique in European experience. It is, of course, possible to criticise, and to question the relevance of sophisticated modern art in a society of starving peasants and badly-housed factory workers. Yet the art was no more or less relevant than the revolution, which was itself totally outside normal past experience. The aim, both of the revolution and its art, was to *work towards* the creation of a new society and not, after centuries of alienation, to produce one ready-made. As Lenin said, 'now for the first time a non-bourgeois form of state has been discovered. Maybe our apparatus is pretty bad, but they say the first steam engine invented was bad too . . . the point is that now we have steam engines.' Thousands of bourgeois newspapers, Lenin declared, 'carry news about the horrors and poverty and sufferings which the workers endure in our country – still all over the world all workers are attracted to the Soviet state'.

Over the next few years, to most architects and commentators in the west, modern architecture became associated with socialism. Those opposed to modernism or marxism, or both, took the opportunity of using the one to discredit the other; but to those who saw socialism as a hope for the future, modern architecture became a way forward. The danger lay in imagining that one was a substitute for the other, that rebuilding cities could alone create a fairer society or that the necessity of social revolution could be avoided by producing a revolutionary architecture.

This was the attitude adopted by the French architect Charles-Edouard Jeanneret (1887–1965). As a purist painter Jeanneret had a close association with Ozenfant and together they had founded the journal *L'Esprit Nouveau* (1920) in which they set out in a succession of brilliant articles their philosophy of design. They synthesised a number of distinct ideas: a total rejection of past styles; their own post-cubist attitude to purity of form; the ancient Greeks' theories of harmonious proportion; an enthusiasm for the achievements of modern structural and mechanical engineers; a utopian sense of human progress. Jeanneret's contributions to *L'Esprit Nouveau* under the nom-de-plume of Le Corbusier were published in 1923 as a book, *Vers une Architecture*. It was a manifesto in support of modern architecture as the determinant of a new social order. Attributing the social unrest of the period to a contradiction between the great potential of modern technology and the fact that too few people benefited from it, Le

l'Esprit Nouveau

before Constructivism: the pre-Corbusian Jeanneret's **Villa Schwob** at Chaux-les-Fonds (1916)

Ozenfant and **Le Corbusier** at the Eiffel Tower in 1923

the 'Maison blanche' emerges: the early **Citrohan house** depicted at the Salon d'Automne (1922) and its first realisation, the **Ozenfant Studio** built in Paris the same year

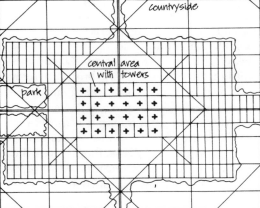

the 1922 Salon d'Automne also saw the emergence of Le Corbusier's ideas on urbanism, in the design for a **Ville contemporaine de 3 millions d'habitants**, a powerful vision of tower blocks and freeways

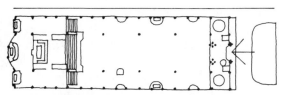

the engineering aesthetic, which captured the enthusiasm of the Esprit Nouveau designers: the plan of **Notre Dame du Raincy** (1922) by Le Corbusier's teacher, Perret; a section of Matté-Trucco's dynamic roof-top testing track at the **Fiat factory** in Turin (1920-23); and the vast **airship hangars** at Orly (1916-23) by Eugene Freyssinet

Corbusier tried to show how the introduction of new building forms would create new ways of living and how the standardisation and mass-production of high-quality dwellings would iron out social differences. This way, he said, 'revolution can be avoided'.

Le Corbusier's few pre-war designs for bourgeois houses had been interesting but derivative, reminiscent of Behrens in his neo-classical vein. But in the immediate post-war, post-revolutionary period, his new theories became clearer in a number of theoretical projects which demonstrated the great range of his thought; on the one hand, plans for cities of three million inhabitants; on the other, detailed designs for individual dwellings; above all an awareness of the relationship between the two scales of thought, of the small as a component of the large, and the large as the product of the small. In 1922 at the Salon d'Automne in Paris he exhibited plans for his 'Ville contemporaine'. With its high rise, high density centre, its sophisticated traffic network and its emphasis on space and greenery, it brought together the ideas of the garden city and the dynamic metropolis, owing something to Howard, to Garnier and to Sant'Elia yet more comprehensive in its vision than any of them.

At the same time, he was working on house designs which would use modern techniques to provide the basic requirements of 'sun, space and greenery' too often missing from contemporary city life. The design he called 'Maison Citrohan' comprised a simple cubist house with large areas of glazing, double-height living spaces and all the internal freedom of planning offered by a reinforced concrete construction. The house would be raised on concrete columns or *pilotis* which would allow the landscape to flow under the building. His first buildings in his new role as Le Corbusier were Ozenfant's studio in Paris (1922) and La Roche-Jeanneret house in Paris (1923), both of which demonstrated the constructional and spatial concepts of the Citrohan house and provided domestic architecture with a whole vocabulary of new ideas.

Le Corbusier recognised the great potential of reinforced concrete. He admired the work of his engineering contemporaries, especailly Perret with whom he worked for a time and whose concrete church of Notre Dame du Raincy (1922) demonstrated the great elegance of which the material was capable. In *Vers une Architecture* he quoted with approval the automobile and aircraft engineers for their direct approach to functional problems and cited the structural engineers as the only ones to have translated this into architecture, taking as examples Giacomo Matté-Trucco's roof-top testing track for Fiat of Turin (1920–23) and Freyssinet and Limousin's parabolic airship hangars at Orly (1916–23). Yet Le Corbusier was no Constructivist; as a sculptor and painter, he approached architecture from the standpoint of formalism and was never unduly affected by theories of absolute structural honesty. For him it was sufficient to create the appearance of modernity; if the right spaces and forms could be obtained equally well with traditional materials, such as bricks and blocks rendered over to resemble concrete, they were none the worse.

In Russia the Constructivists and Rationalists were the only artists to work for the revolution, creating the unusual situation of modern art in the service of the state. In the west the reverse was true; historicist designers continued to serve the state, and the avant-garde was looked on with suspicion, either because its abstract architecture was not stylistically explicit enough to create the associations required in civic building, or because it was thought to be Bolshevik, or both. But though they were still very much in the minority, modernism had its champions. In 1920 Lethaby might have been writing for *L'Esprit Nouveau* when he said: 'Our airplanes and motors and even bicycles are in their way perfect. We need to bring this ambition for perfect solutions into

the use of historicism

Lutyens' **Cenotaph**
war memorial
in London (1919-20)

Scott's **Liverpool Anglican cathedral**, the world's largest
gothic church, begun in 1903 and recently completed

Lutyens' monumental baroque **Britannic house**
in London (1920-26)

Mewès and Davis'
winter garden in the
Ritz Hotel, London
(1903-6)

though obviously inspired
by pre-Columbian
design, Wright's
Millard house in
Pasadena (1923) was
structurally innovatory–
Wright belongs in no
historicist category

the **Wrigley building** in Chicago
(1921-24) by Graham, Anderson,
Probst and
White

Hood and Howells' gothic-style
Chicago Tribune Tower (1925)
won in competition in 1922 against a
number of adventurous designs

housing of all sorts and scales. . . To be concerned with style imitations . . . is not only irrational in itself, but it blocks the way to any possibility of true development.' He was criticising the sub-baroque and simplified classical work still being carried out by commercial architects as though there had been no social change since Victorian times. It was seen in Mewès and Davis' numerous hotels in the style of Italian palazzi (1922–9), in Lutyens' equally numerous buildings for the Midland Bank (1922–9) and his massive office block Britannic House (1920–6), and in the many academically designed war memorials which, like Lutyens' Cenotaph in London (1919–20) and Blomfield's Menin Gate at Ypres (1923–6), were the official response to the Great War.

In Britain the gothic style was by now considered inappropriate for public buildings other than churches, among which the most obvious example was the gigantic Liverpool Cathedral (begun 1903) by Giles Gilbert Scott, grandson of the original gothic-revivalist. Perhaps the finest contemporary European building in the gothic tradition was Ragnar Östberg's Stockholm City Hall (1911–23), beautifully sited and simply designed in traditional materials, with brick external walls, copper roofs and interiors rich in mosaic. In America, Gothic continued in use for embellishing skyscraper offices. The Wrigley building in Chicago (1921–4) by Graham, Anderson, Probst and White used baroque ornament, but the entry for the *Chicago Tribune* competition chosen in preference to those of Loos, Gropius and Meyer was a gothic design by Hood and Howells. Le Corbusier preferred the simple grandeur of the Chicago grain elevators. 'Let us listen to the counsels of American engineers. But let us beware of American architects.'

His strictures would possibly have included even Wright, who was still going through his 'baroque' period; his rich decoration, though highly integrated into the structure of his buildings, was certainly not consonant with Purism. In 1922 Wright built the monumental Imperial Hotel in Tokyo and the following year the beautiful and decorative Millard houses in Pasadena, CA. More to Le Corbusier's taste would have been the architect-engineer Albert Kahn's glass plant building (1922) for the Ford motor company at Dearborn, MI, a magnificently functional steel-framed and glass-clad fabrication shop of great size and simplicity.

In America, industry was less depressed than in Europe and unemployment generally lower – an average of 3.9% between 1923 and 1929, in contrast to 11% in Britain over the same period. As a result, unionisation made some ground. In response to the spread of mass-production there was a general shift from a union system dominated by Samuel Gompers' AFL, with its predominance of craftsmen and building workers, organised on a craft basis, to a system based on the workplace organisation in the manufacturing industries. One of the key figures was William Foster, an ex-'Wobbly" who organised Chicago and led strikes in the stockyards (1917) and the steel industry (1919). In the years following the Russian revolution, anti-union activity became more intense; private armies were hired to break strikes and ring-leaders were victimised. Even the moderate AFL was branded 'Bolshevik'.

Industrial productivity continued to expand and the motor industry in particular underwent a period of uniquely rapid growth. The motor vehicle began to affect the environment, most immediately by encouraging the further growth of suburbia. In Victorian times suburban development clustered around the railway stations; interwar suburbia assumed the low-density, dispersed pattern made possible by the increased accessibility brought by the motor car. Just as Ford's aim was to increase the

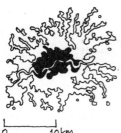

suburban growth—
London in 1860 – and its growth by the year 1920, along the suburban railway lines and arterial roads

0   10km

typical suburban development
in inter-war Britain

close-knit housing within walking distance of suburban station

typical of earlier suburban development designed for rail access

typical of later suburban development, designed for motor access

housing widely spaced, with provision for parking

London 'Underground' poster c 1912

UNDERGROUND

BY DISTRICT RAILWAY.

RIGHT INTO THE HEART OF THE COUNTRY.

BOOK TO HARROW, SUDBURY OR PERIVALE

private garden

street

private garden

typical suburban housing layout—
each house with a 'public' side and a 'private' side

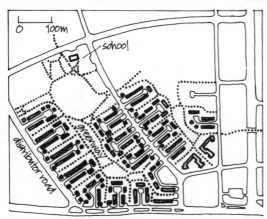

0   100m

school

distributor road

greenway

Radburn New Jersey
Stein and Wright (begun 1929)

Radburn cul-de-sac – each house was approached from two directions

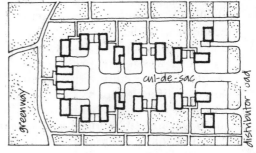

greenway

cul-de-sac

distributor road

vehicle cul-de-sac

pedestrian greenway

vehicle cul-de-sac

typical Radburn housing layout—
vehicles and pedestrians kept separate

suburbia and Radburn

market by widening the social range of car-owners, so realtors sought to extend house-ownerhsip to a wide cross-section of society. The developer Abraham Levitt began in a small way during the inter-war period, building middle-class housing on Long Island, but as the market developed and mass-production of cheaper buildings became possible, his suburban estates grew in size and social range.

Even the best estates tended to be under-provided with community buildings and open spaces which, though socially valuable, were unprofitable for the developer. But worse than the planned estate was the unplanned 'ribbon development' which began to straggle along main arterial highways, cluttering them with local traffic and creating polluted, noisy or unsafe living and working conditions. Answers to both these problems were put forward during the 1920s by Clarence Stein and Henry Wright in their design for the new town of Radburn, NJ, for the City Housing Corporation of New York. They based it on the Perry neighbourhood principle, proposing a grid of main roads at intervals of 300 metres or so with self-contained residential areas between them. Through traffic would be kept to the main roads; local traffic would enter each area by means of a cul-de-sac penetrating only a short distance from each edge, leaving the centre free of traffic, to be devoted to landscape, play spaces and the pedestrian routes which led under the main roads and linked one area with another. No house faced a main road and any part of the town could be reached on foot without walking on a road or even seeing a car. Only a small part of Radburn was built but the principle it established was the starting-point for all subsequent thinking about cars in residential areas.

The suburban syndrome illustrates capitalism at work. Capitalism created the automobile, which it sold to the public as a new amenity providing accessibility. This factor in turn created suburbia and its problems, and led the Radburn designers to try to overcome them. It also affected old city centres which were incapable of taking volumes of traffic without extensive reconstruction. Either way, the motor car demanded considerable capital investment in buildings and land, creating a physical environment in which the motor vehicle was, in its turn, indispensable for survival. It became equally indispensable, in a wider sense, in western economy, which began to depend on keeping the production-lines in operation and the fuel-oil flowing. Capitalism had a self-perpetuating effect, which demanded continuous growth. Only the most radical measures could break the vicious circle.

In 1923 Lenin published his short essay 'On Co-operation' which in effect set out the three tasks for the future of socialism. The first was to guard against bureaucratisation, which at best could create a system *on behalf of* the people but never *by* the people. The second was the development of peasant co-operatives and workers' control of industry, to ensure the peoples' control of their own lives – which alone could lead to socialism. The third was to create the social basis on which co-operative working would be founded: a true cultural revolution. Among many disturbing signs that these tasks would be difficult to carry out was the increasing power of Stalin, whom Lenin saw as a danger to democracy and vainly tried to remove. When Lenin died early in 1924, Stalin was free to build up his personal power. For a few years, the NEP remained in force and continued to provide the parameters for the task of reconstruction.

In 1925 a number of constructivist architects, together with LEF, formed another association, OSA (Union of Contemporary Architects) in Moscow and Leningrad. Alexander Vesnin became chairman and among the members were his brothers Leonid and Viktor, as well as Barsch, Burov, Melnikov, Ilya Golossov and the brilliant young

Constructivism

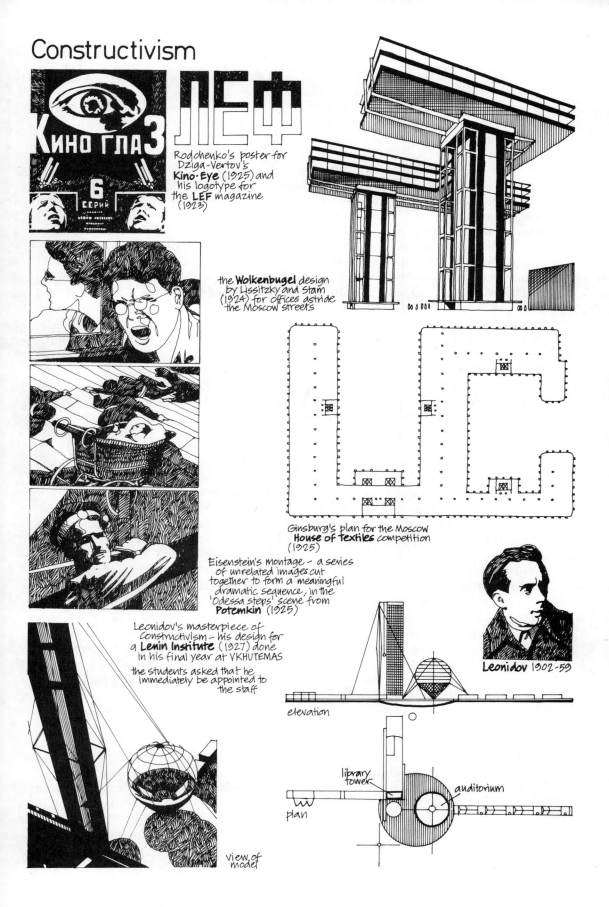

КИНО ГЛА3
ЛЕФ

Rodchenko's poster for
Dziga-Vertov's
Kino-Eye (1925) and
his logotype for
the **LEF** magazine
(1923)

the **Wolkenbugel** design
by Lissitzky and Stam
(1924) for offices astride
the Moscow streets

Ginsburg's plan for the Moscow
House of Textiles competition
(1925)

Eisenstein's montage – a series
of unrelated images cut
together to form a meaningful
dramatic sequence, in the
'Odessa steps' scene from
Potemkin (1925)

Leonidov's masterpiece of
Constructivism – his design for
a **Lenin Institute** (1927) done
in his final year at VKHUTEMAS

the students asked that he
immediately be appointed to
the staff

Leonidov 1902-59

elevation

library
tower

auditorium

plan

view of
model

Ivan Ilich Leonidov (1902–1959). Ginsburg became editor of the group's magazine *Contemporary Architecture* and Le Corbusier contributed to it. OSA successfully spread the ideas of Constructivism both at home and in Europe and made a particular impact through the publication of its members' designs for a number of major architectural competitions in Moscow: the Vesnins, Melnikov and Golossov for the Pravda building (1924); the Vesnins and Melnikov for the Arcos store (1924); Ginsburg and Golossov for the House of Textiles (1925); the Vesnins for the State Telegraph building (1925). Lissitzky continued to forge links with European architects, particularly through his collaboration with the Dutch rationalist Mart Stam in 1924 in the 'Wolkenbugel' design project for vast horizontal skyscrapers to be cantilevered across city streets. The work of Rodchenko at VKHUTEMAS and Breuer at the Bauhaus began to run in parallel: in 1925 both designed the earliest examples of plated tubular-steel-framed furniture. The work of the Russian film-makers made a big impact on the west, particularly their development of documentary techniques. The book *Ten Days that Shook the World*, a vivid account of the October revolution by the American communist John Reed, had created an interest in the techniques of reportage in all the media; in the cinema it found expression in Dziga-Vertov's concept of 'Kino-Eye' and his film *The Man with the Movie Camera* (1929), while Eisenstein's use of real locations, amateur actors and documentary-style cutting in feature films such as *Potemkin* (1925) was in sharp contrast to the artificiality of contemporary films in Berlin and Hollywood.

To the Russian left it was clear that a vast programme of reconstruction lay ahead. Through the especial influence of Ginsburg, OSA became critical of architects who continued to pursue *outré* arguments over the relative merits of 'Rationalism' or 'Constructivism' as separate philosophies, and of the more peripheral designers who began to treat modernism as a 'style' to be followed. The seriousness of the task called for a rigorous approach. Modern architecture, said Ginsburg, should disclaim all pretensions to 'style'; it was a question of *functionalism*: of rational planning, modern constructional techniques, the standardisation and prefabrication of parts and the industrialisation of the building process. Ivan Leonidov's vision of technology's capabilities was the most exciting, at the time, of any architect in the world. His design for a Lenin Institute in Moscow (1927), prepared during his final year at VKHUTEMAS, was the archetypal constructivist building: it consisted principally of a vast spherical auditorium adjoined by a slender library tower and flanked by ancillary buildings. The geometric purity of the idea, the subtlety of arrangement of the various elements on the site, and the structural conception, based essentially on the use of steel tension cables, put the design well in advance of any of its time and created the sharpest possible contrast with academic architectural thought.

The first major constructivist building actually built was, paradoxically, in the west: Melnikov's Soviet Pavilion at the Paris Exposition des Arts Décoratifs of 1925. It was of simple geometric design, making use of flat walls and large areas of glazing. With Le Corbusier's Pavillon de l'Esprit Nouveau – an even simpler, cubist building based on the Citrohan house – it shared the distinction of being the only example of Rationalism. Most of the other pavilions and their exhibits were designed in the modernistic vogue style of the 1920s to which the exhibition gave its name: 'Art Deco'. At the top of the economic scale Deco was the style of the fashionable couturiers and film producers, of modern luxury hotels and the salons of the liner *Normandie*. At a more popular level it affected the design of everything that called for an up-to-the-minute image, from super-cinemas and new suburban houses to jewellery, clocks and radio sets. In

the Paris Exposition 1925

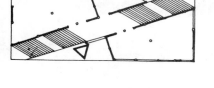

Melnikov's Constructivist **Soviet pavilion –** axonometric view and upper floor plan

Le Corbusier's Purist **Pavillon de l'Esprit Nouveau –** in effect an experiment in housing design

With one or two other exceptions, like the pavilions designed by Stael and Behrens, the rest of the 1925 Exposition was devoted to **Arts Decoratifs** or Art Deco

typical Art Deco artefacts of the period – a **Pye radio** with a fret-cut sunburst design, and a **Meyrowitz clock** in an ancient Egyptian style, post-dating the discovery of the tomb of Tutankhamun (1923)

Art Deco soon became a vogue style for modern buildings –

luxurious drawing-room by the designer Ruhlmann displayed at the Exposition

the archetypal Art Deco building – the **Chrysler building** in New York (1929) by William van Alen

the super-cinema – the Art Deco **Odeon** Leicester Square, London, by Mather and Weedon

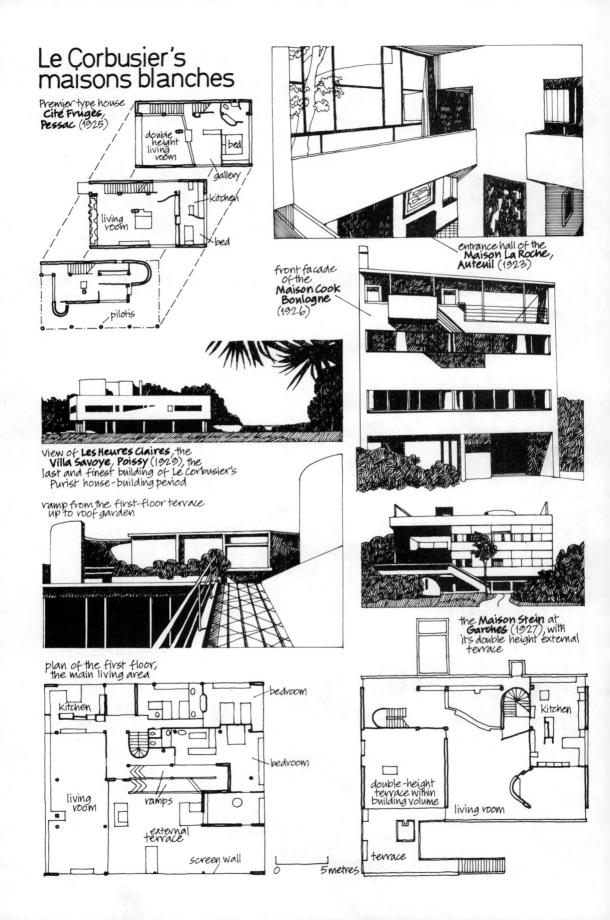

Le Corbusier's maisons blanches

Premier type house **Cité Fruges, Pessac** (1925)

double height living room

bed

gallery

kitchen

living room

bed

pilotis

entrance hall of the **Maison La Roche, Auteuil** (1923)

front facade of the **Maison Cook Boulogne** (1926)

View of **Les Heures Claires**, the **Villa Savoye, Poissy** (1929), the last and finest building of Le Corbusier's Purist house-building period

ramp from the first-floor terrace up to roof garden

the **Maison Stein** at **Garches** (1927), with its double height external terrace

plan of the first floor, the main living area

kitchen

bedroom

bedroom

living room

ramps

external terrace

screen wall

0   5 metres

double-height terrace within building volume

kitchen

living room

terrace

De Stijl

two views of the **workers' housing** at Hoek van Holland (1924-27) by Jacobus Oud – rational and humane

the beautifully ordered **Schroeder house** at Utrecht (1923-24) by Rietveld

the **garage and chauffeur's flat**, Utrecht (1927-28) by Rietveld

Mondriaan in the studio

the Co-operative store **De Volharding** in the Hague (1928) by Buys

Oud's **Café de Unie** in Rotterdam (1924-25)

furniture, the quality of workmanship was often very high, involving the use of exotic woods like satin- and sandal-wood for their smooth finish and beautiful grain. The diverse stylistic origins included the vibrant colour and pattern of Bakst's designs for the Russian ballet, Egyptian motifs popularised by the opening of Tutankhamun's tomb in 1923 and Aztec symbols inspired by the publication in 1926 of Lawrence's *The Plumed Serpent*.

Though a prize was awarded to the Pavillon de l'Esprit Nouveau by an international jury it was later withdrawn at the jealous insistence of the French exhibition authorities. As the pavilion was intended by Le Corbusier to strike a blow at *arts décoratifs*, he himself was partly to blame for this reaction; but modern architecture in general was meeting with increasing opposition, much of it from industrialists with financial interests in traditional building materials or techniques. The stylistic resemblance of Le Corbusier's pavilion to Melnikov's, and their dissimilarity to the other exhibits, enabled the critics to make free with their accusations of Bolshevism – though in Le Corbusier's case it was scarcely merited. Yet his work continued to attract strong criticism throughout the 1920s. With his cousin Pierre Jeanneret he built a small housing scheme for workers and their families at Pessac near Bordeaux (1925) which met with much local opposition, as did his three splendid *chefs-d'œuvres* of the 1920s, the Maison Cook at Boulogne (1926), the Maison Stein at Garches (1927) and the Villa Savoye at Poissy (1929), elegant houses in which Le Corbusier indulged his bourgeois clients with all the spatial luxury that modern architecture could offer – only to be accused of undermining traditional values.

In Holland the Amsterdaamse School continued its work throughout the 1920s, but the small group of Rationalists associated with De Stijl in Rotterdam was gaining international significance. Its most important work, which seemed to summarise all the formal possibilities of modern architecture, was a little house built by Rietveld in a suburb of Utrecht. The Schroeder house (1923–4) was like the projection of a Mondriaan painting into three dimensions. Its walls, floors, partitions, screens, windows were treated as simple planes, some opaque in neo-plasticist colours, some transparent, all overlapping or interlocking at right angles, creating internal spaces which interpenetrated with each other or extended by means of canopies and balconies into the street outside. The façade of Oud's Café de Unie in Rotterdam (1924–5) was also influenced by abstract painting, but his workers' housing at Hoek van Holland (1924–7) was conceived in terms of function as well as abstract form.

By the mid-1920s rationalism had made its way to Britain in Behrens' simple cubist house New Ways, in Northampton, for the industrialist Basset-Lowke. It was built in 1926, a crucial year in British economic life in which the establishment tried to solve the financial crisis by depressing the workers' standard of living. The workforce responded with the first general strike in British history. The British economy crashed and production fell. The British government's policy of cutting wages and public spending, merely betrayed a total lack of comprehension of the depth of crisis that western capitalism as a whole was undergoing. Elsewhere in Europe there were other solutions. In Italy, the ideology of Fascism, promulgated by Rocco and Gentile, was taken up by Mussolini, who seized power in 1922. It asserted the absolute supremacy of the state in law and in morality, and identified the will of the state with that of its leader. The state, it was said, must be centrally organised to achieve both social stability and national discipline. Major public works suddenly became essential, both to create employment and to express the ideology of the state. Mussolini's own preferences lay towards the

Fascism in Italy

We wish to glorify War—the only health-giver in the world—militarism, patriotism...beautiful ideas that can kill...

Marinetti and a statement from his **Foundation Manifesto of Futurism** published in 1909

design for Sant'Elia's **Città Nuova** (1914) which expressed the dynamic yet totalitarian character of Futurism

Terragni's beautiful **Casa del Fascio** in Como (1932-36)

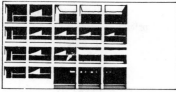

Mussolini

Terragni's **Monument to the Fallen** in Como (completed c.1930) was clearly influenced by Sant'Elia's designs

Terragni's first major work, the **Novocomum** apartments in Como (1928)

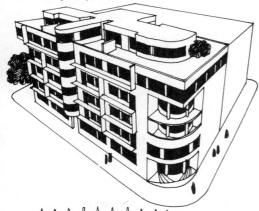

Mussolini's **EUR** (Esposizione Universale di Roma) was to have been held in 1942 to display Fascist achievements to the world and to form a permanent basis for the expansion of Rome towards Ostia and the sea— the plan was prepared by Rossi, Piacentini, Vietti and Pagano— only a section was built

Mussolini's official academicism in Piacentini's hotel, the **Albergo degl'Ambasciatori** in Rome

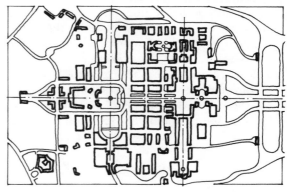

neo-classical and monumental. His schemes for carving processional ways through Rome or building sports stadia to celebrate the health and fitness of Fascist youth received a ready response from traditional architects, notably Piacentini and Del Debbio in Rome and the group in Milan known as '900'.

However, since Matté-Trucco's Fiat works had introduced rationalism to Italy, there was an alternative approach. Gruppo Sette, an association of rationalist architects centred on Milan and Como – of whom the most significant were Luigi Figini (b. 1903), Gino Pollini (b. 1903) and Giuseppe Terragni (1904–42) – was founded in 1926. The group adhered to the idea of the Italian Novecento, a movement intended to combine the rich plasticity of the baroque tradition with 20th-century techniques. In their founding manifesto they attacked Futurism for its 'vain, destructive fury', proposing instead an architecture of 'lucidity and wisdom' whereby 'tradition transforms itself and takes on new aspects, beneath which only a few can recognise it'. Their inspiration came from sources as diverse as Soviet Constructivism and *Vers une Architecture*, but their personal ideals were more in line with Fascism. Amid the arguments and intrigues surrounding the selection of official architects and the official adoption of particular styles for propaganda purposes, Gruppo Sette succeeded in obtaining several government commissions. Terragni's first building was his Novocomum flats at Como (1928), a rich composition of cube and cylinder, solid and void, with a distinct resemblance to Golossov's Workers' Club in Moscow, built the year before.

In Germany too, the strength of Fascism was growing. The abortive Bierkeller Putsch of 1923 was merely a foretaste of Nazi methods. Their ideology was developed in 1925 with the publication of the first volume of *Mein Kampf*, a curious mixture of racial nonsense and political insight. The stated intention was to create a regime based on the superiority of the 'Aryan' race and its finest exemplar, the German people; the method was to assert the supremacy of this master race through the power of its *Führer* by providing it with the *Lebensraum* in which it could develop and an empire which it could dominate. Christians, communists, Russians, Slavs and most particularly Jews stood in the way of this plan and must be removed. The same year, a significant step was taken towards the success of Nazism when Ebert's term as president ended and he was replaced by the conservative Hindenburg, who revived memories of *Junker* Prussia, moved politics to the right and helped to create the conditions under which Hitler could assume power constitutionally. Fear of Bolshevism, encouraged by the right, was so strong that the bourgeoisie were driven towards Hitler, deliberately refusing to recognise what quite plainly he was offering them. As politics polarised between communism and Nazism, it became difficult to occupy middle ground. Left-wing protest art developed a new cutting-edge with the satirical drawings of Georg Grosz, the mordant photo-montages of John Heartfield and a succession of Brecht/Weill masterpieces such as *Kleine Mahagonny* (1927), *Dreigroschenoper* (1928) and *Berliner Requiem* (1928). In opposition to all this, the theories of racially pure art, the glorification on the one hand of the heroic and monumental and on the other of *Kitsch* and folk art, were advanced by the Nazis' main aesthetic theoretician Paul Schultz-Naumberg and by their propaganda newspaper *Volkischer Beobachter*.

The intentions of the Weimar republic, of its main supporter the moderate SPD – and of the rationalist architects of the Bauhaus – lay somewhere between these extremes. They made every effort to achieve the social-progress-without-revolution which seemed so desirable. Government-sponsored housing schemes in Berlin, in Celle – and notably in Frankfurt under the direction of the city architect Ernst May (1886–1970) – attempted to solve manifest social problems by providing rational living conditions for the working class. The setting-up of CIAM (*Congrès Internationaux d'Architecture Moderne*) and its early meetings at La Sarraz, Switzerland (1928), and Frankfurt (1929) were attempts to assert the internationalism of architecture, its transcendence of narrow political attitudes and its concern for social progress. The Werkbund exhibition of 1927, organised by Mies van der Rohe at the Weissenhof in Stuttgart, was a serious attempt to present the public with the reality of modern architecture; in a small park were gathered a number of housing units specially designed by an extraordinary array of architectural talent, including Behrens, Poelzig, Max and Bruno Taut, Oud, Stam, Mies van der Rohe, Gropius and Le Corbusier. In spite of the recent attitudes of many of these, there was no Expressionism to be seen; there seemed no doubt that social progress was synonymous with rationalism. Even Mendelsohn got as near as he ever did to rationalism in his designs for department stores for the Schocken company at Stuttgart (1927) and Chemnitz (1928), in which simplicity of form was combined with richness of detail. The doctrine of *Neue Sachlichkeit*, the new objectivity, though originally coined in relation to the documentary film of the period, seemed to typify its architecture too.

In 1924 the Weimar Bauhaus attracted unwelcome attention from the conservative city and provincial authorities, chiefly because of the unacceptable communistic associations of its work, and at the end of the year it was forced to close. A number of more progressive city councils made approaches to Gropius and the decision was taken to move to Dessau, where he had the unique opportunity of creating a new building to express the Bauhaus philosophy. The Dessau Bauhaus (1925–6) was one of the crucial buildings of the modern movement. Gropius sited the three blocks – workshops, school of design and students' hostel – in a studied yet informal relationship, planning the various spaces in a logical sequence, handling the elevations with their areas of glass and concrete in a way which suited the function of the rooms behind them. Gropius' ideas had developed greatly since his early attempts at rationalism at Alfeld and Cologne; to say that almost everything about the building indicated the influence of Constructivism is not to deny the achievement of actually building the first major example of modern rationalist architecture, east or west. The Bauhaus curriculum was also rebuilt. Itten's foundation course was taken over by Moholy-Nagy and Josef Albers, who moved the emphasis away from hand-craftsmanship to machine production. A number of former students, among them the typographer Herbert Bayer and the furniture designer Marcel Breuer, stayed on to teach, contributing to the development of a distinct, ingrown Bauhaus style, which became the subject of some internal dissent when in 1927 Gropius appointed the Swiss architect Hannes Meyer (1889–1954) as head of a new architectural course. As a communist, Meyer had a scientific approach to problem-solving. He found the Bauhaus unscientific, unduly formalistic, too introverted and consequently lacking in social relevance. Indeed, it was to strengthen the scientific side of the school's work that Gropius had appointed him in the first place.

In the wake of the Bauhaus, rationalism gained ground. Johannes Duiker (1890–1935) emerged as a modern architect of some importance with his Zonnestraal sanatorium in Hilversum (1926–8), while the Constructivism of De Stijl was developed by Rietveld with his garage and flat in Utrecht (1927–8) and by A. W. E. Buys with his De Volharding co-operative store at The Hague (1927–8). Shops offered a special opportunity to use modern glass in an imaginative way, as in Mendelsohn's stores and also those of Lyd Kysela in Prague, the Bata store (1928) and the Commerce House (1928).

187

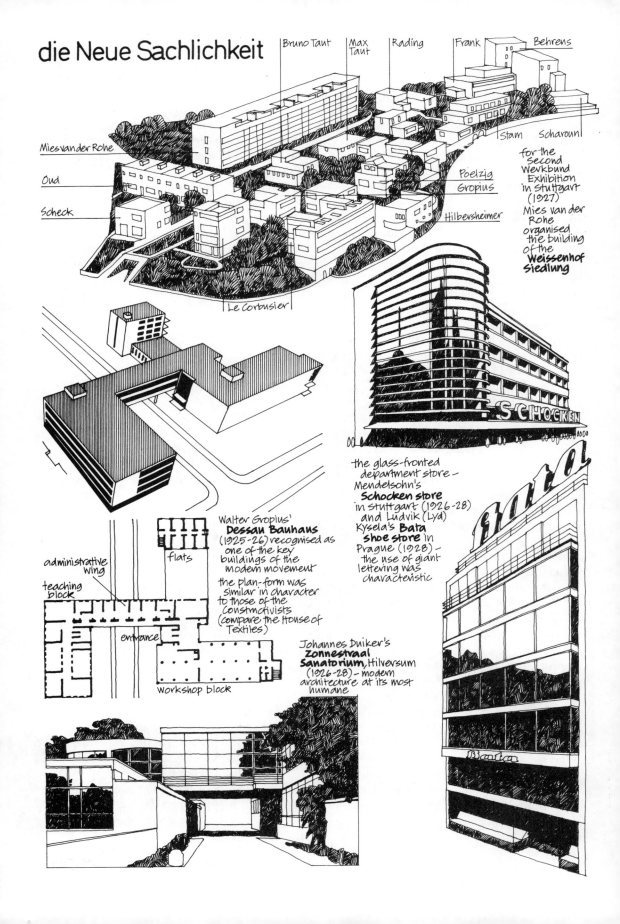

die Neue Sachlichkeit

Bruno Taut

Max Taut

Rading

Frank

Behrens

Stam   Scharoun

Mies van der Rohe

Oud

Scheck

Poelzig
Gropius

Hilbersheimer

Le Corbusier

for the
Second
Werkbund
Exhibition
in Stuttgart
(1927)
Mies van der
Rohe
organised
the building
of the
**Weissenhof
Siedlung**

SCHOCKEN

the glass-fronted
department store –
Mendelsohn's
Schocken store
in Stuttgart (1926-28)
and Ludvik (Lyd)
Kysela's **Bata
shoe store** in
Prague (1928) –
the use of giant
lettering was
characteristic

Walter Gropius'
Dessau Bauhaus
(1925-26) recognised as
one of the key
buildings of the
modern movement

the plan-form was
similar in character
to those of the
Constructivists
(compare the House of
Textiles)

flats

administrative
wing

teaching
block

entrance

workshop block

Johannes Duiker's
**Zonnestraal
Sanatorium**, Hilversum
(1926-28) – modern
architecture at its most
humane

Bata

VKHUTEMAS and the Bauhaus

0   500km

Moscow

May
Meyer
Stam
Taut
(1930-33)

Lissitsky
Chagall
Kandinsky
Gabo
(1920-23)

Amsterdam
Berlin
Dessau
Weimar
Dresden
Paris
Frankfurt
Stuttgart
Vienna

Russian/German links
during the 1920s and 30s

design for propaganda
political kiosk by Alexis Gan (1923) and advertising kiosk for toothpaste by Herbert Bayer (1924)

chinaware for mass production
Lindig's Bauhaus coffee service (1922-25) and Malevich's cups, designed for production in the Lomonosov factory (1923)

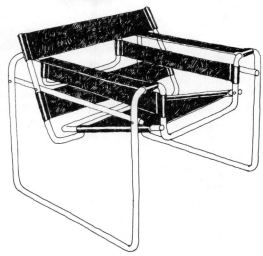

leather and tubular steel chairs
chair designed under the direction of Rodchenko and Breuer's 'Wassily' chair (1925)

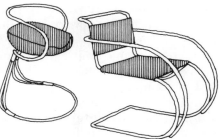

cantilever chairs
prototype cantilever chair designed by Tatlin (1927) and the 'MR' cantilever chair designed by Mies van der Rohe (1926)

МОСКВА 1927

АРХИТЕКТУРА
АРХИТЕКТУРА
ВХУТЕМАС

the art of typography
Lissitzky's cover for the VKHUTEMAS annual (1927) and Herbert Bayer's 'Universal' type (1925)

abcdefghi
jklmnopqr
stuvwxyz

When after Lenin's death Trotsky and Stalin contested the leadership, the struggle lay between, on the one hand, increased local democracy and the 'permanent revolution' of international socialism and, on the other, the increased bureaucracy and centralisation of 'socialism in one country'. Trotsky's banishment in 1929 signified the end of revolutionary Russia and the end of socialism in all but name. Stalin ended the NEP by introducing the First Five-year Plan (1928–32), a programme of large-scale development aimed at exploiting the country's resources, opening up backward areas and co-ordinating its various industries. At the basis of this were to be the *kolkozhoi* or collective farms – owned by the state and run on terms fixed by the state. The system required the dispossession of the peasants and the extermination of the kulaks as a class. It was also necessary to purge the party of the 'old Bolsheviks'; revolutionaries who still held to the ideas of Marx and Lenin, and to replace them with professional bureaucrats who would owe allegiance to Stalin and give him complete control.

OSA proposed a merger of all architectural societies, to unite them in a common task, but dissent over aims and methods prevented unity. These problems increased in 1929 with the formation of VOPRA (the All-Russian Union of Proletarian Architects) which attacked the Constructivists for being too left-wing, too concerned with technology and experiment and not 'proletarian' enough. During the period of the Five-year Plan, experimental architecture continued, but its time was running out. Leonidov continued his brilliant but unexecuted designs with an entry for the competition for the Moscow Centrosoyus (Co-operative) – actually won by Le Corbusier, whose elegant, constructivist design was executed by a Moscow architect. It took from 1929 to 1934 to build, owing, as Le Corbusier drily remarked, to 'a scarcity of materials provoked by the realisation of the Five-year Plan'. Melnikov built the Russakov Club (1928–9) and his own house (1929), both in Moscow. Barsch and Sinavsky built a Planetarium (1929) and Barkhin's *Izvestia* building of 1927 was followed by Ilya Golossov's fine building for *Pravda* (1930–4). Then in 1930 VKHUTEMAS was closed down. The same year, the cult of personality, which Lenin had guarded against, was bestowed by Stalin on Lenin himself by the building of a mausoleum in Red Square. Schussev produced a heavy, monumental, vaguely neo-classical design, an indication of the kind of architecture to come.

The development programme suddenly made it necessary for architects to think on the largest possible scale, to build not only mines, factories, processing-plants and power stations, but also whole new communities in the wilderness. As before, the combination of an urgent task and the opportunity for experiment produced vital results; urban theory developed with a speed and confidence unprecedented in the west. At a time when Europe and the USA were confused and directionless and the concept of economic targets was almost unknown in the west, the planned economy of the Soviet Union provided both the opportunity and the need to evolve an approach to physical planning.

Russian urban planning had a number of distinctive features. The first of these was the importance given to growth and change, a concept which had emerged in the west but had never yet been a significant feature of planning practice – least of all during the depression years. In 1912 the engineer and planner Vladimir Semenov (1874–1960) had published *The Welfare Planning of Towns* which examined this idea in relation both to new cities and to existing ones. It attracted little attention till after the revolution, when it was built into the general body of Soviet planning theory as subsequently developed by Nikolai Miliutin (1889–1942), friend and collaborator of Gins-

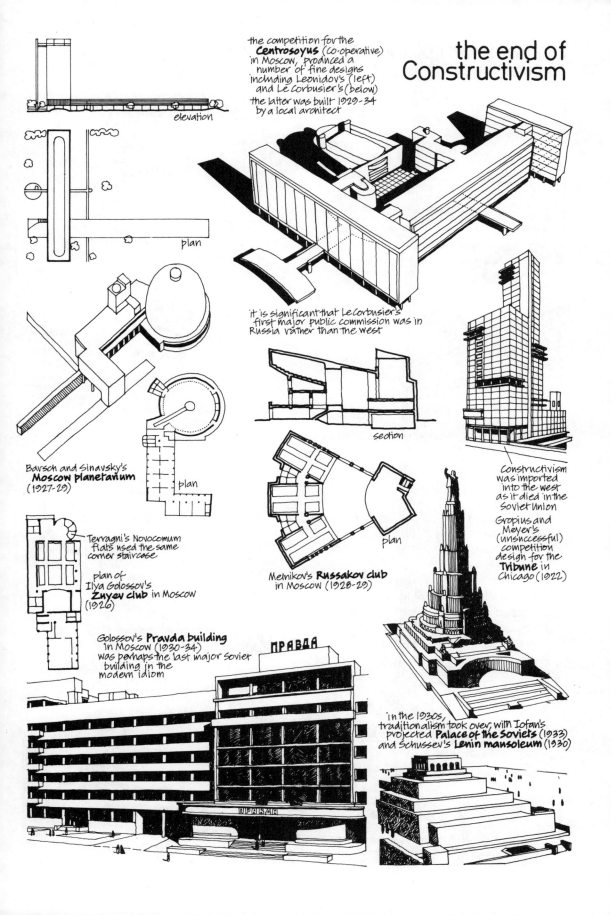

elevation

plan

the end of Constructivism

it is significant that Le Corbusier's first major public commission was in Russia rather than the west

section

plan

Barsch and Sinavsky's **Moscow planetarium** (1927-29)

plan

Terragni's Novocomum flats used the same corner staircase

plan of Ilya Golossov's **Zuyev club** in Moscow (1926)

Melnikov's **Russakov club** in Moscow (1928-29)

Constructivism was imported into the west as it died in the Soviet Union

Gropius and Meyer's (unsuccessful) competition design for the **Tribune** in Chicago (1922)

Golossov's **Pravda building** in Moscow (1930-34) was perhaps the last major Soviet building in the modern idiom

ПРАВДА

in the 1930s, traditionalism took over, with Iofan's projected **Palace of the Soviets** (1933) and Schussev's **Lenin mausoleum** (1930)

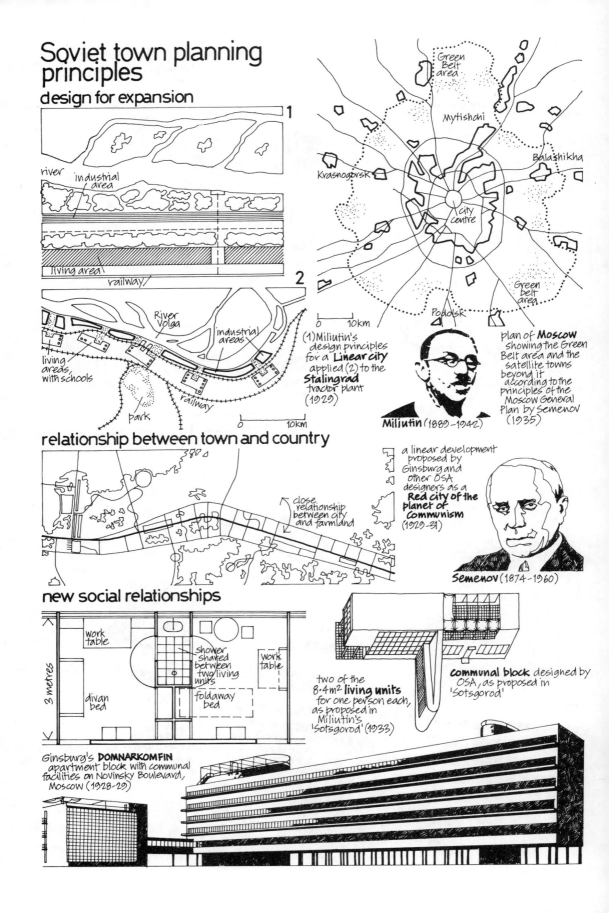

Soviet town planning principles

design for expansion

1

river
industrial area
living area
railway

2

River Volga
industrial areas
living areas, with schools
railway
park

0   10km

(1) Miliutin's design principles for a **Linear city** applied (2) to the **Stalingrad** tractor plant (1929)

Green Belt area
Mytishchi
Balashikha
Krasnogorsk
city centre
Green belt area
Podolsk

0   10km

plan of **Moscow** showing the Green Belt area and the satellite towns beyond it according to the principles of the Moscow General Plan by Semenov (1935)

Miliutin (1889–1942)

relationship between town and country

close relationship between city and farmland

a linear development proposed by Ginsburg and other OSA designers as a **Red city of the planet of Communism** (1929–31)

Semenov (1874–1960)

new social relationships

work table
shower shared between two living units
work table
3 metres
divan bed
foldaway bed

two of the 8.4m² **living units** for one person each, as proposed in Miliutin's 'Sotsgorod' (1933)

communal block designed by OSA, as proposed in 'Sotsgorod'

Ginsburg's **DOMNARKOMFIN** apartment block with communal facilities on Novinsky Boulevard, Moscow (1928–29)

burg and author, under his influence, of *Sotsgorod* (1933) and *Essential Questions of Theory in Soviet Architecture* (1933). In *Sotsgorod*, subtitled 'the problem of building socialist cities', Miliutin outlined his ideas on planning for growth, in particular his famous proposals for a linear city. Mata's city had allowed for expansion but had not incorporated the idea of land-use zoning; Garnier's and Le Corbusier's had involved zoning but had not dealt fully with the question of expansion. Miliutin combined these two ideas into a simple yet effective scheme; he proposed six parallel zones in a ribbon development a few hundred metres in width but of indefinite length: a railway zone; a zone of factories, workshops, stores, research and technical institutes; a green-way with the main highway running along it; a zone of housing, which also contained communal building, local commune offices, clinics, children's homes and nursery schools; a recreation zone with parks and sports areas, ideally also containing lakes and rivers for both recreation and transport; and an agricultural area with gardens, allotments and dairy farms. The linear principle was developed on the ground at Magnitogorsk, Stalingrad and several other new settlements. For existing cities, however, particularly Moscow whose population growth – from 1.7 million in 1917 to 3.7 million in 1935 – had already been phenomenal, another approach was needed. In 1931 it was decided to restrict the growth of the biggest existing cities, and Semenov's Moscow General Plan of 1935 was the earliest city plan in the world to propose a 'green belt' to contain urban expansion, allowing this to take place in satellite towns, or *sputniki*, further out.

A second major feature of Soviet planning was its concern for the relationship between urban and rural areas, an issue raised as early as 1846 by Marx and Engels when they wrote in *The German Ideology* of 'the antagonism between town and country' which creates 'the division of the population into two great classes' and which 'can exist only as a result of private property. It is the most crass expression of the subjection of the individual under the division of labour, under a definite activity forced upon him – a subjection which makes one man into a restricted town-animal, the other into a restricted country-animal, and daily creates anew the conflict between their interests.' Ideologically it became important to offer an alternative. The two main western approaches were rejected, both the policy of *concentration*, which intensified the exploitative effects of the city and increased the tensions between it and the countryside, and also that of *dispersal*, of proposing the escapist, liberal utopia of the garden city while leaving unsolved the dual problem of the distopian city and the exploited countryside. Miliutin's proposal, following Marx and Engels, was to work towards an even spread of population based on an 'industrialised countryside', in accordance with the aims of the Five-year Plan for a gradual transformation of the whole economic structure of the country which would eventually cause the city, as an outmoded capitalist phenomenon, to wither away. Leonidov's unexecuted plan for Magnitogorsk and Miliutin's plan for the Stalingrad tractor plant were examples of the close integration that was intended between industrial and agricultural production.

Thirdly, and perhaps most significant of all, was the completely new set of social relationships envisaged by socialist ideology, which made communal living and working the starting-point for the architecture. The basic residential unit was to be the 'living-cell', a place to sleep and keep private possessions. This would be supported by a whole range of services, collectivised both for efficiency and for social interaction: restaurants, laundries, nurseries, clubs, libraries, repair shops and sports facilities. Communal living would emancipate the woman from housework and would allow special attention to be given to the health and education of the children. As early as

1924 Leonid Vesnin had designed houses for communal living, and there were similar experiments in housing design by Barsch and others at Magnitogorsk (1929) and by Semenov at Stalingrad (1929). But the real archetype was Ginsburg's fine DOMNARKOMFIN apartment house (1928) built in Moscow for government workers, a long, rectangular slab block whose simple façade expressed the repetitive nature of the living cells behind it. The simple, plain aesthetic was that of Gropius' Dessau Bauhaus. There was much interchange of ideas between the Soviet Union and the west: the friendship between Le Corbusier and Ginsburg, and the undoubted effects of the former's Centrosoyus building; visits to Russia by Breuer, Hannes Meyer and Bruno Taut; the work of Ernst May and Mart Stam in Magnitogorsk, where their Frankfurt experience was used to advantage; even the production-line principles of the arch-capitalist Henry Ford had their effects on Soviet industry. Yet it would be a mistake to assume that the architectural intentions were necessarily the same. In general, western architects were using form to make a technological statement, Soviet architects a social one; the Bauhaus was designed in a repetitive way to express its function, the DOMNAR-KOMFIN to express the communality of the new Soviet society.

Other differences between the Soviet Union and the west were sharply underlined by the collapse of the western economy. In the comparative euphoria of the early 1920s, investment in industry had created a spare capacity which the market could not sustain. When the price bubble burst and Wall Street crashed in 1929, western econo-mists were surprised and shocked, having no means of explaining what they saw as an aberration in the history of capitalist growth. Some tried to interpret it in terms of vanishing investment opportunity: falling population, the introduction of new tech-nology with capital-saving effects, or the disappearance of the American frontier. Others, including the economist Schumpeter and both Coolidge and Hoover, blamed the radicals and the 'anti-capitalist' bias of the welfare state. Hoover – republican, conservative and a successful businessman – believed he could bring the rationalism of the business world to his term as President (1929–33). He believed in the capitalist dream: 'We are a happy people – the statistics prove it. We have more cars, more bath tubs, oil furnaces, silk stockings, bank accounts than any other people on earth.' This attitude was given great support by social commentators such as Beard, Veblen and Dewey, who preached 'industrial progressivism' and justified the subjection of the worker to the needs of the factory machine. 'The well-organised factory' said Ford, resulted in 'the reduction of the necessity for thought on the part of the worker and the reduction of his movements to the minimum.' When the crisis came, Hoover claimed that the unsound economy of Europe had been responsible for dragging down that of the USA. He encouraged American isolationism from Europe, though he also believed that Europe was fair game for American neo-colonialism. Welfare he considered an evil; it was better for Americans to starve – as some did during 1929–31 – than to have their moral fibre weakened by charity. In effect, he followed the pattern of most western rulers in times of economic crisis, withdrawing society's support from the most needy in an attempt to maintain profit levels for business.

The effects of the depression were uneven; as the poor starved and smaller capitalists were ruined, the larger ones continued to profit. New York and Chicago mushroomed with skyscrapers during the very worst years: the Chrysler building (1929) by William van Alen, the Palmolive building (1929–30) by Holabird and Root, the Empire State building (1930–2) by Shreve, Lamb and Harmon and the Rockefeller Center (begun 1930), planned by Harrison and Abramovitz, which included the RCA building, the

International building and the Time-Life building. The characteristic tapering silhouette produced by the setbacks on successive floors was required by the City Zoning Ordinance. Following a stylistic controversy over the design of the *Chicago Tribune* tower, modernism had become accepted for skyscrapers, though it was the modernism of Art Deco rather than that of the rationalists, epitomised in the streamlined metal pinnacle of the Chrysler building, in the vast 'sunburst' design of the entrance hall of the Empire State and, at the Rockefeller Center, in the sweeping curves of the Radio City Music Hall.

In Britain, the elegant opulence of Art Deco appeared in prestige commercial buildings like Wallis Gilbert's Hoover factory (1932–5) and Banister Fletcher's Gillette factory (1936), both in west London. It also became the accepted style for every Savoy, Essoldo, Rialto and Odeon, the super-cinemas in which the fantasies of Hollywood could temporarily banish the realities of life. Escapism was a common response to the depression, even among those who called themselves socialists. In 1900 the Webbs were already saying that capitalism had solved the problem of production; all that remained to socialism was to ensure an equitable distribution of the resulting benefits. When the slump came, the Labour party saw its role as helping to stimulate production; the Leninist aim of harnessing the righteous anger of the workers to smash the state and replace it was ignored. 'Socialism', against all the evidence to the contrary, was expected to arrive by negotiation between people. It would live off the surplus of capitalism. The idea of gradual social change for the better through general benevolence was foremost in the growth of the modern movement in Britain. In 1932 the architect Wells Coates wrote: 'As architects of the ultimate human and material scenes of the new order, we are not so much concerned with the formal problems of "style" as with an architectural solution to the social and economic problems of today.' He was expressing the widespread view of progressive bourgeois thinkers that *social* transformation could come through *physical* change.

Modern buildings grew slowly in number: Robertson and Easton's Horticultural Hall in London (1928) with its curved reinforced concrete roof, Thomas Tait's cubist houses at Silver End in Essex (1927–8) for the Crittall manufacturing company, Amyas Connell's fine Corbusian house, High and Over, in Buckinghamshire (1929–30), the glass-walled *Daily Express* office in London (1930–2) by Ellis, Clarke and Williams and the splendidly engineered concrete factory building for Boots the pharmaceutical company in Nottinghamshire (1930–2) by Owen Williams. In 1932 Adams, Holden and Pearson built Arnos Grove station in north London, one of a number of fine buildings for the London Underground. Under its director Frank Pick, London Transport, as it became, built a reputation as an enlightened patron of design. Besides the new stations, which combined modern building techniques with a respect for the traditional London landscape, Pick promoted the use of modern typography, employed the best poster artists of the day and presided over the design of the archetypal STL-model London bus (1933) and of the 1937 'Tube' rolling-stock. London Transport was widely praised by architects and critics for its progressiveness; so closely were high standards of physical design equated with social progress that there was a general failure to recognise London Transport's role during the 1930s in the creation of suburbia, a social phenomenon against which most of the same critics were vehemently arguing.

As suburbia spread, progressive western architects followed Le Corbusier and concerned themselves with city-centre housing, which they saw as the only acceptable

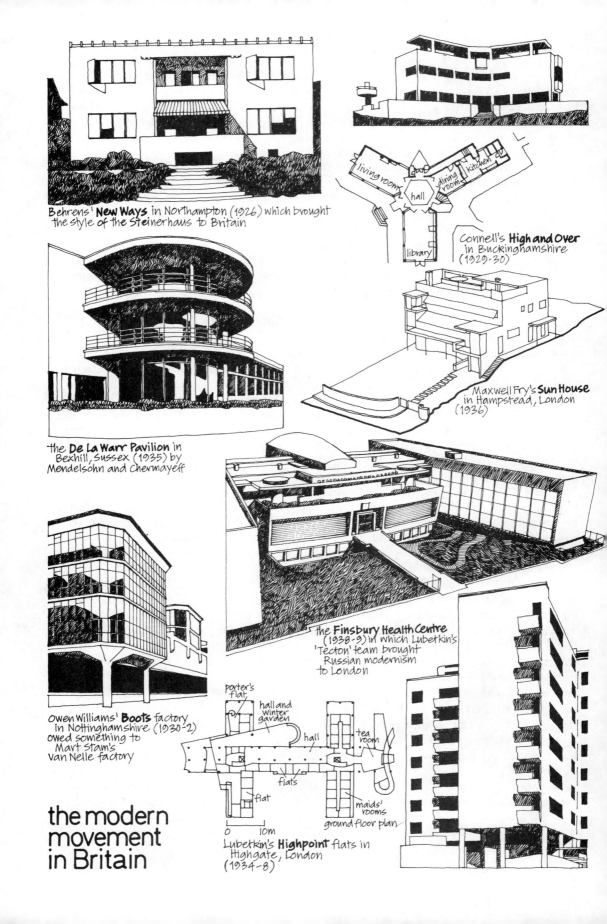

Behrens' **New Ways** in Northampton (1926) which brought the style of the Steinerhaus to Britain

Connell's **High and Over** in Buckinghamshire (1929-30)

living room hall dining room kitchen library

Maxwell Fry's **Sun House** in Hampstead, London (1936)

the **De La Warr Pavilion** in Bexhill, Sussex (1935) by Mendelsohn and Chermayeff

the **Finsbury Health Centre** (1938-9) in which Lubetkin's 'Tecton' team brought Russian modernism to London

Owen Williams' **Boots** factory in Nottinghamshire (1930-2) owed something to Mart Stam's Van Nelle factory

porter's flat hall and winter garden hall tea room flats flat maids' rooms ground floor plan

0 10m

Lubetkin's **Highpoint** flats in Highgate, London (1934-8)

the modern movement in Britain

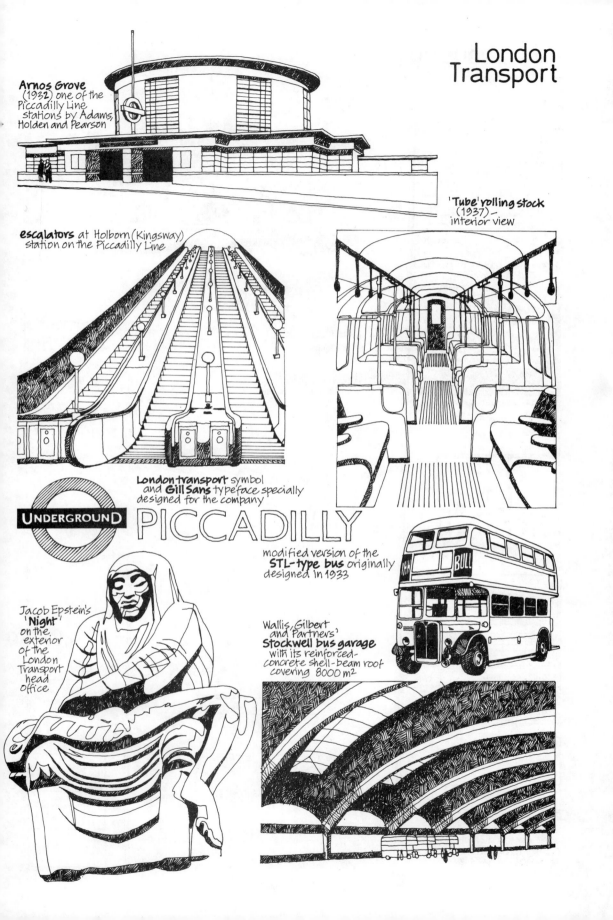

London Transport

Arnos Grove (1932) one of the Piccadilly Line stations by Adams, Holden and Pearson

'Tube' rolling stock (1937) — interior view

escalators at Holborn (Kingsway) station on the Piccadilly Line

London transport symbol and **Gill Sans** typeface specially designed for the company

UNDERGROUND

PICCADILLY

modified version of the **STL-type bus** originally designed in 1933

Jacob Epstein's 'Night' on the exterior of the London Transport head office

Wallis, Gilbert and Partners' **Stockwell bus garage** with its reinforced-concrete shell-beam roof covering 8000 m²

public housing

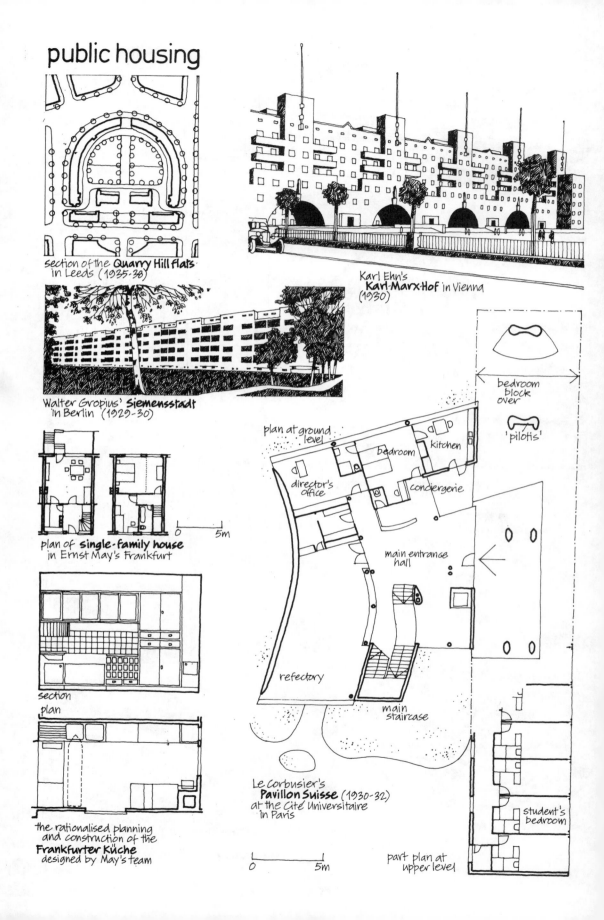

section of the **Quarry Hill flats** in Leeds (1935-38)

Karl Ehn's **Karl-Marx-Hof** in Vienna (1930)

Walter Gropius' **Siemensstadt** in Berlin (1929-30)

plan of **single-family house** in Ernst May's Frankfurt

0   5m

section

plan

the rationalised planning and construction of the **Frankfurter Küche** designed by May's team

0   5m

plan at ground level

director's office

bedroom

kitchen

conciergerie

main entrance hall

refectory

main staircase

bedroom block over

'pilotis'

Le Corbusier's **Pavillon Suisse** (1930-32) at the Cité Universitaire in Paris

student's bedroom

part plan at upper level

alternative. All over Europe, socialist city authorities built housing estates, mostly designed by unknown civic architects or engineers and mostly in the tradition of the LCC, with long, rectangular blocks of walk-up apartments with common staircases. In Britain, the most ambitious project was in Leeds, whose Quarry Hill flats (1935–8) housed 1,000 families on a ten-hectare site. Among the finest architecturally, achieving a feeling of dignity as well as mere size, was the Karl-Marx-Hof in Vienna (1929–30) designed by the city architect Karl Ehn. As yet, few major estates were designed on rationalist principles, and those that existed became objects of pilgrimage to aspiring designers. As well as Ernst May's work in Frankfurt, they included Oud's Kiefhoek estate in Rotterdam (1925–9), Gropius' and Scharoun's Siemensstadt in Berlin (1929–30), Sven Markelius' housing estates with communal facilities on the 'collective' principle in Stockholm, and, at the Cité Universitaire in Paris, Le Corbusier's housing for Swiss students, the Pavillon Suisse (1930–2), which demonstrated an entire range of modern features in a unified design: a repetitively designed bedroom block with glazed front and blank end walls, raised from the ground on *pilotis*, and a free-form communal block nestling underneath, linked by a glazed staircase tower. Like Ginsburg's DOMNARKOMFIN of four years earlier, the Pavillon Suisse was a clear symbol of communal living. It would have considerable influence on the design of working-class housing, even though the social assumptions did not necessarily translate from one situation to the other.

A number of important international exhibitions helped to establish modern architecture as a matter of general public interest and discussion, the subject of enthusiasm or ridicule. The Barcelona exhibition of 1929 was notable for the German pavilion of Mies van der Rohe, a *tour de force* of modernism in which the most luxurious materials – such as chromed steel and polished marble – were used to create the simplest and most elegant of forms. The Stockholm exhibition of 1930, organised by Sven Markelius and Dr Paulsson, was largely designed by Erik Gunnar 'Asplund (1885–1940) whose Paradiset restaurant, with its elegant steelwork and glass, epitomised all that modern architects were trying to do; the exhibition was a view of the city of the future, a complete area of urban landscape demonstrating all the varieties of form, texture and colour made possible by modern materials and methods. In 1931 an exhibition in New York brought the modern movement to a wide American audience, attracting considerable interest, particularly on the east coast. A concurrent book by Henry Russell Hitchcock and Philip Johnson even gave it a new name, *The International Style.*

The authors identified certain characteristics which distinguished the international style from those of the past. They included a concern for the enclosure of space, for volume rather than mass, a concern for regularity rather than symmetry in the ordering of a design, and a rejection of arbitrary surface decoration. In Europe these principles were exemplified in the early 1930s by a number of major buildings of considerable size and complexity in which the use of fully-glazed external walls allowed a total appreciation from outside of the spaces enclosed, and in which the structure itself was clearly displayed, giving regularity and visual order. In Germany they included Mendelsohn's Columbushaus offices in Berlin (1921–31) and Max Taut's Trade Union House in Frankfurt (1929–31). In Holland were Duiker's Open Air school in Amsterdam (1928–30), the Bijenkorf store in Rotterdam (1929–31) by Willem Marinus Dudok (1884–1974) and the fine Van Nelle tobacco factory in Rotterdam (1927–30) by Johannes Brinkman and L. G. van der Vlugt in association with Mart Stam. The Dutch experience underlined the growing internationalism of the international style.

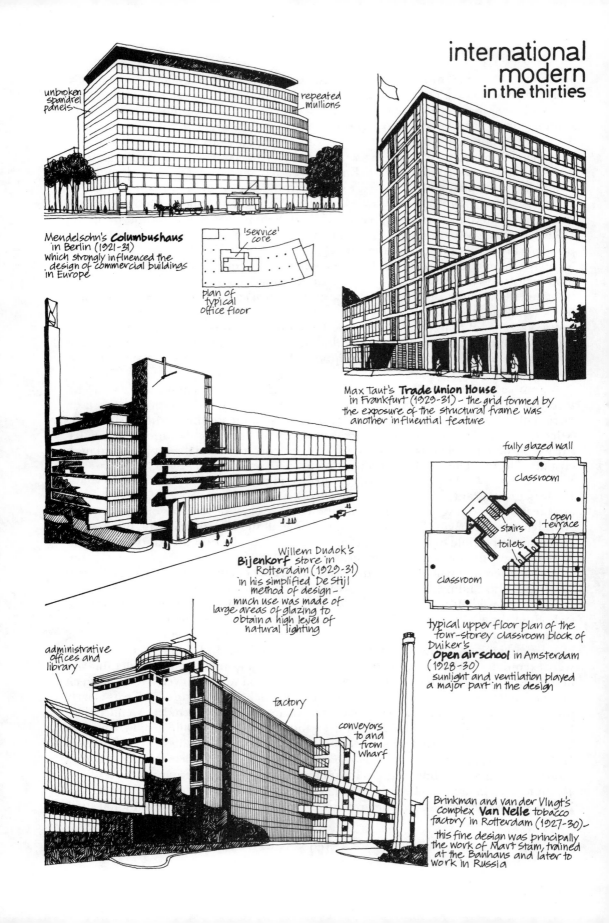

unbroken spandrel panels

repeated mullions

Mendelsohn's **Columbushaus** in Berlin (1921-31) which strongly influenced the design of commercial buildings in Europe

'service' core

plan of typical office floor

Max Taut's **Trade Union House** in Frankfurt (1929-31) - the grid formed by the exposure of the structural frame was another influential feature

fully glazed wall

classroom

open terrace

stairs

toilets

classroom

Willem Dudok's **Bijenkorf** store in Rotterdam (1929-31) in his simplified 'De Stijl' method of design - much use was made of large areas of glazing to obtain a high level of natural lighting

typical upper floor plan of the four-storey classroom block of Duiker's **Open air school** in Amsterdam (1928-30) sunlight and ventilation played a major part in the design

administrative offices and library

factory

conveyors to and from wharf

Brinkman and van der Vlugt's complex **Van Nelle** tobacco factory in Rotterdam (1927-30) - this fine design was principally the work of Mart Stam, trained at the Bauhaus and later to work in Russia

By 1929 the Amsterdaamse School had virtually died out as an identifiable group, De Stijl had disbanded following van Doesburg's departure for Paris and Dutch modernism, dominated by the rationalists, had been assimilated into the mainstream of the modern movement.

The triumph in the early 1930s of both Fascism and Stalinism had a fundamental influence on internationalism in art and architecture. Groups and entire movements were broken up and dispersed, the vacuum being filled by others with more political credibility. The spread of the modern movement was, ironically, Hitler's most significant cultural contribution to the world, a result of his manic crusade against minorities, non-conformists and the left. As Nazi power grew, the progressive elements in society became ever more isolated. Brecht in particular rose to new levels of vitality and abrasiveness as the sa began to sabotage his plays and persecute his supporters. The Nazis had always looked on the modern movement with suspicion. The Weissenhof exhibition had figured in their propaganda for racial purity; its flat roofs and white walls allowed it to be parodied in photomontage as a 'moorish village', complete with Arabs and camels. The Bauhaus, too, ran into trouble; Gropius retired in 1928 and his place was taken by Hannes Meyer, whose socialist views were not acceptable to the Dessau authorities, particularly when he encouraged the students to take part in political activity. In 1930 he was asked to resign and was replaced by Mies van der Rohe whose aim was to find a political compromise with the Nazis. Despite their attitude to modern design in general and to the Bauhaus in particular, and despite the fact that in 1926 Mies himself had designed a monument to the communist martyrs Luxemburg and Liebknecht – albeit for architectural and humanitarian reasons rather than political ones – he hoped to convince the Nazis that his architecture was free from politics and to establish a basis for co-existence. But in 1932, when they became the largest German party, Dessau came under Nazi control and the school was forced to move to Berlin. Hitler's appointment as chancellor in 1933, enabled him to intimidate the Reichstag into agreeing a constitutional change which gave him absolute power both as head of state and commander-in-chief. That year, in which the Gestapo was founded and Dachau opened, the Bauhaus closed down for good. As Hitler began to purge the party of dissidents, to persecute the Jews and to suspend civil rights, it became almost impossible for anyone suspected of leftism to remain in Germany. In 1933 Brecht moved to Prague — later to the usa – Weill and Lotte Lenja to Paris, and Grosz to New York. Breuer and Mendelsohn went to London, to be followed the next year by Gropius. Mies tried to stay, but in 1937 he accepted an invitation from Philip Johnson to teach in Chicago. Gropius and Breuer crossed the Atlantic with him, while Mendelsohn moved to Palestine. Those who did succeed in staying on paid for it with their artistic integrity, their personal freedom and in some cases their lives.

Westerners working in the Soviet Union were unable to return to Germany, though the hardening of the Stalinist regime against human rights, freedom of expression and progressive thought made it impossible for them to remain there long without becoming disillusioned; May ended up in Kenya, Meyer in Switzerland and Stam in Holland. As in Germany, the official line began to promote on the one hand the traditionalism and monumentality of 'social realism', intended to express patriotism and the positive side of life, and on the other hand the *faux-naïveté* of peasant-style art. Constructivism was denounced as leftist, too abstract and formalist; traditional artists, after years in the revolutionary wilderness, returned thankfully to the neo-classical fold. A new group of architects, led by the academics Fomin, Zholtovsky and

A. Tamanian, came to the fore and some Constructivists like Burov or Ilya Golossov began to design in an academic style; those like Leonidov, who could not do so, were consigned to oblivion. Others, like Ginsburg, Lissitsky and the Vesnins, continued to work, though in a more self-effacing way, doing some teaching, writing, or furniture design but no major projects. Lissitzky's *Russia: An Architecture for World Revolution* (1930) was an attempt to sum up the achievements of the preceding decade and state the case for modernism. But the catastasis for the modern movement came the same year when Mayakovsky, the revolutionary, the dedicated communist, was publicly denounced for 'petty-bourgeois leftism', and killed himself. His death marked the virtual end of a culture dedicated to the future and to the creation of an alternative to the state, and its replacement by one which used traditionalism to dignify and perpetuate the state apparatus.

In 1929 and 1930 the peasants resisted collectivisation and persecution with strikes and scorched earth. The eventual destruction of the kulaks robbed agriculture of most of its best technicians, bringing famine and ruining the agricultural industry. The Second Five-year Plan (1933–7) also intensified the effect on urban life. Industrialisation created a proletariat, but there was no corresponding increase in workers' power; Stalin's bureaucrats were becoming a new ruling class, perpetuating capitalist conditions. The workers were exploited, taking lower and lower wages, losing their right to strike or to change jobs without permission. In 1929 in the aftermath of the civil war there were 30,000 political prisoners; by 1933 there were 5 million and by 1942 15 million. Semenov's urban planning work in Moscow continued, but Miliutin's ideas found less support; it can be assumed that his association with Ginsburg and the modern movement condemned him, that the essential flexibility of his linear city concept was inimical to a centralised bureaucracy and its egalitarianism incompatible with the distortions of socialism now being promoted by the regime. As Molotov said, in a direct reversal of the principles of the revolution: 'Bolshevik policy demands a resolute struggle against egalitarians as accomplices of the class enemy, as elements hostile to socialism.'

Communist parties abroad were now expected to take a Stalinist line – to support the Russian state rather than to create international revolution. In the tragic débâcle of the Spanish Civil War (1936) they worked against the interests of the republic and were partly responsible for the success of Franco's Falange, which condemned Spain to decades of social regression and crushed the Catalan political and cultural renaissance. Russian communism retained the support of those European intellectuals unwilling to recognise the reactionary force it had become, or that in sabotaging international revolution they were lending strength to Fascism.

During the 1930s the socialist ideals of the Russian revolution and the altruism of German social democracy, although both were almost dead, continued to shape the ideas of progressive European architects. In Britain the Russians Berthold Lubetkin and Serge Chermayeff brought the experience of VKHUTEMAS to interact with that of the German designers, but the social conditions were totally different and it was impossible to create a genuinely socialist architecture. A few public commissions came along: Connell, Ward and Lucas's Kent House in London, for the St Pancras Housing Association (1935), Mendelsohn and Chermayeff's De La Warr entertainment pavilion at Bexhill (1935), Impington Village College for the Cambridge education authority, by Gropius and Fry (1936), and Lubetkin's fine health centre for the socialist London borough of Finsbury (1938–9). But on the whole the work consisted of residential

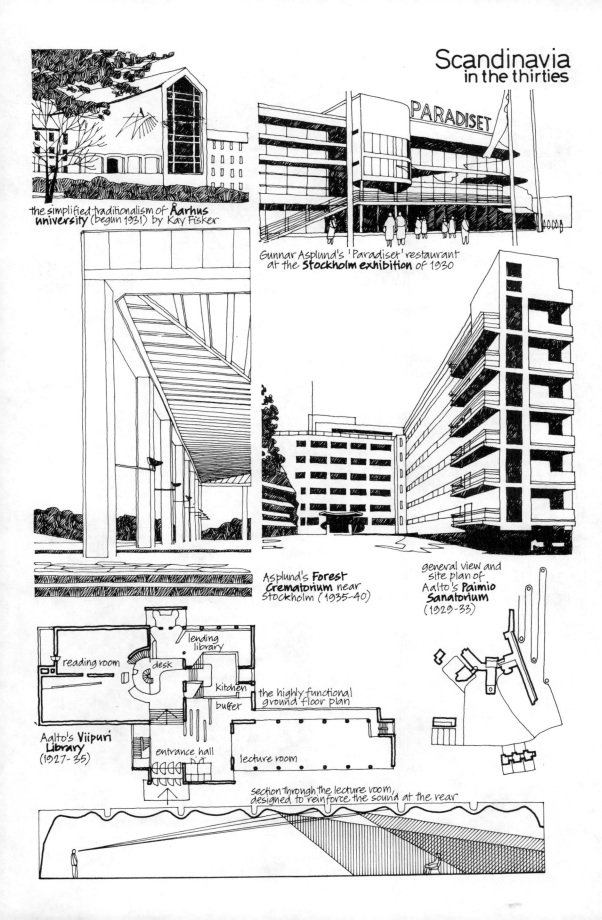

the simplified traditionalism of **Aarhus university** (begun 1931) by Kay Fisker

Gunnar Asplund's 'Paradiset' restaurant at the **Stockholm exhibition** of 1930

PARADISET

Asplund's **Forest Crematorium** near Stockholm (1935-40)

general view and site plan of Aalto's **Paimio Sanatorium** (1929-33)

Aalto's **Viipuri Library** (1927-35)

reading room

lending library

desk

kitchen

buffer

entrance hall

lecture room

the highly functional ground floor plan

section through the lecture room, designed to reinforce the sound at the rear

Aalto and Finnish design

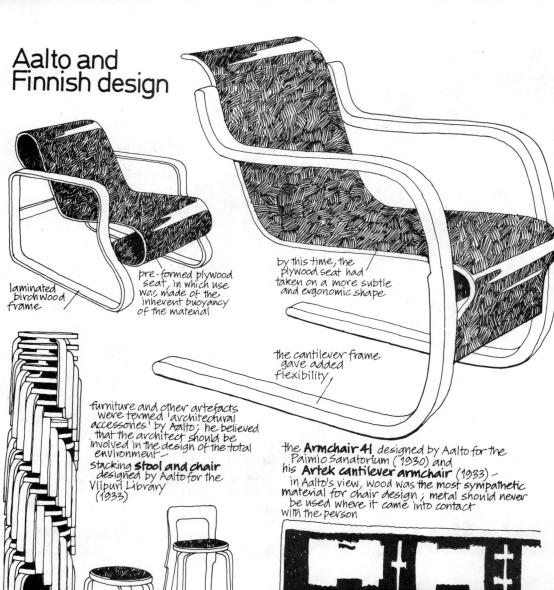

laminated birchwood frame.

pre-formed plywood seat, in which use was made of the inherent buoyancy of the material

by this time, the plywood seat had taken on a more subtle and ergonomic shape

the cantilever frame gave added flexibility

furniture and other artefacts were termed 'architectural accessories' by Aalto; he believed that the architect should be involved in the design of the total environment—

stacking stool and chair designed by Aalto for the Viipuri Library (1933)

the **Armchair 41** designed by Aalto for the Paimio Sanatorium (1930) and his **Artek cantilever armchair** (1933) — in Aalto's view, wood was the most sympathetic material for chair design; metal should never be used where it came into contact with the person

during the 1930's Finnish design consisted mainly of reinterpreting simple, traditional forms in terms of modern techniques

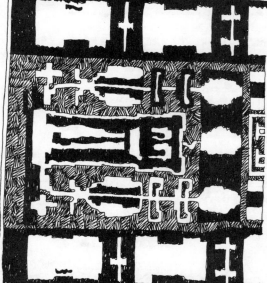

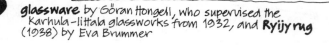

glassware by Göran Hongell, who supervised the Karhula-Iittala glassworks from 1932, and **Ryijy rug** (1938) by Eva Brummer

property for private clients, houses like those in Chelsea by Mendelsohn and Chermayeff (1936) and Gropius and Fry (1936), Maxwell Fry's Sun House (1936) and Connell Ward and Lucas's 66 Frognal, both in Hampstead (1938), and luxury flats such as Wells Coates' Lawn Road flats in Hampstead (1934) and Embassy Court in Brighton (1935) and Lubetkin's Highpoint in Highgate (1934–8). There was an element of self-delusion about the idea of creating a fairer society by such means.

In the meantime, the Scandinavian countries were proceeding steadily towards a social-democratic utopia. In general they had entered a period of freedom and stability; Norway and Sweden had come to an agreement over independence in 1905, Finland had achieved in 1917 both independence from Russia and recognition from the new regime, and Denmark had regained Schleswig from Germany after the First World War. During the inter-war period their economies prospered: Sweden's agriculture and manufacturing, Norway's merchant trading, Finland's forest products and Denmark's dairy industry. In each country an enlightened liberal bourgeoisie was achieving sufficient social responsibility to ensure a contented workforce and encourage productivity. Standards of welfare and education were reflected in the building of workers' housing, community buildings and schools. In Sweden, the social democrats dominated politics continuously after 1932 and at about the same time the modern movement in architecture was established as a visual expression of social progress. The older styles of each country were in their different ways adapted or superseded to meet the new needs. In Denmark the traditional brick architecture of Ivar Bentsen and Kay Fisker (1893–1965), which reached its peak with Peter Klint's highly expressionist Grundtvig church in Copenhagen (1920–40), took on a new dimension when in 1931 Fisker began Aarhus university – later taken over by Møller and Stegman – which combined traditional brick techniques with a new simplicity and rigour of approach. Asplund's modern work in Sweden, beginning with the 1930 exhibition, went from strength to strength with his Law Court extension in Gothenburg (1934–7) and his beautiful Forest Crematorium near Stockholm (1935–40).

Most significant of all was the Finnish architect Alvar Aalto (1898–1976). Like Asplund and many others he was classically trained but adopted modernism in the late 1920s. The most important works of his early 'white' period were the Viipuri library (1927–35), the Turun Sanomat newspaper offices (1929–30), the Paimio sanatorium (1929–33) and the Sunila cellulose works and its associated housing (1936–9). Aalto's adoption of the international style, even at this early stage in his career, was uncompromising and highly assured, despite the fact that Finland, with its highly localised economy unused to large-scale production and its traditional reliance on timber for building, was perhaps the least likely of the Scandinavian countries to take to it.

In America the reverse was true. The growth of monopoly capitalism, despite the depression, continued to increase the scale and rationalisation of industry and the centralisation of control by the monopolists. Whole sectors of the economy, especially in backward rural areas and the inner cities, became redundant, a problem worsened by the high level of unemployment caused by the depression. Roosevelt became president in 1933, determined to save capitalism; his approach was based on that of the British economist Keynes, whose *General Theory of Employment, Interest and Money* (1936) became the bible of Roosevelt's 'New Deal', a massive programme of federal intervention in industry in a spirit of courageous, not to say reckless, experiment. The New Deal was criticised by conservatives as a communists' charter, but in fact conflict with the working class intensified rather than slackened during this period. The FERA pro-

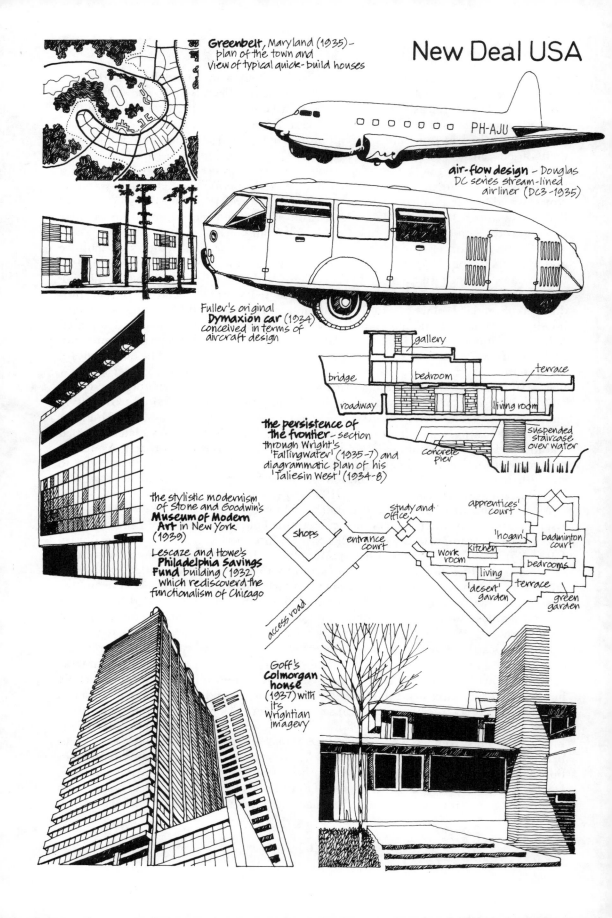

Greenbelt, Maryland (1935) - plan of the town and view of typical quick-build houses

air-flow design - Douglas DC series stream-lined airliner (DC3 - 1935)

PH-AJU

Fuller's original **Dymaxion car** (1934) conceived in terms of aircraft design

the persistence of the frontier - section through Wright's 'Fallingwater' (1935-7) and diagrammatic plan of his 'Taliesin West' (1934-8)

gallery

bridge

bedroom

terrace

roadway

living room

suspended staircase over water

concrete pier

the stylistic modernism of Stone and Goodwin's **Museum of Modern Art** in New York (1939)

Lescaze and Howe's **Philadelphia Savings Fund** building (1932) which rediscovered the functionalism of Chicago

shops

study and office

apprentices' court

entrance court

'hogan'

badminton court

Work room

kitchen

bedrooms

living

'desert' garden

terrace

green garden

access road

Goff's **Colmorgan house** (1937) with its Wrightian imagery

ject offered state-funded poor relief for the unemployed and starving but anti-union legislation remained draconian and unemployment high. The unions demanded 'justice, not charity', and the moderate AFL, with its building and craft unions, was dominated by the new, militant Congress of Industrial Organisations (1936) which staged communist-led strikes in the crucial auto, steel, textile and rubber industries and provoked counter-measures from the employers. General Motors was willing to spend $1million a year on spies and private armies of strike-breakers.

The relative building boom of the late 1920s had ignored the needs of the poor, but the New Deal made significant progress in some areas, despite a general decline in building activity during the 1930s. The setting-up of the Civilian Conservation Corps (1933) created new jobs and carried through a number of reforestation and flood control projects. Greenbelt in Maryland (1935) was one of three pioneering garden suburbs built by the Federal Resettlement Administration. In the face of strong opposition from the power companies the state-run Tenessee Valley Authority (1933) was set up to reclaim one of the most backward and devastated areas of the country, returning 90,000 square km of land to productive industry and agriculture. Its urgent building programme stimulated designers to develop a number of ingenious quick-build dwelling types: trailer-homes that could be towed into position, and homes built from factory-made sections that could be assembled and occupied a few hours after arriving on site.

It was an attractive idea to apply the techniques of the production-line to house-building; builders had much to learn from automobile and aircraft manufacture, now becoming highly sophisticated. The work of the Boeing and Douglas companies during the 1930s culminated in the production in 1935 of the DC-3, whose stressed-skin construction contrasted with the framing and strutting of earlier aircraft design. Chrysler and General Motors emerged to challenge the early supremacy of Ford. The concern of the designers Buckminster Fuller and Norman Bel Geddes for air-flow design, or 'streamlining', was carried over into automobile design for the mass market. Though used for functional reasons, for example the fuel savings of 50% claimed by Fuller for his Dymaxion car of 1934, it was generally applied more superficially as a 'styling' technique to give the appearance of modernity and speed.

Talented contemporary architects such as Philip Johnson and Edward Stone, though broadly within the mainstream of modern design, were more receptive to stylism than the more serious European functionalists. At best, their buildings were less dogmatic, at worst, more superficial and arbitrary. Norman Bel Geddes' General Motors complex, Highways and Horizons, was the success of the New York World's Fair of 1939; its slick and sophisticated imagery of the city of the future contrasted with the serious and didactic Finnish pavilion by Aalto, designed to promote the country's timber industry and way of life.

Amid this drive for industrialisation the myth of the frontier persisted, and Frank Lloyd Wright remained one of its most persuasive architectural advocates. For Edgar Kaufmann he built Fallingwater at Bear Run, PA (1935–7), a house cantilevered over a waterfall and one of his finest works, with an ingenious structure treated in a dramatic way. Taliesin West (1934–8) near Phoenix, on the edge of the Arizona Desert, was Wright's own winter house, studio and workshop, a community home where he could gather disciples around him; the remote landscape and the organic building with its redwood beams, canvas awnings and rough piers of stone created an appropriately Mosaic setting for Wright's handed-down teachings. One of his pupils was Bruce Goff

(b. 1904); his Colmorgan house at Glenview. IL (1937), was a Wrightian concept with overhanging roofs counterpointed by masonry piers, but he went on to develop his own distinctive organic style, using free-form planning and natural materials 'as found'.

In the late 1930s and early 1940s the arrival in America of Mies van der Rohe, Gropius, Mendelsohn and Breuer, as well as Chermayeff and the Catalan modernist José Luis Sert (b. 1902), gave impetus to the international style. Gropius, Breuer and Sert worked at Cambridge, MA, and Mies van der Rohe in Chicago, where he began to lay out the campus of the Armour Institute, later the Illinois Institute of Technology. An earlier example of American architects leaning towards the European style was the office tower by William Lescaze and George Howe for the Philadelphia Savings Fund (1932), a clear expression of structure distinct from contemporary Art Deco skyscrapers in New York. Wright's Fallingwater was another – his nearest approach to the international style; but the first identifiable example occurred after the arrival of the European designers: the Museum of Modern Art in New York (1939) by Edward Stone and Philip Goodwin, with its rational planning and simple elevational expression of the functions within.

In Germany, the vacuum left by the departing modernists had been filled by Hitler's architects Paul Ludwig Troost and Albert Speer. The official Nazi approach produced nothing comparable with Terragni's beautiful, rationalist Casa del Fascio in Como (1932–6); instead, a heavy, derivative neo-classical style was employed, to link the Third Reich with imperial Rome. Early examples in Bavaria, the birthplace of Nazism, included Troost's House of German Art in Munich, based on Schinkel's Altes Museum, his unfinished Colosseum-like Congress Hall in Nuremburg, his Temples of Honour in Munich to commemorate the sixteen 'heroes' killed in the putsch of 1932, and Speer's Zeppelin Field in Nuremburg, a ceremonial stadium for party rallies. Hitler also had a monumental stadium specially built for the Berlin Olympics of 1936. The ethos behind both the rallies and the Olympics was captured in the propaganda films of Leni Riefenstahl, *Triumph of the Will* and *Berlin Olympiad* which, together with Speer's searchlit *mise-en-scène* for the 1934 Nuremburg rally, were among the few genuine works of art produced by the regime, conveying the terrible beauty of the demagoguery and mass-hysteria. In general, Nazi art was deliberately banal with a strong *Volkisch* element, taking architectural form in the numerous 'Hansel and Gretel' houses built for party workers all over Germany. Speer's main building project was to have been the reconstruction of Berlin to a plan devised in collaboration with Hitler, incorporating broad processional ways, arches of triumph and a gigantic domed hall 200 metres in width; but it was overtaken in 1939 by Hitler's invasion of Czechoslovakia and Poland.

The Second World War greatly stimulated technological development, mainly for its destructive power, though with a useful spin-off into the civilian world. The science of structures, for example, benefited from the researches of Buckminster Fuller and Barnes Wallis into 'geodetics', used by the former in lightweight dome buildings and by the latter in aircraft fuselage design. Mitchell's Spitfire fighter set new standards for aerodynamic design, and Whittle's jet engine, produced under wartime pressure, was developed to great effect in the ensuing years. The war gave great impetus to communications technology, especially radar, and ended with the first demonstration of the terrible effects of atomic fission. Even assuming the social benefits of jet propulsion and nuclear energy, the financial and human cost of their development for use in war is never 'worthwhile' in social or economic terms. The only beneficiary is the military-industrial complex itself.

Troost's **House of German Art** in Munich was based on Schinkel's Altes Museum

Speer discussing a plan with **Hitler**

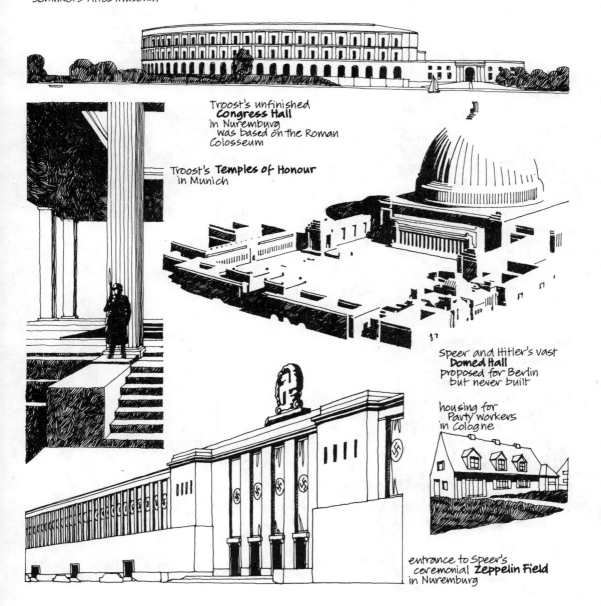

Troost's unfinished **Congress Hall** in Nuremburg was based on the Roman Colosseum

Troost's **Temples of Honour** in Munich

Speer and Hitler's vast **Domed Hall** proposed for Berlin but never built

housing for Party workers in Cologne

entrance to Speer's ceremonial **Zeppelin Field** in Nuremburg

the Second World War

the geodetic framework of the
Wellington bomber and the aerodynamic
construction of the **Spitfire** and other aircraft
stimulated structural ideas after the war

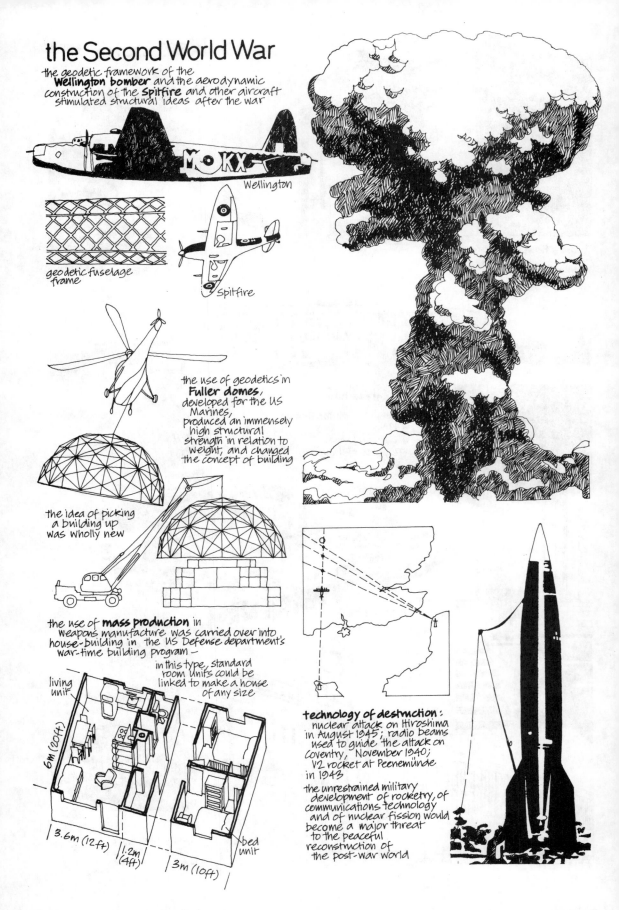

Wellington

geodetic fuselage
frame

Spitfire

the use of geodetics in
Fuller domes,
developed for the US
Marines,
produced an immensely
high structural
strength in relation to
weight, and changed
the concept of building

the idea of picking
a building up
was wholly new

the use of **mass production** in
weapons manufacture was carried over into
house-building in the US Defense department's
war-time building program –

in this type, standard
room units could be
linked to make a house
of any size

living
unit

6m (20ft)

3.6m (12ft) 1.2m (4ft) 3m (10ft)

bed
unit

technology of destruction:
nuclear attack on Hiroshima
in August 1945; radio beams
used to guide the attack on
Coventry, November 1940;
V2 rocket at Peenemünde
in 1943

the unrestrained military
development of rocketry, of
communications technology
and of nuclear fission would
become a major threat
to the peaceful
reconstruction of
the post-war world

The fact remains, however, that such technical advances are made in wartime because it becomes politically acceptable to mobilise industry on a national scale and to control the economy centrally. Governments feel able to spend massively and to reduce unemployment dramatically, in a way they are unwilling to do in peacetime. This was widely recognised during the earliest months of the Second World War; the possibility of carrying over the high levels of central control, of investment, employment and social cohesion into peace-time years, was seen as a way to reconstruct society and to ensure that 'never again' the depression years of slum living, poverty and underprivilege would return.

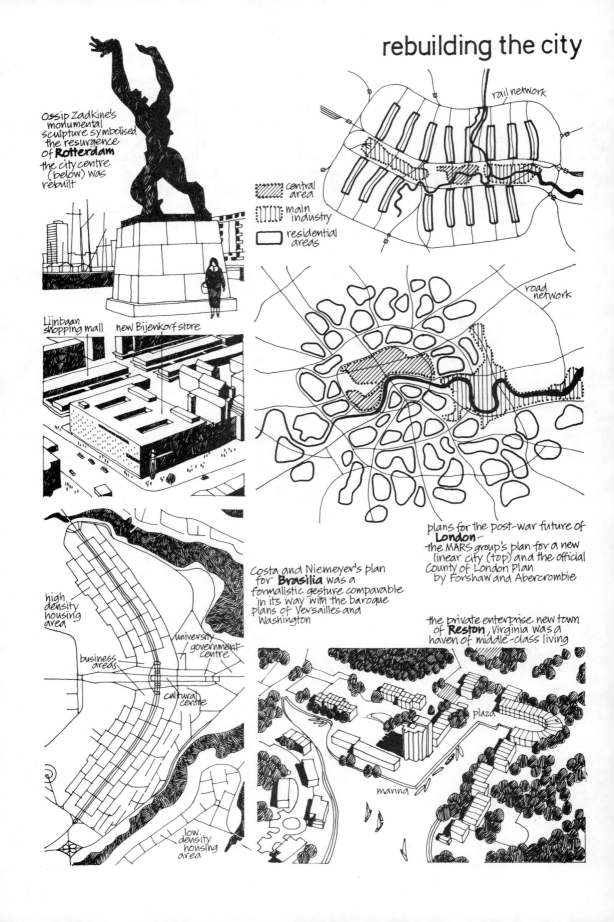

Ossip Zadkine's monumental sculpture symbolised the resurgence of **Rotterdam**, the city centre (below) was rebuilt

rail network

central area

main industry

residential areas

Lijnbaan shopping mall   new Bijenkorf store

road network

plans for the post-war future of **London** — the MARS group's plan for a new linear city (top) and the official County of London Plan by Forshaw and Abercrombie

high density housing area

business areas

university government centre

cultural centre

Costa and Niemeyer's plan for **Brasilia** was a formalistic gesture comparable in its way with the baroque plans of Versailles and Washington

the private enterprise new town of **Reston**, Virginia was a haven of middle-class living

plaza

marina

low density housing area

Brave new world
The Second World War and after

The great cities destroyed in the Second World War were the focus of society's collective guilt about the past as well as of its hopes for the future. It became important to rebuild Rotterdam, Warsaw, Dresden, Coventry, Stalingrad and Hiroshima as quickly and effectively as possible, but at the same time to treat them as shrines to the millions of dead, as if the memory would ensure a saner future for the world. In Coventry the burned-out ruins of the medieval cathedral, and in Hiroshima the domed steel skeleton of the Museum of Science and Industry which inexplicably had withstood the blast, were retained as reminders. In Germany and Poland, concentration camps provided poignant symbols. At Dachau, a chapel of atonement was built in memory of the dead, and the camp itself, in all its ugliness and squalor, provided a more fitting reminder of Nazism than any of the grandiose works of Troost or Speer.

Plans for rebuilding were being prepared even during the early years of the war. It became part of the conventional wisdom of reconstruction that so much destruction provided not only the need to rebuild but also the opportunity to create cities of greater beauty and order than those of the pre-war years, with their memories of depression. Patrick Abercrombie's County of London Plan was prepared as early as 1943. The working-class East End devastated during the *Blitzkreig*, now formed the centre piece of Abercrombie's proposed reconstruction; numerous parks and gardens, and the rational planning of residential neighbourhoods, would create a sharp contrast with the slum conditions of the depression years. A major feature of the plan was the Green Belt, which was intended to contain the city's outward growth, decentralising the surplus population to a ring of new towns some 50 kilometres from the centre.

Abercrombie's plan was based on expediency and attempted to retain the old character of London; a much more radical plan, which would have changed the city out of all recognition, had been prepared in 1941 by the MARS group of architects and planners, a British affiliate of CIAM, proposing a re-shaping of the old concentric city into a linear pattern. A main spine of central-area uses, industry and transport routes would run east-west along the Thames. Perpendicular to this would be ribs of residential development, separated by bands of open space which would bring greenery and growing-land to the heart of the city. The linear idea, and the idea of closely linking town and country, were concepts of Russian dimensions. It was calculated that the immense cost of re-casting the shape of the city would be more than offset by the reductions in transport costs and land-values, but the MARS plan remained an academic exercise; in common with all major cities, the economic forces demanding that London retain its old form were too strong to resist.

The requirements of international finance dictated the ways cities developed. The most significant feature of post-war western economy was the rise of the international corporation, to the extent of rivalling or even surpassing the nation-state in economic and political power. The biggest multi-nationals began to owe allegiance to no country and to pursue their aims across national boundaries, using and discarding international labour and international markets with no more regard for local effects than was necessary to maintain profits. The international corporation prompted the technological 'revolution' of the post-war decades, as a means of reducing labour costs through automation. The demand of the corporation for a general level of political stability within which to operate implicated it heavily in counter-revolution, both in east and west, and encouraged the growth of an international 'military-industrial complex' to develop and sell the high technology of communication, surveillance and destruction. Because high technology is necessary to capitalist expansion, the virtues of moon-shots, of Concorde and of nuclear power are publicly extolled to demonstrate that we live in a 'technological age', though in global terms most people are unable to benefit from high technology, which at best stands in the way of the development of 'appropriate' technology and at worst is mis-used by the industrial sector, with harmful effects.

The effects of northern capitalism and its technologies have been felt most in the Third World, where they have dramatically changed both rural and urban economies. As in the 19th century, falling levels of employment in agriculture have driven masses of people into the big cities in search of work in the new industries. But unlike the 19th-century factory system, the increasingly technological bias of modern industry offers fewer and fewer jobs. The result is uncontrolled urbanisation allied with chronic unemployment, poverty and depressing living conditions, in cities throughout the Third World.

In the developed world, official policies of containment of urban growth and of decentralisation began to fail soon after the war, in the face of mounting pressures for financial concentration. Cities continued to expand as centres of national and international exchange and began to employ ever larger numbers of office employees and of workers in the service industries needed to support them. City authorities with decentralisation policies found that their large working populations had to travel from farther and farther afield, commuting daily across the green belts which separated the work centres from their satellite towns and suburbs. The biggest cities now lay at the economic centre of whole regions and even began to coalesce, growing into vast conurbations like the 600 km urban complex linking Boston with New York, Philadelphia and Washington.

The economic function of the post-war city was as a commercial rather than an industrial centre. With the increased speed and efficiency of road transport it became uneconomic to continue to locate industry in expensive and congested city centres. Instead, industrial growth was directed to the outer suburbs and increasingly to new towns. Many countries had massive town-building programmes in the post-war years. Apart from such unusual cases as Costa and Niemeyer's Brasilia, and Le Corbusier's Chandigarh, both of which were conceived as administrative centres, and satellite towns such as Reston, VA, and Farsta in Sweden, designed as dormitory suburbs to Washington and Stockholm respectively, most new towns had an industrial *raison d'être*. Finance came from a variety of sources: for the company town of Kitimat, BC, from private enterprise; for Toulouse-le-Mirail in Haute Garonne from the parent city of Toulouse; for Elizabeth in South Australia from the state government; and for the Dutch, Israeli, Japanese and British new towns from the national government. New towns were able to offer efficient modern industrial premises and services at low cost, and to attract young skilled workers and their families with guarantees of modern housing and attractive, even luxurious, surroundings. The numerous British new towns, from Stevenage to Milton Keynes, did this with such success that they emptied the cities of much of their industry and jobs, and many of their most skilled and active

214

workers, leaving behind a society increasingly polarised between a comfortable suburban middle class and an inner-city poor. The 'bourgeoisification' of the workers in the new towns distanced them further from the poor of the cities who, unskilled immigrants or elderly, usually badly housed, were left behind in a cycle of deprivation made all the more intense by contrast with the relative affluence elsewhere.

The archetype of suburban affluence, universally known through films, books and the media, was Los Angeles. By the 1940s it had become a paradigm of everything promised by suburbia but rarely attained elsewhere: an equable climate, outdoor living among beaches and mountains, luxurious purpose-built houses, an elegant life-style and above all the speed and mobility of a city fully adapted to the needs of the automobile. Los Angeles cut across the conventional European concept of what a city should be. It was vast and sprawling, 200 square kilometres in extent. It had no coherent architectural form in the conventional sense, and its downtown area, with two-thirds of the land given over to roads and parking, was the exact reverse of the high-density European city centre. Instead it had its own inherent structural logic provided by the freeway system. Nor was there any consistency of architectural style; individualism demanded infinite novelty and variety, and encouraged many talented architects to discover new ways of creating living environments for a society in pursuit of self-gratification. Among them were Richard Neutra's Tremaine house at Santa Barbara (1947–8) and his own house at Silver Lake Boulevard (1932), and the house in Santa Monica (1949) designed by Charles Eames (1907–78) for himself, using industrial components. The problem of building on the steeply sloping foothills was met by John Lautner in his Chemosphere house (1960), a mushroom-shaped structure cantilevered out from one central column, and by houses of Craig Ellwood, especially his Hale house, Beverly Hills (1951), and his Smith house, West Los Angeles (1955), a single-storey house perched on two extra storeys of steel framing. Though they were conceived in terms of the Californian climate and landscape, the source of architectural style for many of these houses was the east coast, where the European emigrés were developing the ideas of the modern movement in its new American context. Mies van der Rohe's work on the campus of Illinois Institute of Technology established the beautifully-designed steel-and-glass box as an acceptable architectural form. This was developed by Philip Johnson in his own house at New Canaan, CT (1949), and by Mies himself in the Farnsworth house at Plano, IL (1950). Gropius and Breuer continued to promote rationalism in their house designs in Connecticut and Massachusetts; they trained younger American designers such as John Johansen, whose own houses in Connecticut picked up their idiom.

In the mid-west, by contrast, Paul Schweikher's Upton House at Scottsdale was inspired by Wright's earlier Taliesin West, while Wright's follower Bruce Goff developed his own personal elemental style, seen at its best in the Bavinger house at Norman, OK (1950–5). Paolo Soleri and Mark Mills pursued similar aims with their Desert House (1951–2) at Cave Creek, AZ, while Goff's admirer Herb Greene built himself a house at Norman, OK (1960–1), whose crouching outline was extraordinarily expressive of some giant raven on the prairie.

Houses of this quality and character were relatively rare amid the vast suburban areas which grew up on the edge of every town, assisted by the universal sale of the motor car. Unlike Los Angeles, most cities were unable to adapt fully to car ownership; the suburbs might be designed for driving in, but most city centres were not, and it was necessary to expand or build suburban railways to carry commuters in and out of the

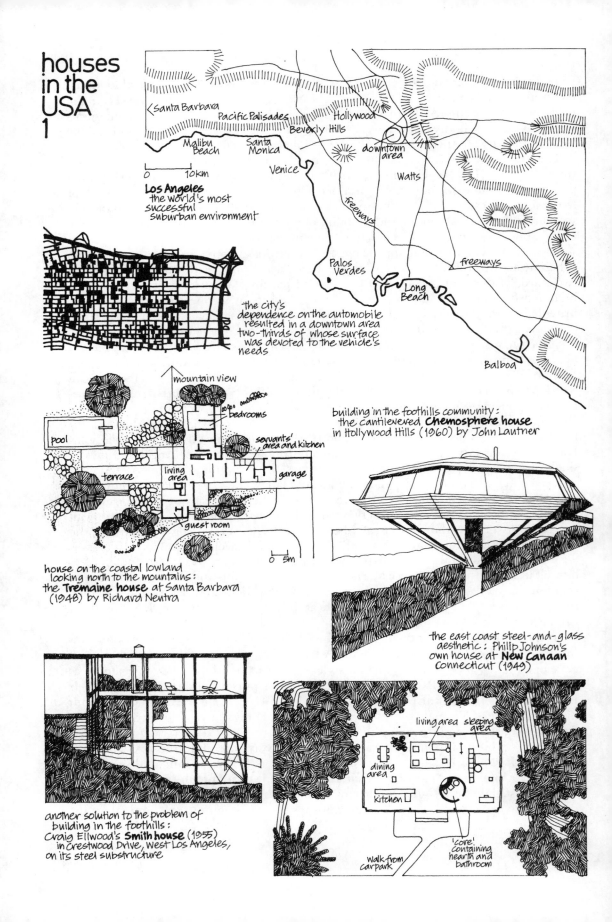

houses in the USA 1

Santa Barbara

Pacific Palisades

Malibu Beach

Santa Monica

Venice

Hollywood

Beverly Hills

downtown area

Watts

freeways

Palos Verdes

Long Beach

freeways

Balboa

Los Angeles the world's most successful suburban environment

the city's dependence on the automobile resulted in a downtown area two-thirds of whose surface was devoted to the vehicle's needs

mountain view

pool

bedrooms

servants' area and kitchen

terrace

living area

garage

guest room

0   5m

house on the coastal lowland looking north to the mountains: the **Tremaine house** at Santa Barbara (1948) by Richard Neutra

building in the foothills community: the cantilevered **Chemosphere house** in Hollywood Hills (1960) by John Lautner

the east coast steel-and-glass aesthetic: Philip Johnson's own house at **New Canaan** Connecticut (1949)

another solution to the problem of building in the foothills: Craig Ellwood's **Smith house** (1955) in Crestwood Drive, West Los Angeles, on its steel substructure

living area   sleeping area

dining area

kitchen

'core' containing hearth and bathroom

walk from carpark

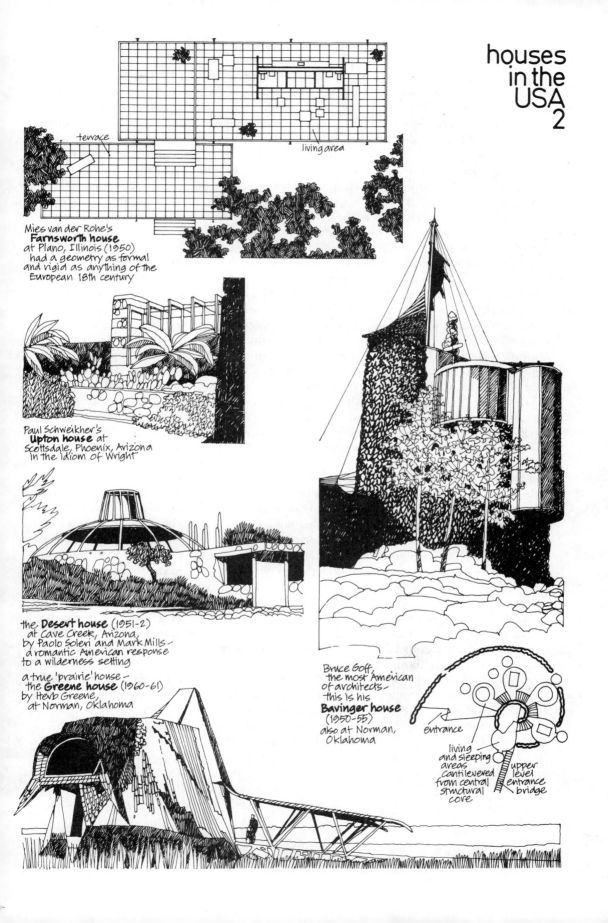

terrace

living area

Mies van der Rohe's
Farnsworth house
at Plano, Illinois (1950)
had a geometry as formal
and rigid as anything of the
European 18th century

Paul Schweikher's
Upton house at
Scottsdale, Phoenix, Arizona
in the idiom of Wright

the **Desert house** (1951-2)
at Cave Creek, Arizona,
by Paolo Soleri and Mark Mills –
a romantic American response
to a wilderness setting

a true 'prairie' house –
the **Greene house** (1960-61)
by Herb Greene,
at Norman, Oklahoma

Bruce Goff,
the most American
of architects –
this is his
Bavinger house
(1950-55)
also at Norman,
Oklahoma

entrance

living
and sleeping
areas
cantilevered
from central
structural
core

upper
level
entrance
bridge

business area. Alongside the older railways of London, Paris and New York came the post-war 'metro' systems of Moscow, Montreal and Milan and the 'rapid-transit' systems of San Francisco and Hong Kong. Although in most big cities as many as 90% of commuters travelled by public transport, it was still necessary to adapt city centres for commercial road transport and for 'essential' car users; the cost of maintaining such complex transport systems was often immense, not only financially but also in their inefficiency and the drastic effects on the environment and townscape.

Another factor that began to change the face of cities, often more radically than at any other time in their history, was the enormous financial profit that began to accrue from post-war commercial growth. City centres were convenient outlets for investment capital. In central areas, land was a scarce resource, needed for working-space, for living-space for the low-paid among the working population who could not afford to live in the suburbs and travel in, and for schools, hospitals and recreation. It was ostensibly to establish in a disinterested way the relative social importance of all these competing claims that most countries developed a land-use planning system, the most comprehensive and frequently-cited example of which was that set out in the British Town and Country Planning Act of 1947. In practice, however, the planning system was yet one more arm of the state; in capitalist economies the investment ethic began to dominate that of social need. The system uncritically accepted the principle of re-development without reference to the fact that it allowed land values to escalate out of control. There was an undue concentration on the physical rather than the social effects of new development. In the competition for land it was the big investors who won; luxury housing, shopping precincts and most particularly office blocks were the result, and in the face of welcome proposals to enlarge the rate-base by investing money in their city each local authority tended to relax density restrictions and to abolish controls on building height. A new generation of tower blocks appeared; the characteristic New York skyscraper of the 1930s was superseded by the rectangular slab block inside an almost featureless glass skin, whose seemingly endless design was the *reductio ad absurdum* of the need to provide many repetitive floors of offices or apartments in a logical, economical way. Glass skins were prone to heat loss in winter and solar heat gain in summer; buildings often had to be heavily serviced, consuming large amounts of energy in heating and ventilation. Economical use could be made of deep sites if the buildings were correspondingly deepened, placing many workers at such a distance from windows that they worked permanently under artificial light.

Many tower blocks were extremely elegant and expensive in detail and proportion, if bland and uninspiring in their general conception. Pietro Belluschi's building for the Equitable Savings and Loan Association of Portland, OR (1948), had one of the earliest glass skins, and Wright's laboratory tower for the Johnson Wax Company at Racine, WI (1947–50), was a highly individualistic variant, in which the glazing was not sheet-glass but Pyrex tubing. Mies van der Rohe's luxury apartment blocks at 860 and 880 Lake Shore Drive in Chicago (1948–51) were a development of his own elegant steel-and-glass aesthetic. The cigar-box-shaped slab block became a common form; Le Corbusier and others designed one for the United Nations in New York (1947–52), Skidmore, Owings and Merrill for the Lever company (1952) and Mies van der Rohe and Philip Johnson for the Seagram Company (1958), both in New York. For a slab block, the 'House of Seagram' was beautifully designed and ostentatiously costly, not only in the marble, bronze and tinted glass in which it was clothed, but in the fact that it devoted a large proportion of its expensive Park Avenue site to a public plaza.

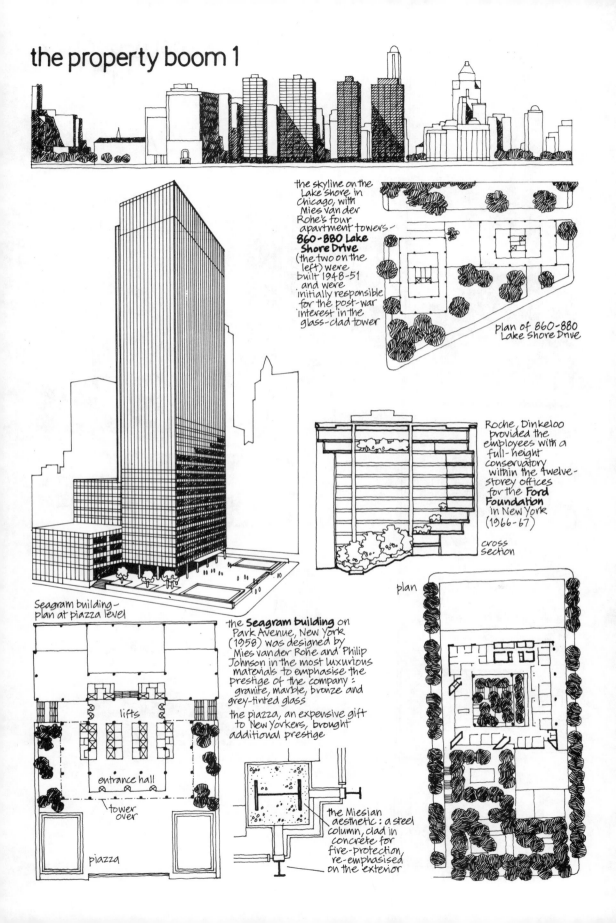

the skyline on the Lake Shore in Chicago, with Mies van der Rohe's four apartment towers – **860-880 Lake Shore Drive** (the two on the left) were built 1948-51 and were initially responsible for the post-war interest in the glass-clad tower

plan of 860-880 Lake Shore Drive

Roche, Dinkeloo provided the employees with a full-height conservatory within the twelve-storey offices for the **Ford Foundation** in New York (1966-67)

cross section

plan

Seagram building – plan at piazza level

the **Seagram building** on Park Avenue, New York (1958) was designed by Mies van der Rohe and Philip Johnson in the most luxurious materials to emphasise the prestige of the company: granite, marble, bronze and grey-tinted glass

the piazza, an expensive gift to New Yorkers, brought additional prestige

lifts

entrance hall

tower over

piazza

the Miesian aesthetic: a steel column, clad in concrete for fire-protection, re-emphasised on the exterior

Heutrich and Petschigg's
Phoenix tower
in Düsseldorf (1957-60)

Revell and Parkin's
Toronto City Hall (1958-65)

council chamber

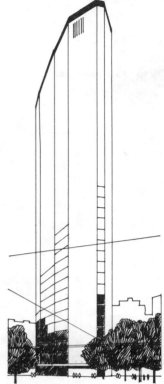

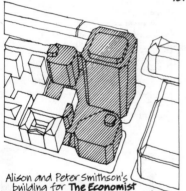

Alison and Peter Smithson's
building for **The Economist**
newspaper in London (1962-64)
which interrupted the traditional
street-scene to provide a plazza

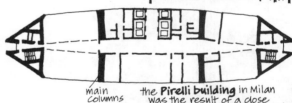

main columns

the **Pirelli building** in Milan
was the result of a close
partnership between the architect
Gio Ponti and the structural
engineer Pier Luigi Nervi

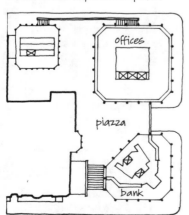

offices

piazza

bank

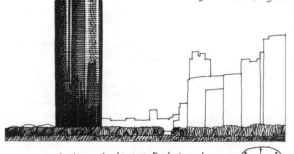

Graham, Anderson, Probst and
White's **Lake Point tower**
in Chicago (1968)
containing luxury apartments
and commercial offices

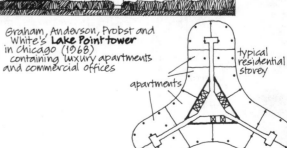

typical
residential
storey

apartments

Largesse of this kind became a prestigious feature of many subsequent office towers, from Skidmore, Owings and Merrill's Union Carbide building and Chase Manhattan building in New York (both 1957–60) to Alison and Peter Smithson's building for *The Economist* in London (1962–4).

In Milan, the architect Gio Ponti (1891–1979) designed an elegant office slab for the Pirelli company (1955–9). Here was a deliberate attempt to escape from the endless repetition of glass-skin walling and to create a building with a finite and satisfying shape. The inherent form of the building derived partly from Ponti's rationalist planning and partly from the imaginative structure of Pier Luigi Nervi (1891–1979). The nearby Torre Velasca by the firm BBPR (1956–7) was an even greater departure in skyscraper design. In contrast to the Miesian approach, whose architectural anonymity suited the facelessness of multi-nationalism, the Milanese philosophy belonged to the earlier, more primitive phase of capitalism in which deliberate use was made of historical reference to create a sense of civic pride. The post-war affluence of the Roman, Torinese and Milanese bourgeoisie gave rise to a minor artistic revival, in the cinema, in literature and in design. Furniture design became imaginative and slightly outrageous, like the transparent inflatable chair and the flexible 'sacco' chair produced by Zanotta of Milan, or the mildly decadent and historicist furniture of Vico Magistretti, all of which seemed to overturn the rationalist principles of the modern movement. In architecture, too, there was a concern for historicism; the work of Ignazio Gardella (b. 1905), such as his house of the Zattere in Venice (1957), and of Franco Albini (1905–77) and Franca Helg, as in their department store for La Rinascente in Rome (1961), reminded some critics of the 'Liberty' style of the Art Nouveau period. The historicism of the Torre Velasca was that of the late middle ages; its cantilevered upper storeys and slightly castellated roof-line were reminiscent of the Florentine Palazzo Vecchio.

As in the middle ages, a high tower demonstrated the pride and prestige of its owner and consequently had to be distinguishable from its neighbours. As beautifully-detailed slab blocks grew more common, architects sought – while retaining the essential economies of scale and repetition – to vary the basic shapes for greater identity. Hentrich and Petschnigg's Phoenix tower in Düsseldorf (1957–60) consisted of two slabs, one large, one small, placed side by side. Revell and Parkin's City Hall in Toronto (1958–65) also had two slabs, but they were curved round a central, circular council-chamber. For Lake Point Tower in Chicago (1968) Graham, Anderson, Probst and White went back to Mies van der Rohe's early 'design for a glass skyscraper' to produce a tall tower with a serpentine outer wall of glass. Larger still was the 100-storey John Hancock tower in Chicago (1969) by Skidmore, Owings and Merrill, a giant monolith whose rectangular form was relieved by large diagonal wind-braces on the outside. Yet this was exceeded in height by Minoru Yamasaki's twin towers for the World Trade Center in New York (1962–77) and again by Skidmore, Owings and Merrill's gigantic Sears tower in Chicago (1968–70), currently the highest building in the world.

Among the most interesting of the prestige office buildings was the headquarters for the Ford Foundation in New York (1966–7) designed by Roche, Dinkeloo and Associates as a broad twelve-storey block whose main feature was an equally high internal conservatory into which the offices opened at each level. The creation of this benign kind of internal environment, as an antidote to the noise and pollution of the busy streets, became a feature of office design. It was seen, for example, in the work of

neo-Liberty

Michele Achilli, Daniele Brigidini and Guido Canella: **house** near Seveso (1965)

Ignazio Gardella's **house** on the Zattere in Venice (1957)

studio BBPR: the **Torre Velasca** in Milan (1956-7), the archetype of the neo-Liberty style

Gatti, Paolini and Teodoro: the **Sacco** chair (1967) manufactured by Zanotta of Milan

De Pas, D'Urbino, Lomazzi and Scholari: the **Blow** chair, in inflatable plastic (1967) also manufactured by Zanotta

Franco Albini and Franca Helg: **La Rinascente** store in Rome (1961)

Vico Magistretti's red lacquer **chair** (1960) made by Cassina

Norman Foster, his Willis Faber Dumas offices in Ipswich (1973) and his proposed glass tower in Hong Kong for the Shanghai and Hong Kong Bank, zones of private affluence insulated from the public spaces outside.

During the 1960s, schemes for central area redevelopment in western cities reached an extravagant climax. In Montreal the Place Bonaventure (1967), by Affleck, Desbarats, Dimakopoulos, Lebensold and Sise, was a multi-level complex housing 100,000 square metres of commercial floorspace. In London speculative commercial proposals by land-owners, beginning with those designed by the architects Cotton, Ballard and Blow for the 'Monico' site in Piccadilly Circus (1954), had proliferated by the mid-1960s into separate but linked development schemes covering the whole of the Covent Garden area, part of Leicester Square, all of Piccadilly Circus, most of Regent Street and large areas of Oxford Street and Mayfair, involving high-level decks and walk-ways, moving pavements, underground roads and millions of square metres of new commercial floorspace. In Paris, too, though most new development was being directed towards the vast, 700-hectare inner suburban site of La Défense just west of the Étoile, the winding-up of the market at Les Halles offered a rare opportunity for redevelopment in the centre. A number of ambitious and bizarre schemes were prepared, which met with increasing local hostility. In Paris, London and elsewhere there was growing concern at the very principle of redevelopment, both among middle-class conservationists wishing to keep the old buildings and from local working-class communities anxious to protect the existing social structure of the central area. They were assisted by the over-ambitious and impracticable nature of many of the schemes themselves. In Covent Garden, the conservationists won; most of the old buildings were kept and renovated. At Les Halles, they lost; Baltard's buildings went, to be replaced by new commercial developments of which the magnificent centre-piece was the high-technology Centre Beaubourg (1976) by Piano and Rogers. In both cases the old social structure was destroyed; expensive rehabilitation was just as inimical as expensive redevelopment to a precarious local economy based on low land-values.

Speculative property development was the most flagrant example of capitalism at work. The buildings the system produced could be seen for what they were, not designed to meet human need but to act as financial assets. It hardly mattered that the London office tower of Centre Point (1959–63), designed by Richard Seifert, remained empty for fifteen years; though not housing workers or even earning rent, it was still increasing in value and borrowing-power. Like multi-national corporations, the property investors began to cross national boundaries in search of better financial returns: Americans to invest in Europe, Europeans in America, and both in the exploited, artificially booming cities of the Third World.

Most architects were in no doubt about the direction in which their role lay. For the sake of critical acclaim or professional success it was possible to ignore the social effects of commercial redevelopment or even to convince themselves and others of its social value, that it brought 'new life' to 'outworn' areas, that it was possible to 'exploit' the capitalist system to create public benefits. Plazas in front of tower blocks were somehow thought adequate recompense for the drastic economic effects created by their corporate owners. The highest architectural quality thus often emerged from a background of social and economic injustice.

The post-war years were remarkable too for an extraordinary number of public buildings of a variety, originality and technical quality surpassing even those of the Victorian age. For fifty years, depression, political turmoil and war had provided fertile ground for the theories of the modern movement but little possibility of their realisation. Now, an affluent, post-war society provided the economic and political opportunity. There was no longer any reason to associate modern architecture with socialism. The dominance in the east of state-controlled capitalism and in the west of monopoly capitalism served by the state had pushed revolutionary politics to the periphery of public life. Public and private sectors were now joined together in an ever more complex web of economic relationships, in which state intervention, as Keynes had proposed, was used to increase rather than diminish the strength of capitalism. The architectural expression of this strength, whether commissioned by public or private clients, was both lavish and imaginative, exploring all the structural and spatial possibilities of modern design.

The post-war commercial promotion of bourgeois art-forms – especially of classical music, popularised by the gramophone and radio, and of the visual arts, by publishing and television – was reflected in the building of concert halls, galleries and arts centres. The Royal Festival Hall in London (1949–51) was built as part of an exhibition of British production to celebrate the centenary of the Great Exhibition. It was designed by a group of LCC architects under Robert Matthew, including Leslie Martin, Edwin Williams and Peter Moro. Acoustically it was a technical achievement and, until the drastic alterations during the 1960s which eroded much of its character, it was a showpiece of all the spatial techniques of the international style. The Guggenheim Museum in New York (1943–59) was Frank Lloyd Wright's personal approach to exhibition design, planned as a large spiral ramp around a central domed space. Kuneo Maekawa's Festival Hall in Tokyo (1959–61) and Kenzo Tange's Cultural Centre at Nichinan (1961–3) were dramatic, monumental concrete buildings owing something both to Le Corbusier and to the constructivist timber buildings of Japanese tradition. Hans Scharoun's Philharmonic Hall in Berlin (1960–3) was a rich, expressionist building, tailored to the needs of a particular conductor and orchestra. The Lincoln Center in New York (1957–66) by Abramovitz and Harrison, in association with Philip Johnson and Eero Saarinen, was a group of buildings forming an elaborate and specialised cultural 'ghetto', as if to emphasise the apartness of fine art from the everyday life of the city. London's version, much less opulent with its dour concrete buildings, was the South Bank complex, where the Royal Festival Hall was augmented by the LCC's Queen Elizabeth Hall, Purcell Room and Hayward Gallery (1961–3) and later by Denys Lasdun's National Theatre. Most dramatic of all was Jørn Utzon's Sydney Opera House (1956–73), its beautiful sail-like concrete roofs, engineered by Ove Arup, dominating the harbour front. A different kind of opulence was seen in Norman Foster's Sainsbury Gallery at the University of East Anglia (1978), an elegant high-technology shed, whose sensory equipment adapted the enclosing lightweight membrane to changes in the weather. The building, like many of its genre, was a quid pro quo to the public from a family of successful businessmen, one of a long line of architectural monuments which discreetly combined altruism with advertisement.

The growth of international sport, promoted both for reasons of national prestige and for the profits to be made from television and sponsorship, was seen especially in the increasing popularity of football and athletics. In the Latin-American countries, where soccer offered aspiring young players an escape route out of poverty and spectators a temporary respite from it, the game almost became a religion. The Maracaña Stadium in Rio, holding 200,000 people, was the largest in the world and the Aztec Stadium in Mexico City, built in 1968, one of the best-appointed. National govern-

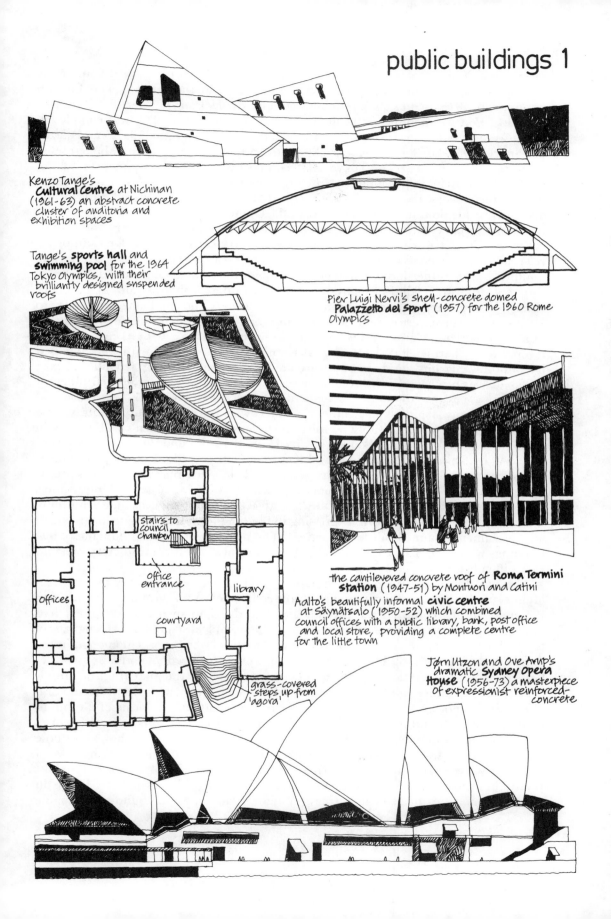

Kenzo Tange's **Cultural Centre** at Nichinan (1961-63) an abstract concrete cluster of auditoria and exhibition spaces

Tange's **sports hall** and **swimming pool** for the 1964 Tokyo Olympics, with their brilliantly designed suspended roofs

Pier Luigi Nervi's shell-concrete domed **Palazzetto del Sport** (1957) for the 1960 Rome Olympics

stairs to council chamber

office entrance

library

Offices

courtyard

the cantilevered concrete roof of **Roma Termini Station** (1947-51) by Montuori and Catini

Aalto's beautifully informal **civic centre** at Säynätsalo (1950-52) which combined council offices with a public library, bank, post office and local store, providing a complete centre for the little town

grass-covered steps up from 'agora'

Jørn Utzon and Ove Arup's dramatic **Sydney Opera House** (1956-73) a masterpiece of expressionist reinforced-concrete

ments and city corporations bid vast sums of money to stage the World Cup or the Olympic Games, sometimes bankrupting themselves in the process. The London Olympics of 1948 used existing buildings, and for the Helsinki Games of 1952 Lindegren and Jäntti's small-scale and informal stadium, begun in 1933, was completed. These were outdone, however, by Nervi's elegant domed Palazzetto (1957) and Palazzo del Sport (1958–60) for the Rome Olympics of 1960, by the fine parabolic-roofed stadium of Kenzo Tange for Tokyo in 1964, and by Frei Otto's Munich stadium of 1972, with its 90,000-square-metre tented roof on masts and steel cables. In Montreal in 1976 the costs escalated to such an extent that they caused a political crisis locally and world-wide doubts about the future of the Games.

The Victorian civic building had imparted its message through literary and historical association; it was necessary to be reasonably educated to read, for example, a reference to the Medici in the Villard houses. The expressiveness of the modern civic building, on the other hand, came either through the functionalism of its design, or through an abstract kind of expressionism which offered oblique, almost Freudian clues to its meaning. Nervi's exhibition halls (1947–9) and his Palazzo del Lavoro (1959–61) in Turin were pure structure, refined and developed into geometric abstraction. Montuori and Catini's railway station in Rome (1947–51) with its curved, cantilevered roof, Saarinen's TWA building at Kennedy airport (1961) with its roof poised like an alighting bird, and the same architect's terminal building at Dulles airport (1958–62), its heavy concrete roof floating above walls of glass, were in their different ways abstract expressions of the excitement of travel, totally removed from the literal references of, say, Pennsylvania station, with its overtones of romantic antiquity.

Buildings with a recognisably political purpose, such as Saarinen's US Embassy in London (1956–60), Tange's Kurashiki City Hall (1958–60) and the Boston City Hall (1962–9) by Kallmann, McKinnell and Knowles all displayed the formal, monumental and ultimately forbidding dignity with which modern bureaucracy, despite its pretensions to accessibility and democracy, continued to invest itself. Only Aalto's little civic centre at Säynätsalo (1950–2), with its homely materials and beautifully informal planning came near to expressing in building form the humane ideals which all governments claimed but few practised. The problem of creating humane public buildings which were also formal and monumental was a self-contradictory one and very difficult to solve.

This was especially true of church design, where it seemed necessary to evolve an architectural language which not only expressed ideas of cosmic grandeur but also met the most intimate individual psychological needs. The medieval designers had managed this, but it was impossible now to use the complex, symbolic, lost language of the gothic architect; the dangers of attempting to do so were apparent enough in the failure of the buildings of the gothic revival to capture the original gothic spirit. Giles Gilbert Scott's Liverpool cathedral (1903–80), exemplifies the anachronistic emptiness of the imitation gothic style; while Basil Spence's new Coventry cathedral (1951–62) demonstrates the inadequacy of trying to adapt the forms of Gothic to modern materials and techniques. What the modern architect could offer, of course, was a rational approach to planning, and the most successful churches were those which solved the spatial and dynamic needs of the liturgy in functional terms. Two of the finest were designed as multi-purpose buildings: Aalto's Vuoksenniska church at Imatra in Finland (1956–8) and Le Corbusier's pilgrimage chapel of Notre Dame du Haut at Ronchamp, near Besançon in the Vosges (1950–5). Aalto's building is capable

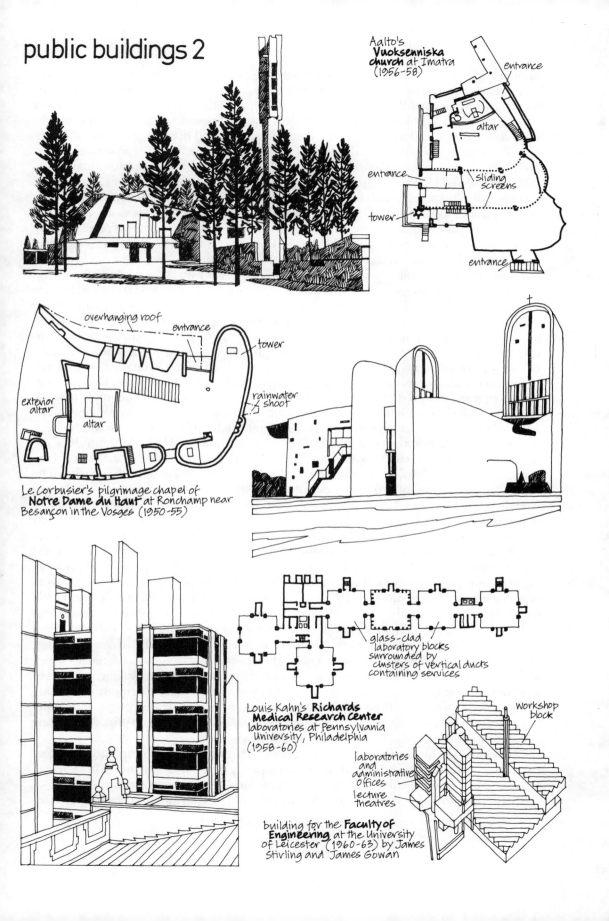

public buildings 2

Aalto's **Vuoksenniska church** at Imatra (1956-58)

entrance

altar

entrance

Sliding screens

tower

entrance

overhanging roof

entrance

tower

exterior altar

altar

rainwater shoot

Le Corbusier's pilgrimage chapel of **Notre Dame du Haut** at Ronchamp near Besançon in the Vosges (1950-55)

glass-clad laboratory blocks surrounded by clusters of vertical ducts containing services

Louis Kahn's **Richards Medical Research Center** laboratories at Pennsylvania University, Philadelphia (1958-60)

workshop block

laboratories and administrative offices

lecture theatres

building for the **Faculty of Engineering** at the University of Leicester (1960-63) by James Stirling and James Gowan

of subdivision by screens into three separate cells, and of simultaneous use as a church and a community centre; Le Corbusier's chapel has an internal focus for intimate worship and an external one for open-air gatherings of thousands of pilgrims. Rational planning provided part of the answer, but it was still necessary to evolve a symbolic language; the two buildings reflect the cultural background in each case – one northern and Protestant, the other southern and Catholic – as well as the character of the architects themselves. Aalto's approach was Apollonian; his building is calm and rational, flooded with clear light from large, high-level windows. The unusual detailed complexity of his architectural language resulted in a building of intellectual intensity. Le Corbusier's approach, by contrast, was Dionysian, using form, texture, patches of colour and shafts of light to create a numinous, theatrical effect; panels of painted glass, set in thick masonry walls, glow like jewels in a cave, and the heavy whale-back roof floats above the walls on narrow strips of sunlight.

One of the most significant areas of architectural effort was seen at universities and colleges as they rapidly expanded to provide the administrative and technical leaders of the growing industrial states. As land-owners, many older colleges suddenly found themselves financial beneficiaries of the wild property boom of the post-war years; money flowed in from other sources too: from governments investing in the technological future or in prestige, and from successful businessmen investing in immortality by endowing colleges and faculties. In most countries, including some of the most advanced industrially, elementary education remained short of resources, but universities – the most cultured of clients – became showplaces of all that the finest modern architects could do with an open brief and a deep purse. It was financially possible to import major foreign architects if they were thought right for the job; Aalto was brought to MIT to design a dormitory block (1947–9), Le Corbusier to Harvard to produce the Carpenter Center (1961–3) with Luis Sert, and the foremost Danish architect Arne Jacobsen to Oxford to design the new St Catherine's College (1959 onwards). The controlling influence of Mies van der Rohe at IIT ensured a consistency of design; elsewhere, universities became architectural zoos, displaying an exotic variety of modern styles. At Yale, Kahn and Orr designed the Art Gallery and Design Center (1954) as a four-storey high concrete box, Saarinen's skating rink (1958) had a magnificent parabolic roof and Paul Rudolph's Art and Architecture building (1959–63) was a monumental essay in post-Constructivism. At Cambridge University there were new colleges, such as Richard Sheppard's Churchill College, and major extensions to older ones, like Powell and Moya's work at St John's. There were also a number of major buildings, including the calm, formal Harvey Court at Gonville and Caius (1959–62) by Leslie Martin and Colin St John Wilson, and the extraordinary brick and glass History Faculty Library (1966–8) by James Stirling. Major new buildings appeared at universities everywhere: Yamasaki's elegant McGregor Conference Center at Wayne, Detroit (1958), Louis Kahn's powerful, functionalist Richards Medical Research Center at Pennsylvania (1958–60), Stirling and Gowan's Engineering building at Leicester University (1960–3), its harsh, industrial materials expressive of its function, Dunelm House at Durham (1966) by the Architects' Co-Partnership, Aalto's fine auditorium at the Polytechnic Institute in Helsinki (1963–5).

The aim of all this environmental privilege was to help produce an intellectual élite, particularly the élite on whom industrial prosperity depended. By the 1970s science, engineering, administrative and business graduates comprised two-thirds or more of the collective annual output of universities, both in industrial and industrialising coun-

production line working in an auto plant of the 1930s

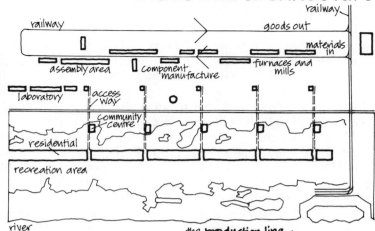

railway

railway

goods out

materials in

assembly area

component manufacture

furnaces and mills

laboratory

access way

Community centre

residential

recreation area

river

the production line – the logical layout of OSA's design for the Nizhninovgorod auto plant (1930)

the industrial aesthetic which derives from functional design – the Ford Glass Plant at Dearborn, Michigan (1922) by Albert Kahn

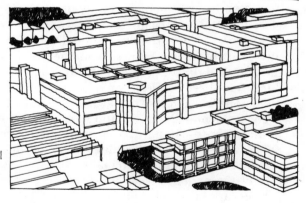

Figini and Pollini's **rational design** aiding the industrial process – the Olivetti Works at Ivrea (1934-57)

simple utility in a functional building designed with little thought for architectural effect – the NASA space vehicle assembly building in Florida (1962-66) by Urbahn

design for prestige in Eero Saarinen's GM Technical Center, Warren, Michigan (1949-55) – the water tower

tries. In the design of industrial buildings, as in the 19th century, it was unusual to involve a major architect – or even any kind of architect – unless there was a need for prestige, or for a treatment of special environmental sensitivity such as the architectural camouflage of the off-shore oil rigs at Long Beach to make them 'acceptable'. Saarinen's General Motors Technical Center at Warren, MI (1949–55), came clearly into the category of 'prestige', a group of elegant Miesian buildings calculated to impress the visitor and to inculcate in the employee a sense of corporate pride. Fuller's domed 'rotunda' building for Ford at Dearborn (1953) and his vast 100-metre domed repair shop (1958) for the Union Tank-car company at Baton Rouge, LA, had the added advantage of a remarkably short construction period. It was possible for the skilled designer to provide all kinds of economies and efficiencies through careful analysis of the industrial process and rationality of design. The Architects' Co-Partnership did this for the Brynmawr rubber factory (1945–52), as did Egon Eiermann in his cotton mill at Blumberg (1951), Figini and Pollini for their multi-phased Administrative and Technical Center for Olivetti at Ivrea (1934–57), Marco Zanuso for his Buenos Aires factory (1964) also for Olivetti, and Foster and Rogers for their Reliance Electronics factory at Swindon (1964–5). Philip Johnson's work on the nuclear reactor at Rehovet in Israel (1961), where he provided heavy concrete redoubts in an archaic style, and even a walled garden, must be categorised as beautification. The very opposite was true of the space vehicle assembly building (1962–6) designed by Max Urbahn and engineered by Roberts and Schaefer for Cape Kennedy, FL. Two hundred metres in height and capable of housing four Saturn rockets, the building was the biggest and most expensive shed in the world, designed almost entirely for utility and architecturally impressive mainly for its extraordinary size.

Over the four decades since the end of the war there has been a complete economic cycle, from post-war austerity and recovery, through the wild boom conditions of the 1960s, to the growing uncertainty of the early 1970s which by the late 1970s made it clear that the industrialised world was entering one of the worst self-inflicted crises in its history. Flexible, responsive and diverse, the multi-national corporation has generally been able to protect itself from the worst effects, while its policies have had unpredictable and drastic effects on local economies. National governments, on the other hand, have been helpless, partly because of the intensity of the crisis and partly because all national economies are now interdependent and have been affected simultaneously. A government wishing to adjust its economy has been able to do so only in areas under its direct control, mainly public spending and welfare. The welfare state has continued only as a spin-off from capitalist success, declining rapidly in times of recession when its resources are withdrawn to maintain profit-levels in the private sector. The architecture of the period reflects this tendency; whereas major commercial and industrial projects appear to continue unaffected, the building of schools, hospitals and public housing is noticeably subject to the condition of the national economy. The capitalist's self-justification has always been that he alone creates wealth. The 'liberal' conservatives and the social democrats of the 1960s and early 1970s – from Kennedy, Johnson and Trudeau in north America to Brandt, Wilson and Heath in Europe – claimed that this wealth was for the benefit of the whole of society, that capitalism was and should be used in an egalitarian way. Anthony Crosland's *The Future of Socialism* (1956) had expressed the widespread view that social progress depended on the maintenance of a healthy capitalist system, but by the late 1970s it was clear that if wealth had ever reached society as a whole it was not doing so now, even in the most advanced industrial countries. The ideology underwent a significant shift: capitalism should never have been seen as egalitarian. Society thrived on élitism and inequality, which alone could restore the wealth on which equality depended. The welfare state must be dismantled in order to save the system which provided the welfare state.

In addition to the large-scale post-war investment in commercial and industrial buildings, it was necessary to make an attack on the problems of poor housing and homelessness; these were intensified not only by the extensive wartime destruction and the general resolve to banish the slum conditions of the inter-war years, but also by the sudden recognition of the existence of a 'population problem'. This was the starting point of much planning theory; it was based on the undoubted problem of population growth in Third World countries and was extended by implication to those of the industrial north, where a similar growth was predicted.

An extensive body of architectural theory was developed to meet these actual and imagined problems. The desired higher standards, it was thought, could be met by modern industrialised building methods, by rational building design, and by the 'proper' planning of towns as offered by the emerging land-use planning systems. 'Higher standards' would include land-use zoning to separate the dirt and pollution of industry from residential areas, a major problem of Victorian cities; it would also include the introduction of sunlight, space and greenery as an antidote to their gloom and harshness. An ideal image of the city emerged, expressed in a million perspective drawings, of white, rationalist buildings with flat roofs and plenty of glass to let in the healing sun, set in spacious areas of municipal greenery.

Setting aside the appearance of the buildings, this kind of standard continued to be met in most suburbs and new towns but the economic logic of the system made it impossible to obtain in the cities themselves. High land values, the great investment potential of the building industry for major commercial interests and its emergence as a legitimate area for technical experiment ensured that working-class inner-city housing had a different set of criteria. The persistent imagery of the Futurists and Le Corbusier, which expressed the teeming dynamism of city centre life, together with the perceived need to match the scale of the 'population problem', gave an architectural respectability to high buildings at high density. So when in the 1950s and 1960s governments and city authorities began to call for higher residential densities they found an architectural profession swept away by its own propaganda and ready to justify its visual preferences for tower blocks and high-level walkways with theories of 'neighbourliness' and 'community' – which in effect meant putting a lot of people on a small amount of land. Though social issues were discussed, and even given considerable philosophical importance, they were very rarely analysed in terms of the economic facts; the whole intellectual basis for post-war design theory was essentially a visual and architectural one, coming predominantly from the great art historians such as Pevsner and Giedion, who appeared not to doubt that modern architecture alone was capable of answering 'the serious questions which it is the responsibility of the architect to answer'.

The generally accepted heroes of this serious quest were the architects of the Bauhaus and CIAM, Gropius, Mies van der Rohe and above all Le Corbusier who had crystallised all the current ideas on housing design in one of the most significant buildings of the post-war world. The Unité d'Habitation (1945–52), a great concrete slab block containing seventeen storeys of flats and duplex apartments, was set in open land near the edge of Marseille. On the roof were free-form concrete constructions containing sports facilities, laundry and crèche; in the middle of the building was a storey of local shops

231

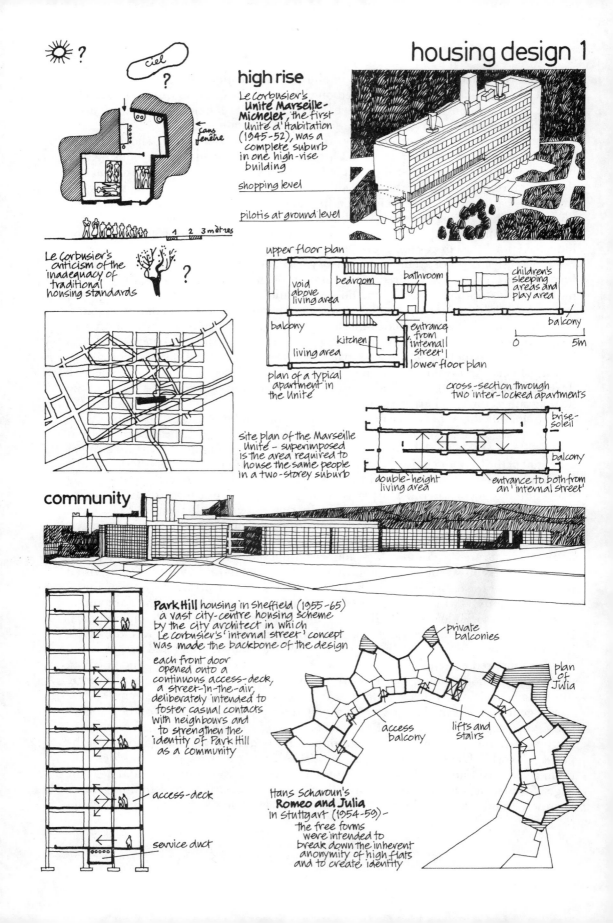

? ciel ?

sans fenêtre

1 2 3 mètres

high rise

Le Corbusier's **Unité Marseille-Michelet**, the first Unité d'Habitation (1945-52), was a complete suburb in one high-rise building

shopping level

pilotis at ground level

Le Corbusier's criticism of the inadequacy of traditional housing standards ?

upper floor plan

void above living area

bedroom

bathroom

children's sleeping areas and play area

balcony

entrance from internal street

balcony

kitchen

living area

lower floor plan

0   5m

plan of a typical apartment in the Unité

Site plan of the Marseille Unité — superimposed is the area required to house the same people in a two-storey suburb

cross-section through two inter-locked apartments

brise-soleil

balcony

double-height living area

entrance to both from an 'internal street'

community

Park Hill housing in Sheffield (1955-65) a vast city-centre housing scheme by the city architect in which Le Corbusier's 'internal street' concept was made the backbone of the design

each front door opened onto a continuous access-deck, a street-in-the-air, deliberately intended to foster casual contacts with neighbours and to strengthen the identity of Park Hill as a community

access-deck

service duct

private balconies

plan of Julia

access balcony

lifts and stairs

Hans Scharoun's **Romeo and Julia** in Stuttgart (1954-59) — the free forms were intended to break down the inherent anonymity of high flats and to create identity

housing design 2

British Ministry of Works emergency 'Portal' house (1944)

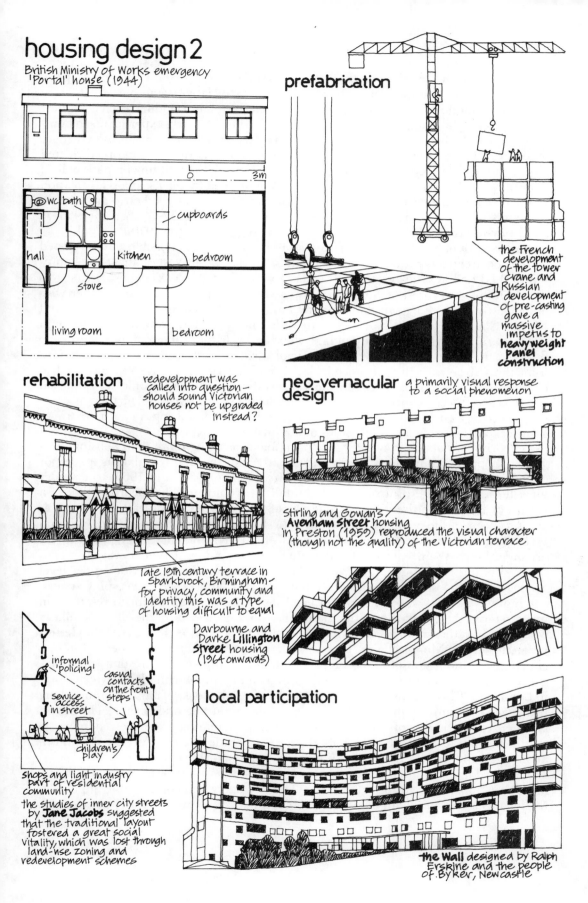

0 3m

wc bath
cupboards
hall
kitchen
bedroom
stove
living room
bedroom

prefabrication

the French development of the tower crane and Russian development of pre-casting gave a massive impetus to **heavy weight panel construction**

rehabilitation

redevelopment was called into question — should sound Victorian houses not be upgraded instead?

late 19th century terrace in Sparkbrook, Birmingham — for privacy, community and identity this was a type of housing difficult to equal

informal 'policing'
casual contacts on the front steps
service access in street
children's play

shops and light industry part of residential community

the studies of inner city streets by **Jane Jacobs** suggested that the traditional layout fostered a great social vitality, which was lost through land-use zoning and redevelopment schemes

neo-vernacular design

a primarily visual response to a social phenomenon

Stirling and Gowan's **Avenham Street** housing in Preston (1959) reproduced the visual character (though not the quality) of the Victorian terrace

Darbourne and Darke **Lillington Street** housing (1964 onwards)

local participation

the **Wall** designed by Ralph Erskine and the people of Byker, Newcastle

and the ground storey was raised up on elephantine *pilotis* to allow the landscape to flow underneath. The apartments, entered from an artificially-lit 'internal street', were ingeniously interlocked to obtain an aspect on each side of the building; each contained the double-height living-space familiar from Le Corbusier's early experiments in housing design and incorporated a balcony to form a link with the sun, space and greenery of the Provençal landscape outside. Each dwelling unit was designed in prefabricated pieces and set into the main reinforced-concrete frame of the building on pads of lead to insulate sound. The dimensional co-ordination implied by the use of prefabrication was evolved according to Le Corbusier's 'Modulor' system of geometric proportion. The Unité, other examples of which were built in Nantes (1952–5), Berlin (1956–7) and Briey-la-Fôret (1957–9), influenced housing design until the 1970s.

The concept of building high to retain as much landscape as possible was developed by the LCC architects Lucas, Howell and Killick at the Alton West estate at Roehampton in the London suburbs (1955–9) where tower and slab blocks, whose design was clearly influenced by the Unité, were disposed in an organised group together with other, low-rise dwellings, in the romantic landscape of Richmond Park. Powell and Moya's Churchill Gardens housing estate in Pimlico, London, won in competition in 1951, was another regular group of high slab blocks, without the romantic landscape but on a fine riverside site. For pseudo-sociological reasons, Denys Lasdun departed from the slab form in his 'cluster-blocks' in Bethnal Green (1954–60), designed to create upper-level spaces between the various dwellings which would foster casual contacts and 'neighbourliness'. In Stuttgart, Hans Scharoun went further; his two tower blocks 'Romeo' and 'Julia' (1954–9), on their open, hill-top site, were extravagantly expressionist in form, full of Freudian imagery.

Le Corbusier conceived of a large housing block as being more than housing, providing shopping, community needs and a pattern of internal circulation spaces for casual contact. It was common for an architect in the 1950s and 1960s to consider himself the legitimate controller of the 'total' environment. The incorporation of a variety of uses into one building was one way of extending architectural control over as many aspects of life as possible. The gigantic hilltop development of Park Hill and Hyde Park in Sheffield (1955–65) was indeed a total environment, designed by the city architect Lewis Womersley, and his assistants Jack Lynn and Ivor Smith, as a continuous complex of slab blocks of varying heights, linked together by wide, upper-level 'streets' and enclosing within their enfolding forms landscaped areas, play spaces, community facilities, school, pub and local shops. It was an attempt to re-create in modern terms the complexity of the traditional working-class life of the city. A similarly complex but rather more idyllic scheme was built by Atelier 5 – Fritz, Gerber, Hesterberg, Hostettler, Morgenthaler, Pini and Thormann – at Halen near Bern (1960), a close-knit, hillside group of low-rise private houses complete with restaurant, shops, garage and sports facilities. Patrick Hodgkinson and Leslie Martin's Brunswick Centre in London (1967–70) consisted of two stepped-back slab blocks of flats enclosing a long pedestrian concourse on to which faced shops, pub, restaurants and cinema. The heavy, symmetrical formality of the blocks and their punctuating towers owed more to Sant'Elia than to Le Corbusier, though there was little enough Futurist dynamism about the building's location in its quiet corner of Bloomsbury.

The third main strand of Le Corbusier's thought was his concern, like that of many of his contemporaries, for prefabrication. The war had given considerable impetus to the idea as a way of solving logistical problems in a short time. Apart from the new structural techniques learned from weapons technology, there had been emergency military building programmes, to which the British 'Nissen' hut, constructed from curved sheets of corrugated steel, and its American equivalent the 'Quonset', had considerably contributed. There had been Roosevelt's wartime housing programme for factory and munitions workers to which a number of architects, including Gropius and Breuer, had brought new ideas on quick-build and prefabrication. There was also Britain's post-war emergency rehousing programme in which the 'Arcon' short-life, single-storey 'prefab' house was invaluable.

In the post-war boom in school building, British achievements were exemplary, particularly the work of the Hertfordshire and Nottinghamshire County Councils and their respective architects Charles Aslin and Donald Gibson. Cheshunt primary school in Hertfordshire (1947) was the first of many humane, informal buildings systematically designed and constructed in a semi-military operation. Max Bill also used prefabricated construction in his new buildings for the Hochschule für Gestaltung at Ulm (1950–5), the self-styled successor to the Bauhaus; but the most acclaimed example was the British CLASP system, devised for the Consortium of Local Authorities Special Programme and used for many schools in the English midlands, which was awarded a *gran premio* at the Milan Triennale of 1960.

Prefabrication is useful when a large number of well-designed buildings are needed in a short time. It may be less appropriate for longer-term programmes. It has the effect of altering the pattern of labour needs, transferring much of the skilled work from the building site to the factory, a consideration of less importance in temperate countries than in northern ones, where the longer winters make site-work difficult. Those who benefit most are the manufacturers of components and the largest building contractors, capable of investing in new production methods. Those who benefit least are the smaller contractors and their workers, especially those in public labour forces, whose work fluctuates wildly as the larger contractors move in and out of the public sector in search of the best profits. Profits are to be made by the fortunate few, particularly when, as in many European countries after the Second World War, governments provide subsidies to aid the development of industrialised building. But subsidised or not, industrialised building methods have seldom been found to be cheap and with honourable exceptions like CLASP the end product has often been bad value for money.

Industrialised building became a political weapon in the fight to achieve high annual housing statistics. A number of systems, such as the Danish Larsen and Neilsen, the French Camus and the English Reema methods, had long and successful histories, but as industrialisation was officially promoted during the 1960s and manufacturers sensed the profits to be made, literally hundreds of new systems appeared on the international market. The housing estates of the sixties are legacies of this part-political, part-economic promotional exercise. The grim thirty-one-storey towers and slabs of Glasgow's Red Road estate (1964–8) by Sam Bunton Associates were steel-framed with clip-on asbestos panels, to a specially-designed system. The British Ministry of Housing's endless terraces at St Mary's, Oldham (1965–7), were built in pre-cast concrete panels to the 12M-Jespersen system. They were exceeded in anonymity and vastness only by the Southwark Council's Aylesbury estate (1965–70). Elsewhere in Europe, similar strides were being made, particularly in heavyweight pre-cast concrete construction, from the suburbs of Paris where the serpentine block at Bobigny was one of the longest in the world, to those of Moscow, where at the height of the boom 500 identical flats were being built in a day.

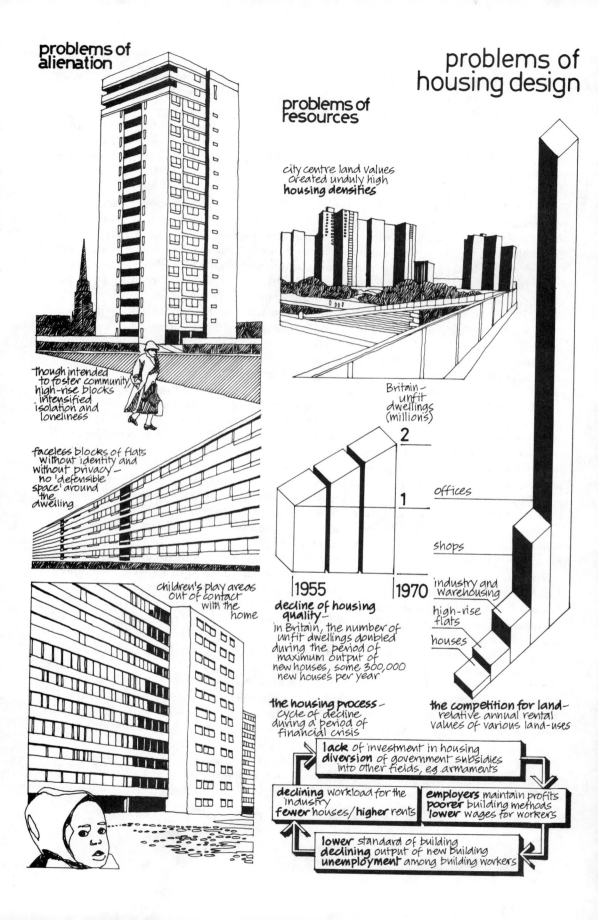

problems of alienation

problems of housing design

problems of resources

though intended to foster community, high-rise blocks intensified isolation and loneliness

city centre land values created unduly high **housing densities**

faceless blocks of flats without identity and without privacy — no 'defensible space' around the dwelling

children's play areas out of contact with the home

Britain — unfit dwellings (millions)

2

1

1955   1970

offices

shops

industry and warehousing

high-rise flats

houses

decline of housing quality — in Britain, the number of unfit dwellings doubled during the period of maximum output of new houses, some 300,000 new houses per year

the housing process — cycle of decline during a period of financial crisis

the competition for land — relative annual rental values of various land-uses

lack of investment in housing
diversion of government subsidies into other fields, eg. armaments

declining workload for the industry
fewer houses/**higher** rents

employers maintain profits
poorer building methods
lower wages for workers

lower standard of building
declining output of new building
unemployment among building workers

Industrialised building attracted investment for political and economic reasons, but the professionals were engaged in it because they believed in their own ability to predict, quantify, analyse and propose the optimum solution to any problem, independently of political considerations. This view had its counterpart in urban planning; here there was an urge to systematise decision-making, which led to the adoption of many numerical techniques, ranging from the familiar critical path analysis for charting programmes to the selection of preferred solutions to problems by using 'balance-sheets', 'goals-achievement matrices' or cost-benefit analysis, the most ambitious example of which was probably the Roskill Commission's examination of four alternative sites for London's third airport. This belief in the independence of the man of science, and of architecture and planning as some Panglossian exercise in optimisation, took a hard knock when the architectural achievements of the 1960s began to be examined. They were revealed as not being all for the best in the best of all possible worlds.

As in the 19th century, the architectural focus of all the doubts and questions was the environment of the inner city. It was becoming obvious, despite all the new investment and the architectural theorising, that slums were not disappearing as fast as they should; while some were being replaced, other old houses were falling further into disrepair, forming a stock of dilapidated accommodation which although over-priced was all that certain sections of the inner-city poor, notably the recent immigrants, could either obtain or afford. Yet it was also obvious that many of the new buildings, particularly the untried, system-built blocks, deteriorated almost as fast. There were also increasing doubts about the environment they offered; Le Corbusier's vision was one thing, but vast concrete warrens without balconies, without open space, without community halls or local shops, were another. Reports were received of the malaise of life in tower blocks, of tenants marooned by faulty lifts, of children's playgrounds too remote from the homes to be safely supervised, of lonely old people dying unnoticed. The problem of vandalism particularly concerned the authorities; it was bad enough even at pleasant, spacious Roehampton, let alone the bleak towers of Hutchestown-Gorbals in Glasgow, the giant Pruitt-Igoe flats in St Louis, or the crowded multi-racial estates of New York's lower East Side.

The biggest doubt of all was raised over the very principle of redevelopment. In the drive for quantity it was recognised that certain qualities were being lost as existing communities were broken up and dispersed and their old neighbourhoods laid waste, to remain in some cases, such as Liverpool, as vast areas of dereliction in the middle of the city. Young and Willmott's *Family and Kinship in East London* (1957) and Jane Jacob's *The Death and Life of Great American Cities* (1961) were two pioneering studies discovered by urbanists in the 1960s amid a growing interest in the rehabilitation, rather than redevelopment, of older working-class areas. The response of architects to this was to rediscover in visual terms the romance of the working-class community. As early as 1959 Lyons, Israel and Ellis, with Stirling and Gowan, had attempted to reproduce the character of Victorian Preston in their Avenham Street terrace housing. Darbourne and Darke's Lillington Street Phase 1 in London (1964–8), with its broken outlines and warm red brickwork, began to set a pattern for what erroneously became known as a 'neo-vernacular' style, in which smallness of scale, intimacy of space and the use of 'natural' materials – that is, brickwork – was offered as an antidote to the barren megalomania of the big housing estates. This approach persisted for the next decade or more, becoming the accepted technique for housing design, though its signi-

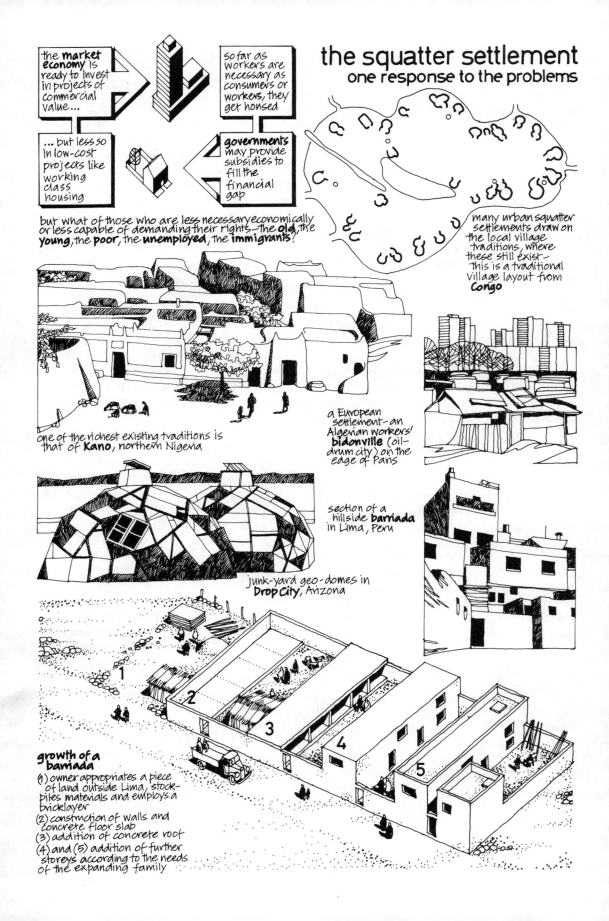

the **market economy** is ready to invest in projects of commercial value...

...but less so in low-cost projects like working class housing

so far as workers are necessary as consumers or workers, they get housed

governments may provide subsidies to fill the financial gap

the squatter settlement
one response to the problems

but what of those who are less necessary economically or less capable of demanding their rights—the **old**, the **young**, the **poor**, the **unemployed**, the **immigrants**?

many urban squatter settlements draw on the local village traditions, where these still exist—this is a traditional village layout from **Congo**

one of the richest existing traditions is that of **Kano**, northern Nigeria

a European settlement—an Algerian workers' **bidonville** (oil-drum city) on the edge of Paris

junk-yard geo-domes in **Drop City**, Arizona

section of a hillside **barriada** in Lima, Peru

growth of a barriada

(1) owner appropriates a piece of land outside Lima, stock-piles materials and employs a bricklayer
(2) construction of walls and concrete floor slab
(3) addition of concrete roof
(4) and (5) addition of further storeys according to the needs of the expanding family

ficance was a visual and architectural rather than social one.

But there were more fundamental criticisms of the processes at work in the city. Increasingly, land-use planning assumptions were being questioned; zoning was seen to create sterile, unsocial environments, and development seen to benefit the developer rather than the community; the emphasis placed by planning on the physical and quantifiable was seen to be at the expense of the social and less tangible values of life; in particular, the 'systems approach', with its implied message that somewhere a 'preferred' solution to every planning problem lay hidden only to be discovered by logic, ran counter to the growing recognition among radical critics that there was no 'correct' solution to urban problems, merely solutions which favoured one group at the expense of another, the choice between them being political rather than a scientific act.

The 'science' of sociology offered a more rigorous analysis of the city than architects had been able to give, not only by building up a fuller picture of the dynamics of urban problems but also by its criticisms of the simplistic 'environmental determinism' which architects so far had offered as solutions. Both planners and architects began to take more seriously the real rather than the imagined needs of those for whom they were designing. The work of the 'Shelter' Neighbourhood Action Project in Liverpool, of the GLC architects at Swinbrook in North Kensington, and of Ralph Erskine at Byker in Newcastle, were three honest attempts to create designs matched to the needs of the people they were intended for. Though something of a contradiction in terms, many governments began to set up urban programmes. Predictably, none of them were allowed to go too far; the American Office of Economic Opportunity was kept tightly under control, and the British Community Development project was disbanded when it began to get too radical.

But architecture, planning and sociology were after all bourgeois sciences and dedicated, despite all their attempts to ameliorate the problems, to the continuation of the status quo from which the problems stemmed in the first place. The intensifying protest movement of the late 1960s and 1970s against the monolithic, corporate system firmly placed the professionals, well-meaning as they may have been, on the wrong side of the fence. One aspect of this protest was the growing interest in informal environments. From the junkyard geodesic domes of Drop City in Arizona, to People's Park in Berkeley, to Tent City in Boston, environmental comments were being made by groups of local people which demonstrated their dissatisfaction both with the system and with the repressive environments its agents created.

An even bigger comment was being made by countless city-dwellers in the Third World, whose desperation at their city authorities' refusal to recognise their plight gave rise to a dramatic and spontaneous self-help movement. Squatting was a world-wide phenomenon from Paris to Istanbul and London to Congo-Kinshasa but was especially typical of South America, with its contrast between repressive, right-wing regimes and a radicalised poor. In Santiago de Chile, *pobliaciones* of timber and cardboard shacks were thrown up in 1970 on empty suburban land forcibly seized from the city authorities; in three or four years they housed one-sixth of the city's entire population, and became a recognised and influential part of the city's structure. On an international scale, squatter groups were only one part of an entire 'community action' movement through which bureaucratic decisions were challenged and improvements demanded. The dispossessed working class everywhere, stimulated by the abortive revolutions of 1968 and the challenge they posed to the values and methods of the capitalist world, both east and west, learned the virtues of solidarity.

Then, in the early 1970s, came yet another cyclical crisis in the world economy, as the bubble of over-production burst. The problems began to penetrate western consciousness through the sudden shortages of fossil fuel, and the realisation that the Club of Rome's warnings about the finite nature of the earth's resources were at least to be taken seriously. There were opposing views however: whether to begin an intensive search for alternative sources of energy in order to keep up the level of growth, or whether to question the very principle of growth and to formulate an alternative life-style. The latter course, whose main champion was E. F. Schumacher, author of *Small is Beautiful* (1973), was in tune with conclusions being reached independently by many individuals and small groups, critical of official policies and determined to discover their own practical solutions to the problems of the conservation of energy and other resources. Many of these were in the USA and Canada, where the problems of over-consumption could be seen at their most acute. One of a number of practical projects was the 'Ecology house' in Toronto (1980), an old family house converted by the Pollution Probe Foundation to demonstrate techniques of heat and energy conservation, waste recycling and solar greenhousing. Though the project, typically, was the work of enthusiastic volunteers, its list of industrial sponsors indicated a further twist, that official bodies were themselves becoming interested in conservation. Even entrepreneurs were beginning to look on conservation as a potential commodity, to be sold to consumers on the basis of their susceptibility to alarmism. With a few exceptions, however, notably the experiments in tidal power by the French and Canadian governments, the continued development in Sweden and Russia of hydro-electric power, and various isolated official experiments in wave and ocean thermal power, in wind machinery and in solar collectors, most governments failed to take conservation seriously, and instead pinned their hopes on a massive expansion of the ecologically dangerous nuclear industry, ignoring the potential long-term effects in favour of the short-term profits to be made by the military-industrial complex.

As the crisis deepened, all the paradoxes of capitalism were thrown into sharper relief: rapidly mounting inflation accompanied by deepening unemployment in industrialised countries; the over-production and dumping of foodstuffs by the USA and the EEC while mass starvation threatened the Third World; international banks and investment houses making enormous profits while productive industry rapidly declined; multi-national corporations continuing to prosper while aid to underdeveloped countries was withdrawn; a rapid increase in arms spending while investment in hospitals, schools and public housing was cut.

Architects and planners reacted to the crisis in a variety of ways. To those most closely identified with the establishment, economic crisis was something to be endured, in the hope of capitalism recovering its strength – and even to be profited from if possible. There was more short-term profit to be made from designing and marketing fall-out shelters than there was in questioning the priorities of a system which made them necessary in the first place. The oil-rich Near East, where investment capital was still available in a way it no longer was in the west, became a focus of attention. Western architects who ten years before might have been working on the problems of the urban poor were now competing to design palaces, luxury hotels and cultural centres in Oman or Saudi Arabia. That these problems had not evaporated was evidenced by the mounting tensions in the inner cities of the west as chronic unemployment grew and people's hopes faded; fair-weather remedies were not good enough.

Architectural theory too was becoming more remote from the real world. The his-

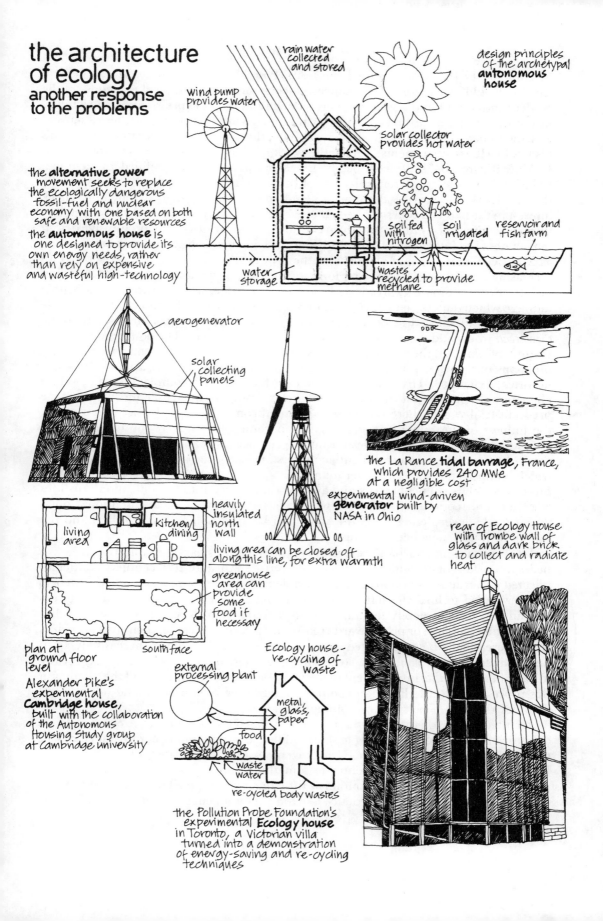

the architecture of ecology
another response to the problems

rain water collected and stored

wind pump provides water

design principles of the archetypal **autonomous house**

solar collector provides hot water

the **alternative power** movement seeks to replace the ecologically dangerous fossil-fuel and nuclear economy with one based on both safe and renewable resources

the **autonomous house** is one designed to provide its own energy needs, rather than rely on expensive and wasteful high-technology

soil fed with nitrogen

soil irrigated

reservoir and fish farm

water storage

wastes recycled to provide methane

aerogenerator

solar collecting panels

the La Rance **tidal barrage**, France, which provides 240 MWe at a negligible cost

experimental wind-driven **generator** built by NASA in Ohio

heavily insulated north wall

living area can be closed off along this line, for extra warmth

greenhouse area can provide some food if necessary

living area

kitchen/dining

rear of Ecology House with Trombe wall of glass and dark brick to collect and radiate heat

plan at ground floor level

south face

Alexander Pike's experimental **Cambridge house,** built with the collaboration of the Autonomous Housing Study group at Cambridge university

Ecology house - re-cycling of waste

external processing plant

metal, glass, paper

food

waste water

re-cycled body wastes

the Pollution Probe Foundation's experimental **Ecology house** in Toronto, a Victorian villa turned into a demonstration of energy-saving and re-cycling techniques

torian Charles Jencks had coined the term 'Post-Modernism' to describe a general trend he could see emerging: less concern for the serious, puritanical principles of the modern movement and a greater interest in self-indulgent expressionism, in richness, in the frivolous and bizarre. There was no underlying theory; the earlier designs of Saarinen, such as his Kennedy airport terminal, the designs of Robert Venturi, such as his Guild House apartments (1960), the work of Charles Moore, Bruce Goff, Ralph Erskine, Ricardo Bofill, Vincent Scully, Lucien Kroll and others qualified for inclusion, linked only by their apparent rejection of the principles of the international style. By the mid 1970s, the Post-Modern movement had developed a slightly tongue-in-cheek interest in the neo-classical style, seen mainly in the unbuilt work of schools of architecture and competition entries but given considerable vicarious life by progressive design magazines. The later work of James Stirling, and the theorising of urban designers such as Maurice Culot, Oswald Ungers and the brothers Leon and Rob Krier showed an increasing tendency to Beaux-Arts formalism. In its original context, neo-Classicism had been the ultimate expression of bourgeois prestige, architecture with a legible message which only the educated and privileged could read. The choice of such a style as today's academic diversion was an equally elitist gesture, appealing mainly to the *cognoscenti* who could appreciate the witty historical references. The bourgeois architect might have failed in the recent past, and still be failing, to come to terms with the social problems of the city, but there could be no denying that he was a master of witty historical reference. His work now demonstrated all the complexities of modern alienation. In place of the simple, personal relationship between user and artisan of the pre-industrial world, there was now impersonal commodity production. As a result, the fullness of the human personality had become restricted by the narrowness of individual knowledge or skill. Despite man's great scientific and technological achievements, he found it ever more difficult to understand the social relationships around him which had become objective rather than subjective, relationships between commodities rather than between people. Art and architecture drifted into 'mystification'; realities were ignored; committed attitudes were rejected in favour of unconditional ones, which made fewer demands on the artist and kept a distance between him and the society he might have been serving.

This retreat from the complex realities of the world was part of a collective failure of nerve in the face of the widespread economic crisis of the late 20th century. Politicians rejected constructive solutions to social problems in favour of repression and violence; industry failed to find alternative, socially useful outlets for investment; trade union bureaucrats sought merely to gain what they could from the capitalist system rather than pose a challenge or put forward creative alternatives. People, their lives and ideas have increasingly been exploited; local cultures and skills have increasingly been undermined, to be replaced by a corporate technology used deliberately and cynically to harmful effect. The involvement of the technologist, the architect and the planner in this process has been a Faustian compact, the trading of one's own and others' freedoms for the sake of short-term professional success.

Architecturally, this attitude has been encouraged by the emergence of new schools of historians and theorists seeking to shake off the persistent influence of Pevsner and all those other defenders of the modern movement and emphasisers of its social role. Instead, rationalism was represented as something unacceptably alien, and architectural history was re-written to contain as little reference as possible either to the movement itself or to its direct antecedents, like the Victorian engineers or William Morris.

242

the new historicism

in contrast to the serious modern movement,
it became architecturally respectable to
design historicist frivolities
like **Port Grimaud**

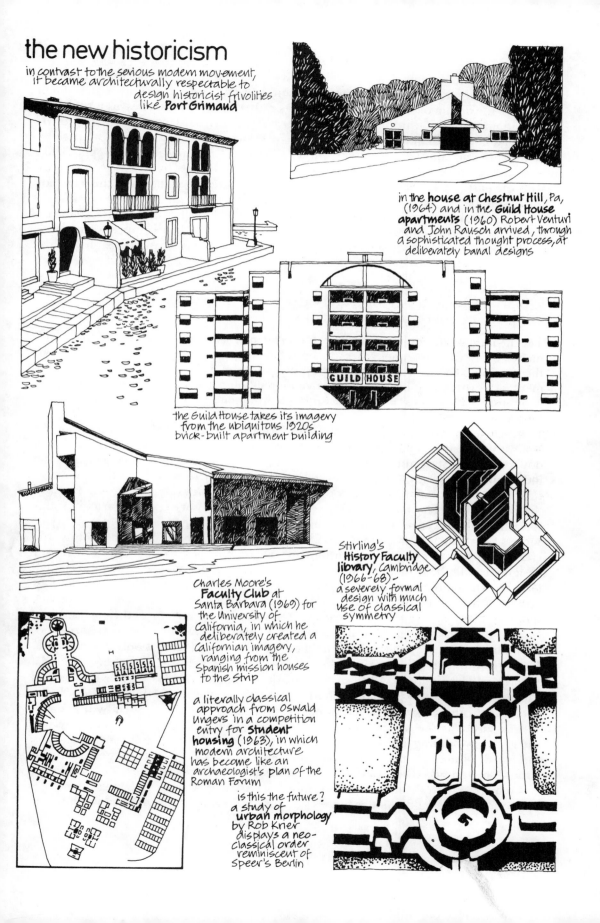

in the **house at Chestnut Hill**, Pa,
(1964) and in the **Guild House
apartments** (1960) Robert Venturi
and John Rausch arrived, through
a sophisticated thought process, at
deliberately banal designs

GUILD HOUSE

the Guild House takes its imagery
from the ubiquitous 1920s
brick-built apartment building

Stirling's
**History Faculty
library**, Cambridge
(1966-68) -
a severely formal
design with much
use of classical
symmetry

Charles Moore's
Faculty Club at
Santa Barbara (1969) for
the University of
California, in which he
deliberately created a
Californian imagery,
ranging from the
Spanish mission houses
to the Strip

a literally classical
approach from Oswald
Ungers in a competition
entry for **Student
housing** (1963), in which
modern architecture
has become like an
archaeologist's plan of the
Roman Forum

is this the future?
a study of
urban morphology
by Rob Krier
displays a neo-
classical order
reminiscent of
Speer's Berlin

New heroes and monuments were revived from the bourgeois past: Schinkel, Lutyens, the Victorian mansion, the Ritz hotel. Architecture was seen as mainly a question of style, as the design of monumental buildings rather than humble ones, as a matter of individual inspiration rather than of co-operative effort. History was studied 'for its own sake', as a rarefied specialism divorced from common life, and as a supposedly apolitical, uncommitted and 'value-free' discipline – behind which a politically tendentious attitude nonetheless lay concealed. Above all, history was concerned only with the past; the present was not to be studied the better to understand the past, nor the past to be used as a way into the future.

The effect, in short, was to exclude from architectural theory and practice any sense of doubt about conventional ways of looking at environmental questions, and any sense of challenge to the existing social order. It was to ignore the questions of Brecht's 'worker who reads' when he asked,

> Who built Thebes of the seven gates?
> In the books you find the names of kings.
> Was it kings who hauled chunks of rock to the place?

Yet the large-scale environmental problems facing society today – the squatter settlements, the devastated inner cities, the hostile new central areas, the traffic congestion, the declining services, the emphasis on arms production rather than social investment – clearly cannot be solved by conventional bourgeois means; the very concept of capitalism solving, rather than creating, environmental problems has so far proved illusory.

Nevertheless there are alternative ways forward: the early building unions fought against the destruction of their system; Morris, like Marx, saw a vital need to break down the élitist state apparatus in order to restore the autonomy and creativity of the individual; the Constructivists worked to this end, to overhaul existing property relations, to treat buildings as needs rather than commodities, to put the real needs of the people first. The Bauhaus designers and their successors at least partook of this social idealism, even if working within the capitalist system made the possibility of success that much more remote. It is becoming increasingly clear today that the creation of a better physical environment will require political action, as well as a designer's skill: the urban poor of the squatter communities, creating their alternative local economies; the community activists of the inner cities, challenging the authorities; groups of trade unionists like the Upper Clyde shipbuilders or the Lucas Aerospace shop stewards, putting forward creative alternatives to the mis-use of their skills. If the current trend in architectural theory gives little help in this direction, there are other possibilities. The work of the French school of urban sociologists is only one example. Deriving its impetus from 1968 and its philosophical background of the classic marxist theories of Gramsci and Althusser, the work of Lojkine and Castells in France and Pickvance in Britain placed a responsibility on the professional, the 'new petit bourgeois', to recognise his real place in society, to see that he was exploited by the system just as surely as the factory worker or the poor of the inner city. If he really was interested in creating a better world he could do so only by becoming part, as Castells indicated, of an 'organisation of popular classes *objectively interested* in going beyond capitalism and *subjectively conscious* of this necessity and possibility'.

Architects, both theorists and practitioners, ought perhaps to be asking themselves such questions. Would it not be more sane, for example, to begin with people and their needs, recognising the fundamental part in human life which the building process plays, meeting not only functional needs but also evolutionary ones, by helping all people develop their inherent skills and spirituality? The treating of land and buildings as commodities, and the alienation inherent in the building process, would be seen as failures of our present system. Should we not recognise that the economic structure of society is the base from which any analysis must start, rather than from the half-truths of political dogma or the dogmas of architectural design? Should we not recognise that there is no automatic connection between technical progress and social progress, even though bourgeois ideology pretends there is? Instead, history is contingent, offering us opportunities which we can grasp or not, depending on our readiness to act. Should we not recognise the dynamic, dialectical nature of society? Bourgeois culture conceals the existence of class conflict; if we recognise this we can re-create, with Morris, the reality of the class struggle and through it alone the possibility of a better future. Should we not attempt to define 'architecture' and 'architectural history' more broadly? Resisting the tendency of bourgeois criticism towards élitism and academicism, we should perhaps be discovering a more basic and common culture than is depicted in monumental buildings and in purely stylistic criticism. Above all, should we not be concerned equally with the past, present and future? We should perhaps understand that it is only our knowledge of present problems that teaches us what is historically significant; if the past somehow seems remote from us, maybe this is because we are concerned only with its irrelevancies. We should become aware of the real traditions of which we are inheritors, rather than the ones capitalism forces upon us. It is with them rather than with the profane and dangerous ideas of the bourgeois system that we must learn to create the future.

Select Bibliography

GENERAL BACKGROUND: THE WRITING OF HISTORY

Marx, Karl *Capital*, vol. 1 Penguin, London, 1976; Progress Publishers, c/o Imported Publications, Chicago, 1979
Marx, Karl and Engels, Friedrich *The German Ideology, Part 1* Lawrence & Wishart, London, 1974; Progress Publishers, c/o Imported Publications, Chicago, 1976

SOCIAL AND ECONOMIC HISTORY

Cipolla, Carlo M. (ed.) *The Fontana Economic History of Europe* (vols 4, 5 and 6) Collins, Glasgow, 1973; Barnes & Noble, New York, 1976–7
Cochran, Thomas C. and Miller, William *The Age of Enterprise: a social history of industrial America* Harper & Row, London and New York, 1968
Hobsbawm, Eric *Industry and Empire: the economic history of Britain since 1750* Weidenfeld & Nicolson, London, 1968; Penguin, New York, 1970
Miller, William *A New History of the United States* Dell Publishing Co. Inc., New York, 1969
Morton, A. L. *A People's History of England* Lawrence & Wishart, London, 1966; International Publ. Co., New York, 1980

GENERAL HISTORY: ARCHITECTURE AND DESIGN

Benevolo, Leonardo *History of Modern Architecture* (2 vols) Routledge, London, 1971; MIT Press, Cambridge, Mass., 1977
Fitch, James M. *American Building: the historical forces that shaped it* Schocken, New York, 1973
Fletcher, Banister *History of Architecture* (18th edn ed. J. C. Palmes) Athlone Press, London, and Scribner, New York, 1975
Heskett, John *Industrial Design* Thames & Hudson, London and New York, 1980
Hitchcock, Henry Russell *Architecture: Nineteenth and Twentieth Centuries* Penguin, London 1971, New York 1977
Lucie-Smith, Edward *Furniture: a concise history* Thames & Hudson, London and New York, 1979
Oates, Phyllis Bennett *The Story of Western Furniture* Herbert Press, London, and Harper & Row, New York, 1981
Pevsner, Nikolaus *An Outline of European Architecture* Penguin, London, 1970; Allen Lane, London and New York, 1974
Risebero, Bill *The Story of Western Architecture* Herbert Press, London, and Scribner, New York, 1979

CHAPTER 1

Hobsbawm, Eric *The Age of Revolution 1789–1848* Weidenfeld & Nicolson, London, and New American Library, New York, 1962
Klingender, Francis D., rev. edn Arthur Elton (ed.) *Art and the Industrial Revolution* Granada, London, 1972; Academy Press, Chicago, 1981
Rosenau, Helen *Social Purpose in Architecture* Studio Vista, London, 1970

CHAPTER 2

Clark, Kenneth *The Gothic Revival* Murray, London, 1962; Harper & Row, New York, 1974
Coleman, Terry *The Railway Navvies* Hutchinson, London, 1965; Penguin, London, 1970
Furneaux Jordan, Robert *Victorian Architecture* Penguin, London and New York, 1966
Kasson, John F. *Civilising the Machine   Technology and Republican Values in America 1776–1900* Penguin, London and New York, 1977
Morton, A. L. *The Life and Ideas of Robert Owen* Lawrence & Wishart, London, and Beckman Publishers, New York, 1969
Pelling, Henry *A History of British Trade Unionism* Macmillan, London, 1963; St Martin's Press, New York, 1977
Rolt, L. T. C. *Victorian Engineering* Allen Lane, London, 1970; Penguin, 1974

CHAPTER 3

Beaver, Patrick *The Crystal Palace 1851–1936: A Portrait of Victorian enterprise* Hugh Evelyn, London, 1970; British Book Centre, New York, 1974

Engels, Friedrich *The Condition of the Working Class in England* Granada, London, and Academy Press, Chicago, 1979
Oliver, Paul (ed.) *Shelter and Society* Barrie & Jenkins, London, 1978; distr. US by Arco, New York

CHAPTER 4

Morris, William *Political Writings* (ed. A. L. Morton), Lawrence & Wishart, London and International Publ. Co., New York, 1973
Rubinstein, David (ed.) *People for the People* Ithaca Press, London, 1973; Humanities Press New York, 1974 (contains 'William Morris; Art and Revolution' by Anthony Arblaster)
Thompson, E. P. *William Morris: Romantic to Revolutionary* Merlin Press, London, 1977; Pantheon, New York, 1978

CHAPTER 5

Guérin, Daniel *One Hundred Years of Labor in the USA*, Ink Links, London, 1979

CHAPTER 6

Baran, Paul A. and Sweezy, Paul M. *Monopoly Capital: an essay on the American economic and social order* Monthly Review Press, New York, and Penguin, London, 1968
Bell, Colin and Rose *City Fathers: town planning in Britain from Roman times to 1900* Barrie & Jenkins, London 1969; Humanities Press, NJ, 1974
Davey, Norman *Building in Britain* Evans, London, 1964
Pevsner, Nikolaus *Pioneers of Modern Design* Penguin, London and New York, 1961
Pevsner, Nikolaus and Richards, J. M. *The Anti-Rationalists: Art Nouveau Architecture and Design* Architectural Press, London, 1973; Harper & Row, New York, 1976
Sharp, Dennis *A Visual History of Twentieth Century Architecture* Heinemann/Secker & Warburg, London, and New York Graphic, New York, 1972
Siegel, Arthur *Chicago's Famous Buildings* (2nd edn) University of Chicago Press, 1970

CHAPTER 7

Berger, John *Art and Revolution* Readers & Writers Co-operative, London, 1979; as *Art in Revolution* Pantheon, New York, 1969
Gray, Camilla *The Russian Experiment in Art 1863–1922* Thames & Hudson, London, 1962
Gropius, Walter *The New Architecture and the Bauhaus* Faber, London, 1935; MIT Press, Cambridge, Mass, 1965
Lenin, Vladimir Ilich *The State and Revolution* Progress Publishers, c/o Imported Publications, Chicago, 1972; Greenwood, Westport, Conn., 1978
Lissitzky, El *Russia; an Architecture for World Revolution* Lund Humphries, London, and MIT Press, Cambridge, Mass, 1970
Miliutin, Nikolai A., *Sotsgorod: The Problem of Building Socialist Cities* MIT Press, Cambridge, Mass, 1974
Richards, J. M. *An Introduction to Modern Architecture* Penguin, London, 1940
Shvidkevsky, Oleg A. (ed.) *Building in the USSR 1917–32* special edition of 'Architectural Design', London, Feb. 1970
Willett, John *The New Sobriety: Art and Politics in the Weimar Period 1917–33* Thames & Hudson, London, 1979; Pantheon, New York, 1980

CHAPTER 8

Ambrose, Peter and Colenutt, Bob *The Property Machine* Penguin, London, 1975
Banham, Reyner *Los Angeles: the architecture of four ecologies* Allen Lane, London, and Harper & Row, New York, 1971
Barnet, Richard J. and Müller, Ronald E. *Global Reach: the power of the multi-national corporations* Cape, London, and Simon & Schuster, New York, 1975
Castells, Manuel *City, Class and Power*, Macmillan, London, 1978; St Martin's Press, New York, 1979
Chesneaux, Jean *Pasts and Futures or What is History for?* Thames & Hudson, London and New York, 1978
Coolley, Mike *Architect or Bee? The Human Technology Relationship* Langley Technical Services, Slough, England, 1979; South End Press, Boston, 1982
Gramsci, Antonio *The Modern Prince, and other writings* International Publ. Co., New York, 1959
Hall, Peter *The World Cities* Weidenfeld & Nicolson, London, 1977; McGraw Hill, New York, 1979
Hayter, Theresa *The Creation of World Poverty* Pluto Press, London, 1981
Le Corbusier *L'Unité d'Habitation de Marseilles* special edition of 'Le Point', Mulhouse, Nov. 1950
Schell, Jonathan *The Fate of the Earth* Pan Books/Cape, London, and Knopf, New York, 1982
Schumacher, E. F. *Small is Beautiful* Blond and Briggs, London, and Harper & Row, New York, 1973

Index

Numbers in italics refer to illustrations

Aalto, Alvar, 205, 207, 226, 228; chairs by, *204*
Aarhus university, 205; *203*
Abadie, Paul, 126
Abercrombie, Patrick, 213
Abramovitz and Harrison, 224
Achilli, Brigidini and Canella, house at Saveso, *222*
Adam, Robert, 29
Adams, Holden and Pearson, 195
Adler, Dankmar, 130, 140
Adler and Sullivan, 140, 152
AEG, Berlin, turbine hall, 154, 155; *153*
Affleck, Desbarats, Dimakopoulos, Lebensold and Sise, 223
Alarcón, Francisco Jareño y, 126
Ala-Urpala, Karelia, 65
Albergo degl' Ambasciatori, Rome, *185*
Albers, Josef, 187
Albert, Prince Consort, 72, 73, 76; Memorial, 91, 94; *90*
Albini, Franco, 221
Albrechtsburg villa, Dresden, 56
Alden House, Long Island, *124*
Alexander II of Russia, 78
Allerheiligen royal church, 50
All Saints, Margaret St, London, 94; *96*
Altes Museum, Berlin, 53, 208; *54*
Alte Pinakothek art gallery, 50
Althusser, 244
Altman, 166
Alton West estate, Roehampton, 234, 237
American Civil War, 15, 114
Amstel hotel, Amsterdam, 126
'Amsterdaamse School', 169, 184, 201
Amsterdam, Stock Exchange, 150
Amsterdam-Zuid, apartments in, 169
Andrews House, Newport, RI, *124*
Anhalter railway station, Berlin, 108
Antonelli, Alessandro, 86
Appleton, Nathan, 41
applied arts, 142, 143, 146, 167, 180, 184; *204*
Arc de Triomphe, Paris, 15; *12*
archaeology, influence on style, 13, 29
architect, position in society, 11, 13, 58, 110, 119; architect engineers, 84; 'crafts-

man-', 13, 23; 'gentleman-', 11, 13, 23, 25
Architects' Co-Partnership, 228, 230
Arcon house, 235
Arcos store, Moscow, 180
Arkay, Aladár, 146
Armour Institute, 208
Arnos Grove station, London, 195; *197*
Art Deco, 180, 195; *181*
Artisans' and Labourers' Dwellings Im-(1868), 136
Artisans' an Labourers' Dwellings Improvement Act (1875), 136
Art Nouveau, 142, 143, 146, 148, 150, 152, 158, 162, 171, 221
'Art Nouveau, L'', 143
Arts and Crafts Movement, 121, 138, 142, 158
Art Workers' Guild, 121
Arup, Ove, 224
Ashbee, Charles, 138
Aslin, Charles, 235
ASNOVA, 167
Asplund, Erik Gunnar, 199, 205
Assize Courts, Manchester, 89
Associated Artists, 146
Astor House, New York, 43
Atelier, 5, 234
Atelier Elvira, Munich, 146; *145*
Athenaeum Club, London, 29; *28*
Atwood (Charles) and Snook (John), *115*
Atwood, Daniel Burnham and Olmstead, design by, *115*
Auditorium building, Chicago, 130; *132*
autonomous house, *241*
Aveling, 104
Avenham Street, Preston, 237; *233*
Aylesbury estate, Southwalk, 235
Aztec Stadium, Mexico City, 224

Baird, John, 91
Baker, Benjamin, 128
Baker, Herbert, 155, 157
Bakunin, Mikhail, 78
Baldwin locomotive, *44*
Baltard, Victor, 84, 223
Baltimore cathedral, 14
Banca d'Italia, Rome, 89

Bank of England, City of London, 14, 16, 25; *17*
Bank of England, Liverpool branch, 25; *27*
Barcelona exhibition (1888), 148; *147*; —(1929) 199
Barcelona: apartment blocks, 146; church of the Holy Family, 146; *147*
Barkhin, 190
Barlow, W. H., 91
'Barn, The', Exmouth, 121; *122*
Barnett, Henrietta, 158
baroque style, in Bavaria, 108
barriada, *238*
Barry, Sir Charles, 29, 32, 34, 50, 73
Barsch, Mikhail, 167, 178, 190, 194
Basile, Ernesto, 146
Bassi, Carlo, 65
Bata shoe store, Prague, 187; *188*
Bath railway station, *39*
Baudot, Anatole de, 152
Bauhaus (Weimar), 169, 171, 180, 186, 187, 201, 231, 235, 244; *170*
Bauhaus (Dessau), 187, 194, 201; *188*
Bavinger house, Norman, OK, 215; *216*
Bax, Ernest Belfort, 104
Bayer, Friedrich, 106
Bayer, Herbert, 187; *189*
Bay State Mills, Lawrence, MA, 41; *42*
Bazaar de l'Industrie, 86
BBPR, firm of architects, 221
Bedford Park, London, 99
Behrens, Peter, 154, 174, 184, 187
Belcher, John, 155
Bell, Alexander Graham, 117
Bellamy, Richard, *Looking Backward*, 117, 118, 158
Belluschi, Pietro, 218
Belter, John Henry, 45
Bentsen, Ivar, 205
Benyon and Marshall, 36
Berenguer, Francesc, 148
Berg, Max, 154
Berg-en-Dal, Nijmegen, 126
Berger, John, 164
Berlage, Hendrikus, 150, 169
Berlin, 53, housing schemes, 186; city plan, 208; *209*
Bernstein, Eduard, *Suppositions of Socialism*, 157

248

Bessemer process, 82
Bethnal Green estate, 234
Bianchi, Pietro, 63
Bibliothèque Nationale, Paris, 58
Biedermeier furniture, 63; *64*
Bijenkorf store, Rotterdam, 199; *200*
Bill, Max, 235
Biltmore, Ashville, NC, 121; *115*
Birmingham, Sparkbrook, *233*
Bismarck, 106, 108, 123
Blake, William, 142
Blomfield, Reginald, 155, 176
Blumberg, cotton mill at, 230
Boccioni, 162
Bofill, Ricardo, 242
Bogardus, James, 111
Boileau, Louis Auguste, 61, 84
Bois de Boulogne, 79
Bois de Vincennes, 79
Bollati, Giuseppe, 86
Bon Marché, Paris, 84
Boodle's Club, London, 29
Boots factory, Nottingham, 195; *196*
Borgund church, Norway, *68*
Bouch, Thomas, 128
Bouchot, 86
Boulevard de Sébastopol, 82
Boullée, Etienne Louis, 13
Boundary Street estate, Bethnal Green, 158, *159*
Bournville Estates, 136; *137*
Box railway tunnel, 38; *39*
Brandenburg Gate, Berlin, 14; *12*
Brasilia, 214; *212*
Brassey, Thomas, 36
Brecht, Berthold, 167, 171, 186, 201, 244
Breslau, office building, 154
Breuer, Marcel, 180, 187, 194, 201, 208, 215, 235
bridges, 86, 91; iron, 16, 38, 91; reinforced concrete, 152; steel, 128; suspension, 38, 49, 114, 117; trestle, 117; trussed, 49; viaducts, 84, 86
Bright, John, 21
Brik, Ossip, 167
Brinkman, Johannes, 199
Britannia railway bridge, 40, 91; *39*
Britannic House, London, 176; *175*
British Museum, London, 25; *27*;
—Reading Room, 38
Broadleys, Lake Windermere, *122*
Brodrick, Cuthbert, 89
Brooklyn Bridge, New York, 117; *116*
Brummer, Eva: Ryijyrug, *204*
Brunel, Isambard Kingdom, 38, 73, 91
Brunswick Centre, London, 234
Brussels, Exchange, 126
Bryanston, Dorset, 121; *120*
Brynmawr rubber factory, 230
Buckingham Palace, London, 157
Builder, The, 158
building industry, development in Britain, 23, 25, 40, 119
building materials, 69, 97, 148, 176; brick, 169, 205; cast iron, 16, 19, 36, 38, 58, 61, 73, 76, 84, 86, 91, 111, 114; glass, 164, 169, 176, 187, 218, 221; iron and glass, 19, 36, 38, 58, 61, 73, 76, 77, 84, 86, 126; reinforced concrete, 152, 160, 174; steel, 49, 84, 89, 106, 114, 117, 128, 130, 218; timber, 65, 67, 69, 117, 123; wrought iron, 38, 40, 76, 91, 128

building societies, 121
Building Societies Act, The, (1874), 121
Buntes-theater, Berlin, 146
Bulfinch, Charles, 15
Bunning, James, 38
Burden, Jane, 102
Bureau of Indian Affairs, 43
Burne-Jones, Sir Edward, 102
Burnet, John, 155
Burnet House hotel, Cincinnati, *44*
Burnham and Company, 130
Burnham and Root, 126, 128, 152
Buron and Durand-Gasselin, 86·
Burov, Andrei, 167, 178, 202
Burton, Decimus, 38
Busseau, railway viaduct at, 84
Butterfield, William, 94, 99
Buys, A. W. E., 187
Byker, Newcastle, 239; *233*
Byzantine influence on style, 50, 56, 78, 126

Cadbury, George, 136
Cadbury, Richard, 136
Café de Unie, Rotterdam, 184; *183*
Caffe Pedrocchi, Padua, 63; *62*
Caledonia Road Free Church, Glasgow, 89; *90*
Calvinist church, Budapest, 146; *145*
Cambridge house, *241*
Camus system, 235
Capitol, Columbus, 43
Capitol, Richmond, VA, 50; *52*
Capitol, Washington, 15, 111, *113*
Capricho, El, at Comillas, 146
Cardiff, Civic Centre, 155
Carlton House, London, conservatory, 36
Carlton House Terrace, *26*
Carlyle, Thomas, 97, 102, 104
Carnegie, Andrew, 117, 136
Carson, Pirie, Scott and Company store, Chicago, 130; *133*
Carstenson and Gildermeister, 114
Casa Battlo, 146
Casa del Fascio, Como, 208; *185*
Casa Lleo Morera, Barcelona, 148
Casa Milá, Barcelona, 146; *147*
Casa Navás, Reus, 148
Casa Thomas, Reus, 148
Casa Vicens, Barcelona, 146
Castel Béranger, Brussels, 143; *144*
Castells, 244
Castle Drogo, 138
Catherine the Great, 13
Cavour, 86
Celle, housing in, 186
Cenotaph, Whitehall, 176; *175*
Centrale railway station, Milan, 86
Central Hall, Westminster, 155; *156*
Central Pacific Railroad, 114
Central Station, Amsterdam, 126
Centre Beaubourg, Paris, 223
Centre Point, London, 223
Centrosoyus, Moscow, 190; *191*
Ceppi, 86
Chadwick, Edwin, *71*
Chamberlain, Joseph, 78
Chandigarh, 214
Charles X of France, 56
Charlottenhof Palace, Potsdam, 53; court gardener's house, 53; *54*
Charnley house, Chicago, 140; *125*

Chartist movement, 41, 73, 97
Chase Manhattan building, New York, 221
château de Pierrefonds, *60*
Chatsworth House, Derbyshire, conservatory, 36, 38
Chelsea Hospital, Soane's extension to, 14
Chemosphere house, Hollywood Hills, 215; *216*
Chermayeff, Serge, 202, 205, 208
Cheshunt primary school, Hertfordshire, 235
Chesters, Northumberland, 121; *120*
Cheyne Walk, Chelsea, nos. 37, 38–9, 138
Chiattone, Mario, 162
Chicago Tribune office building, 171, 195; *175, 191*
Chile shipping office, Hamburg, *170*
Chrysler building, 194, 195; *181*
church design, 29, 53, 61, 65, 67, 226, 228
Churchill College, Cambridge, 228
Churchill Gardens estate, Pimlico, 234
CIAM, 187, 213, 231
cinema, 180, 208; buildings, 180, 195; *181*
'cité industrielle', 160; *159*
Città Nuova, *185*
city-centre planning, 195, 199, 218, 221, 223, 231, 234, 237; *232, 233, 236*
City Hall, Boston, 226
City Hall, Kurashiki, 226
City Hall, Philadelphia, 111
City Hall, Stockholm, 176; *156*
City Hall, Toronto, 221; *220*
city plans, 21, 41, 123, 130, 134, 158, 160, 178, 190, 193, 202, 208, 213, 223, 231; Berlin, 208; Chicago, 128; *135*; Madrid, 134; Paris, 79; Rome, 89; Vienna, 106; Washington, 15
ciudad lineal, 134, 193; *135*
civil engineer, 23, 25, 58, 76, 84, 91, 111, 119
CLASP, 235
Cleveland, OH: court-house, 43
Clifton suspension bridge, 38; *39*
Clouds, Wiltshire, 99
Coal Exchange, London, 38; *37*
coal industry, 16, 34, 43
Coalpitheath, vicarage at, 99; *100*
Cobden, Richard, 21
Cockerell, Charles, 25
Coignet, François, 152
Colmorgan house, Glenview, ILL. 208; *206*
Cologne Cathedral, 56; *55*
colonial expansion, 78, 79, 104
Colonna, Eugène, 143
Colonnade Row, New York, 43, *42*
Columbushaus offices, Berlin, 199; *200*
Commerce House, Prague, 187
'Communist Manifesto', 73
Compagnie des Forges de Franche-Comté, 82
'concentric' city, 130, 134, 213; *135*
Congress Hall, Nuremburg, 208; *209*
Congress of Vienna, 61, 69
Connell, Amyas, 195
Connell, Ward and Lucas, 202, 205
constructivism, 164, 167, 169, 171, 172, 174, 180, 186, 187, 190, 201, 202, 244
'constructivist international', 171
Contamin, Victor, 128, 152
Contemporary Architecture, magazine of OSA, 180

Conwy suspension bridge, 38
Conyhurst, Surrey, 99
Coonley (Avery) house, 140
Cooper, Edwin, 155
co-operative movement, 23, 97; in Russia, 178
corporations, development of, 49
Costa and Niemeyer, plans for Brasilia, 214; *212*
Cottage, The, Bishop's Itchington, Warwickshire, 121; *122*
Cotton, Ballard and Blow, 223
cotton industry: in England, 16, 19, 21, 23, 89; *17, 22*; in USA, 41, 43, 45
country houses: in England, 32, 34, 99, 138, 148; in Finland, 65
Covent Garden, London, 223
Coventry Cathedral, 226
Cragside, Northumberland, 99; *101*
Crane, Walter, 142
Crazy Horse, Sioux leader, 43
Crimean War, 78, 86
Crosland, Anthony *The Future of Socialism*, 230
Crunden, John, 29
Crystal Palace, Hyde Park, 73, 76, 126, 128; *74*; competition designs for, 73, 111, 114; *113*
cubism, 162
Cubitt, Lewis, 91
Cubitt, William, 38
Cuijpers, P. J. H., 126
Culot, Maurice, 242
Cultural Centre, Nichinan, 224; *225*
Cumberland, W. C., 111
Cumberland Terrace, London, 25; *26*
Cummings, G. P., 114

Daily Express office, London, 195
Daimler, Gottlieb, 106
Darbourne and Darke, 237
Darby III, Abraham, 16
Darmstadt, 150, 154
d'Aronco, Raimondo, 146
Darwin, Charles *The Origin of Species*, 110, 123
Davis, A. J., 43
Deane and Woodward, 94
Deanery Gardens, 138; *139*
de Dageraad housing association, 169
Dee bridge, 91
Défense, La, Paris, 223
de Fleury and Blondel, 82
Delaware breakwater, 111
De La Warr pavilion, Bexhill, 202; *196*
Del Debbio, 186
Desert House, Cave Creek, AZ, 215; *216*
De Stijl, 162, 167, 171, 184, 187, 201
Deutscher Werkbund, 154, 155, 164, 171
Diamond Workers Union building, Amsterdam, 150
Disraeli, Benjamin *Sybil*, 134
Dobson, John, 91
Doesburg, Theo Van, 162, 171, 172, 201
Dollman, Georg von, 108
Domènech y Montaner, 146, 148, 150
domes, 111, 164, 208; *113, 163, 209, 210, 238*
Domnarkomfin, Moscow, 194, 199; *192*
Douro, railway viaduct at, 84
Dresden 56; art school, 143; military hospital, 106

Drop City, AZ, 239; *238*
Duban, J.-F., 79
Dudok, Willem Marinus, 199
Duiker, Johannes, 187, 199
Dulles airport terminal building, 226
Dulwich Picture Gallery, 14
Dunelm House, Durham University, 228
Dunrobin Castle, Scotland, 34
Duquesney, F.-A., 58
Durand, J.-N.-L., *Receuil et parallele des édifices en tout genre*, 58; *Précis et leçons d'architecture*, 58
Durand-Gasselin, 86
Durkheim, Emile, 130
Dziga-Vertov, 180

Eames, Charles, 215
Eastern State Penitentiary, Philadelphia, 111
Ecole Centrale des Travaux Publiques, Paris, 58, 84
Ecole des Beaux-Arts, 79, 123, 161, 242
'Ecology house', Toronto, 240; *241*
Economist building, London, 221; *220*
Ehn, Karl, 199
Ehrenström, Albert, 65
Eiermann, Egon, 230
Eiffel, Gustave, 84, 86, 128, 142
Eiffel Tower, 128, 142, 166; *129*
Eigenhaard housing, Amsterdam, 169; *170*
Einsteinturm, Potsdam, 169
Eisenstein, 167, 171, 180
Elizabeth, South Australia, 214
Elizabethan style, 34
Ellerdale Road, Hampstead, 99
Ellis, Peter, 91
Ellis, Clarke and Williams, 195
Ellwood, Craig, 215
Elmes, Harvey Lonsdale, 25
Elmslie, George, 130, 140, 146
Embassy Court, Brighton, 205
Empire State building, 194, 195
'Empire' style, 15
Endell, August, 146
Engel, Carl Ludwig, 65
Engels, Friedrich, 11, 18, 69, 72, 73, 104, 111, 118; *The Condition of the Working Class in England*, 69; *The German Ideology*, 193
Epstein, Jacob, 'Night', *197*
Equitable Savings building, Portland, OR, 218
Ermolaeva, 167
Erskine, Ralph, 239, 242
Esedra, Rome, 89; *87*
Espirit Nouveau, L', 172, 174
Euston station, London, 91; *92*
Exchange, Berlin, 108; *107*
Exchange, Oslo, 65; *66*
Expressionism, 162, 169, 171, 187

façades, 111, 130
Fagus factory at Alfeld, 164; *163*
Fairbairn's textile mill, Manchester, 152
Fallingwater, Bear Run, PA, 207, 208; *206*
Farmers' and Mechanics' Bank, Pottsville, 111
Farnsworth house, Plano, ILL. 215; *217*
fascism, 184, 186, 201, 202
Federal Resettlement Administration, 207
Ferdinand II, *62*
Festival Hall, Tokyo, 224

Festspielhaus, Bayreuth, 108, 110; *109*
Feure, Georges de, 143
Fiat testing track, Turin, 174, 186; *173*
Figini, Luigi, 186
Figini and Pollini, 230
Finlay, James, 49
Finnish pavilion, New York World's Fair (1939), 207
Finsbury health centre, 202; *196*
First Leiter building, Chicago, *131*
First World War, 164, 169
Firth of Forth bridge, 128; *129*
Firth of Tay bridge, 128
Fischer, Johann Michael, 108
Fisk, Jim, 114
Fisker, Kay, 205
Fletcher, Bannister, 195
Folkwang Museum, Hagen, 143
Folly Farm, 138
Fomin, I., 172, 201
Fontaine, P. F. L., 15, 58, 86
Ford, Henry, 117, 136, 178, 194
Ford Foundation, New York, 221; *219*
Ford Motor Company building, Dearborn, 176, 230; *229*
Foreign Office, London, 91
Forest Crematorium, Stockholm, 205; *203*
formalism, 174
Forshaw and Abercrombie: County of London plan, *212*
Foster, Norman, 223, 224
Foster, William, 176
Foster and Rogers, 230
Fouquet, Georges, *144*
Fowler, John, 128
Fox, Sir Charles, 76
framed buildings, 84, 108, 126, 128
Franco, 202
Frankfurt: housing, 186, 199; *198*
Franz Josef, emperor, 106
Frederick the Great, 13; design for his memorial, 14, 50
Free Trade Hall, Manchester, 89
Freyssinet and Limousin, 174
Friedenskirche, Potsdam, 53; *55*
Frizzi, Giuseppe, 63
Froelicher, 86
Frognal, Hampstead, 205
Fry, Maxwell, 202, 205
Fuller, Buckminster, 207, 208, 230; domes, 208; *210*; Dymaxion car, 207; *206*
Fuller, Thomas, 111
Furness, Frank, 111
functionalism, 180
furniture, 34, 45, 63, 102, 121, 138, 143, 154, 171, 180, 221; *189, 204, 222*
Futurists, 162, 171, 172, 186, 231, 234

Gabo, Naum, 167, 169
Gage building, Chicago, 130; *133*
Gaillard, Eugène, 143
Gainswood, Demopolis, AL, 45
Galleria de Cristoforis, Milan, 86
Galleria Vittorio Emanuele, Milan, 86; *88*
Galérie des Machines, 128; *129*
Galerie d'Orléans, Paris, 58, 86
Galéries du Commerce et de l'Industrie, 86
Gallé, Emile, 143
Gamble (D. B.) house, Pasadena, 140; *141*
Gan, Alexis, *189*
Garabit, railway viaduct at, 86, 128; *85*

Gardella, Ignazio, 221
garden city, 158
Garden City Association, The, 158
garden suburbs, 99
Gare de l'Est, Paris, 58; *59*
Gare du Nord, Paris, 58; *59*
Garibaldi, 86
Garnier, Charles, 82
Garnier, Tony, 160, 174, 193
Gärtner, Friedrich von, 50, 58
Gaskell, Elizabeth *Mary Barton*, 72
Gau, Franz Christian, 61
Gaudí, Antoni y Cornet, 146, 148
Geddes, Norman Bel, 207
Geiger, Theodore, 126
General Builders' Association, 119
General Motors Technical Center, Warren,
  MI, 230; *229*
geodetics, 208, 239
German pavilion, Barcelona exhibition
  (1929), 199
Gibson, Donald, 235
Giedion, 231
Gilbert, Cass, 155
Gilbert, Wallace, 195
Gilchrist-Thomas process, 106, 114
Gillette factory, London, 195
Gilly, Friedrich, 14, 50; *52*
Ginsburg, Moisei, 167, 180, 190, 194, 199,
  202; *168*
Girault, Charles, 143
Gjörwell, 65
'Glasgow School', 148
Glasgow School of Art, 148; *149*
Glasgow tea-rooms, 148
Glass Industries pavilion, Cologne, 164;
  163
Glen Andred, Sussex, 99
Glessner house, Chicago, 123; *125*
Glyptothek, Munich, 50; *51*
Godwin, E. W., 121
Goff, Bruce, 207, 208, 215, 242
Goldman offices, Vienna, 152
Golossov, Ilya, 167, 178, 180, 186, 190,
  202
Gompers, Samuel, 176
Gonville and Caius College, Cambridge;
  Harvey Court, 228
Goodwin, Francis, 19
Goodwin, Philip, 208
Goodyear's rubber tyre, 117
gothic revival style, 29, 32, 34, 56, 61, 91,
  94, 97, 102, 146, 176; *30, 33*; Italian
  gothic, 94; Venetian gothic, 94
Gould, Jay, 114
Graham, Anderson, Probst and White,
  176, 221
Gramsci, 244
Grand Central station, New York, 114,
  155; *113*
Grand Union Hotel, Saratoga Springs,
  114
grannelag, 67
Great Exhibition (1851), 73, 76, 102;
  75
Great Northern Hotel, King's Cross, 91
Great Western Railway, 38
Great Western Hotel, Paddington, 91
Greenbelt, Maryland, 207; *206*
Green Belt, London's, 213
Greene, Charles and Henry, 140
Greene, G. T., 91

Greene, Herb, 215; Greene house, 215;
  216
Grisart, 86
Gropius, Walter, 164, 169, 171, 176, 187,
  194, 201, 208, 215, 231, 235; *163*
Gropius and Fry, 202, 205
Gropius and Meyer, *163, 170, 191*
Gropius and Scharoun, 199
Grosch, Christian Heinrich, 65
Grosses Schauspielhaus, Berlin, 154
Grosvenor Place, nos. 1–5, 126
Grundtvig church, Copenhagen, 205; *156*
Gruppo Sette, 186
Gruschenko, tower, 168
Guaranty building, Buffalo, 130; *132*
Güell, Count, 146
Guggenheim Museum, New York, 224
Guild and School of Handicraft, London,
  138
Guild House apartments, 242; *243*
Guimard, Hector, 143
Guinness Trust, 136

Hakola, Antti, 67
Hale house, Beverly Hills, 215
Halen housing estate, Bern, 234
Halles Centrales, Paris, 84, 223; *85*
Hampstead Garden Suburb, 158
Hansen, Theophil von, 106
Hardwick, Philip, 91
Harlaxton Hall, Lincolnshire, 34; *33*
Harper Brothers' printing works, New
  York, 111
Harrison and Abramovitz, 194
Harvard, Carpenter Centre, 228
Haussmann, Baron Eugène Georges, 79,
  82, 84; *80*
Haviland, John, 111
Haymarket Theatre, London, *26*
Hayward Gallery, London, 224
Haywood, William, 157
Heathcote, 138
Heinrichshof, Vienna, 106; *107*
Heise, 106
Helg, Franca, 221
Helsinki Cathedral, 65; *66*; Senate Square
  and public buildings, 65
Henderson, 76
Hennebique, François, 152
Henriette Ronnerplein apartments, Am-
  sterdam, 169
Hentrich and Petschnigg, 221
Hermitage, Nashville, 45
Herrenchiemsee, 108
Herzen, Alexander, 78
High and Over, Buckinghamshire, 195;
  196
Highclere, Hampshire, 34
High Level bridge, Newcastle, 38
Highpoint, Highgate, 205; *196*
Highways and Horizons, 207
Hill, Octavia, 138
Hill House, Helensburgh, 148
historicism, 221
Hitchcock, Henry Russell and Johnson,
  Philip *The International Style*, 199
Hitler, 186, 201, 208; *209*; *Mein Kampf*, 186
Hittorf, Jakob Ignaz, 58, 123
Hitzig, 108
Hochschule fur Gestaltung, Ulm, 235
Hochzeitsturm, Darmstadt, 150
Hodgkinson, Patrick, 234

Hoek van Holland, housing at, 184; *183*
Hoff, Rob van t', 162
Hoffmann, Josef, 150, 152
Höger, Fritz, *170*
Holabird and Roche, 130
Holabird and Root, 194
Holden, Charles, 155
Hollola, church at, 65
Home Insurance Company office, Chicago,
  126, 130
Hongell, Göran: glassware, *204*
Honka, Matti, 67
Hood and Howells, 176
Hoover, President, 194
Hoover factory, London, 195
Hopper, Thomas, 36
Horniman Museum, London, 148
Horta, Baron Victor, 143
Horticultural Halls, London, 195
Hotel Cecil, London, 97; *98*
Hôtel Solvay, 143
Hôtel Tassel, Brussels, 143
House of German Art, Munich, 208; *209*
House of Seagram, New York, 218; *219*
House of Textiles, Moscow, 180; *179*
Houses of Parliament, 32; *31*
housing associations, 134, 136
housing design, 157, 158, 160, 193, 194,
  199, 231, 234, 237, 239; *232, 233, 236*
Howard, Ebenezer, 158, 160, 174; *159;
  Tomorrow*, 158
Howe, George, 208
Huis ter Heide, Utrecht, 162
Humboldt, 53
Hunt, Richard, 114, 121
Hutchestown-Gorbals, Glasgow, 237
Huxley, Thomas, 123
Hyndman, 104

Illinois Institute of Technology, 208, 215
Imperial Hotel, Tokyo, 176
Impington Village College, Cambridge-
  shire, 202
Impressionists, 161, 162
industrialised building, 237
INKHUK, 167
'Innovation, L'', 143
Institute of British Architects, 25
Institut Pere Mata, Reus, 148
interiors, 34, 53, 140, 150
International building, New York, 195
Iron Bridge, Coalbrookdale, 16; *17*
iron industry, 16, 34, 43, 65, 106, 117
Islamic influence on design, 46
Italian renaissance style, 29, 56, 111
Itten, Johannes, 171, 187
Izvestia building, Moscow, 190; *168*

Jackson, Patrick, 41
Jacobean style, 34
'Jacobethan' style, 34
Jacobs, Jane *The Death and Life of Great
  American Cities*, 237; *233*
Jacob's creek bridge, *48*
Jacobsen, Arne, 228
Jacquard loom, 56
Jahrhunderthalle, Breslau, 152, 154; *153*
Jamaica Street warehouse, Glasgow, 91
James William, 138
Japanese influence on style, 140, 142
Japelli, Giuseppe, 63
Jaurès, 157

Jeanneret, Charles-Edouard, 172
Jeanneret, Pierre, 184
Jefferson, President, 14, 50
Jekyll, Gertrude, 138
Jencks, Charles, 242
Jenkontovets, Stockholm, 126
Jenney, William Le Baron, 126, 152
Jenney and Mundie, 130
Johansen, John, 215
John Hancock tower, Chicago, 221
Johnson, Philip, 199, 201, 207, 215, 218,
  224, 230
Johnson Wax Company building, Racine,
  218
Joldwyns, Surrey, 99
Jugendstil, 142
July Monarchy, 56

Kahn, Albert, 176
Kahn, Louis, 228
Kahn and Orr, 228
Kallman, McKinnell and Knowles, 226
Kandinsky, 167, 169, 171
Karl-Marx-Hof, Vienna, 199; *198*
Keble College Chapel, Oxford, 94; *96*
Kellum, John, 114
Kent House, London, 202
Keuruu, church at, 67
Keynes, Maynard, 205, 224; *General Theory
  of Employment, Interest and Money*, 205
Kiefhoek estate, Rotterdam, 199
King's Cross station, London, 91; *93*
Kinmel Park, Denbighshire, 121; *101, 120*
Kirvu, church at, 67; *68*
Kitimat, BC, 214
Kivennapa, church at, 67
Kleiviloft, Telemark, *68*
Klenze, Leo von, 50, 58
Klerk, Michel de, 169
Klint, Peter, 205
Knights of Labor, 118
Koch, Gaetano, 89
Königsbau, Royal Palace, Munich, 50
Königsplatz, Munich, 50
Kornhäusel, Josef, 63
Kramer, Piet, 169
Krier, Leon and Rob, 242
Krier, Rob, 242; *243*
Kroll, Lucien, 242
Krupps iron and steel works, Essen, 106,
  155
Kumlien brothers, 126
Kysela, Lyd, 187

Labrouste, Henri, 58, 111, 123
Ladovsky, Nikolai, 167; *168*
laftehus, 67, 69
La Garrof, bodega and chapel at, 148; *147*
Laing Stores, New York, 111
Lake Point Tower, Chicago, 221; *220*
Lake Shore Drive, Chicago, apartment
  blocks, 218; *219*
Lalique, René, 143; *144*
Lamkov, water tower, *168*
Lanchester and Rickards, 155
Langhans, Carl Gotthard, 14
Laon, 61
Larkin building, Buffalo, 140; *141*
Larsen-Neilsen system, 235
Lasdun, Denys, 224, 234
Lassalle, Ferdinand, 108
Latrobe, Benjamin, 14, 111

Lautner, John, 215
Law Court extension, Gothenburg, 205
Lawn Road flats, Hampstead, 205
Law Society building, London, 155
Le Blanc, 73
Lechner, Odön, 146
Le Corbusier, 172, 174, 176, 180, 184, 187,
  190, 193, 194, 195, 199, 214, 218, 224,
  226, 228, 231; *173, 232*; designs, *191; Vers
  une Architecture*, 172, 174, 186
Ledoux, Claude Nicolas, 13, 14
Lee, Robert E., his house at Arlington, 45
LEF, 167
Lefuel, Hector Martin, 79
Léger, Fernand, 162
Leipzig Fair (1913), pavilion for, *153*
Lelong, 86
Lemercier, Jacques, 82
L'Enfant, Pierre Charles, 15
Lenin, 164, 166, 167, 169, 172, 178, 190;
  'On Co-operation', 178; *The State and
  Revolution*, 164; mausoleum, 190; *191*
Lenin Institute, design, 180; *179*
Lenin Tribune, *165*
Lenné, P. J. 53
Leonidov, Ivan Ilich, 180, 190, 193, 202;
  designs by, *191*
Lescaze, William, 208
Leslie, 34
Lesseps, Ferdinand de, 84
Letchworth garden city, 158
Lethaby, William, 121, 158, 174
Lever, W. H., 136
Lever Company building, New York, 218
Levitt, Abraham, 178
Leys Wood, Sussex, 99; *101, 124*
Liebknecht, 108, 201
Lillington Street, Phase I, London, 237;
  233
Lincoln Center, New York, 224
Lincoln's Inn Fields, no. 19, 99; *100*
Lindegren and Jantli, 226
Lindig, *189*
Lindisfarne Castle, 138
'linear' city, 193, 202, 213; *192*
Lissitzky, Eleazar (El), 166, 167, 169, 171,
  180, 202; *165, 189: Russia: An Architecture
  for World Revolution*, 202
Liszt, Friedrich, 50
Liverpool Anglican Cathedral, 176, 226:
  175
Locke, Joseph, 38
Lockwood and Mawson, 134
Lojkine, 244
Lokrestue, Norway, *68*
Lomonosov factory, *189*
London, 25; Abercrombie and MARS plans
  for, 213; *212*; clubs, 29; *28*
London County Council, 158, 199, 224,
  234
London Transport, 195
Long Beach, oil rigs, 230
Loos, Adolf, 150, 152, 160, 176
Los Angeles, 215; *216*
Loudoun, J. C., *70*
Louis XIV, 13, 108
Louis XV, 13
Louis XVI, 13
Louis Napoleon (later Napoleon III), 73,
  79
Louis Philippe, 56, 73
Louvre, Paris, enlargement: 79, 82; *81*

Low (W. G.) house at Bristol, RI, 123; *125*
Lowell, MA, growth of, 41, 134
Lowell, Francis Cabot, 41, 134; *42*
Lowther Lodge, Kensington, 99, 121; *101*
Luban, chemical factory, 154
Lubetkin, Berthold, 202, 205
Lucas, Howell and Killick, 234
Lucy Furnace, Pittsburgh, 117
Ludwig I of Bavaria, 50
Ludwig II of Bavaria, 108
Ludwigskirche, Munich, 50; *52*
Lutyens, Sir Edwin, 138, 157, 176, 244
Lynn, Jack, 234
Lyons, Israel and Ellis, 237

McArthur, John, 111
McCormick House, Richfield Springs, NY,
  125
McDonald, Frances, 148
McDonald, Margaret, 148
McGregor Conference Center, Wayne,
  Detroit, 228
McKim, Charles, 123
McKim, Mead and Bigelow, *124*
McKim, Mead and White, 111, 114, 155
Mackintosh, Charles Rennie, 148, 150
Mackmurdo, Arthur, 121, 142; exhibition
  stand, Century Guild, *122*
McNair, Herbert, 148
Madeleine, La, Paris, 15
Madrid, Spanish National Library and
  Museum, 126
Maekawa, Kuneo, 224
Magnitogorsk, USSR, 193, 194
Maillart, Robert, 152
'Maison Citrohan', 174, 180; *173*
Maison Cook, Boulogne, 184; *182*
Maison du Peuple, Brussels, 143; *144*
Maison La Roche, Auteuil, *182*
Maison Stein, Garches, 184; *182*
Majorelle, Louis, 143
Malevich, Kasimir, 162, 167, 169; *189;
  Suprematist Manifesto*, 162
Manchester, 19, 25, 29, 89, 152; *71*;
  working-class housing, 69, 72
Manifesto dell' Archittetura Futurista, 162
Maracana Stadium, Rio, 224
Maria Magdalenakerk, Amsterdam, 126
Marinetti, 162; *185*
Markelius, Sven, 199
Market Hall, Oslo, 65
Marktplatz, Karlsruhe, 50; *51*
MARS plan for London, 213; *212*
Marshall Field warehouse, Chicago, 128,
  130; *131*
Martin, Sir Leslie, 224, 228, 234
Marx, Eleanor, 104
Marx, Karl, 11, 18, 40, 73, 99, 108, 110,
  111, 118, 130, 142, 157, 190, 244; *Capital*,
  104; *The German Ideology*, 193; *Grundrisse*,
  99
Mata, Arturo Soria y, 134, 193
Mathildenhöhe, Darmstadt, 150, 154; *149*
Matthew, Sir Robert, 224
Matté-Trucco, Giacomo, 174, 186
May, Ernst, 186, 194, 199, 201
Mayakovsky, 166, 202
Mazzuchetti and Ceppi, 86
Mead, W. R., 123
medievalism, 29, 34, 56, 61, 102
Melnikov, Konstantin, 167, 178, 180, 184,
  190

Menai Straits suspension bridge, 38; *26*
Mendelsohn, Erich, 169, 187, 199, 201, 208
Mendelsohn and Chermayeff, 202, 205
Mengoni, Giuseppe, 86
Menin Gate, Ypres, 176
Mérimée, Prosper, 61
Merlshanger, 138; *139*
Metropolitan tower, New York, *156*
Metternich, 61, 63, 73
Mewès and Davis, 157, 176
Meyer, Adolf, 164, 171, 176
Meyer, Hannes, 187, 194, 201
Meyerhold, 166, 167, 171
Midland Bank buildings, 176
Midland Hotel, London, 91
Midway Gardens entertainment centre, Chicago, 155
Mies van der Rohe, Ludwig, 171, 187, 199, 201, 208, 215, 218, 221, 228, 230, 231; chair, *189*; designs for glass skyscrapers, 169, 221; *170*
Miliutin, Nikolai, 190, 202; *Essential Questions of Theory in Soviet Architecture*, 193; *Sotsgorod*, 193; *192*
Millard houses, Pasadena, 176; *175*
Millbank estate, Pimlico, 158; *159*
Mills, Mark, 215
Mills, Robert, 111
MIT (Massachusetts Institute of Technology), 228
Model factory, Cologne, 164; *163*
model theatre, Cologne, 164; *163*
Modernisme, El, 142, 146, 148
Modulor system, 234
Modulor, La, 234
Moholy-Nagy, László, 171, 172, 187
Mole Antonelliana, Turin, 86
Møller and Stegman, 205
Molotov, 202
Monadnock building, Chicago, 128; *131*
Mondriaan, 162, 184; *183*
monopoly capitalism, 49, 114, 118, 154, 155
Montaner y Simón building, Barcelona, 148
Montauk building, Chicago, 126
Montuori and Catini, 226
Monument to the Fallen, Como, *185*
Moore, Charles, work of, 242; *243*
Moro, Peter, 224
Morris, William, 102, 104, 105, 110, 118, 121, 138, 142, 143, 148, 150, 242, 244, 245; *103*; *A Dream of John Ball*, 104; *The Earthly Paradise*, 102; 'The Society of the Future', 150; *News from Nowhere*, 104, 118
Morse, Samuel, 89, 117
Mortier, 82
Moscow, 235; Cathedral of the Redeemer, 78; Melnikov's house, 190
Moscow General Plan (Semenov), 193; *192*
Mucha, Alphonse, 143; *144*
Munich, 50; War Office, *52*
Munstead Wood, 138
Museum of Modern Art, New York, 208; *206*
Mussolini, 184
Muthesius, Hermann, 142, 154; *Das Englishe Haus*, 142

Napoleon Bonaparte, 15
Napoleon III, 79, 82, 89, 106
NASA, space vehicle assembly building, Cape Kennedy, 230; *229*
NASA generator, Ohio, *241*
Nash, John, 19, 25; *20*, *26*
Nashdom, 138
National Academy of Design, New York, 111; *112*
National Farmers' Bank, Owatonna, MN, *133*
National Federation of Building Trades Employers, 119
National Gallery, London, 25
National Theatre, London, 224
'neighbourhood unit', 160, 178; *159*
neo-baroque, 155, 161
neo-classical, 25, 29, 50, 53, 63, 65, 111, 155; *66*
neo-Greek, 14, 15, 19, 43, 45
Neo-Plasticism, 162
neo-renaissance, 50, 58, 78, 86
Nervi, Pier Luigi, 221, 226
Nesfield, Eden, 99, 121
Neue Wache guard house, Berlin, 53
Neumann, Johanne Balthasar, 108
Neuschwanstein, Bavaria, 108, 109
Neutra, Richard, 215
'New' Academy, Turku, 65; *66*
New Canaan, Connecticut: Philip Johnson's house, 215; *216*
Newcastle Central station, 91; *92*
New Delhi, 157
New Harmony, Indiana, 23
New Lanark cotton mills, 21, 41, 134; *22*
New Orleans, *46*
New Scotland Yard, London, 99, 126
new towns, post-war, 193, 214, 215
New Ways, Northampton, 184; *196*
New York exhibition (1931), 199
New Zealand Chambers, London, 99
Niagara railway bridge, 117; *116*
Niccolini, Antonio, 63
Nicholas I of Russia, 78
Nietzsche, 110, 130
Nietzsche Archiv, Dresden, 143
Nikolaikirche, Hamburg, 56; *55*
Noisiel: turbine building at, 84; *85*
Norman, OK: house at, 215
Notre Dame de Paris, 61
Notre Dame du Haut, Ronchamp, 226; *227*
Notre Dame du Raincy, 174; *173*
Novecento (900), 186
Novocomum flats, Como, 186; *191*
Nyrop, Martin, 126

Odeon cinema, London, *181*
Ohio River bridge, Cincinnati, 117; *116*
Olbrich, Josef Maria, 150, 152
'Old' Church, Helsinki, 65
Old Oak estate, Wormwood Scrubbs, 160; *159*
Olivetti: Administrative and Technical Centre, Ivrea, 230; *229*; factory, Buenos Aires, 230
Olympic Games, 208, 226; *225*
Open Air school, Amsterdam, 199; *200*
opera, 82, 86
Opéra, Paris, 82, 108; *83*
Opera House, Cologne, 106; *107*
Opera House, Dresden, 56; *55*

Opera House, Sydney, 224; *225*
Oppenheim Palace, Dresden, 56
Orange hotel, Scheveningen, 126
Orchard, The, Chorley Wood, 138; *139*
Orchards, The, Godalming, 138; *139*
'organic' architecture, 140, 142
Oriel Chambers, Liverpool, 91
Orly, airship hangars at, 174; *173*
OSA, 178, 180, 190; proposal for Red City, *192*; proposal for Nizhninovgorod auto plant, *229*
Oslo, public buildings, 65
Østberg, Ragnar, 176
Otis elevator, 117, 128
Ottawa: parliament building, 111; *112*
Otto, Frei, 226
Otto I of Greece, 50
Oud, Jacobus Johannes Pieter, 184, 187, 199
Outshoorn, Cornelis, 126
Owen, Robert, 21, 23, 41, 134; *22*: *A New View of Society*, 21
Owen, William, 136
Oxford, suburbs, 97; University museum, 94; *95*
Ozenfant, Amédée, 162, 172; *173*; Paris studio, 174; *173*

Paddington station, London, train shed, 91; *92*
Paimio Sanatorium, Finland, 205; *203*
Palace Green, no. 1, London, 99
Palace of the People, USSR, 167; *168*
Palace of the Soviets, *191*
Palace of Westminster, 32
Palacio Güell, 146
Palais de Justice, Brussels, 126; *127*
Palais Stoclet, Brussels, 150; *149*
Palais vor Volksvlijt, Amsterdam, 126
Palau de la Musica Catalana, Barcelona, 148; *147*
Palazzetto, Rome, 226
Palazzo Boncampagni, Rome, 89
Palazzo del Lavoro, Turin, 226
Palazzo delle Belle Arti, Rome, 89
Palazzo del Sport, Rome, 226; *225*
Palazzo Salmoivaghi, Milan, *145*
Palgrin, 15
Palmer, Norman, chair by, *28*
Palm House, Kew Gardens, 38; *37*
Palmolive building, 194
Paradiset restaurant, 199; *203*
Paris, 58, 79, 82, 84, 136, 152, 235; *80*; toll-gates, 14
Paris Commune, 84, 118
Paris Exposition (1889), 128; *129*
Paris Exposition des Arts Décoratifs (1925), 180
Paris international exhibition (1900), 143; *144*
Park, Robert, 130
Parker, Barry, 158
Park Hill and Hyde Park estate, Sheffield, 234; *232*
Park Village, London, 25
Parque Güell, Barcelona, 146
Parris, Alexander, 43
Passage Pomeraye, Nantes, 86
Pastures, The, North Luffenham, Rutland, 138; *139*
Patent Office, Washington, 111
Paul, Bruno, 154

Paulsson, Dr., 199
Pavillon de l'Esprit Nouveau, 180, 184; *181*
Pavillon de l'Horloge, Paris, 82
Pavillon Suisse, Paris, 199; *198*
Paxton, Joseph, 38, 76, 114
Peabody Donation Fund, 136
Peabody Estates, 157, 158
Pearson, John, 94
Peckforton Castle, Cheshire, 34
Pellechet, 58
Penn Mutual Life Insurance Building, Philadelphia, 114
Pennsylvania Academy of Fine Arts, Philadelphia, 111
Pennsylvania station, New York, 155, 226; *156*
People's Park, Berkeley, 239
Percier, Charles, 15, 58
Perret, August, 152, 174
Perry, Clarence, 160, 178
Persius, Ludwig, 53, 58
Pessac housing scheme, 184; *182*
Peter the Great, 13
Petersen and Jensen, 126
Peto, Samuel, 36
Pevsner, A., 167, 169
Pevsner, Nikolaus, 231, 242
Philadelphia, 14; Exchange, 111; *42*
Philadelphia Exposition (1876), 126
Philadelphia Savings Fund office tower, 208; *206*
Philharmonic Hall, Berlin, 224
Phoenix tower, Düsseldorf, 221; *220*
Piacentini, Pio, 89, 186; *185*
Piano and Rogers, 223
Piazza Carlo Felice, Turin, 63
Piazza del Statuto, Turin, 86
Piazza Vittorio Veneto, Turin, 63
Piccadilly Circus, London, 223
Piccadilly Hotel, London, 157
Pick, Frank, 195
Pickvance, 244
Pike, Alexander, *241*
Piranesi, Giovanni Battista, 13, 14
Pirelli Company building, Milan, 221; *220*
Pizzala, Andrea, 86
Place Bonaventure, Montreal, 223
Place de la Bourse, Paris, 58
Place de l'Opéra, Paris, 82; *81*
Planetarium, Moscow, 190; *191*
Poelaert, Joseph, 126
Poelzig, Hans, 154, 187
Poggi, Giuseppe, 89
Pollini, Gino, 186
Pollution Probe Foundation, 240; *241*
Polytechnic Institute, Helsinki, 228
Ponti, Gio, 221
Poor Law Amendment Act (1834), 32
Popova, Liubov, 167, 171
Porta Nuova, Turin, 86; *87*
Port Grimaud, *243*
Port Sunlight, 136; *137*
Postal Savings Bank, Kecskemet, 146; *145*
Post-Constructivism, 228
Post-Modernism, 242
Post Office, Washington, 111
Post Office Savings Bank, Vienna, 150; *149*
Powell and Moya, 228, 234
Powers' 'Greek Slave', *76*
Poznan, water tower, 154; *153*

Pratt, Thomas, 49
Pravda building, Moscow, 190; design for, 180; *168, 191*
prefabrication, 76, 180, 234, 235; *233*
Pre-Raphaelites, 94, 102
Prince Regent, 19, 25; *20, 26*
Prior, E. S., 121
Promis, Carlo, 63
Proudhon, 160
PROUN, 167
Prouvé, Victor, 143
Provident Life and Trust Company, Philadelphia, *112*
Pruitt-Igoe flats, St. Louis, 237
Prussian National theatre, design for, 14; *12*
Public Health Act (1848), 72
Public Library, Boston, 111; *115*
Pugin, Augustus Welby, 29, 32, 34, 91, 94, 102; his house, 99; *The True Principles of Pointed, or Christian Architecture*, 29, 32
Purcell, William, 140
Purcell Room, London, 224
Purism, 162, 172, 176
Purkersdorf, convalescent home at, 150

Quarry Hill Flats, Leeds, 199; *198*
'Queen Anne' style, 121, 158
Queen Elizabeth Hall, London, 224
Queen's Gate, no. 170, London, 121; *120*
Quincy Market, Boston, 43; *42*

Radburn, NJ, 178; *177*
Radio City Music Hall, 195
railways, 36, 38, 40, 43, 49, 50, 56, 61, 86, 89, 91, 114, 117, 215, 218; *35*
Ramsgate, Pugin's house at, 99
Rance, La, tidal barrage, *241*
Raschdorf, Julius, 106
rationalism, 164, 167, 169, 174, 180, 184, 186, 187, 199, 201, 208, 215, 221, 242
Rattle and Snap (Polk mansion), Tennessee, 45; *46*
RCA building, 194
Red House, Bexleyheath, 99, 102; *100*
Red Road estate, Glasgow, 235
Reed, John, *Ten Days that Shook the World*, 180
Reed and Stem, 155
Reema system, 235
Reform Club, London, 29; *28*
Regent Street, London, 25; *26*
Rehovet, Israel, nuclear reactor at, 230
Reichstag, Berlin, 126
Reliance building, Chicago, 130; *131*
Reliance Electronics factory, Swindon, 230
Renwick, James, 111
Reston, VA, 214; *212*
Revell and Parkin, 221
Richards Medical Research Center, Pennsylvania, 228; *227*
Richardson, Henry Hobson, 111, 123, 126, 128, 130, 150
Rickman and Cragg, 36
Riefenstahl, Leni, 208
Rietveld, Gerrit, 162, 184, 187
Rijf, Jacob, 67
Rijks Museum, Amsterdam, 126
Rinascente store, Rome, 221; *222*
Risorgimento, 86
Ritz Hotel, London, 157; *175*
roads, 38, 79, 82

Roberts and Schaefer, 230
Robertson and Easton, 195
Robie house, 140; *141*
Roche, Dinkeloo and Associates, 221
Roche-Jeanneret house, Paris, 174
Rockefeller, John D., 118
Rockefeller Center, 194, 195
'Rocket' locomotive, 38; *35*
Rodchenko, 167, 171, 180; *168, 189*
Roebling, John, 49, 114, 117, 126
Rogers, Isaiah, 43
romanesque, 50, 56, 111, 123; Italian romanesque, 94
Romantic movement, 14, 16, 21, 29, 32
Rome, railway station, 226; *225*
'Romeo' and 'Julia', Stuttgart, 234; *232*
roofs: iron vaulting, 36, 91; glass, 38, 58; mansard, 58, 82; modern, 226, 228
Roosevelt, President F. D., 205, 235
Rowntree Trust, 136
Royal Albert bridge, Saltash, 91
Royal Courts of Justice, London, 94
Royal Festival Hall, London, 224
Royal Institute of British Architects, 25
Royal Palace, Athens, 50; *51*
Royal Pavilion, Brighton, 19; *20*
Royal Society of Arts, 29
Rudolph, Paul, 228
rue de Milan, Paris, 82
rue de Rivoli, Paris, 58; *57*
rue Franklin, Paris, 152; *151*
rue Ponthieu, Paris: garage, 152; *151*
Rugby School, 94
Rundbogenstil, 50, 56
Ruskin, John, 94, 97, 99, 102, 104, 142; *95*; *Modern Painters*, 94; *The Seven Lamps of Architecture*, 94, 97; *The Stones of Venice*, 94; *Unto this Last*, 94
Russakov Club, Moscow, 190; *191*
Russian revolution, 164, 166, 167, 169, 171, 172, 202
Rütschi-Bleuler house, Zurich, 126

Saarinen, Eero, 224, 226, 228, 230, 242
Sacconi, Giuseppe, 126
Sacré-Coeur, Paris, 126; *127*
Sainsbury Gallery, University of East Anglia, 224
St Augustine's, Kilburn, 94; *96*
St Catherine's College, Oxford, 228
St Denys-de-l'Estrée, 61; *60*
Sainte Chapelle, Paris, 61
Ste Clotilde, Paris, 61; *59*
Ste Eugène, Paris, 61
Ste Geneviève library, Paris, 58, 79, 111; *57*
St Elizabeth, Bratislava, *145*
Ste Madeleine, Vézelay, 61
St George's church, Everton, Liverpool, 36
St George's Hall, Liverpool, 25; *27*
St Giles, Camberwell, 29; *30*
St Giles, Cheadle, 29; *30*
St Jean-de-Montmartre, Paris, 152
St John's, Bethnal Green, 14
St John's College, Cambridge, 228
St Louis, MO: Cathedral, 43
St Mary's Oldham: terrace housing, 235
St Pancras station, London, 91; *93*
St Patrick's Cathedral, New York, 111
St Philip and St James, Oxford, 94; *95*
St Stephen's, Rosslyn Hill, London, 94; *96*

254

St Wilfred, Hulme, Manchester, 29; *30*
Salgina Gorge, bridge, 152; *151*
'Saline, La', Besançon, 14; *12*
Salon d'Automne, Paris (1922), 174; *173*
Salonen family, 67
Salt, Titus, 134
Saltaire, 134, 136; *137*
Salvin, Anthony, 34
'Samaritaine', 143
Sam Bunton Associates, 235
San Carlo Opera House, Naples, 63; *62*
San Francesco di Paola, Naples, 63; *62*
San Gaudenzio, Turin, 86
San Paolo fuori le Mura, Rome, 63; *62*
San Pau hospital, Barcelona, 148; *147*
Santa Coloma chapel, 146
Santa Monica, Eames house, 215
Sant' Elia, Antonio, 162, 174, 234; *185*
Saulnier, Jules, 84
Savannah, Georgia, *46*
Säynatsälo civic centre, 226; *225*
Scarisbrick Hall, Lancashire, 34; *33*
Scharoun, Hans, 199, 224, 234
Schauspielhaus, Berlin, 53; *54*
Schinkel, Karl Friedrich, 53, 56, 58, 65, 106, 208, 244
Schlesinger-Mayer store, Chicago, 130
Schloss Linderof, 108; *109*
Schocken stores, Stuttgart and Chemnitz, 187; *188*
Schottenhof, Vienna, 63
Schroeder house, Utrecht, 184; *183*
Schumacher, E. F., *Small is Beautiful*, 240
Schussev, A., 172, 190
Schwechten, Franz, 108
Schweikher, Paul, 215
Scott, Sir George Gilbert, 29, 56, 91, 94
Scott, Sir Giles Gilbert, 176, 226
Scully, Vincent, 242
Sears tower, Chicago, 221
Second Empire style, 79, 82, 106, 111, 123, 126; *81*
Second Leiter building, Chicago, 130; *131*
Second World War, 208, 211, 213
Seifert, Richard, 223
Semenov, Vladimir, 167, 193, 194, 202; *The Welfare Planning of Towns*, 190
Semper, Gottfried, 56, 58
Senate, Helsinki, 65
Sert, José Luis, 208, 228
Sezession, 150, 162
Sezession House, Vienna, 150; *149*
Shaftesbury, 7th Earl of, 21
Shaker Barn, Hancock, MA, *47*; Shaker furniture, 45; *47*
Shanghai and Hong Kong Bank, design for, 222
Shaw, G. B., 138
Shaw, Richard Norman, 99, 102, 105, 121, 126, 138, 157, 158; his Hampstead house, 99
Sheerness, naval boat-store at, 91
Shelter Neighbourhood Action Project, 239
Sheppard, Richard, 228
shipbuilding industry, 36, 89, 97
Shklovsky, Viktor, 172
Shreve, Lamb and Harmon, 194
Shrewsbury, flax mill, 36
Siemens, Werner von, 106
Siemens-Martin open hearth, 114
Siemensstadt, Berlin, 199; *198*

Silver End, Essex, houses at, 195
Silver Lake Boulevard, 215
Sinavsky, 190
Skidmore, Owings and Merrill, 218, 221
skyscrapers, 126, 128, 130, 155, 169, 176, 194, 195, 208, 218, 221
slums, 136, 158, 237
Small (Ralph) house, 45
Smeaton, Yorkshire, 99
Smirke, Robert, 25
Smirke, Sidney, 38
Smith, Ivor, 234
Smith house, West Los Angeles, 215; *216*
Smithson, Alison and Peter, 221
Smithsonian Institution, Washington, 111
Snook, John, 114
Soane, Sir John, 14, 16
Social Democratic Federation, 104
Socialist League, 104
Society for Improving the Condition of the Labouring Classes, 72
Society for the Protection of Ancient Buildings, 102
Soleri, Paolo, 215
Sommaruga, Giuseppe, 146
Sommerfeld House, *170*
Søtorvet, apartment blocks, Copenhagen, 126; *127*
South Bank, London, 224
Soviet Pavilion, Paris Exposition (1925), 180; *181*
Spanish Civil War, 202
Speer, Albert, 208, 213
Spence, Basil, 226
Spencer, Herbert, 110
Sports Hall, Tokyo Olympics, 226; *225*
squatters, 239; *238*
Staatsbibliothek, Munich, 50; *52*
Stalin, 178, 190, 202
Stalingrad, 193, 194
Stalinism, 201
Stam, Mart, 180, 187, 194, 199, 201; *200*
standardisation, 117, 154, 155, 174, 180
State Capitol, Indianapolis, 43; *44*
State Telegraph building, Moscow, 180
statics, 36
stave churches, 67
Stein, Clarence, 178
Steinberg-Hermann factory, Luckenwalde, *170*
Steinerhaus, Vienna, 152; *151*
Stepanova, Varvara, 167, 171
Stephenson, George, 38; 'Rocket', *35*
Stephenson, Robert, 38, 40, 91; *37*
Stern, Raffaelle, 63
Stewart (A. T.) Store, (Wanamaker's), New York, 114; *113*
stile Liberty, 143, 146, 221
Stirling, James, 228, 242
Stirling and Gowan, 228, 237
Stockholm: housing estates, 199
Stockholm exhibition (1930), 199
Stockwell bus garage, London, *197*
Stone, Edward, 207, 208
Stoughton House, Cambridge, MA, 123; *124*
Straub, Daniel, 143
Street, George Edmund, 94, 99: *95*
Strickland, William, 111
Strutt's Milford Cotton Mill, Derbyshire, *17*
Studio, London, *122*

suburbs, 97, 99, 134, 176, 178, 215; garden suburb, 158, 207
Suez Canal, 84; *85*
Sullivan, Louis, 130, 140, 146, 161
Sun House, Hampstead, 205; *196*
Sunila cellulose works and housing, 205
suprematism, 162, 166
Sutton Dwellings, 136
Suys, L.-P., 126
Swan House, Chelsea, 99; *101*
Swinbrook, North Kensington, 239

Tacoma building, Chicago, 130
Tait, Thomas, 195
Taliesin West, Phoenix, 207, 215; *206*
Tamanian, A., 202
Tange, Kenzo, 224, 226
Tatlin, Vladimir, 166, 171; chair, *189*; steel tower, 166, 167; *165*
Taut, Bruno, 164, 187, 194; *153*
Taut, Max, 187, 199
Tavenasa, bridge at, 152
Taylor house, Newport, RI, *125*
Tegel, Germany, 53
Telford, Thomas, 38
Temples of Honour, Munich, 208; *209*
Tennessee Valley Authority, 207
Tent City, Boston, 239
Terragni, Giuseppe, 186, 208
Teulon, Samuel Sanders, 94
Théâtre des Champs-Elysées, 152
Third World, 214, 239; *238*
Thompson, James, *26*
Thomson, Alexander 'Greek', 89
Thon, Konstantin, 78
Thonet, Michael, 63; *64*
Tiffany, Louis Comfort, 143, 146
Tigbourne Court, 138
Time-Life building, New York, 195
Tolstoy, *The Cossacks*, 78
Tombs, The, New York, 111
Torre Velasca, Milan, 221; *222*
Toulouse-le-Mirail, Haute Garonne, 214
tower blocks, 218, 221, 231, 234, 235: *232, 236*
Town and Country Planning Act (1947), 218
Town and Davis, 43
Town Hall, Colchester, 155
Town Hall, Copenhagen, 126; *127*
Town Hall, Leeds, 89; *90*
Town Hall, Manchester, 19, 89; *20, 90*
Townsend, Charles Harrison, 148
Tractarian movement, 29
Trade Union House, Frankfurt, 199; *200*
trade unions, 13, 14, 23, 40, 41, 97, 104, 119, 121, 242, 244; in USA, 41, 45, 117, 118, 176, 207
Traveller's Club, London, 29; *28*
Treaty of Amiens, 19
Tremaine house, Santa Barbara, 215; *216*
Tremont House hotel, Boston, 43; *42*
Trentham Hall, Staffordshire, 34
Trenton viaduct, *48*
Trinity Church, Boston, 111; *112*
Troost, Paul Ludwig, 208, 213
Trotsky, 190
Turcoing, mill at, 152
Turku, Finland, 65
Turin exhibition (1902), buildings for, 146; *145*
Turner, Richard, 38

Turun Sanomat newspaper officers, 205
Tuscan style, 14
TWA building, Kennedy airport, 226
12M-Jespersen system, 235

Ungers, Oswald, 242; *243*
Union Carbide building, New York, 221
Union Tank-car building, Baton Rouge, LA, 230
Unité d'Habitation, Marseille, 231, 234; *232*
United Nations building, New York, 218
United States Embassy, London, 226
United States Mint, Washington, 111
United States Treasury, Washington, 111
Unity Temple, Oak Park, ILL, 140; *141*
University of California, Faculty Club, *243*
University of Cambridge, History Faculty Library, 228; *243*
University of Helsinki, Library, 65; *66*
University of Leicester: Faculty of Engineering, 228; *227*
University, Oslo, 65
University College, London, 25; *27*
University College of Toronto, 111
UNOVIS, 167; *165*
Unwin, Raymond, 158
Upton House, Scottsdale, Phoenix, 215; *217*
Urbahn, Max, 230
urban sociology, 130, 134, 244
urbanisation, 67, 69, 72, 214
Utrecht: garage and flat, 187
Utzon, Jørn, 224

Van Alen, William, 194
Vanderbilt, Cornelius, 117
Vanderbilt Mansion, New York, 114; *115*; houses, New York, *115*
Van Nelle tobacco factory, Rotterdam, 199; *200*
Vassar College, 111
Vatican Museum: sculpture hall, 63
vaulting, 61, 91
Velde, Henri van de, 142, 143, 154, 164, 169
Venice, 94; house on Zattere, 221; *222*
Venturi, Robert, 242
Verdi, 86
vernacular tradition, 13, 67, 69
Versailles, 13, 15, 136; *12*
Vesnin, Alexander, 167, 178, 180, 202: *168*
Vesnin, Leonid, 167, 178, 180, 194, 202
Vesnin, Viktor, 178, 180, 202
via Nazionale, Rome, 89
via Venti Settembre, Rome, 89
Viceroy's Palace, New Delhi, 157; *156*
Vico Magistretti, 221; *222*
Victoria and Albert Museum, London, 157

Vienna, 148, 150; Ringstrasse, 106; Stadtbahn stations, 150
Vignoles, Charles, 38
Vignon, Pierre, 15
Viipuri library, 205; *203*; chairs for, *204*
Villard houses, New York, 114, 226; *115*
Villa Karma, Montreux, 152
Villa Rose, Dresden, 56
Villa Savoye, Poissy, 184; *182*
Villa Schwob, Chaux-les-Fonds, *173*
'Ville contemporaine', 174
Viollet-le-Duc, Eugène Emanuel, 61, 84, 148; *Dictionnaire raisonné de l'architecture française*, 61; *Entretiens*, 61
Visconti, Louis, and Lefuel, 79
Vittorio Emanuele, 86; monument in Rome, 126; *127*
Viurila, Turku, 65
VKHUTEMAS, Moscow, 167, 171, 180, 190, 202
Vlugt, L. C. van der, 199
Volharding store, The Hague, 187; *183*
VOPRA, 190
Votivkirche, Vienna, *107*
Voysey, Charles F. Annesley, 121, 138, 142
Vuojoki, near Turku, 65
Vuoksenniska church, Imatra, 226; *227*

Wagner, Otto, 148, 150, 152
Wagner, Richard, 108, 110
Wainwright building, St. Louis, 130; *132*
Walhalla, Regensburg, 50; *52*
Wallis, Barnes, 208
Wallis, Gilbert and Partners, work by, *197*
Wallot, Paul, 126
Walter, Thomas, 111
Walters, Edward, 89
Washington Monument, Washington, 111
'Wassily' chair, *189*
Waterhouse, Alfred, 89
Watt, James, *17*
Watts Sherman house, Newport, RI, *124*
Webb, Aston, 155, 157
Webb, Philip, 99, 102, 105, 121
Webb, Sidney, 157, 158, 195
Weber, Max, 130
Weimar, monument to dead of March Rising, 169
Weimar Republic, 169, 186
Weinbrenner, Friedrich, 50
Weissenhof Seidlung, 187; *188*
Wells Coates, 195, 205
Werkbund Exhibition (1914), Cologne, 164; *163*
Werkbund Exhibition (1927), Weissenhof, Stuttgart, 187, 201; *188*
Westminster Abbey, 32
Westminster Hall, 32

Whistler, James McNeill, 121
White, Stanford, 123
Whitechapel Art Gallery, London, 148
White House, Chelsea, 121
White House, The, Washington, 15
White tenements, Brooklyn, 157
Wiener Werkstätte, 150, 152
Wight, P. B., 111
Wilde, Oscar, 138, 143
Wilkins, Williams, 25
Williams, Edwin, 224
Williams, Owen, 195
Willis Faber Dumas offices, Ipswich, 223
Willitts house, Highland Park, ILL. 140; *141*
Wilson, Colin St. John, 228
'Windsor' chair, 45; *47*
Windy Hill, Kilmalcolm, 148
Winslow house, River Forest, ILL. 123, 140; *125*
'Wispers', Midhurst, Sussex, *120*
'Wolkenbugel' design, 180; *179*
Womersley, Lewis, 234
Wood, J. A., 114
Woolworth building, New York, 155; *156*
Wordsworth, William, 14, 21
Workers' Club, Moscow, 186
World's Fair, Chicago, design for, *115*
World's Fair, New York (1939), 207
World Trade Center, New York, 221
Wren, Sir Christopher, 14, 25
'Wrenaissance' style, 121
Wright, Frank Lloyd, 123, 140, 155, 164, 176, 207, 208, 215, 218, 224
Wright, Henry, 178
Wrigley building, Chicago, 176; *175*
Württemburgische Metallwarenfabrik, 143
Wyatt, Sir Matthew Digby, 76, 91; 'Bagshaw', 76; *75*

Yale University: Art and Architecture building, Art Gallery and Design Center, skating rink, 228
Yamasaki, Minoru, 221, 228
Young and Willmott *Family and Kinship in East London*, 237

Zadkine, Ossip, sculpture by, *212*
Zanotta: 'Blow' chair, *222*; 'sacco' chair, 221; *222*
Zanuso, Marco, 230
Zeppelin Field, Nuremburg, 208; *209*
Zholtovsky, I., 172; 201
Zollverein, 53, 106
Zonnestraal sanatorium, Hilversum, 187; *188*
Zuoz, bridge at, 152; *151*
Zuyev club, Moscow, *191*